MCSA Guide to Managing a Microsoft® Windows® 2000 Network

Conan Kezema

Australia • Canada • Mexico • Singapore • Spain • United Kingdom • United States

MCSA Guide to Managing a Microsoft® Windows® 2000 Network

by Conan Kezema

Managing Editor:
Will Pitkin

Product Manager:
Charles Blum

Technical Editor:
Jason West

Production Editor:
Brooke Albright

Quality Assurance Manager:
John Bosco

Associate Product Manager:
Tim Gleeson

Editorial Assistant:
Nick Lombardi

Marketing Manager:
Jason Sakos

Text Designer:
GEX Publishing Services

Compositor:
GEX Publishing Services

Cover Design:
Efrat Reis

Printed in Canada

1 2 3 4 5 6 7 8 9 WC 06 05 04 03 02

For more information, contact Course Technology, 25 Thomson Place, Boston, Massachusetts, 02210.

Or find us on the World Wide Web at: www.course.com.

ISBN 0-619-13012-1

BRIEF

Contents

TABLE OF

Contents

CHAPTER FIVE
Administering File and Print Resources 145

CHAPTER SIX
Administering Web Resources in Windows 2000 215

Preface

Welcome to the *MCSA Guide to Managing a Microsoft Windows 2000 Network.* This book provides in-depth coverage of the knowledge and skills required to pass Microsoft Certification Exam #70-218: *Managing a Microsoft Windows 2000 Network Environment.* This course of study prepares a network professional to manage a network. These solutions include configuring, administering, and troubleshooting the services available within a network infrastructure such as DNS, DHCP, and Routing and Remote Access Services. You also learn how to create, configure, and manage network resources such as file, print, and Web resources, as well as various Active Directory objects such as users and groups.

The Intended Audience

The goal of this book is to teach strategies for network management to individuals who desire to learn about that topic for practical purposes, as well as those who wish to pass Microsoft Certification Exam, #70-218. This book provides the content for all the skills measured on that exam, but also provides related information that is not directly tested.

Chapter 1, "Windows 2000 Network Administration," provides an overview of network administration and procedures, and introduces Windows 2000 Active Directory. **Chapter 2**, "Managing Windows 2000 Hardware and Software," emphasizes the importance of planning an installation and assessing hardware and software needs in advance. It shows how to install and configure hardware devices, as well as how to install and manage Windows 2000 updates. **Chapter 3**, "Administering Active Directory," outlines how to administer Active Directory Objects and group types. Various permissions in Active Directory are described and information is provided about how to manage Active Directory replication.

Chapter 4, "Managing Group Policy," introduces Group Policy and explains how to manage Group Policy inheritance and how to deploy software using Group Policy. **Chapter 5**, "Administering File and Print Resources," focuses on creating and managing shared folders and monitoring access to them. This chapter also teaches how to configure Web folders and shared printers, and how to publish resources into Active Directory. In addition, auditing access to shared resources and managing data storage are explained.

Chapter 6, "Administering Web Resources in Windows 2000," describes how to install and configure Internet Information Services (IIS), and how to create and configure Web site virtual servers, as well as how to configure authentication for Web sites. It also focuses on configuring FTP virtual servers, updating and maintaining security for an IIS server, and troubleshooting Web client connectivity problems. **Chapter 7**, "Administering the Network Infrastructure," explains TCP/IP and how to configure TCP/IP on Windows 2000 computers, as well as how to troubleshoot TCP/IP and network connectivity. This chapter also teaches how to administer DHCP and DNS in Windows 2000, and how to troubleshoot name resolution problems.

Chapter 8, "Monitoring and Troubleshooting Windows 2000," outlines issues involving monitoring Windows 2000 Server health and performance. It also discusses troubleshooting Windows 2000 startup procedures and Advanced Startup options.

Chapter 9, "Administering Remote Access Services," explains how to configure remote access and Virtual Private Network connections and how to implement and troubleshoot remote access policies. This chapter also outlines how to configure Network Address Translation, Internet connection sharing, and Terminal Services for remote access.

Features

To ensure a successful learning experience, this book includes the following pedagogical features:

- **Chapter Objectives:** Each chapter in this book begins with a detailed list of the concepts to be mastered within that chapter. This list provides you with a quick reference to the contents of that chapter, as well as a useful study aid.
- **Illustrations and Tables:** Numerous illustrations of server screens and components aid you in the visualization of common setup steps, theories, and concepts. In addition, many tables provide details and comparisons of both practical and theoretical information and can be used for a quick review of topics.
- **End of Chapter Material:** The end of each chapter includes the following features to reinforce the material covered in the chapter:
  - **Summary:** A bulleted list is provided which gives a brief but complete summary of the chapter
  - **Review Questions:** A list of review questions tests your knowledge of the most important concepts covered in the chapter
  - **Key Terms List:** All new terms and their definitions are listed
  - **Hands-on Projects:** Hands-on projects help you to apply the knowledge gained in the chapter
  - **Case Study Projects:** Case study projects take you through real world scenarios

- **On the CD-ROM:** On the CD-ROM, you will find **CoursePrep®** exam preparation software, which provides 50 sample MCSE exam questions mirroring the look and feel of the MCSE exams, and **CourseSim®** simulation software, which allows you to perform tasks in a simulated Windows 2000 network environment.

Text and Graphic Conventions

Wherever appropriate, additional information and exercises have been added to this book to help you better understand what is being discussed in the chapter. Icons throughout the text alert you to additional materials. The icons used in this textbook are as follows:

Tips are included from the author's experience and provide extra information on resources related to network design.

The Note icon is used to present additional helpful material related to the subject being described.

Each Hands-on Project in this book is preceded by the Hands-on icon and a description of the exercise that follows.

Case project icons mark the case project. These are more involved, scenario-based assignments. In this extensive case example, you are asked to implement independently what you have learned.

Instructor's Materials

The following supplemental materials are available when this book is used in a classroom setting. All of the supplements available with this book are provided to the instructor on a single CD-ROM.

Electronic Instructor's Manual. The Instructor's Manual that accompanies this textbook includes:

- Additional instructional material to assist in class preparation, including suggestions for classroom activities, discussion topics, and additional projects.
- Solutions to all end-of-chapter materials, including the Review Questions, Hands-on Projects, and Case Projects.

ExamView® This textbook is accompanied by ExamView, a powerful testing software package that allows instructors to create and administer printed, computer (LAN-based), and Internet exams. ExamView includes hundreds of questions that correspond to the topics covered in this text, enabling students to generate detailed study guides that include page references for further review. The computer-based and Internet testing components allow students to take exams at their computers, and also save the instructor time by grading each exam automatically.

PowerPoint presentations. This book comes with Microsoft PowerPoint slides for each chapter. These are included as a teaching aid for classroom presentation, to make available to students on the network for chapter review, or to be printed for classroom distribution. Instructors, please feel at liberty to add your own slides for additional topics you introduce to the class.

Read This Before You Begin

To the User

This book was written with the network professional in mind. It provides an excellent preparation for the Microsoft Certification Exam #70-218, and also for the real-life tasks involved in managing today's networks and the ever-increasing variety of applications supported by them. To fully benefit from the content and projects presented here, you must have access to a classroom lab containing computers configured as follows:

- Windows 2000 Server installed with the default settings. Name each computer server1, server2, etc. It is recommended to have two network cards in each computer.
- Run dcpromo.exe to upgrade the server to a domain controller. Install DNS when prompted. Use Bayside.net as the domain name. Change the zone type to standard primary.
- For the Domain Users group, add the right to log on locally to the domain controllers security policy.

Visit our World Wide Web Site

Additional materials designed especially for you might be available for your course on the World Wide Web. Go to *www.course.com*. Search for this book title periodically on the Course Technology Web site for more details.

To the Instructor

The hand-on projects should meet the hardware requirements listed below:

Hardware Component	Windows 2000 Server
CPU	Pentium II 200 or higher
Memory	128 MB RAM
Disk Space	Minimum of two 2 GB partitions (C and D)
Drives	CD-ROM Floppy disk
Networking	All lab computers should be networked and placed within groups of two. If you are completing the labs as a single user, two computers are recommended. Connect each pair of computers with either a hub or crossover cable. Make sure to have Windows 2000 compatible network adapters. A connection to the Internet via some sort of NAT or proxy server is assumed.

Software Needed

The following software is needed for proper setup of the labs:

- Windows 2000 Server
- Windows 2000 Professional
- Windows 2000 service pack 2
- The following tools from the Microsoft Security site (*www.microsoft.com/security*):
  - Hotfix Checker (nshc332.exe)
  - IIS Lockdown Tool (iislockd.exe)
  - IIS Security Rollup (Q301625_W2K_SP3_)

Setup Procedure

To successfully complete the lab exercises, set up each computer as listed below:

1. Create two NTFS partitions labeled C and D. There should be at least two gigabytes of space available on each partition.
2. Install Windows 2000 Server onto drive C: with the following parameters:

Parameter	Setting
Name	Server1, Server2, Server3, etc.
Admin Password	Password
Components	Default Settings
Network Adapter	IP Address: 131.107.2.1, 2.2, 2.3, etc. Subnet Mask: 255.255.255.0 DNS: its own IP address
Workgroup	workgroup

3. Copy the entire contents of the Windows 2000 Server CD to a folder called W2KAS on drive D: on the computer.
4. Copy the I386 folder from the Windows 2000 Professional CD to a folder called W2KPro on drive D:.
5. Copy the Windows 2000 service pack files to a folder called SP2 on drive D:, and make sure that the service pack files are extracted. (There should be a folder and file called Update.) To extract the service pack files, type **w2ksp2.exe -x**
6. Copy all files downloaded from the Microsoft Security Web site to a folder on drive D: called IIS Security. Rename each file as listed in the Software Needed section. (As an alternative, students can be asked to download these files themselves.)
7. Run DCPROMO to install Active Directory and a new domain. Name the new domain Bayside.net. For multiple computers, add a consecutive number next to Bayside. (i.e.: Bayside1.net). Install DNS when prompted.
8. Switch the domain to native mode.
9. Adjust the domain controller security policy to allow domain users to log on locally.
10. Install Windows 2000 Professional as a dual boot configuration on the computer.

CHAPTER

1

WINDOWS 2000 NETWORK ADMINISTRATION

After reading this chapter and completing the exercises, you will be able to:

- List the various tasks of a Windows 2000 Network Administrator
- Understand general troubleshooting techniques
- Ease network management with the help of various Windows 2000 Administration Tools
- Explain Windows 2000 Active Directory concepts

Windows 2000 Network Administration consists of two major goals. The first goal is to ensure availability of network resources, such as files, folders, e-mail, and printers, to users whenever they need access. The second goal is to secure the network so that available resources are only accessible to users that have been granted the proper permissions. Most day-to-day network administration tasks focus on achieving these two goals to ensure an efficient and secure computer network infrastructure.

To acquire the skills needed to meet your network administration goals, you need to understand a number of basic concepts, from the account creation process to server and resource management. You also need to master troubleshooting techniques. In addition, a Windows 2000 Network Administrator requires an understanding of Active Directory (AD) concepts and management. These objectives are covered in three parts throughout the chapter.

The first section of this chapter outlines the tasks network administrators are expected to understand and carry out to successfully manage a Windows 2000 Network. This section provides a basic outline of the concepts and procedures covered in the subsequent chapters of this book.

It is very important for you to be able to quickly troubleshoot problems and resolve any issues that may interfere with your network resource availability and security goals. The second section of this chapter outlines a network troubleshooting process that can assist you. This section also introduces you to common Windows 2000 management Tools for routine administration activities, such as creating Microsoft management consoles and using the secondary logon feature.

Since most network management tasks take place within a domain environment, it is also essential to understand the basic concepts of Windows 2000 Active Directory, and how Active Directory influences your network management procedures. The final section of this chapter discusses basic Active Directory concepts to give you a solid foundation on which to build the rest of your network administration skills.

NETWORK ADMINISTRATION OVERVIEW

As a Windows 2000 Network Administrator, you are expected to possess a wide range of networking knowledge. This knowledge can help you to successfully complete the tasks needed to provide efficient and reliable network operations. Some of these tasks include:

- Installing and maintaining the operating system
- Administering Active Directory
- Administering file and print resources
- Administering Internet resources
- Administering the network infrastructure
- Monitoring and troubleshooting Windows 2000
- Administering routing and remote access services

Operating System Installation and Maintenance

The first skill required to become a successful network administrator is the ability to install the operating systems that your environment uses. You need to be able to install the client workstation operating systems, as well as have the ability to install and configure the server environment. In the event that an installation fails, you have to be able to troubleshoot and resolve the cause of the failure. As security and software updates become available, you must also be able to efficiently install and manage the required service packs and hot fixes.

Chapter 2 provides you with information on verifying hardware compatibility, the configuration of drive signing options, and the installation and maintenance of Windows 2000 service packs and hot fixes.

Administering Active Directory

One of the most important responsibilities related to Windows 2000 Network Management is the administration of Active Directory. Administering Active Directory includes such tasks as creating or modifying user, computer, and group objects. In addition, you must also be able to manage Active Directory container and object permissions to make sure that only authorized users can access or manage the objects stored within Active Directory.

Active Directory provides the ability to easily enforce desktop restrictions and security, or deploy software through the use of **Group Policy**. This is a Windows 2000 feature that allows for policy creation that affects domain users and computers. The ability to create and troubleshoot group policies adds much to your value as a Windows 2000 Network Administrator.

Chapters 3 and 4 provide all of the information needed to manage users, groups, computers, and group policy objects within Active Directory. Applying security by using group policy is also discussed, including the configuration and analysis of security templates. An Active Directory overview is discussed later in this chapter to benefit those who do not have previous Active Directory knowledge.

Administering File and Print Resources

Many daily operations involve troubleshooting user access to files and printers. This can easily consume a large portion of your administrative duties as users contact you about printing problems or not being able to gain access to files that are needed on the network. It will be your job to plan and maintain the most efficient and secure way for users to work with the file and print resources available on the network.

Chapter 5 provides you with information on configuring shared folders and printers for both a local network and for Web access. Information is also provided to assist you in creating a Distributed File Sharing (DFS) environment and securing file resources by using methods such as the Encrypted File System (EFS).

Administering Internet Resources

The Internet has become one of the most important business tools available to an organization. Business-to-Business (B2B) and Business-to-Consumer (B2C) online commerce opportunities require that network administrators not only understand local network management, but also understand Internet administration as well. The first step in this task is to master the configuration options within the Windows 2000 Internet

Information Services. Important concepts to understand include providing secure access to Internet-accessible resources, as well as troubleshooting client connectivity problems.

Chapter 6 provides you with information on configuring and maintaining Internet Information Services (IIS).

Administering the Network Infrastructure

The network infrastructure consists of a number of network services and protocols that may require regular maintenance and periodic troubleshooting. Windows 2000 primarily uses the TCP/IP protocol for network communications throughout the infrastructure and the Internet. To properly administer and troubleshoot connectivity problems, a solid understanding of TCP/IP is required.

The most important service on a Windows 2000 Network is the Domain Name System (DNS), which provides name resolution and network service location capabilities to other Windows 2000 network servers and clients. Other services or hardware that may be present in your network include routers, DHCP servers, and WINS servers. Each of these requires the administrator to be able to configure, monitor, and troubleshoot problems as they arise.

Chapter 7 provides you with information on configuring and troubleshooting TCP/IP connectivity and configuring various network services such as DHCP and DNS.

Monitoring and Troubleshooting Windows 2000

Routine maintenance includes monitoring server health and system performance. This can be accomplished by using management tools such as System Monitor or Event Viewer. To assist in troubleshooting any problems that occur when you start a system, Windows 2000 also provides advanced troubleshooting tools such as Recovery Console and safe mode. Network administrators can become proactive and decrease disaster recovery time by learning how to utilize these tools to assist in management and recovery procedures.

Chapter 8 provides you with information on using tools such as System Monitor, Event Viewer, and Task Manager. The Recovery Console and safe mode are also covered to assist you in troubleshooting the startup of client computers and servers.

Administering Routing and Remote Access Services

Windows 2000 **Routing and Remote Access Services (RRAS)** includes a wide variety of features. Basic routing and remote access services allow access to the company network by use of dial-up modems. For example, if a user needs to access the company network from home, a modem might be used to dial into the network to access the desired resources. Windows 2000 has built upon this basic RRAS concept by providing additional services, such as **Virtual Private Networking (VPN)**, Internet Connection Sharing (ICS), and **Network Address Translation (NAT)**. Each of these services assists in allowing remote access over public networks such as the Internet. Windows 2000 also includes a new feature called Terminal Services, which enables administrators to provide resources or manage the network remotely.

Chapter 9 provides you with information on configuring various remote access connections such as virtual private network connections, network address translation, and terminal services. This chapter also discusses the troubleshooting of Routing and Remote Access priorities.

Network Administration Procedures

Once the network is operational, you inevitably run into connectivity or availability issues within the network. There may be various reasons for network problems, including hardware failures, security or virus attacks, or file corruption. Being able to quickly solve these problems is a valuable asset.

Network Troubleshooting Process

A major task for you, as a network administrator, is troubleshooting computer and network problems. A systematic approach to troubleshooting helps to define the exact problem and quickly solve it.

A successful troubleshooting process involves the following steps:

1. Define the problem
2. Gather detailed information about what has changed
3. Devise a plan to solve the problem
4. Implement the plan, and observe the results
5. Document all changes and results

Define the Problem

Problems are often indicated by some cryptic error message or by a general complaint from a user. The first step is to ask questions of the user or person having the problem. Be specific in your questioning; you want answers from the user on exactly what the problem is and how long the problem has been evident. If possible, you should also try to recreate the problem in a test lab to enable you to attempt various solutions.

Windows 2000 provides the Net utility to assist you in identifying specific error messages. At a command prompt, type net helpmsg *number* (where *number* is the number associated with the error message) to give you additional information about a specific error message. You can also access the Microsoft web site at *www.microsoft.com/windows2000/support/search* to discover the specifics on various error messages.

Gather Detailed Information About What Has Changed

Once the problem has been identified, it is important to find out what has changed recently to cause the issue. Important factors to consider include any new components that have been installed on the computer, who has access to the computer and might have changed previous settings, and whether any software or service patches that have been installed recently might be causing conflicts. Knowing about any changes that have occurred makes it easier for you to devise a plan to solve the problem, which is the next step in the troubleshooting process.

Devise a Plan to Solve the Problem

Before making any additional changes to the system, a plan should be adopted to ensure that no additional problems are created. A rollback strategy should also be in place in case the proposed fix does not work.

When devising the plan to solve the problem, you should consider the following:

- Interruptions to the network or its components (e.g., restarting the server)
- Possible changes to the network security policy (e.g., permission or group membership changes, firewall adjustments, etc.)
- The necessity for documentation detailing all changes and troubleshooting steps

Implement the Plan, and Observe Results

Once you have devised a plan, be sure to notify all users on the network if network availability will be interrupted. As you implement your plan, do not make too many configuration changes at one time. It is difficult to roll back or test a specific step if too many changes have taken place.

Once you implement your plan, if the problem still occurs, you must document what was tested or adjusted up to this point, and start the troubleshooting process all over again.

Document All Changes and Results

It is essential that all troubleshooting steps, results, and configuration changes be documented to keep track of what has changed on the network. If the problem should occur again, the documentation helps to explain the possible cause and provide the solution that was discovered during the previous troubleshooting phase.

Windows 2000 Management Tools

As you read through all of the tasks that a network administrator performs, it becomes clear that any tool that can assist in making network management more efficient is valuable. Windows 2000 provides a number of new features and utilities to assist in your daily management tasks. Some of these features include:

- The Microsoft Management Console
- The secondary logon feature
- Additional management utilities, such as the task scheduler or the netdiag command

The Microsoft Management Console

The **Microsoft Management Console (MMC)** is a customizable management interface that can contain a number of management tools thus providing a single, unified application for network administration. The management tools that are added to the interface are called **snap-ins**, and can be obtained from Microsoft or a variety of third-party companies. For example, if you need to create a console to administer your DNS and DHCP servers, you might add the DNS and DHCP snap-ins to an MMC interface. This would provide you with an administration tool to manage both DNS and DHCP.

The advantage of using the MMC is that you can add or remove management tools as necessary, and save custom tools for use by authorized administrators. The console is saved as a **Microsoft Saved Console (MSC)** file with the .msc extension.

The supplied Windows 2000 Administration Tools, such as Computer Management or Active Directory Users and Computers, are actually prebuilt Microsoft Management Consoles with various snap-ins added.

Perform a search for *.msc to view all of the prebuilt consoles available in Windows 2000.

To create a custom MMC console, use the following steps:

1. Click **Start**, click **Run**, and then type **mmc** in the Open text box. Click **OK**. Figure 1-1 illustrates an empty MMC window.

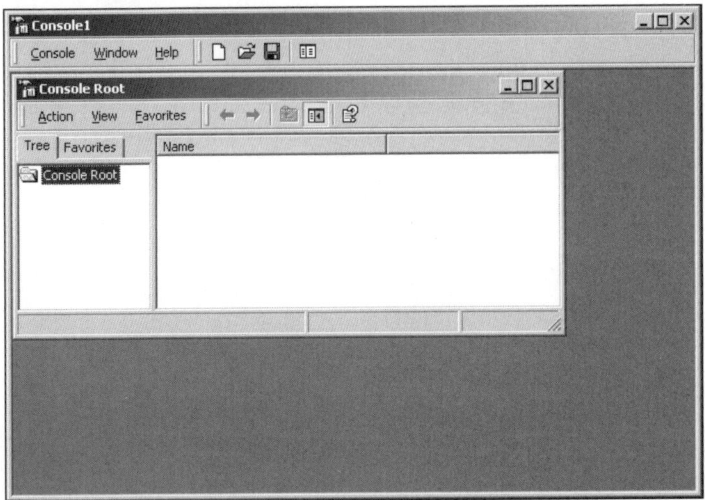

Figure 1-1 An empty MMC console

2. Click the **Console** menu, and click **Add/Remove Snap-in**. Figure 1-2 shows an open Add/Remove Snap-in dialog box.

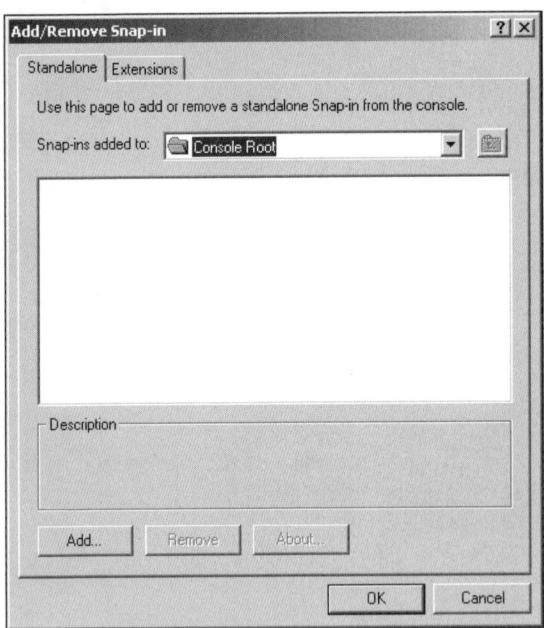

Figure 1-2 The Add/Remove Snap-in dialog box

3. Click the **Add** button to open a dialog box listing the available snap-ins, as shown in Figure 1-3.

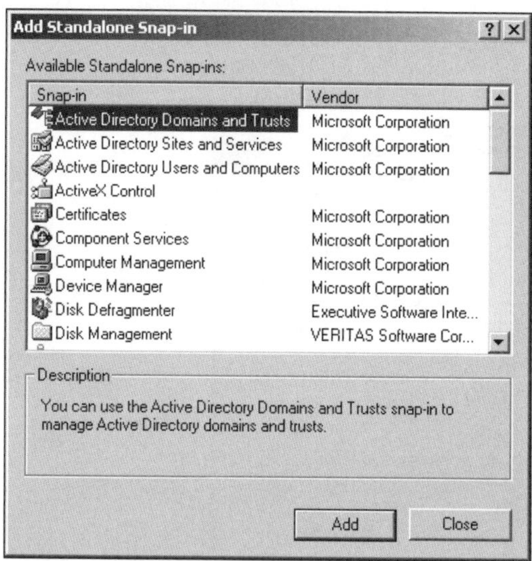

Figure 1-3 The Add Standalone Snap-in dialog box

4. Choose the snap-in that you want to add to the console, and click **Add**. Depending upon the console that you add, you may be asked to choose the computer that will manage use of the snap-in, as shown in Figure 1-4. Click **Finish**, and then click **Close**.

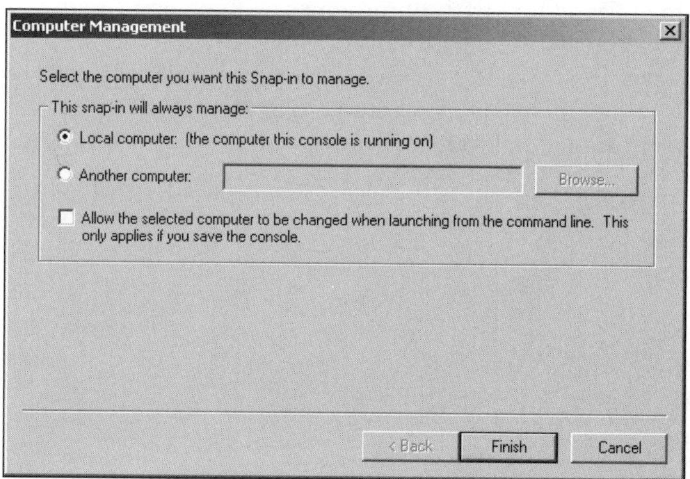

Figure 1-4 Selecting the snap-in focus

5. Repeat steps 3 and 4 for any additional snap-ins that you want to have available in your custom console. When finished, click **OK**.
6. To save the console, click the **Console** menu, and click **Save As**. Provide a name and a location for storing the console, and click **Save**. A finished console is shown in Figure 1-5.

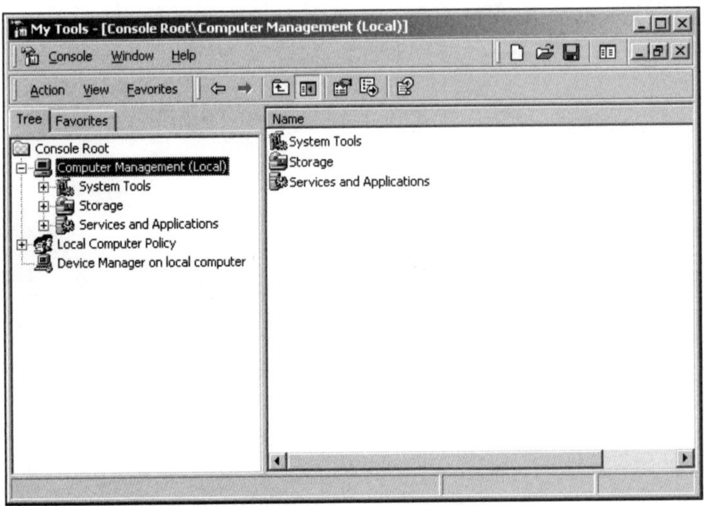

Figure 1-5 A customized MMC console

Some of the management snap-in tools may be confusing to an inexperienced administrator. To better understand these tools, you can create a **taskpad** view of the console. The taskpad view simplifies administrative procedures by providing you with a graphical representation of the tasks that can be performed in an MMC console. See Figure 1-6 for an example of a taskpad view of the Services snap-in. To create a taskpad view, right-click the snap-in. Then click New Taskpad View to start the New Taskpad View Wizard. (For detailed steps in creating a taskpad, consult the end-of-chapter projects.)

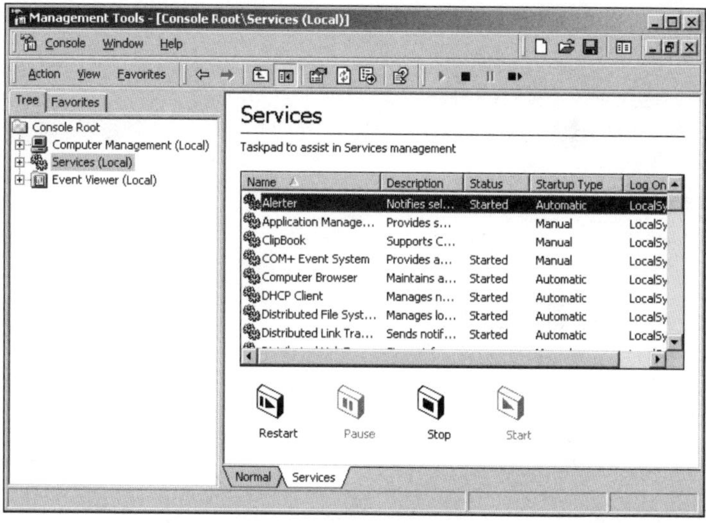

Figure 1-6 A taskpad view of the Services snap-in

The Secondary Logon Feature

It is a recommended best practice for network administrators to have two logon accounts. One account is granted administrative rights and is only used for network management. A second account has normal user rights and is used for any nonadministrative tasks. The problem with this recommendation is that you may have to log on and off many times throughout the day to gain the rights needed to complete your tasks.

To save the time required to log on and off, Windows 2000 provides the secondary logon feature. This feature allows you to log on with your regular user account and then open administrative tools as an administrator.

You can disable this feature by stopping the Run As service found in the Services administrative console.

To use the secondary logon feature, follow these steps:

1. Click **Start**, point to **Programs**, point to **Administrative Tools**, and then right-click the tool that you want to open.
2. Click **Run as**. The Run As Other User dialog box opens, as shown in Figure 1-7. Type the Administrator user name and password, and then click **OK**.

If Run as does not appear, hold down the Shift key and right-click the icon.

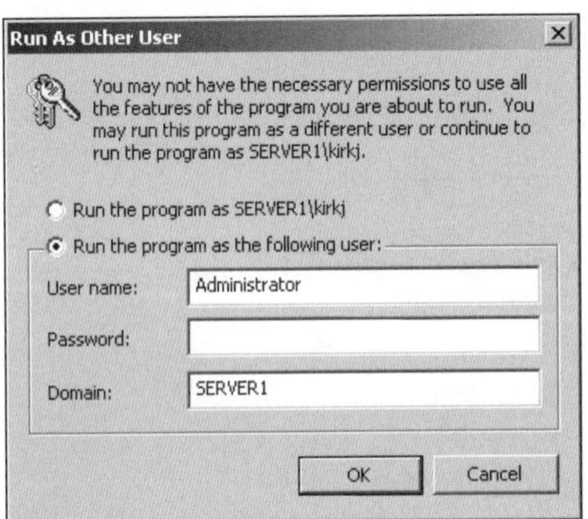

Figure 1-7 The Run As Other User dialog box

You can also use a command prompt to start applications under the Administrator account. Open a command prompt and type the following syntax (without the ending period): runas /user:<*domain\username*> *cmd*. The *domain\username* is the domain and user account in which you want to start the application, and *cmd* is the command used to start the application.

Additional Administrator Utilities

There are many additional utilities available with Windows 2000 or the Windows 2000 Resource Kit that can assist you in troubleshooting or general network management. Following are a few interesting utilities that you may want to investigate further:

- *The Windows 2000 task scheduler*—This utility can be used to schedule various tasks to run at certain times and intervals. The task scheduler service is started when you switch on your machine and runs in the background. To use the task scheduler, open the Control Panel, and double-click the Scheduled Tasks folder.
- *netdiag*—This troubleshooting tool reports on a number of functions such as WINS, trust relationships, IP configuration, DCHP, routing, running tests on DNS, and more. This tool is available from Windows 2000 Support Tools, which can be installed from the Support\Tools folder of the Windows 2000 CD-ROM. To run the utility, open a command prompt and type netdiag. Use the /l switch to send results to c:\netdiag.log, as the output may become quite lengthy. The /v switch provides extensive and verbose information.
- *The NET command*—The NET command can be used to perform a variety of management tasks such as starting and stopping services, viewing shares on the computer, and viewing the system time. For a list of the options that can be used with the NET command, open a command prompt, and type NET ?.

INTRODUCTION TO WINDOWS 2000 ACTIVE DIRECTORY

Active Directory is a directory service database provided with Windows 2000 server-based operating systems. Active Directory provides the following services and features to the network environment:

- A central point for storing, organizing, managing, and controlling network objects, such as users, computers, and groups
- A single point of administration of objects, such as users, groups, computers, and Active Directory-published resources, such as printers or shared folders
- Logon and authentication services for users
- Delegation of administration to allow for decentralized administration of Active Directory objects, such as users and groups

The Active Directory database is stored on any Windows 2000 server that has been promoted to a domain controller. Each domain controller throughout the network has a writable copy of the directory database. This means that you can make Active Directory changes to any domain controller within your network, and those changes are replicated to all of the other domain controllers. This process is called **multi-master replication**, which also provides a form of fault tolerance because every domain controller has a copy of the directory database. If a single server fails, Active Directory does not fail because replicated copies of the database are available from other servers within the network.

Active Directory uses the **Domain Name System (DNS)** as a method for maintaining domain naming structure and locating network resources. What this means to a network designer is that all Active Directory names must follow standard DNS naming conventions. An example of a standard DNS naming convention would be *Bayside.net*. A child domain of *Bayside.net* would add its name as a prefix, such as *Winnipeg.Bayside.net*.

Active Directory Objects

Active Directory stores a variety of objects within the database. An **object** represents network resources such as users, groups, computers, and printers. When an object is created in Active Directory, various attributes are assigned to it to provide information about the object. For example, Figure 1-8 illustrates the creation of a new user object and the ability to add various attributes, such as First name, Last name, and User logon name.

If you need to locate information about an object from Active Directory, a search can be performed on specific attributes relating to the object. For example, Figure 1-9 shows how you can find the e-mail address of a user object by searching for the specific user name and then viewing the attributes for the object.

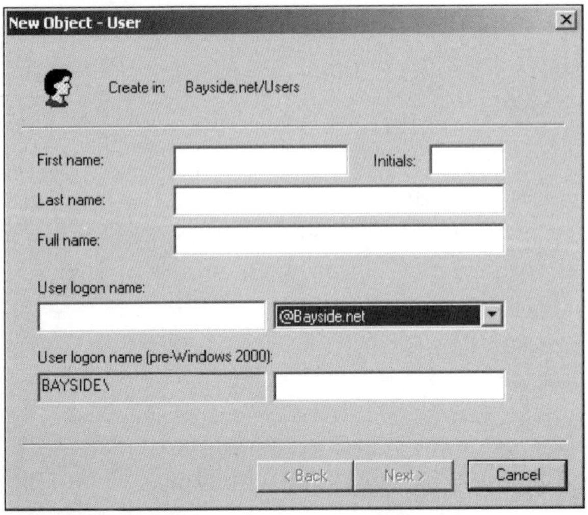

Figure 1-8 Viewing object attributes

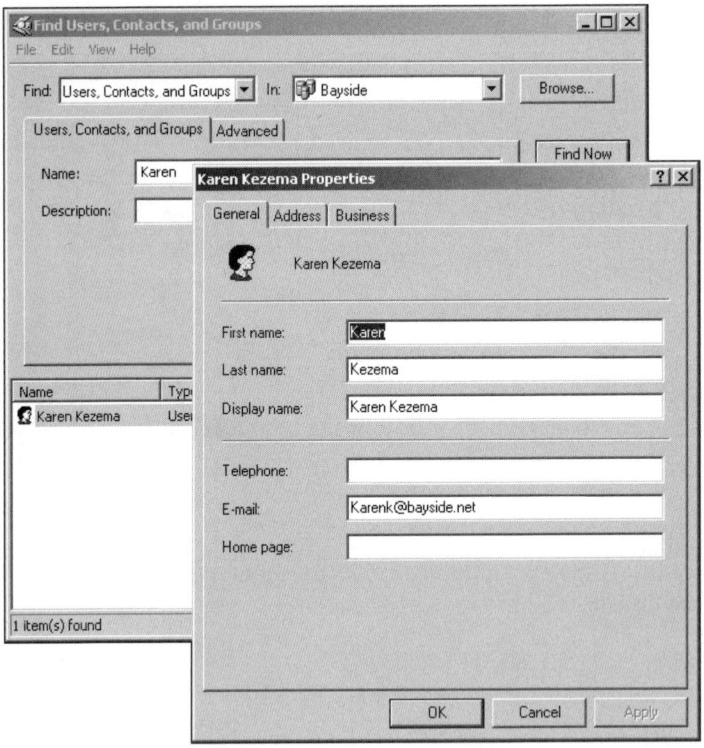

Figure 1-9 Searching for the e-mail address of a user object

The Active Directory Schema

All of the objects and attributes that are available in Active Directory are defined in the **Active Directory schema**. In Windows 2000, the schema defines the objects for the entire Active Directory structure. This means that there is only one schema for the entire Active Directory, and this schema is replicated among all domain controllers within the network.

The Active Directory schema consists of two main definitions: **object classes** and **attributes**. Object classes define which types of objects can be created within Active Directory, such as user objects and printer objects. All object classes consist of various attributes that describe the object itself. For example, the user and printer object classes may both have an attribute called description, which is used to describe the use of the object. Attributes are created and stored separately in the schema and can be used with multiple object classes to maintain consistency.

The Active Directory database stores and replicates the schema partition throughout the entire infrastructure. Storing the schema within the Active Directory database provides the ability to dynamically update and extend the schema, as well as provide instant access to information for user applications that need to read the schema properties.

Active Directory Components

Active Directory is made of several components that provide a way of designing and administering the hierarchical, logical structure of the network. The logical components that make up an Active Directory structure include:

- Domains and organizational units
- Trees and forests
- The Global Catalog

To ensure efficient maintenance and troubleshooting within Active Directory, it is essential that you understand the logical components listed above. The next few sections discuss each component in greater detail.

Domains and Organizational Units

A Windows 2000 **Domain** is a logically structured organization of objects, such as users, computers, groups, and printers that are part of a network and share a common directory database. Each domain has a unique name, and is organized in levels and administered as a unit with common rules and procedures. On the Internet, domains are defined by an IP address. A domain in Windows 2000 is considered a security and replication boundary. This means that objects, such as user accounts, and security settings, such as password policies, are assigned at the domain level, and do not replicate to other domains. By default, members of the Administrators group are only allowed to manage the objects within their own domain. As mentioned earlier, all the domain controllers within a single domain store a copy of the Active Directory database, and domain-specific information is only replicated between the domain controllers of the same domain.

An **organizational unit (OU)** is an Active Directory logical container used to organize objects within a single domain. Objects such as users, groups, computers, and other OUs, can be stored in an OU. For example, you may want to organize your users based upon the department in which they work. You might create a Sales OU to store all of your Sales Department users and objects. You might also create a Marketing OU to store all of your Marketing Department users and objects. Not only does this make it easier to locate and manage the Active Directory objects, you can then apply a Group Policy to define more advanced features such as software deployment or desktop restrictions based upon department. Figure 1-10 illustrates a domain with several OUs.

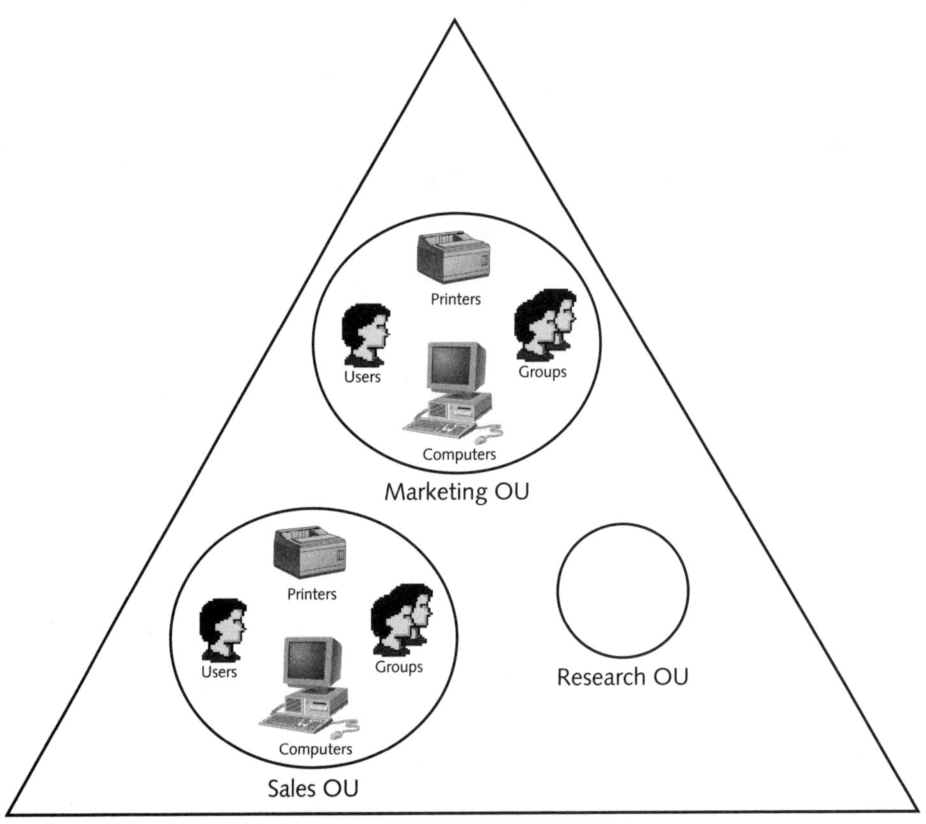

Figure 1-10 An Active Directory domain and OU structure

Another main advantage of using an OU structure is the ability to delegate administrative control over organizational units. For example, you may want to give a set of users the right to add or remove new users within the Sales OU. You do not have to provide the group with full administrative rights to accomplish this task, as Active Directory allows you to delegate very specific tasks, if necessary.

Trees and Forests

When designing the Windows 2000 network infrastructure, there might be times when you are required to create multiple domains within an organization. Reasons for creating multiple domains within an organization include the following:

- Divisions within the company may be separated geographically. To make administration easier, a separate domain is created for each division.
- Different password policies are needed between divisions within an organization.
- Language settings differ between company divisions.
- Replication performance needs to be improved.

Although domains are replication boundaries, there is another way to control replication by using site objects. Site objects are discussed later in the chapter.

The first Active Directory domain created in an organization is called the **forest root domain**. When multiple domains are needed, they are connected to the forest root to form either a single tree or multiple trees, depending upon the design of the domain name structure. A **tree** is a hierarchical collection of domains that share a contiguous DNS namespace. For example, Bayside Detailing has its head office in Winnipeg with a forest root domain called *Bayside.net*. Bayside has two divisions, one located in Vancouver and the other located in Montreal. Because of geographical and language differences, you might decide to create a distinct domain for each division. Two child domains can be created off of the forest root domain. The Vancouver domain can be named *Vancouver.Bayside.net*, which follows the contiguous DNS namespace design. Similarly the Montreal domain can be called *Montreal.Bayside.net*. See Figure 1-11 for an example of this structure.

Whenever a child domain is created, a two-way, transitive trust relationship is automatically created between the child and parent domains. A **transitive trust** means that all other trusted domains implicitly trust one another. For example, since *Vancouver.Bayside.net* trusts the *Bayside.net* forest root domain, Vancouver also trusts the *Montreal.Bayside.net* domain automatically. These two-way, transitive trusts allow for resource access anywhere throughout the Active Directory structure.

A **forest** is a collection of trees that do not share a contiguous DNS naming structure. For example, Bayside Detailing purchases a large, international company called Washex Incorporated. It does not make sense to make the Washex domain a child of *Bayside.net* because of the renaming required to maintain a contiguous naming convention based on *Bayside.net*. Instead, you should create a new tree and allow Washex to start its own contiguous naming hierarchy. Both trees make up an Active Directory forest. See Figure 1-12 for an illustration.

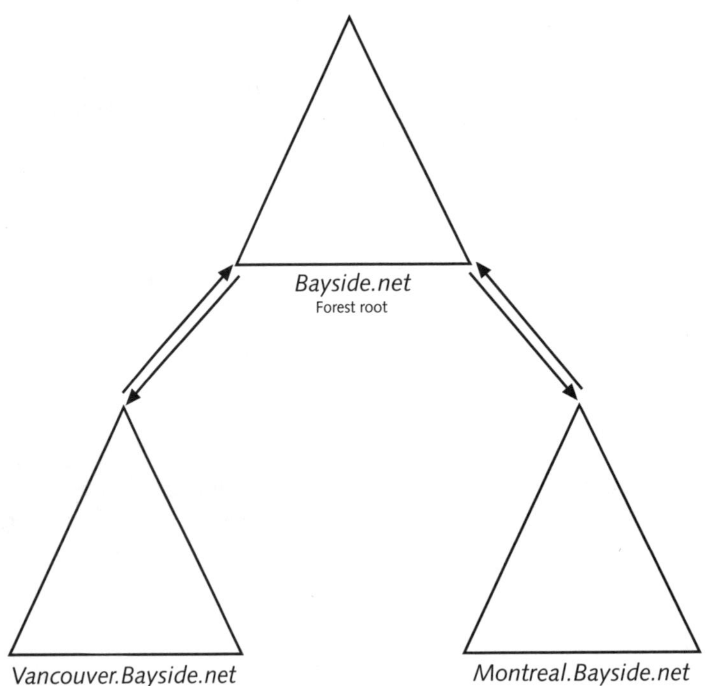

Figure 1-11 The *Bayside.net* domain tree

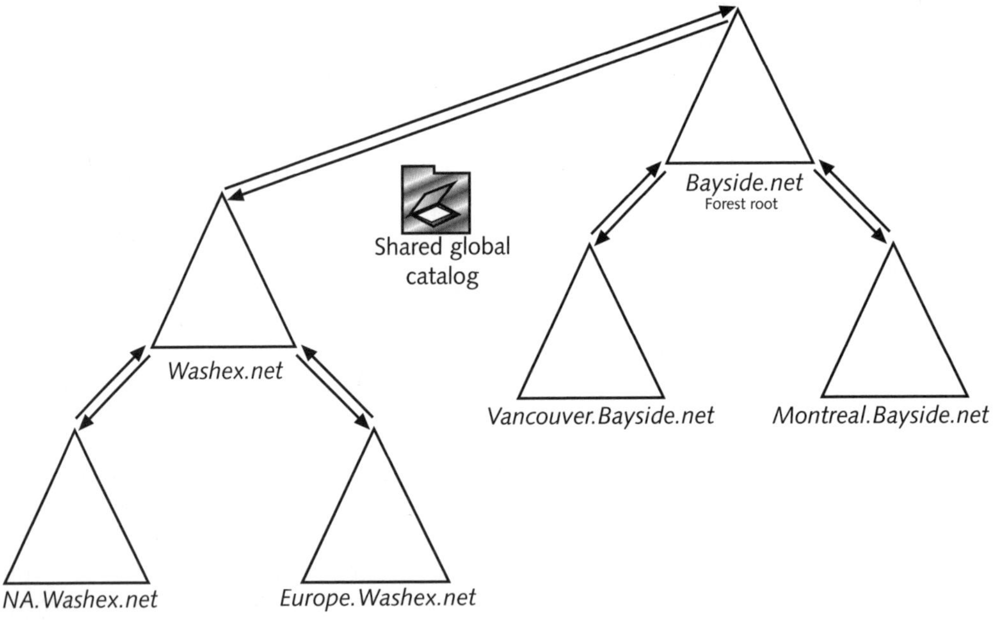

Figure 1-12 Creating an Active Directory forest

Even though the trees within a forest do not share a common namespace, they do share a single Active Directory schema, which ensures that all object classes and attributes are consistent throughout the entire structure. A special user group called the Enterprise Admins is also created, which allows members to manage objects throughout the entire forest. The Enterprise Admins group is created within the initial forest root domain and has a scope throughout the entire forest. Another component that is shared throughout the forest is the Global Catalog.

The Global Catalog

The **Global Catalog** is an index and partial replica of the objects and attributes most frequently used throughout the entire Active Directory structure. Some of the common attributes that are stored in the Global Catalog include a user's first and last name, logon name, or e-mail address. The Global Catalog is replicated to any server within the forest that is configured to be a global Catalog server.

The Global Catalog is used primarily for three main functions:

- Enables users to find Active Directory information from anywhere in the forest
- Provides Universal Group membership information to facilitate logging on to the network
- Provides the global address list for Exchange 2000 e-mail systems

The first domain controller in Active Directory automatically becomes a global catalog server. To provide redundancy, additional domain controllers can easily be configured to also be global catalog servers. Multiple global catalogs can improve user query and logon authentication performance.

Active Directory Communication Standards

As mentioned previously, Active Directory uses the DNS naming standard for IP name resolution and for providing information on the location of network services and resources. For example, if you need to locate a server called *apps.bayside.net*, your workstation first queries a DNS server to resolve the IP address of the apps server. Once the IP address is known, then a direct communication session can take place.

The same process occurs when you need to log on to the domain. Your workstation queries DNS to find a domain controller that can perform the authentication. Once the location of a domain controller is known, then the authentication process can take place thus allowing access to the network resources.

When users need to access Active Directory, the **Lightweight Directory Access Protocol (LDAP)** is used to query or update the Active Directory database directly. Just as a DNS name contains a specific naming convention (e.g., *bayside.net*), LDAP also follows a specific naming convention. LDAP naming paths are used when referring to objects stored within the Active Directory. Two main components of the naming paths include:

- *Distinguished Name* —Every object in Active Directory has a unique **distinguished name (DN)**. For example, the *Bayside.net* domain component (DC) has a user object with a common name (CN) of Karen Kezema that is stored within the Sales OU. The distinguished name for the object would be:
  CN=Karen Kezema, OU=Sales, DC=Bayside, DC=net
- *Relative Distinguished Name* — A portion of the distinguished name that uniquely identifies the object within the container is referred to as the **relative distinguished name**. For example, the distinguished name OU=Sales, DC=Bayside, DC=net would have a relative distinguished name of OU=Sales. For the distinguished name CN=Karen Kezema, OU=Sales, DC=Bayside, DC=net, the relative distinguished name would be CN=Karen Kezema.

The Active Directory Physical Structure

The Active Directory physical structure relates to the actual connectivity of the physical network itself. Since the Active Directory database is stored on multiple servers, you need to make sure that any modification to the database is replicated as quickly as possible between domain controllers. You must also design your topology so that replication does not saturate the available network bandwidth. One replication problem that you may encounter is when domain controllers are separated over a slow WAN connection. In this scenario, you likely want to control the frequency and the time that replication takes place.

In addition to replication, you may also want to control logon traffic. Referring back to the previous scenario, you do not want any users to have to cross the slow WAN link when obtaining authentication to log on to the network. Users should have to authenticate to a domain controller on their side of the WAN connection.

Keep in mind that the physical structure of Active Directory is totally separate from the logical structure. The logical structure is used to organize your network resources, whereas the physical structure is used to control network traffic.

You can control Active Directory replication traffic and network logon traffic by configuring sites and site links. An Active Directory **site** is a combination of one or more Internet Protocol (IP) subnets connected by a high-speed connection. It is assumed that domain controllers that belong to the same site all have a common network connection. It is also assumed that any connection between sites that are not reliable at all times must have replication controlled through replication schedules and frequency intervals.

A **site link** is a low bandwidth or unreliable/occasional connection between sites. Site links created using the AD Sites and Services snap-in are the core of Active Directory replication. The site links can be adjusted for replication availability, bandwidth costs, and replication frequency. Windows 2000 uses this information to generate the replication topology for the sites, including the schedule for replication.. Figure 1-13 shows an example of a site structure within a domain. Each site contains domain controllers that share a high-speed connection. Because of a slower WAN connection between Vancouver, Winnipeg, and Ottawa, sites and site links have been created to enable control over replication and logon traffic.

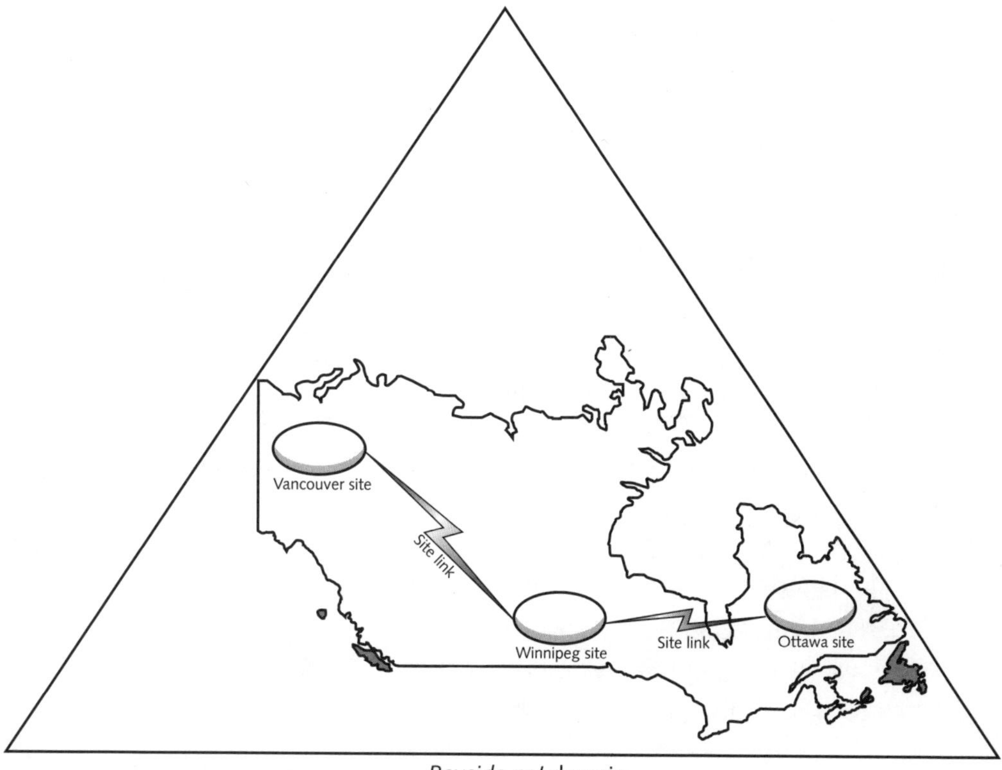

Figure 1-13 The site structure of *Bayside.net*

Replication within a site takes place based on a change notification process. If any change is made within Active Directory, the server waits five minutes and then announces the changes to the other domain controllers. If no changes have been made, replication takes place within an hour. Replication between sites is initially set at every three hours, but can easily be changed by editing the properties of the site link object.

CHAPTER SUMMARY

- There are many tasks and procedures that a network administrator is expected to be able to perform on a daily basis. Some of these tasks include software installation, Active Directory administration, file and print administration, Internet and remote access administration, network performance monitoring, and troubleshooting.
- A network administrator needs to follow a systematic approach to troubleshooting network problems. This requires defining the problem, gathering detailed information on what has changed, devising a plan to solve the problem, implementing the plan, observing what happens, and documenting all changes and results.
- Some of the tools that a network administrator can use to help with routine network management include the Microsoft Management Console, the secondary logon service, and various command-line utilities such as netdiag.exe and the NET command.
- Active Directory is a directory service database provided with Windows 2000 Server-Based Operating Systems. Active Directory provides the following services to the network environment:
  - A central point for storing, organizing, managing, and controlling network objects such as users, computers, and groups
  - A single point of administration of objects such as users, groups, computers, and Active Directory-published resources, such as printers or shared folders
  - Logon and authentication services for users
  - Delegation of administration to allow for decentralized administration of Active Directory objects such as users and groups.
- The logical components that make up an Active Directory structure include:
  - Domains and organizational units
  - Trees and forests
  - The Global Catalog
- Active Directory uses the DNS naming standard for IP name resolution and provides information on the location of network services. When users need to access Active Directory, the Lightweight Directory Access Protocol (LDAP) is used to query or update the Active Directory database directly.
- Active Directory replication traffic and network logon traffic can be controlled by configuring sites and site links. An Active Directory site is a combination of one or more Internet Protocol (IP) subnets connected with a high-speed connection. A site link is a low bandwidth or unreliable/occasional connection between sites. The site links can be adjusted for replication availability, bandwidth costs, and replication frequency. They enable control over replication and logon traffic.

Key Terms

Active Directory (AD) — A directory service included with Windows 2000 server-based systems that provides a single point of administration, authentication, and storage for user, group, and computer objects.

Active Directory schema — Contains the definition of all object classes and attributes used in the Active Directory database.

attributes — Used to define the characteristics of an object class within Active Directory.

distinguished name (DN) — An LDAP component used to uniquely identify an object throughout the entire LDAP hierarchy by referring to the relative distinguished name, domain name, and the container holding the object.

domain — A logically structured organization of objects, such as users, computers, groups, and printers, that are part of a network and share a common directory database. Domains are defined by an administrator and administered as a unit with common rules and procedures.

Domain Name System (DNS) — A hierarchical name resolution system that resolves host names into IP addresses and vice versa. It is a method for maintaining domain naming structure and locating network resources.

forest — A collection of Active Directory trees that do not share a contiguous DNS naming convention, but do share a common global catalog and schema.

forest root domain — The first domain created within the Active Directory structure.

global catalog — An index of the objects and attributes used throughout the Active Directory structure. It contains a partial replica of every Windows 2000 domain within Active Directory, enabling users to find any object in the directory.

Group Policy — The Windows 2000 feature that allows for policy creation that affects domain users and computers. Policies can be anything from desktop settings to application assignment to security settings and more.

Internet Connection Sharing (ICS) — A Windows 2000 service that allows the use of a single, live Internet IP address to be shared among multiple clients. DHCP and DNS cannot be configured.

Lightweight Directory Access Protocol (LDAP) — An access protocol that defines how users can access or update directory service objects.

Microsoft Management Console (MMC) — A customizable management interface that can contain a number of management tools to provide a single, unified application for network administration.

Microsoft Saved Console (MSC) — The filename extension of a console saved using the Microsoft Management Console.

multi-master replication — A replication model in which any domain controller accepts and replicates directory changes to any other domain controller. This differs from other replication models in which one computer stores the single modifiable copy of the directory and other computers store backup copies.

Network Address Translation (NAT) — The process of converting between IP addresses used within an intranet or other private network (called a stub domain) and Internet IP addresses. This approach makes it possible to use a large number of addresses within the stub domain without depleting the limited number of available numeric Internet IP addresses. Also, the network is protected when NAT replaces the source internal address and ports of all outgoing packets with a single public IP address.

object — A collection of attributes that represent items within Active Directory, such as users, groups, computers, and printers.

object classes — Define which types of objects can be created within Active Directory, such as users, groups, and printers.

organizational unit (OU) — An Active Directory logical container used to organize objects within a single domain. Objects such as users, groups, computers, and other OUs, can be stored in an OU.

relative distinguished name (RDN) — An LDAP component used to identify an object within the object's container.

Routing and Remote Access Services (RRAS) — A Windows 2000 service that allows users to access a company network or access the Internet through a variety of ways such as dial-up, VPN, or NAT services.

site — A combination of one or more Internet Protocol (IP) subnets connected by a high-speed connection.

site link — A low bandwidth or unreliable/occasional connection between sites. The site links can be adjusted for replication availability, bandwidth costs, and replication frequency. They enable control over replication and logon traffic.

snap-ins — The management tools that are added to a Microsoft Management Console interface.

taskpad — Allows you to simplify administrative procedures by providing a graphical representation of the tasks that can be performed in an MMC console.

transitive trust — The ability for domains to trust one another, even though they do not have a direct explicit trust between them.

tree — A hierarchical collection of domains that share a contiguous DNS namespace.

Virtual Private Networking (VPN) — A Windows 2000 service that allows a private and secure connection with a company network over the Internet.

Review Questions

1. What service does Active Directory use for name resolution and locating network resources?

    a. DHCP

    b. DNS

    c. WINS

    d. None of the above

2. What is the name of the first domain installed within the Active Directory database?
   a. master root domain
   b. principal root domain
   c. primary root domain
   d. forest root domain
3. Domains in a tree share a contiguous DNS namespace. Trees in a forest do not share a contiguous DNS naming structure. True or False?
4. In Windows 2000, a two-way, transitive trust relationship is maintained between:
   a. child and parent forests
   b. child and parent groups
   c. child and parent domains
   d. none of the above
5. An Active Directory object can contain users, groups, computers, and printers. True or False?
6. Which of the following logical components make up an Active Directory structure? (Choose all that apply.)
   a. domain
   b. global catalog
   c. forest
   d. tree
   e. schema
   f. all of the above
7. Each tree in a forest shares a contiguous namespace. True or False?
8. Which of the following describe advantages of the secondary logon feature? (Choose all that apply.)
   a. Two users can access a group at the same time.
   b. The administrator can log on with a user account and then as an administrator.
   c. A user can access more than one group at a time.
   d. It saves the administrator having to log off and then log back on to perform administrative tasks.
9. Some of the administrative utilities available with Windows 2000 include:
   a. the Windows 2000 task scheduler
   b. netdiag
   c. the NET command
   d. all of the above
   e. none of the above

10. *Bayside.net* has two child domains named *East.Bayside.net* and *West.Bayside.net.* You already know that these domains automatically trust *Bayside.net.* As well, they trust each other automatically. True or False?

11. Which step of the troubleshooting process is associated with the task of investigating whether software has been installed recently on the workstation?

    a. define the problem

    b. gather detailed information on what has changed

    c. devise a plan to solve the problem

    d. implement the plan and observe results

12. You need to search for all custom MMC consoles on your server. What extension should you search for?

    a. .mcs

    b. .mmc

    c. .msc

    d. .mcm

13. The management tool that can be added to customize an MMC is called a:

    a. snap-let

    b. snap-in

    c. plug-in

    d. none of the above

14. The global address list for Exchange 2000 e-mail systems can be found in:

    a. the universal group

    b. a transitive trust

    c. the global catalog

    d. a global group

15. Which of the following tasks does a network administrator not usually perform? (Choose all that apply.)

    a. installing and maintaining the operating system

    b. administering Active Directory

    c. keeping adequate documentation

    d. troubleshooting Windows 2000

    e. a and d

16. Active Directory is:
    a. a group
    b. a database
    c. a forest
    d. a folder
    e. none of the above
17. An organizational unit structure is useful because it allows the administrator to:
    a. administer one large corporation at a time
    b. delegate specific tasks
    c. dictate the maximum number of trees in a forest
    d. none of the above
18. You are currently logged in with your regular user account. At a command prompt, which command would you type to start the Event Viewer console under the context of the administrator?
    a. runas /user:<*domain\username*> eventvwr
    b. runas /console:<*domain\username*> eventvwr
    c. start /user:<*domain\username*> eventvwr
    d. start/console:<*domain\username*> eventvwr
19. Distinguished name is a component of Lightweight Directory Access Protocol (LDAP). True or False?
20. Which of the following are valid reasons for creating more than one domain for an organization?
    a. replication issues
    b. language needs
    c. geographical separation
    d. all of the above
21. Active Directory is stored on multiple servers. True or False?
22. Which of the following objects can be stored within an organizational unit? (Choose all that apply.)
    a. Active Directory
    b. printer objects
    c. user objects
    d. a and c
23. The first domain controller in Active Directory cannot become a global catalog server. True or False?

24. Terminal Services is a feature in Windows 2000 used by network administrators. True or False?
25. In Windows 2000, the Active Directory schema defines:
    a. how to access System Monitor
    b. the rules for accessing e-mail through Exchange 2000
    c. the objects for the entire Active Directory structure
    d. none of the above

HANDS-ON PROJECTS

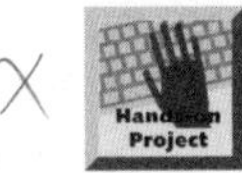

Project 1-1

In this Hands-on Project, you experiment with the runas / command to open Event Viewer.

1. Log on to your Windows 2000 computer.
2. Click **Start**, and then click **Run**.
3. In the Open text box, type **cmd** to open a command prompt.
4. At the command prompt, type the following:
   runas /user:<*servername*>\administrator eventvwr
5. Type the Administrator's password at the prompt.
6. The Event Viewer opens. Browse the various logs in the Event Viewer.
7. Close all open windows.

Project 1-2

In this Hands-on Project, you will create a new MMC console.

1. With an Administrator account, log on to your Windows 2000 computer.
2. Click **Start**, click **Run**, and then type **mmc** in the Run text box. Click **OK**. Maximize the Console Root window by double-clicking the title bar or clicking the **Maximize** button.
3. Click the **Console** menu, and then click **Add/Remove Snap-in**. The Add/Remove Snap-in dialog box opens.
4. Click the **Add** button. Click **Computer Management**, and then click **Add**.
5. Click **Local computer**, and then click **Finish**. Click **Close**, and then click **OK**.
6. To save the custom console, click the **Console** menu, and click **Save As**. Name the console **My Management Tools**, and click **Save**.
7. Continue to the next project.

Project 1-3

In this Hands-on Project, you will create a taskpad based upon the custom MMC created in the previous project.

1. In the My Management Tools console, expand **Computer Management** by clicking the plus sign.
2. Expand **System Tools** by clicking the plus sign.
3. Click **Shared Folders**.
4. Right-click **Shared Folders**, and click **New Taskpad View**. Click **Next** at the Welcome screen.
5. In the Taskpad Display dialog box, accept the defaults, and click **Next**.
6. On the Taskpad Target dialog box, accept the defaults, and click **Next**.
7. Type a name and description for the taskpad. Click **Next**.
8. At the Completing the New Taskpad View Wizard, check the **Start New Task Wizard** option if it is not already checked. Click **Finish**.
9. Click **Next** at the Welcome screen.
10. Click **Menu**, and click **Next**.
11. At the Shortcut Menu Command screen, click **List in details pane** under Command source if it is not already selected.
12. Click **Shares** in the left pane, and then click **New File Share**. Click **Next**.
13. Leave the Task name and Description as the defaults. Click **Next**.
14. Choose an icon for the task, and click **Next**.
15. At the Completing the New Task Wizard, click **Finish**.

Project 1-4

In this Hands-on Project, you will install the Windows 2000 Support Tools. (This project assumes that you have set up your computer as listed in the lab setup guide.)

1. Right-click **My Computer**, and click **Explore**.
2. Click drive D: on your computer.
3. Double-click the **W2KAS** folder, and browse to the Support\Tools folder.
4. Double-click **Setup**.
5. Click **Next** at the Welcome dialog box.
6. Click **Next** at the User Information screen.
7. Click **Typical**, and click **Next**.
8. Click **Next** to begin the installation.

9. To test a specific support tool, click **Start**, and click **Run** to open a command prompt. Type **cmd** in the Open text box.
10. Type **netdiag** to perform diagnostic tests on your computer.
11. Close all windows and log off.

CASE PROJECTS

Case Project 1-1

Bayside Detailing is upgrading their network infrastructure to Windows 2000 Active Directory. They have three divisions, with the main office located in Melfort, Saskatchewan, one office in Montreal, Quebec, and the third located in Winnipeg, Manitoba. The Montreal office is primarily a French-speaking division. The physical network connection between Melfort and Winnipeg is 100 Mbps whereas the connection to Montreal is a 56k ISDN connection. You have been asked to come up with a general Active Directory plan for the company.

1. What factors influence the decision on how the logical Active Directory structure is to be designed?
2. What type of domain structure do you suggest for Bayside Detailing?
3. What is a possible naming convention for the suggested domain structure?
4. How many sites will likely be created for the organization?

Case Project 1-2

A user phones you and states that she cannot log on to the network. Using the troubleshooting procedures discussed in this chapter, list each step and state what questions you would ask or procedures you would follow for each of the steps to attempt to solve the problem.

CHAPTER

2

MANAGING WINDOWS 2000 HARDWARE AND SOFTWARE

After reading this chapter and completing the exercises, you will be able to:

- Plan your operating system installation to ensure Windows 2000 hardware and software compatibility
- Assess your hardware and software needs by using the Windows 2000 qualifier tools
- Install and configure computer hardware devices and drivers
- Configure driver signing options and verify digital signatures on existing drivers
- Install and manage Windows 2000 Updates using service packs and hot fixes

A Windows 2000 installation and deployment is not always a straightforward process. Many companies have complex networking needs and diverse environments that can present challenges for the administrator. However, with the proper installation and maintenance plan, you can become proactive in discovering any potential problem areas that may interfere with a successful server or workstation deployment.

As you deploy Windows 2000 throughout your network, you need to be sure that all existing hardware and software is compatible with the new operating system. This chapter introduces you to the Microsoft qualifier tools that assist in determining if your current hardware is compatible with Windows 2000. These tools can also help in assessing any new hardware that is to be purchased and verifying its compatibility with Windows 2000.

After the operating system installation is complete, there may be a number of additional tasks that need to take place before the server or workstation is ready for the production environment. For example, there may be hardware or components that were not automatically detected during the installation. You may need to obtain and update device drivers to ensure the functionality expected under the new operating system. To ensure that a Windows 2000-compatible driver is installed, you can configure driver code signing options to only allow tested and verified device drivers to be incorporated into the installation. This chapter describes how to install and troubleshoot hardware devices, as well as how to configure and verify driver signatures and signing options.

Microsoft periodically releases service pack updates and hot fixes to secure potential security or software problems with Windows 2000. You should be aware of how to obtain and install these updates and how to slipstream the service packs into the installation point to make sure that all future installations incorporate the updates. The final portion of this chapter discusses how to install and manage Windows 2000 updates such as service packs and hot fixes.

Planning the Installation

To be sure that a deployment of Windows 2000 Server or Windows 2000 Professional goes as smoothly as possible, it is important for you to plan your installation. Planning helps ensure that all aspects of the installation are thought out before the start of the setup process, and that all problem areas can be identified and minimized.

As you are analyzing your environment, there is a variety of information that you need to collect and document to prepare for your Windows 2000 deployment. This information includes:

- Computer hardware configurations: It is vital to know exactly what computer hardware configurations are deployed throughout the organization. As discussed in the next section, Windows 2000 installations must meet the minimum hardware requirements for a successful and reliable installation.
- Network infrastructure configuration: It is very helpful to understand the physical layout of servers, workstations, routers, and hubs. All LAN and WAN speeds, bandwidth, and latency issues should also be documented. In addition, you should also create or obtain a diagram and listing of the IP subnets and network addresses. This information can assist you when configuring TCP/IP settings on the machines.
- A diagram illustrating each organizational unit (OU) is also helpful. This can assist you in network configurations such as domain and OU memberships.
- Network interoperability issues: It is important to understand which network operating systems are integrated within your organization. Specific configurations

are needed when incorporating Windows 2000 with Novell Netware, UNIX, or a Macintosh environment.

- Existing applications: All applications should be analyzed to ensure that they work within a Windows 2000 environment. Custom applications may need to be rewritten to function correctly within the Windows 2000 environment.

In addition to analyzing the network for Windows 2000 compatibility and functionality issues, keep in mind the risks associated with deploying a new network system. A proactive approach to risk management means that you are able to predict and possibly prevent trouble before it happens. A reactive approach is when you fix the problem after it has happened. A reactive approach to problem solving causes user frustration, network downtime, company expenditures, and possibly the loss of your job. Therefore, a thoroughly thought out Windows 2000 installation or deployment plan is part of a proactive approach that allows you to know exactly what can go wrong, and how to prevent or minimize disruption if something does go wrong.

Assessing the Hardware and Software Needs

Your Windows 2000 infrastructure is only as reliable as the hardware upon which it is based. This is why it is vital that you understand the system requirements of Windows 2000. Before you install Windows 2000, make sure that your hardware meets and, if possible, exceeds the minimum requirements set forth by Microsoft. It is also wise to buy hardware that is listed in the **Microsoft Hardware Compatibility List (HCL)**. Although you may find that most hardware devices perform well with Windows 2000, if the hardware has not been specifically tested and registered with the HCL, Microsoft may not provide troubleshooting support. As a rule, only buy servers that have hardware listed on the HCL. Non-HCL computers or hardware can be used as workstations, because they do not require the reliability or performance that a server may need.

You can check the Hardware Compatibility List on the Microsoft Web site at *www.microsoft.com/hcl*.

Windows 2000 minimum system requirements on new servers may not matter as much as they did in the past, because most computers sold today exceed the minimum requirements. However, in the event that you need to upgrade an older server to Windows 2000, you need to make sure that the minimum requirements are met to ensure constant reliability and performance. Meeting the minimum hardware requirements also helps to ensure that Windows 2000 functions as expected.

Table 2-1 lists both the minimum and recommended system requirements for Windows 2000 Server and Windows 2000 Professional products.

Table 2-1 Minimum hardware requirements for Windows 2000

Component	Minimum	Recommendation
processor	Intel Pentium 133 MHz	Intel Pentium II 300 MHz or faster
memory	64 MB for Server, 32 MB for Professional	256 MB for Server, 128 MB for Professional
hard disk	850 MB partition with 650 MB of free space	2 GB of free disk space
display	VGA monitor	Super VGA at 800 by 600 resolution
CD-ROM	bootable CD-ROM support	bootable CD-ROM or DVD-ROM
network adapters	PCI-based fast Ethernet	PCI based and PXE compatible

Accessing the BIOS Configuration

Another aspect that is often overlooked is whether or not the computer's **Basic Input/Output System (BIOS)** is compatible and configured to work properly with Windows 2000. The BIOS is a program stored on a flash memory chip attached to the motherboard. This program establishes the initial communication between the components of the computer, such as the hard drive, CD-ROM, floppy disk, video, and memory. An illustration of a sample BIOS configuration screen is shown in Figure 2-1.

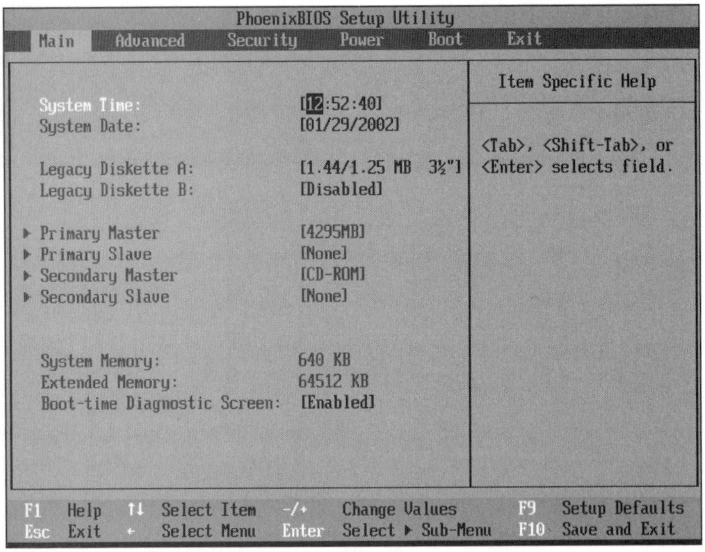

Figure 2-1 Sample computer BIOS configuration screen

Accessing the BIOS is usually done by pressing the Delete key or F2 on the keyboard during the initial startup of the computer before the operating system loads. Some obvious settings that may need to be adjusted in the BIOS include the order in which devices start when you start your system from CD-ROM during setup. If you have a legacy component in your computer that is not compatible with Plug and Play, you may also have to reserve a specific **interrupt request (IRQ)**, which will ensure that conflicts do not take place. For example, you may have an old ISA-based sound card that requires interrupt 5. When your Plug and Play components come online, there may be one that prefers and attempts to use interrupt 5 and causes a conflict with the sound card. If you reserve the interrupt in the BIOS for devices that are not Plug and Play compatible, the Plug and Play component must choose an alternate configuration and give first priority to the ISA card to use interrupt 5.

In addition to configuration settings, you may also need to download a BIOS flash update from your computer motherboard manufacturer to ensure that all Windows 2000 settings, such as Advanced Power Management and device configuration features, are supported.

For more information on BIOS compatibility and Windows 2000, access the following Web page: *www.microsoft.com/windows2000/server/howtobuy/upgrading/compat/biosissue.asp*

Verifying Hardware and Software Compatibility

In addition to verifying that your computer meets the minimum hardware requirements of Windows 2000, it is important to ensure that all of your individual components, such as your video card and network adapter, are also supported. You also need to ensure that your current software supports Windows 2000. There are two ways in which you can evaluate the compatibility of your existing components and software: by utilizing the Windows 2000 Readiness Analyzer, or by accessing the Microsoft Hardware and Software Compatibility Web site.

The Microsoft Windows 2000 Readiness Analyzer

The **Windows 2000 Readiness Analyzer** utility launches the first part of Windows 2000 setup, but only checks for hardware and software compatibility and does not actually install Windows 2000. It then generates a report based upon results of the check. You can run this check by inserting the Windows 2000 CD-ROM or accessing the installation point, and typing winnt32.exe /checkupgradeonly at a command prompt. The analyzer starts, as shown in Figure 2-2.

Be sure to run the analyzer on compatible systems. For example, you cannot run a Windows 2000 Advanced Server Readiness Analyzer on a Windows 98 machine. Windows 98 only allows you to upgrade to Windows 2000 Professional, and so you must use the Windows 2000 Professional version of the analyzer.

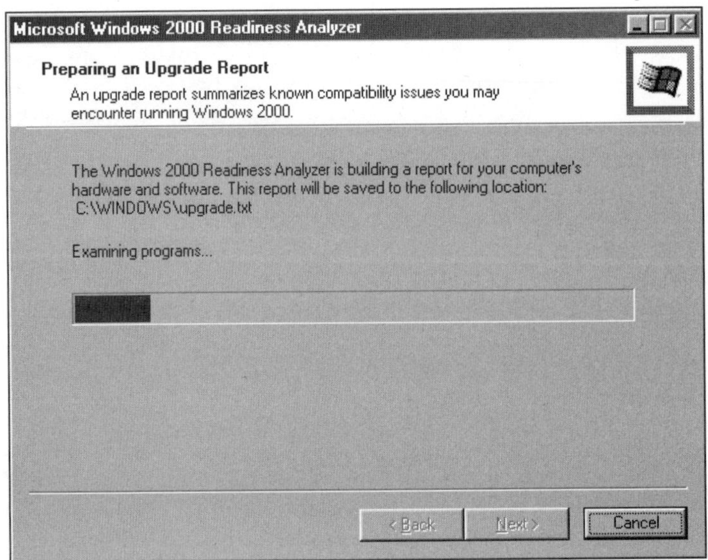

Figure 2-2 Running the Windows 2000 Readiness Analyzer

As stated in the analyzer dialog box, a report is saved at C:\windows\upgrade.txt. After the analyzer finishes, a report is also displayed, as shown in Figure 2-3.

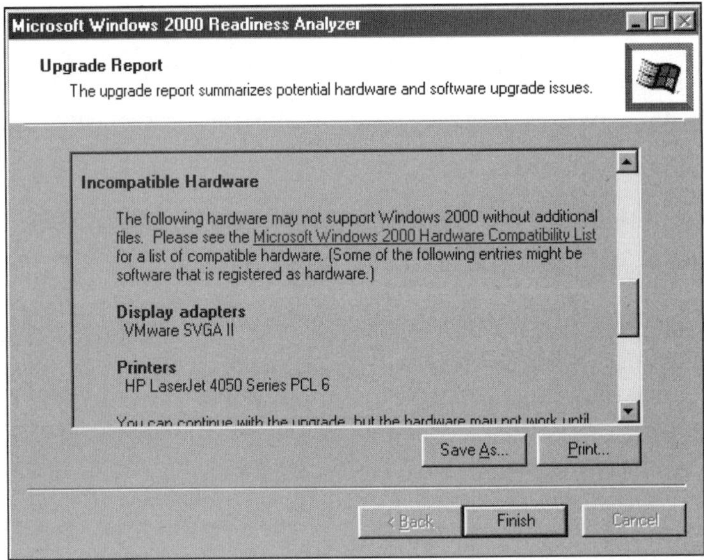

Figure 2-3 The Readiness Analyzer report

2

The Hardware and Software Compatibility Web Site

As shown in Figure 2-4, Microsoft provides a Web page that you can query to evaluate current or future hardware and software compatibility. The Web page can be accessed at:

www.microsoft.com/windows2000/server/howtobuy/upgrading/compat/default.asp

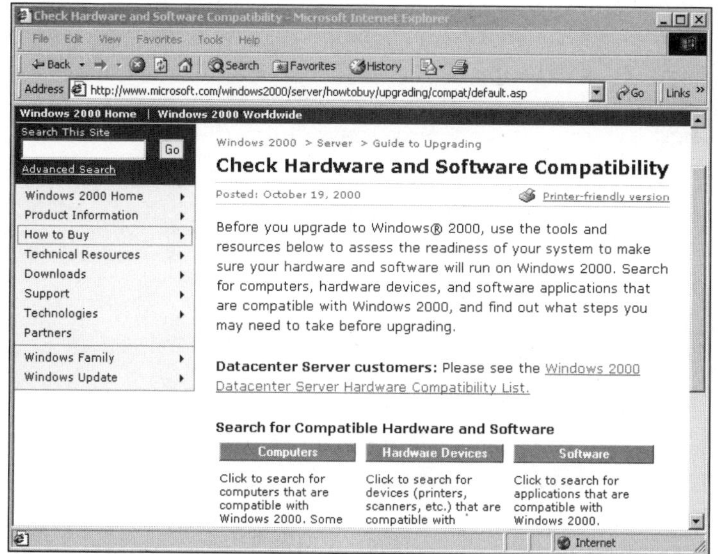

Figure 2-4 Accessing the Check Hardware and Software Web site

This online utility allows you to type in a specific manufacturer or model of a hardware or software component, and then it indicates whether the component is compatible with Windows 2000 and where to find updated drivers, if necessary.

Prior to the release of Windows 2000, Microsoft tested the top business applications for compatibility. Most applications were successful, but some that were specifically designed for the Windows 9.x platform required specific compatibility updates to be installed. The most popular application compatibility updates have been included with Windows 2000. As Microsoft evaluates additional applications, they provide periodic Windows 2000 compatibility update downloads on their Web site. Some of the newest updates include fixes for minor compatibility issues with some of the more popular entertainment applications. The compatibility update download can be accessed at the following Web site:

/www.microsoft.com/windows2000/downloads/tools/appcompat/default.asp

You can install the update by double-clicking the file that you have downloaded from the Web site. Please note that you must restart your machine after installing the update.

INSTALLING AND CONFIGURING HARDWARE DEVICES

After a successful installation, there are still a few tasks that might need to be completed before assigning the workstation or server to the production environment. Some of these tasks include verifying hardware detection and updating device drivers. You also need to install the latest service packs and hot fixes.

Your first step is to verify that all hardware devices have been detected properly by Windows 2000. To accomplish this task, you can open the Device Manager to view all of the installed devices. The **Device Manager** is used to view and modify hardware device properties, update device drivers, and uninstall unneeded hardware.

To open the Device Manager, right-click My Computer, and click Properties. When you click the Hardware tab, you notice the Device Manager button. Click the button to open the Device Manager as shown in Figure 2-5.

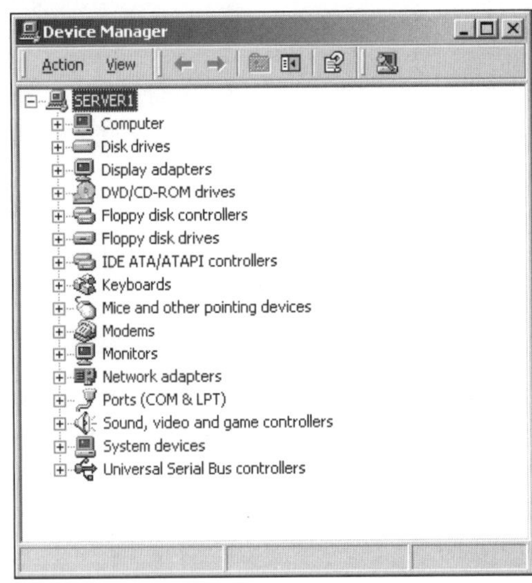

Figure 2-5 Viewing hardware devices using the Device Manager

As shown in Figure 2-6, any device that is not functioning is indicated with a yellow exclamation point. If you have a disabled device, it is indicated with a small red "x" over the device icon. If you double-click the device, you are able to update device drivers or disable the device from the current logon profile.

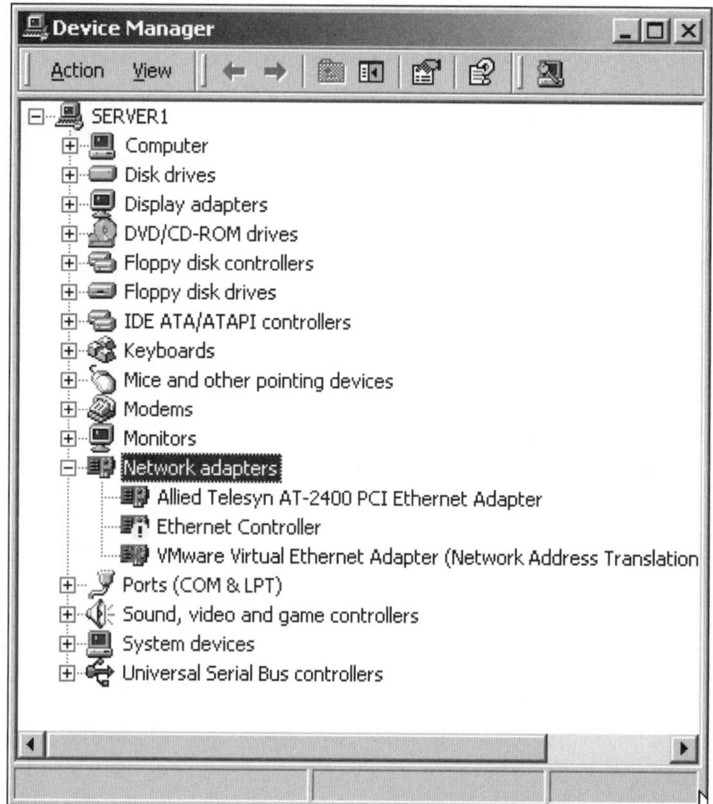

Figure 2-6 Viewing devices that are disabled or have a problem

If a specific device is missing or is not functioning, Windows 2000 provides two ways to troubleshoot or repair the problem. The first method is to obtain a new driver from the manufacturer's Web site, and then install the new driver from within the Device Manager. To install the new driver, double-click the malfunctioning device in the Device Manager. This would be the device with the yellow exclamation mark. Click the Driver tab to view current driver details, and to display the Update Driver button, as shown in Figure 2-7.

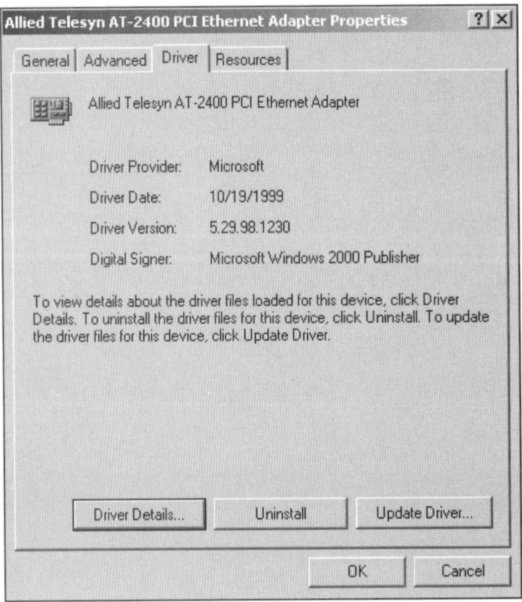

Figure 2-7 Installing an updated device driver

When you click the Update Driver button, the Upgrade Device Driver Wizard opens, as shown in Figure 2-8. This wizard steps you through the task of selecting and installing the updated device driver.

Figure 2-8 Starting the Upgrade Device Driver Wizard

The second method of installing, removing, or repairing a hardware device is to use the **Add/Remove Hardware Wizard**. To start the Add/Remove Hardware Wizard, access Control Panel, and double-click Add/Remove Hardware. The Add/Remove Hardware Wizard opens. When you click Next, you are presented with options to Add/Troubleshoot a device or Uninstall/Unplug a device, as shown in Figure 2-9.

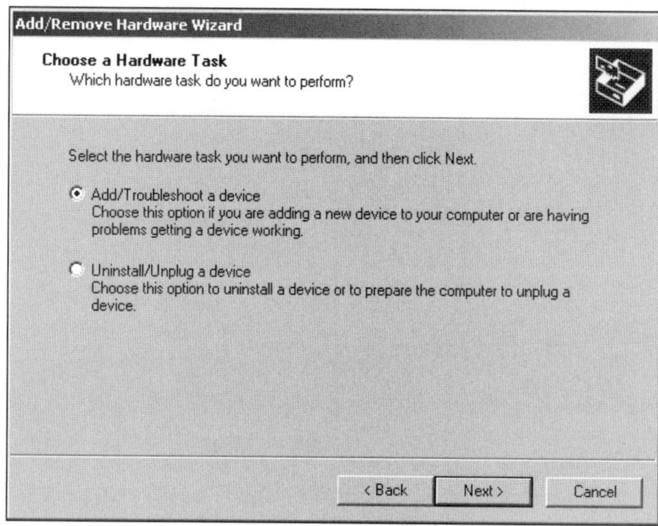

Figure 2-9 Adding or troubleshooting hardware

If you choose to Add/Troubleshoot a device, Windows then performs a Plug and Play search for all devices attached to the computer. After the detection, the Choose a Hardware Device dialog box appears. Click the device that is causing problems, or click Add a new device to install new hardware.

When installing a new device, you are given the opportunity to provide the device drivers needed. If you are troubleshooting a device, a status window appears stating the status of the device and prompting you to start the hardware troubleshooter.

If you choose to Uninstall/Unplug a device, you are presented with a list of devices you can use as you would the Device Manager. You are then able to select the device and have Windows uninstall the drivers associated with the device to be removed.

Configuring Driver Signing Options

Every Windows 2000 operating system file and built-in driver has been digitally signed by Microsoft to ensure compatibility and quality. **Driver signing** ensures that a driver for a specific device has been verified by Microsoft to work with Windows 2000, and a unique digital signature has been incorporated into the driver. This digital signature assures you that it has met a certain quality test standard and that the file has not been altered or overwritten by another program's installation process.

When you configure driver signing options, you are presented with three choices:

- *Ignore*—This option effectively turns off driver and file verification. If this option is selected, driver signing is ignored.
- *Warn*—If this option is selected, a message appears, as shown in Figure 2-10, alerting you that a digital signature was not found and there is no guarantee that the driver is going to work with Windows.

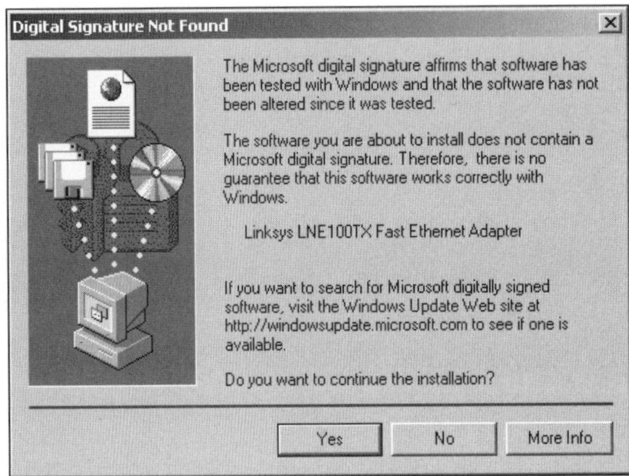

Figure 2-10 Verifying digital signatures

- *Block*—This option prevents the installation of any driver that is not signed. If you attempt to install an unsigned driver, a message appears, as shown in Figure 2-11, that states a digital signature was not found.

Figure 2-11 Denying the installation of drivers without digital signatures

To configure driver signing, right-click My Computer, and click Properties. The Hardware tab contains a button labeled Driver Signing. When you click the Driver Signing button, the Driver Signing Options dialog box opens, as shown in Figure 2-12. It is here that you can choose to ignore, warn about, or block unsigned drivers.

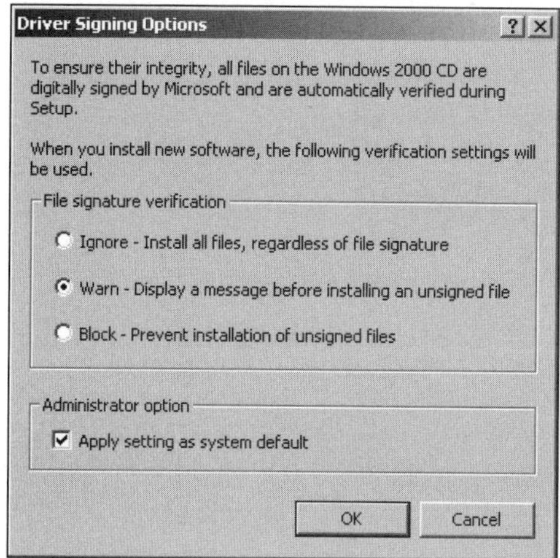

Figure 2-12 Configuring driver signing

After a Windows 2000 installation, the Warn option is selected by default. This can be changed by logging on as the administrator, choosing the signing option, and then selecting the check box next to Apply setting as system default. This setting then applies to all users that log onto the computer.

If you decide to leave the driver signing option set to Warn, it is possible that unsigned or incompatible device drivers can inadvertently be installed. If you are having problems with operating system instability, you can run a verification check to see which existing drivers on your computer are not digitally signed. Windows 2000 includes a utility called the **File Signature Verification**. This utility can identify unsigned files and give you information such as the file name, location, modification date, and version number. To start the File Signature Verification utility, click Start, click Run, and then type sigverif in the Open text box. The File Signature Verification utility opens, as shown in Figure 2-13.

When you click the Start button, your computer is scanned for any system files that have not been digitally signed. The results appear in a dialog box, as shown in Figure 2-14.

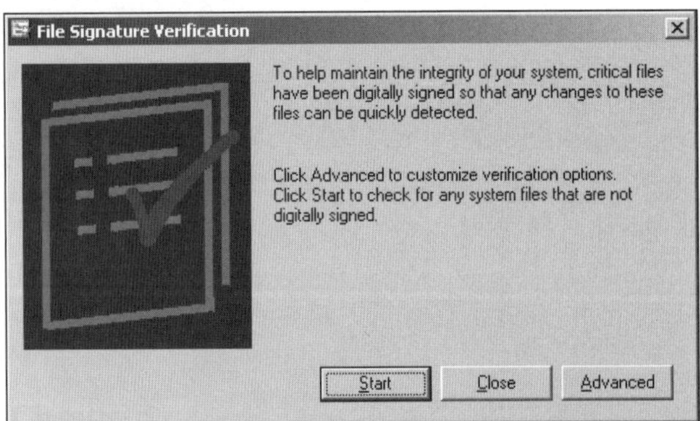

Figure 2-13 Starting the File Signature Verification utility

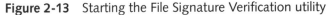

Signature Verification Results

The following files have not been digitally signed:

Name	In Folder	Modified	File Type	Version
netpnic.inf	c:\winnt\inf	6/10/1999	Setup Inf...	None
netvmware.inf	c:\winnt\inf	10/3/2001	Setup Inf...	None
vmnet.sys	c:\winnt\system32\drivers	11/1/2001	System file	2.0.1.0
vmnetx.sys	c:\winnt\system32\drivers	11/1/2001	System file	1.0.0.1
hpv600al.dll	c:\winnt\system32\spool\dri...	8/17/2001	Applicatio...	1.0.0.1
hpvdj200.hlp	c:\winnt\system32\spool\dri...	7/21/2001	Help File	None
hpvdj69x.gpd	c:\winnt\system32\spool\dri...	7/21/2001	GPD File	None
hpvdj6xx.gpd	c:\winnt\system32\spool\dri...	7/21/2001	GPD File	None
hpvimg50.dll	c:\winnt\system32\spool\dri...	8/17/2001	Applicatio...	7.19...
hpvnam50....	c:\winnt\system32\spool\dri...	7/21/2001	GPD File	None

Close

Files found: 675. Signed files: 635. Unsigned files: 24. Files not scanned: 16.

Figure 2-14 The results of the File Signature Verification

By default, the File Signature Verification utility only checks Windows 2000 system files. If you want to check other files to see if they are digitally signed, click the Advanced button, and then click the option button next to Look for other files that are not digitally signed. You can then specify the file type and location of the files to be checked, as shown in Figure 2-15.

Windows 2000 also includes protection for any system files that may be overwritten by installing software. **Windows File Protection** helps to prevent the replacement of protected files such as .sys, .dll, .ocx, .ttf, .fon, and .exe files. When you install an application that attempts to replace a protected file, Windows File Protection checks the file's digital signature to determine if it is a correct Microsoft version. If the file is not the correct version, Windows File Protection replaces the file from a backup of the original file, which is stored in the Winnt\system32\dllcache folder. This feature is enabled by default and only allows the replacement of protected files from signed Windows 2000 service packs, hot fixes, OS upgrades, or the Windows Update Web site.

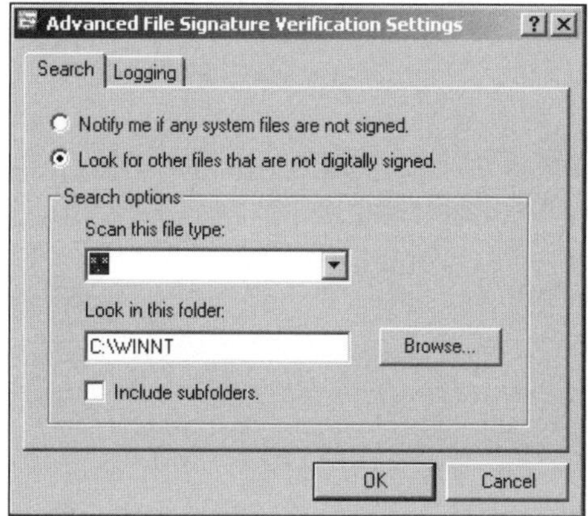

Figure 2-15 Scanning other files for digital signatures

If you want to be sure that all of your Windows system files are the correct versions, Microsoft provides a utility called the System File Checker. The **System File Checker** is a command-line utility that scans and verifies all of the protected system files on your computer. If it discovers that a protected file has been overwritten, it replaces the file with an original backup from the dll cache folder.

To start the System File Checker, open a command prompt, and type sfc /scannow. Note that system performance may be decreased while the utility is running.

INSTALLING AND MANAGING WINDOWS 2000 UPDATES USING SERVICE PACKS AND HOT FIXES

As problems and bugs are discovered with the Windows 2000 operating system, Microsoft provides updates known as **service packs** that can be applied to the current operating system to fix the reported problems. As service packs are released, a version sequence number identifies them. For example, as each service pack is released. it may be called service pack 1, service pack 2, and so on. The latest service pack can be downloaded from the Microsoft Web site or you can order a CD-ROM for a small fee.

As of this writing Windows 2000 Service Pack 2 has been released.

The steps for installing a service pack are as follows:

1. Back up your computer settings, and update your emergency repair disk.
2. Download or obtain the service pack CD, and double-click the executable update file. The Service Pack Setup screen appears, as shown in Figure 2-16.

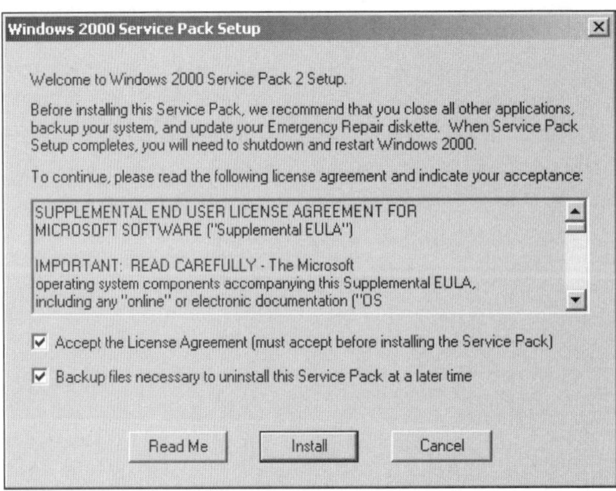

Figure 2-16 Installing a Windows 2000 service pack

3. If you may need to remove this service pack for some reason, be sure to check the option next to Backup files necessary to uninstall the Service Pack at a later time.
4. Accept the License Agreement, and then follow the on-screen instructions for installing the new service pack. The service pack installation begins, as shown in Figure 2-17. You need to restart your machine to finish the installation.

If you insert the service pack CD-ROM into the CD-ROM drive, you can install the service pack from the HTML page that loads automatically when the CD is inserted.

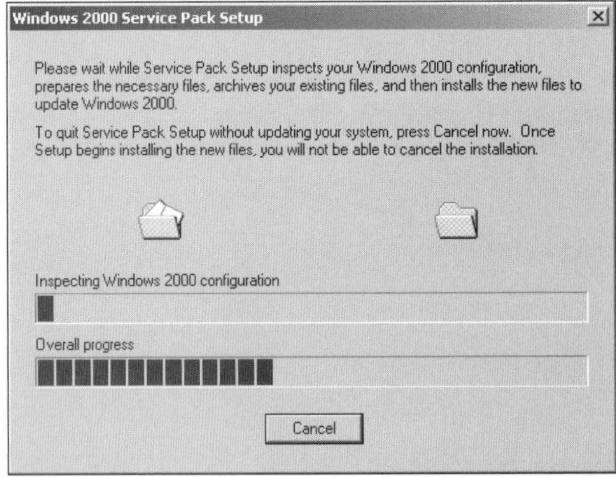

Figure 2-17 The installation of a Windows 2000 service pack

In between service pack releases, there may be bugs or security alerts discovered that require immediate updates. These interim updates are called **hot fixes**. Windows 2000 hot fixes are usually deployed to fix specific problems or security issues with the operating system. When the next service pack is released, it incorporates all of the service packs and hot fixes previously released. Depending upon the type of hot fix available, you usually access a Microsoft Web site to download the patch. The patch is then installed by double-clicking the downloaded file.

You can also use the **Windows Update** Web site to install service packs and hot fixes. To access Windows Update, click Start, and then click Windows Update. The Windows Update Web site opens, as shown in Figure 2-18.

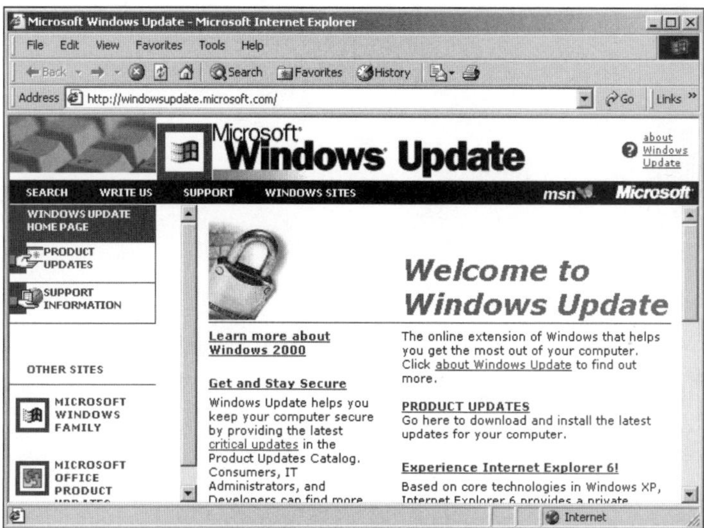

Figure 2-18 Accessing Windows Update

When you click the Product Updates link, Windows Update scans your operating system to determine which service packs and updates are required on your computer. A list of critical updates and service packs is then listed, as shown in Figure 2-19.

When you click the Download button, Windows Update downloads and automatically installs all updates that you had indicated on the main page. If you have the need to uninstall any of the hot fixes or service packs, you can uninstall them by accessing the Add/Remove Programs applet in Control Panel. As shown in Figure 2-20, Add/Remove Programs lists each update installed, and enables you to uninstall them if the need arises.

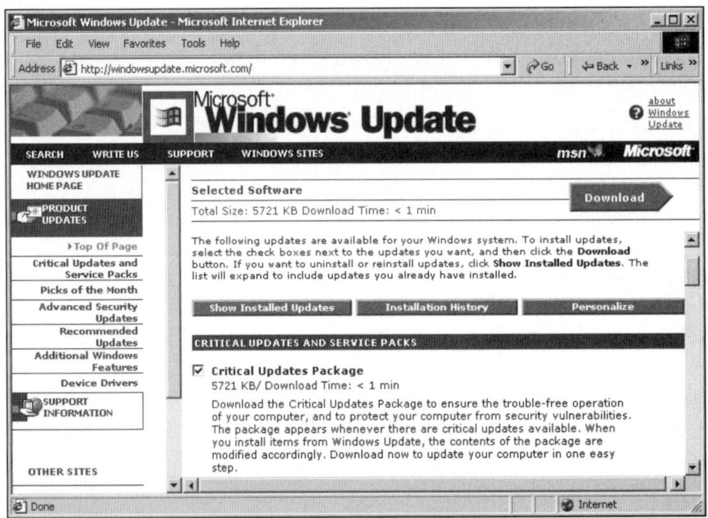

Figure 2-19 Installing Windows hot fixes

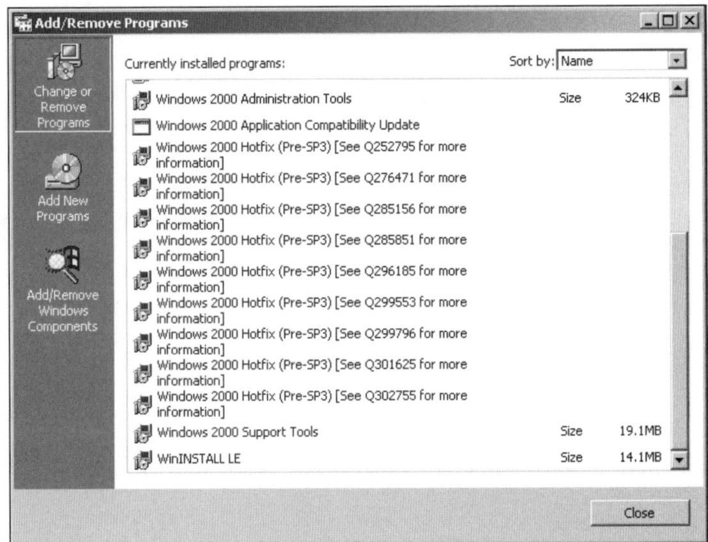

Figure 2-20 The installed hot fixes within Add/Remove programs

To verify which hot fixes and service packs have been installed, you can download a utility called the Microsoft Network Security Hotfix Checker (HFNetCHK). This utility can be downloaded from:

www.microsoft.com/downloads/release.asp?ReleaseID=31154

To run the utility, open a command line, and type hfnetchk. The output appears, as shown in Figure 2-21.

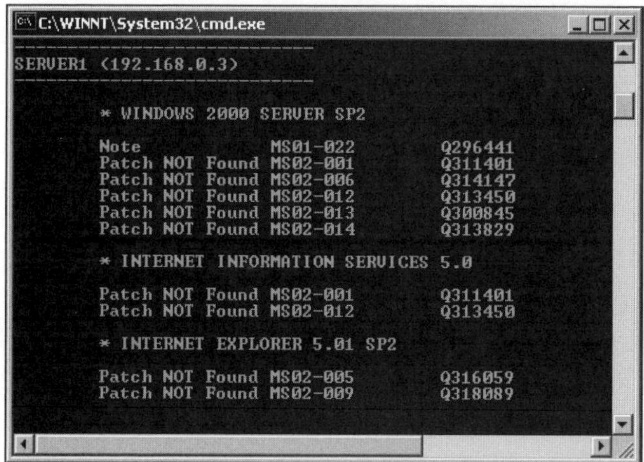

Figure 2-21 Running the HFNetCHK utility

There are a number of parameters that can be used with this utility, including: -r <range>, which specifies a specific IP address range to be scanned, and -d <domain name>, which specifies all of the computers within a domain to be scanned. To view the various options type hfnetchk /? at the command prompt.

Slipstreaming Windows 2000 Service Packs

Slipstreaming is a process that integrates a Windows 2000 service pack with the original Windows 2000 installation files. This is an advantage in that you no longer need to perform separate installations of the operating system and the individual service packs. When you perform a new installation, the service pack is automatically installed with the original setup files.

To slipstream a service pack into a Windows 2000 installation point, follow these steps:

1. Create and share a folder that can be used as a Windows 2000 network installation point.

2. Copy the entire contents of the Windows 2000 CD-ROM to the shared folder created in Step 1.

3. Download or obtain the latest Windows 2000 service pack. To apply the service pack to the installation point, you must first extract the service pack files from the packaged file, and then run the Update.exe program in integrated mode. For example, to extract the service pack 2 package, open a command prompt, and type **W2ksp2.exe /x**. Type an extraction folder name and path when prompted, as shown in Figure 2-22.

Figure 2-22 Extracting the Windows 2000 service pack files

4. After the files have been extracted, browse to the **\i386\update** folder found in the extraction directory, and type **update -s** ***<install point name and path>***. For example, if you have extracted the service pack to a folder called sp2 and you want to integrate sp2 with an installation point on drive E: called W2K, you would either browse to the update folder or type the following at the command prompt: **C:\sp2\i386\update\update.exe -s:e:\w2k**
5. The Windows 2000 Service Pack Setup dialog box appears and starts to integrate the service pack files into the installation point, as shown in Figure 2-23.

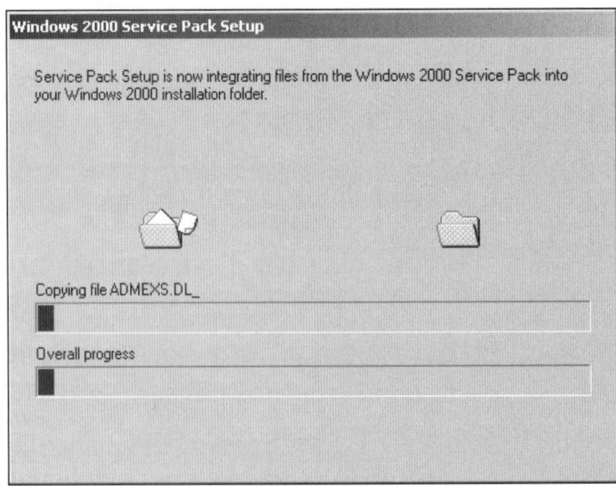

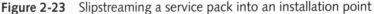

Figure 2-23 Slipstreaming a service pack into an installation point

After the integrated installation point is created, you can install Windows 2000 using the standard installation methods. Windows 2000 is automatically installed at the latest service pack level.

Chapter Summary

- Before installing Windows 2000, there are a number of pre-installation tasks that you must consider that can potentially affect both your organizational and hardware needs. Some of these tasks include understanding the network infrastructure, domain configuration, interoperability issues, existing applications, and current hardware configurations.
- When assessing the organization's current and future hardware needs, check the Microsoft Hardware Compatibility List to verify that Windows 2000 has been tested with the hardware that is to be upgraded or installed. You can also use the Windows 2000 Readiness Analyzer, and the Hardware and Software Compatibility Web site.
- Verify that your system BIOS has been updated and is compatible with Windows 2000. Advanced Configuration and Power Interface (ACPI). ACPI can cause an installation failure if your BIOS does not support ACPI.
- Some post-installation tasks that you might need to perform include checking the Device Manager for device failures, updating device drivers, and installing the latest service pack or hot fix.
- To assist in maintaining computer stability, you can configure driver signing to only allow drivers and system files to be installed if they contain authorized digital signatures.
- A Windows 2000 installation point can be easily integrated with the latest service pack to prevent you from having to perform a separate service pack installation after the operating system installation.

Key Terms

Add/Remove Hardware Wizard — Enables you to add or remove hardware and troubleshoot any hardware-related problems.

Basic Input/Output System (BIOS) — A program stored on a flash memory chip attached to the motherboard that establishes the initial communication between the components of the computer, such as the hard drive, CD-ROM, floppy disk, video, and memory.

Device Manager — Used to view and modify hardware device properties, update device drivers, and uninstall unneeded hardware.

driver signing — Ensures that a driver for a specific device has been verified by Microsoft and a unique digital signature has been incorporated into the driver.

File Signature Verification — This utility can identify unsigned files and give you information such as the file name, location, modification date, and version number.

hot fixes — Interim updates to Windows 2000 that are released between major service pack releases. These are used to fix operating system bugs and security issues.

interrupt request (IRQ) — A signal sent by a device to notify the processor when the device is ready to accept or send information. Each device typically has a unique IRQ number.

Microsoft Hardware Compatibility List (HCL) — A list of hardware devices that have been tested by Microsoft to determine whether they can work with Windows 2000.

service packs — Periodic updates to the Windows 2000 operating system to fix reported bugs and security issues.

slipstreaming — A process that integrates a Windows 2000 service pack with the original Windows 2000 installation files.

System File Checker — A command-line utility that scans and verifies all of the protected system files on your computer.

Windows 2000 Readiness Analyzer — A Windows 2000 utility used to check for hardware and software compatibility.

Windows File Protection — Helps to prevent the replacement of protected Windows 2000 files such as .sys, .dll, .ocx, .ttf, .fon, and .exe files.

Windows Update — A Microsoft Web site used to automatically download and install Windows 2000 service packs and hot fixes.

Review Questions

1. What can be considered the first step to be completed when installing Windows 2000 on a new computer?
   a. typing Winnt32 at the command prompt
   b. typing Winnt at the command prompt
   c. typing ERD at the command prompt
   d. verifying that your hardware is listed in the Hardware Compatibility List
2. Legacy hardware such as an ISA-based sound card should have its own IRQ reserved to ensure a trouble-free Windows 2000 installation. True or False?
3. After installing Windows 2000 on an older computer, you notice that some features such as Advanced Power Management do not work. You are logged in as the administrator. What might be wrong?
   a. You do not have permissions to run any Advanced Power Management features.
   b. The computer BIOS needs to be updated.
   c. Windows 2000 does not support Advanced Power Management.
   d. Advanced Power Management only functions on Pentium III processors.
4. Which command can be used to start the Windows 2000 Readiness Analyzer?
   a. Winnt /checkupgradeonly
   b. Winnt /s

c. Winnt32 /checkupgradeonly

d. Winnt32 /s

5. You want to check the hardware and software of a Windows 98 computer for Windows 2000 compatibility. You insert the Windows 2000 Advanced Server CD-ROM into the drive, and attempt to start the Windows 2000 Readiness Analyzer, but it fails. What is wrong?

   a. Windows 98 cannot run the Windows 2000 Readiness Analyzer,

   b. Windows 98 cannot be upgraded to Windows 2000 Advanced Server. Run the analyzer from a Windows 2000 Professional CD-ROM.

   c. You do not have the proper permissions to run the Readiness Analyzer.

   d. You can only run the Readiness Analyzer after the installation is complete.

6. Which items listed below are included in the *minimum* hardware requirements for Windows 2000 Server? (Choose all that apply.)

   a. 32 MB of RAM

   b. Intel Pentium 133

   c. 850 MB partition with 650 MB free disk space

   d. All of the above

7. Which of the following is used to view and modify hardware device properties, update device drivers, and uninstall unneeded hardware?

   a. Control Panel

   b. Add/Remove Programs

   c. Device Manager

   d. b and c

8. A disabled device is indicated with a small yellow "!" symbol over the device icon. True or False?

9. The Add/Remove Programs Wizard can be used to troubleshoot hardware problems in addition to adding or removing hardware devices. True or False?

10. Most installation problems that occur can be related to hardware device configuration errors or drivers. True or False?

11. Which of the following choices are available driver-signing options? (Choose three.)

    a. Block

    b. Disable

    c. Warn

    d. Ignore

12. Which Windows 2000 tool(s) can assist you in troubleshooting hardware problems?
    a. Device Manager
    b. Add/Remove Programs
    c. Add/Remove Hardware
    d. a and c
13. Which command is used to start the File Signature Verification utility?
    a. sigupdate
    b. verifsig
    c. sfc /verify
    d. sigverif
14. Which switch is used to integrate a service pack into a Windows 2000 installation point?
    a. Update -a
    b. Update -x
    c. Update -s
    d. Update -u
15. A Microsoft Web page called Windows Update can be used to download and install service packs and hot fixes. True or False?
16. Which tool can be used to verify which hot fixes and service packs have been installed on your computer?
    a. Hfnetchk
    b. Sigverif
    c. Winnt32 /verify
    d. Scandisk
17. In addition to hardware compatibility, you must also be concerned with software compatibility when upgrading from Windows 9.x to Windows 2000. True or False?

HANDS-ON PROJECTS

Project 2-1

In this Hands-on Project, you determine if the Matrox Millennium G400 Video adapter is compatible with Windows 2000. Note that an Internet connection is needed to complete this project.

1. Double-click **Internet Explorer**.
2. In the Address bar, type **http://www.microsoft.com/hcl**. Press **Enter**.

3. In the Search for the following text box, type **Matrox Millennium**.
4. Click the list arrow next to In the following types and click **Display**.
5. Click the **Search Now** button.
6. In the results screen, scroll down to Matrox Millennium G400 [AGP]. Notice that this display adapter meets the Microsoft Logo requirements.
7. Click the **Matrox Millennium G400 [AGP]** link to view additional information.
8. Close all windows to return to the desktop.

Project 2-2

In this Hands-on Project, you verify that Windows 2000 detected all hardware components properly.

1. Right-click **My Computer**, and click **Manage**.
2. Click **Device Manager**. Look in the details pane for any yellow exclamation marks. This is an indication that a specific device has not been installed correctly.
3. If there are any devices that have not been installed correctly, access the Internet, and download the newest device drivers for the device. (Consult your instructor for the correct driver version.)
4. You can install the downloaded driver by right-clicking the device icon, clicking **Properties**, clicking the **Driver** tab, and then clicking **Update Driver**. Follow the steps provided by the Upgrade Device Driver Wizard to complete the installation.
5. If all of your devices are installed correctly, close the Computer Management window, and log off.

Project 2-3

In this Hands-on Project, you use the Add/Remove Hardware Wizard to troubleshoot a hardware device.

1. Log on to Windows 2000 as the administrator.
2. Click **Start**, point to **Settings**, and then click **Control Panel**.
3. Double-click **Add/Remove Hardware**. Click **Next**.
4. Click the option button next to Add/Troubleshoot a device and then click **Next**.
5. Scroll down and click the entry representing your display adapter. Click **Next**.
6. You should receive a message stating that the device is working properly. If you were really troubleshooting a malfunctioning device, you would be prompted to supply the updated drivers.
7. Click **Finish**.
8. Close all windows.

Project 2-4

In this Hands-on Project, you check a hardware device to ensure that there are no resource conflicts with another device.

1. Right-click **My Computer**, and click **Manage**.
2. Click **Device Manager**.
3. In the details pane, click the + (plus sign) next to Network adapters.
4. Double-click your network adapter to open the Properties dialog box.
5. Click the **Resources** tab.
6. Ensure that **No conflicts** is stated in the Conflicting device list section.
7. Note the interrupt request (IRQ) number. If two devices were to use the same IRQ, conflicts might occur.
8. Click **Cancel**, close all windows, and log off.

Project 2-5

In this Hands-on Project, you install Windows 2000 service pack 2 and any current hot fixes available online. (This project assumes that you have an Internet connection and that you have set up your computer as described in the project setup guide.)

1. Log on to the computer as the administrator.
2. Right-click **My Computer**, and click **Explore**.
3. Click drive **D:**, and double-click the **SP2** folder.
4. Browse to the i386/update folder, and double-click the **Update.exe** application file.
5. Check the **Accept the License Agreement** option. (You must accept before installing the service pack.) Ensure that the **Backup files necessary to uninstall the Service Pack at a later time** option is also checked. Click **Install**.
6. Click **Restart** to restart the computer.
7. Log on to your computer as the administrator.
8. Right-click **My Computer**, and click **Properties**. Click the **General** tab to view the information and confirm that your server is now installed with service pack 2. Click **OK** when finished.
9. Click **Start**, and then click **Windows Update**.
10. Click the **PRODUCT UPDATES** link. If a security warning appears, click **Yes**. Any critical updates that are available are listed and checked by default. Click the **Download** button at the top right of the screen.
11. Click the **Start Download** button, and then click **Yes** to accept the terms of the License Agreement. All of the security updates are automatically downloaded and installed on your computer.
12. Restart the computer when prompted.

Project 2-6

In this Hands-on Project, you remove the Windows 2000 service pack and hot fixes that were installed in Project 2-5.

1. Log on to the computer as the administrator.
2. Click **Start**, point to **Settings**, and then click **Control Panel**.
3. Double-click **Add/Remove Programs**.
4. Scroll through the Currently installed programs list until you see the service pack that you previously installed.
5. Click the service pack entry in the list, and then click the **Remove** button. Click **Yes** at any prompts.
6. Restart your computer if necessary.
7. Repeat Steps 5 and 6 for any hot fixes that are listed in the Currently installed programs list.

Case Projects

Case Project 2-1

You have been hired by Bayside Detailing to upgrade their Windows NT network to a Windows 2000 network. What information would you want to collect and document before starting the upgrade process? List and explain at least five main points.

Case Project 2-2

One of your clients has two Pentium 200 desktop computers and three Pentium II 400 desktop computers. Your client asks you if it is possible to upgrade these computers to Windows 2000 Professional. What additional information do you need before you can answer her question? What can you do to verify whether Windows 2000 Professional works with these computers?

CHAPTER

3

ADMINISTERING ACTIVE DIRECTORY

After reading this chapter and completing the exercises, you will be able to:

- Create and modify Active Directory objects such as organizational units, users, computers, and groups
- Identify and troubleshoot Active Directory group types and scopes
- Administer Active Directory object permissions
- Manage and troubleshoot Active Directory replication

In the previous chapters, you learned the basics of network administration, Active Directory, and the installation of Windows 2000. Your next step is to understand how to access hardware and software needs for the Active Directory containers, users, groups, and other objects stored within the directory service. The Active Directory Users and Computers console provides you with an administrative tool to help you perform the tasks needed to create and manage these objects. The first part of this chapter discusses how to use this tool to manage your Active Directory domain.

Managing Active Directory also requires a thorough knowledge of how object permissions are inherited and delegated throughout the domain. For example, you may want to allow a specific group of users full control over a particular organizational unit. You can apply these permissions manually or use the Delegation of Control Wizard to assist you in assigning these rights to the group. More information is presented on administering permissions and delegation later in the chapter.

As a Windows 2000 Administrator, you also need to have a good understanding of how the Active Directory replicates throughout the infrastructure. Because Windows 2000 uses a multi-master domain controller concept, you need to understand the implications of an object being modified by two different administrators at the same time. The final section of this chapter discusses the concept of managing and troubleshooting Active Directory replication concepts.

ADMINISTERING ACTIVE DIRECTORY OBJECTS

In reality, administering a Windows 2000 domain means administering Active Directory objects. Objects stored in the Active Directory database can be either a container object or a leaf object. A **container** is an object that is used to contain and organize related objects within the Active Directory hierarchy. Container objects can consist of other child containers or leaf objects. An example of a container object is the organizational unit (OU), which can consist of objects such as users, groups, and other OUs.

A **leaf** is an object that represents resources within a selected domain. Leaf objects are stored within a container, and cannot contain other objects. An example of a leaf object is a user or group object.

After Active Directory is installed on a Windows 2000 server, management tools are automatically installed to assist you in the administration of the directory objects. Look at the Administrative Tools menu to discover a number of new entries such as **Active Directory Users and Computers**, **Active Directory Sites and Services**, and **Active Directory Domains and Trusts**, as shown in Figure 3-1.

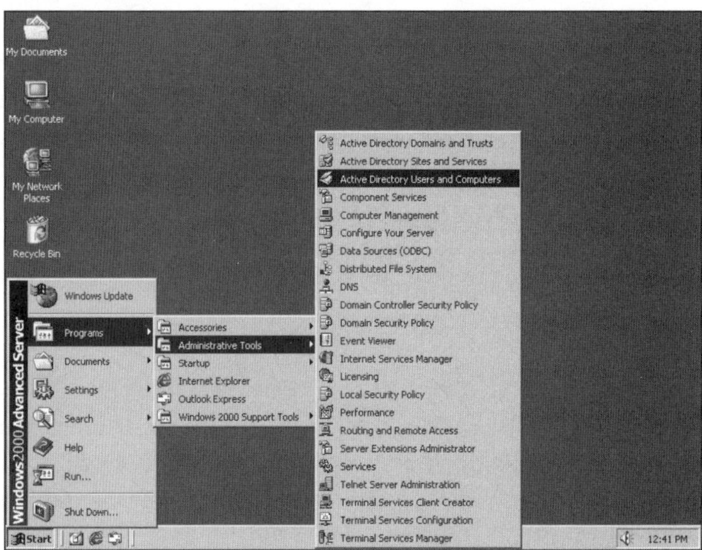

Figure 3-1 Viewing the Administrative Tools menu

Each of these tools assists in the configuration and management of specific areas of the Active Directory. By default, these tools are only installed on Windows 2000 domain controllers. Since each of these tools is a Microsoft Management Console (MMC) application, each can potentially be installed on any Windows 2000 computer. The easiest way to make these tools available to nondomain controller machines is to install the Windows 2000 Admin Pak, which is named Adminpak.msi and is found in the \I386 folder of the Windows 2000 CD-ROM. This installation file can be run locally or made available via

Group Policy. More information on deploying applications with Group Policy is presented later in the chapter.

Most of your time will likely be spent using the Active Directory Users and Computers console, as this is where all organizational unit, user, group, computer, and published information is created and maintained. The next section explores this management console in more detail.

Exploring Active Directory Users and Computers

Active Directory Users and Computers is the primary administration tool used to manage users, groups, organizational units, and published information within an Active Directory domain. It is also one of the tools that can be used to create and manage Group Policy objects, which control such elements as user desktop settings, security, logon/logoff **scripts** (computer programs that automate routine operations), and software deployment. This tool is an MMC application with the filename of Dsa.msc.

To open the Active Directory Users and Computers console, you can either type **Dsa.msc** at the Run command or follow these steps:

1. Click **Start**, point to **Programs**, point to **Administrative Tools**, and then click **Active Directory Users and Computers**. The console opens.
2. Click the plus sign next to your domain name in the left console pane. The default containers appear, as shown in Figure 3-2.

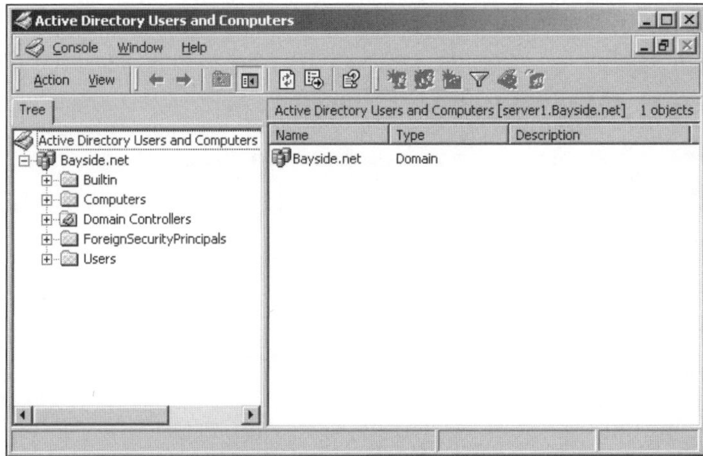

Figure 3-2 Viewing the Active Directory Users and Computers console

When a Windows 2000 server is promoted to domain controller, several container objects are created automatically. During the Active Directory installation, all of the information contained within the local Security Accounts Manager (SAM) database of the server is transferred to these containers.

The **security accounts manager (SAM) database** is the local directory service that stores user and group information for standalone Windows NT and 2000 computers. When a member server is promoted to a domain controller, all information in the SAM database is transferred to the Active Directory database. Even though it may seem that you will never use the SAM database again, do not forget the administrator account and password that are stored in the SAM database. This is the account that is used to boot the computer into the recovery console and directory services restore mode. More information about the recovery console is discussed in Chapter 8, "Monitoring and Troubleshooting Windows 2000."

Table 3-1 lists and explains each default container that is created when Active Directory is installed.

Table 3-1 Purpose of the default container objects in Active Directory

Container Object	Purpose of Container
Builtin	This container holds local security group objects for the domain; during an upgrade, this is where the local groups of the member server are placed
Computers	This container holds all member server and workstation account objects that belong to the domain; during an upgrade, this is where all computer accounts will be placed
Domain Controllers	This organizational unit holds the computer accounts for each Active Directory domain controller within the domain
ForeignSecurityPrincipals	This container is used by the Message Queuing Service to communicate with other trusted Windows 2000 or NT domains outside of the forest
Users	This container holds all user accounts and global groups for the domain; during an upgrade, all user and global groups are placed in this container

Even though the default containers are used initially to store various Active Directory objects, you are free to modify, create, and move objects to any container that is desired, including the root container. The only objects that cannot be moved are the local security groups stored within the Builtin container.

It is recommended to place all domain controllers together within the Domain Controllers OU. Moving domain controllers out of this container may cause replication problems between the individual replicas of the Active Directory database.

New containers or objects can easily be created by following these steps:

1. Right-click the root or container in which the new object is to be placed.

2. Point to **New**, and click the object type that you want to create, as shown in Figure 3-3.
3. Fill in the appropriate attribute information.

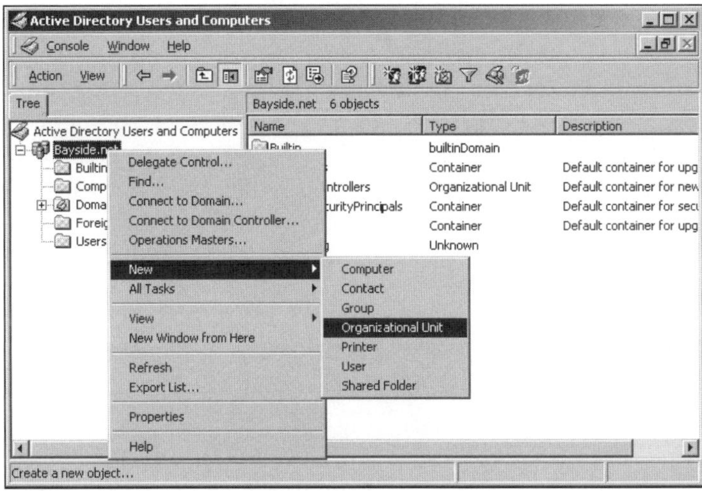

Figure 3-3 Creating a new object in Active Directory

As stated previously, there are a number of objects that can be created within the domain. Table 3-2 lists the objects that can be created with Active Directory Users and Computers.

Table 3-2 Objects available in Active Directory Users And Computers

Object Type	Description
Computer	An object that represents a computer account that is a member of the domain
Contact	An object that represents an account that does not have any logon or security rights within the domain; typically used for e-mail or informational purposes
Group	An object that represents a collection of users, computers, contacts, or other groups; Windows 2000 groups can be used as security groups or e-mail distribution lists
Organizational Unit	A logical container object that can contain and organize users, groups, computers, and other organizational units within a single domain
Printer	An object that represents a shared printer available on the network
User	An object that contains all of the information that defines a user that has access permissions to the network; this includes the user name, password, and group memberships
Shared Folder	An object that represents a shared folder available on the network that has been published into the Active Directory

The following sections discuss the creation and management of the most common objects that you encounter: organizational units, user accounts, groups, and computer objects.

Creating Organizational Units

An **organizational unit (OU)** is a logical container that can contain other objects such as users, groups, computers, published resources, or other OUs. Organizational units can only consist of objects from their home domain. The main reason for creating an organizational unit is to organize and partition a single domain into logical administrative units. For example, a company may have three departments within its organization: Marketing, Sales, and Accounting. You could place the users, groups, and computers from all three of these departments into the root container of Active Directory, as shown in Figure 3-4, but you would most likely have some administrative problems with this structure.

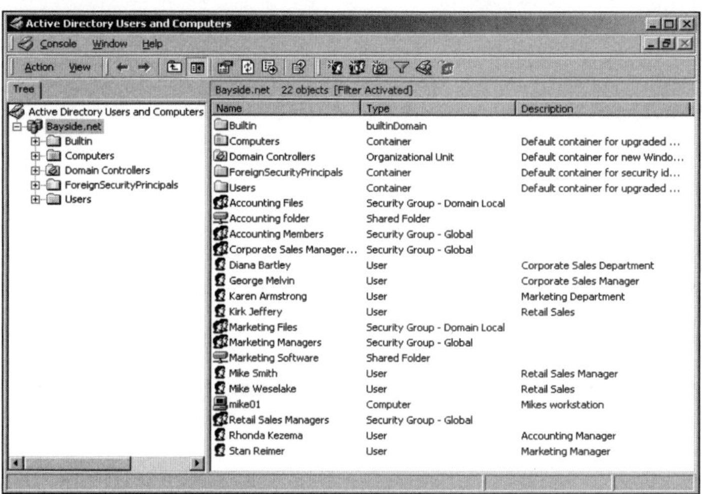

Figure 3-4 Placing objects into the root container

How would you delegate permissions to allow a specific user to only manage the Sales Department objects? How would you control the desktop environment of only the Accounting Department? If you wanted to deploy a specific application to only the Marketing Department, how would you accomplish this task? As you can see, if you do not organize the objects into specific organizational units, administration becomes more difficult. Figure 3-5 illustrates the creation of various organizational units and the placement of related objects within a specific OU.

Organizational units can be useful for a number of management tasks. Administrators can use OUs to create and apply Group Policies to either the entire domain, or specific OUs within a domain. Administration can also be delegated in a very granular fashion to allow specific individuals or groups to have various levels of control over Organizational units, without necessarily requiring full administrative permissions. For example, you may want to allow the office manager to have the ability to unlock or reset user passwords within a specific department. By delegating this task to another individual, you free up your time to do other tasks as well as allow the OU to have local control of its own resources.

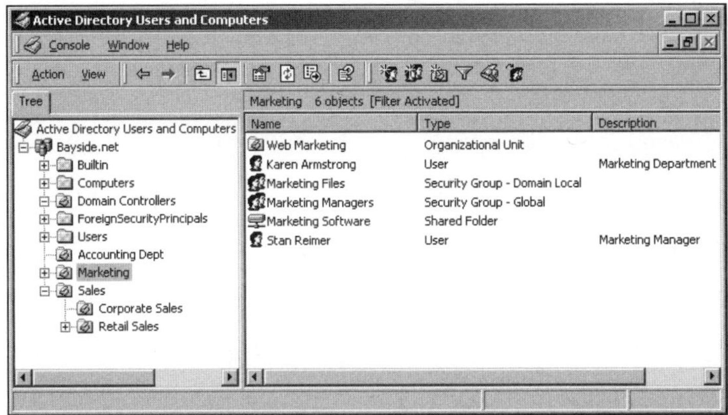

Figure 3-5 Organizing objects within an OU structure

When designing an organizational unit structure, try to design with administrative delegation and Group Policy in mind. Your goal is to design a domain that is logically organized, easy to administer, and easy to control.

Most organizations create an OU structure that is static and does not change for the first level. For example, an international company with a single domain might have the first level of the OU structure based upon physical location. For a smaller company with a single domain, the first level may be based according to department. Again the main goal is to create a granular structure that meets the Group Policy and delegation needs of the organization.

To create an organizational unit follow these steps:

1. Open the **Active Directory Users and Computers** console from the Administrative Tools menu.
2. Right-click the container in which the OU is to be created.
3. Point to **New**, and click **Organizational Unit**. The New Object–Organizational Unit dialog box opens, as shown in Figure 3-6.
4. Type the name of the new OU in the Name text box.
5. Click **OK**.

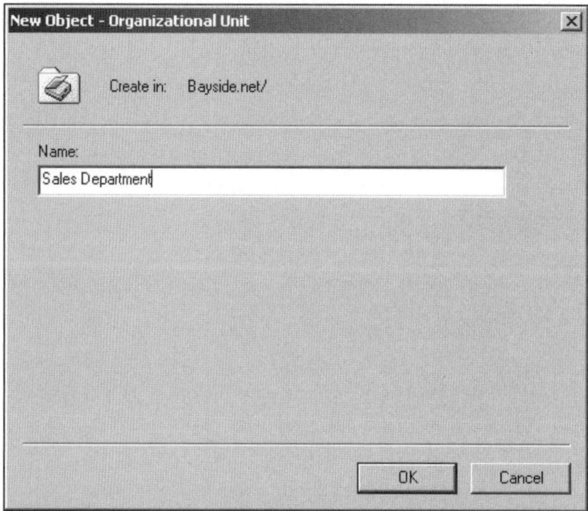

Figure 3-6 Creating a new organizational unit

Creating New User Accounts

A **user account** is an object that is stored in Active Directory that represents all of the information that defines a physical user with access permissions to the network. The information that defines a physical user may include attributes such as first and last name, password, and group memberships, as well as a number of other options.

Any person who needs access to resources available on the network requires a user account. User accounts can assist in the administration and security of the network by making it possible to:

- Require authentication of anyone connecting to the network
- Controlling access to network resources such as file sharing or printers
- Monitoring access to resources by auditing actions performed by a user logged on with a specific account

When creating a new user account, it is important that an organization set standards on the various elements of a user object. Some of these standards might include:

- *Establishing a naming convention*—Each user account name within the domain should follow a consistent naming convention. Common examples include:
  - *First name and last initial*: The account name for Kirk Jefferies would be KirkJ

- *First initial and last name*: The account name for Karen Armstrong would be Karmstrong.
- *Last name and first initial*: The account name for Mike Smith would be Smithm. Users with the same name can be accommodated by adding additional initials such as middle name.

- *Controlling password ownership*—You need to decide on whether you control the password for each user, or allow users to maintain their own passwords. A password policy that requires a password at least six characters long, containing a variety of alphanumeric characters, and which has a password expiration setting is considered best practice by many organizations.
- *Including additional required attributes*—You need to decide which additional attributes should be included with the creation of the user account. For example, will you require that all phone numbers and e-mail addresses be included with the account information? Keep in mind that every additional attribute requires additional replication bandwidth and storage space within Active Directory.

To create a new domain user account, follow these steps:

1. Open the Active Directory Users and Computers console from the Administrative Tools menu.
2. Right-click the container in which the new user account is to be created.
3. Point to **New**, and click **User**. The New Object–User dialog box opens, as shown in Figure 3-7.

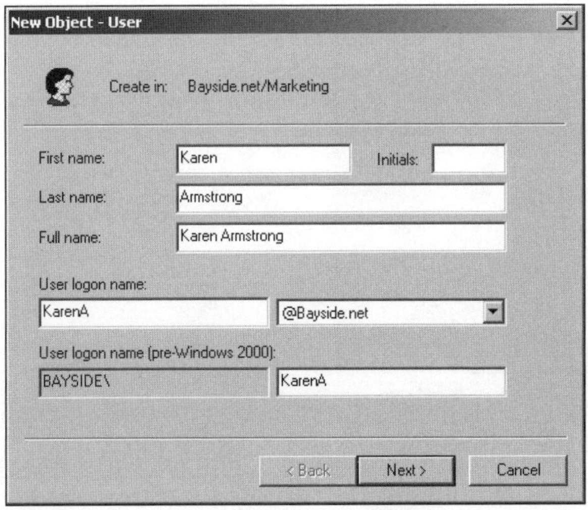

Figure 3-7 Creating new user object

4. Type the first and last name of the new user in the appropriate text boxes. (It is important that this name be unique within the container in which the object is being created.)
5. Type the User logon name based upon the user naming conventions established by the organization. (It is important that this name be in the entire forest.) The user logon name (pre-Windows 2000) entry automatically corresponds to what you have typed in the User Logon name text box. (It is important that the pre-Windows 2000 name be unique within the domain.) Click **Next**.

The user logon name is also called the **user principal name (UPN)** when combined with the domain suffix listed next to the User Logon name text box (e.g., *@bayside.net*). The UPN allows users to log on from any trusted domain within the forest by just providing the UPN name and password in the logon screen. This is a handy feature because administrators can configure the UPN to look like a user's e-mail address and allow users to log on to the network from any location.

6. In the second New Object – User dialog box, provide a password and place a check mark next to any specific account policy to be implemented at this point, as shown in Figure 3-8. Click **Next**.

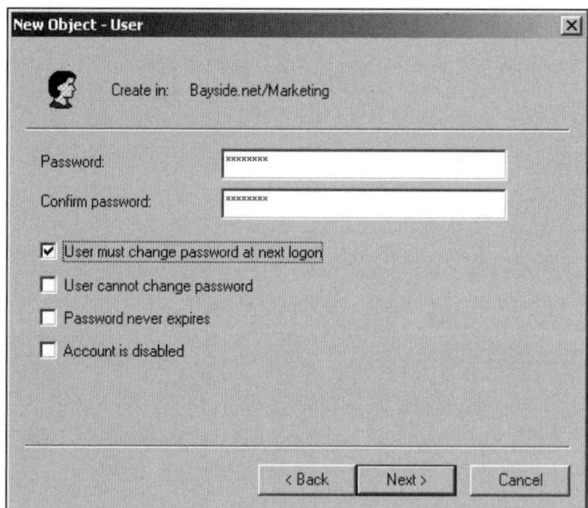

Figure 3-8 Configuring password and initial password policies for a new user object

7. At the final dialog box, read the summary information, and then click **Finish**.

As illustrated in the previous steps, the second dialog box allows you to set a number of initial policies on the new user account. The initial account policy options are listed in Table 3-3.

Table 3-3 Initial account policy options for a new user account

Option	Description
User must change password at next logon	Requires a new user to change their password upon initial logon; this option will be turned off when the password change takes place
User cannot change password	Prevents the user from being able to change the password
Password never expires	Prevents the account from expiring as configured in the password expiration policy of the domain
Account is disabled	If checked, the account cannot be used to log on to the domain

Modifying User Account Attributes

When you create a new user account, the initial attribute options are very basic. After the account is created, there are a number of additional tasks and attributes that can be applied to the user account. Some of the more popular tasks include:

- *Copy*—Used to copy and create a new account based on some of the attributes, such as group memberships
- *Add members to a group*—Used to quickly add selected users to a specific group
- *Disable Account*—Used to disable the selected account deny allow network access
- *Reset Password*—Used to reset the password of the selected user account; the previous password does not have to be known to complete this task
- *Move*—Used to move the selected object to another container within the domain
- *Properties*—Used to access the various attributes of the selected user object

To view the additional tasks, right-click the user account, as shown in Figure 3-9.

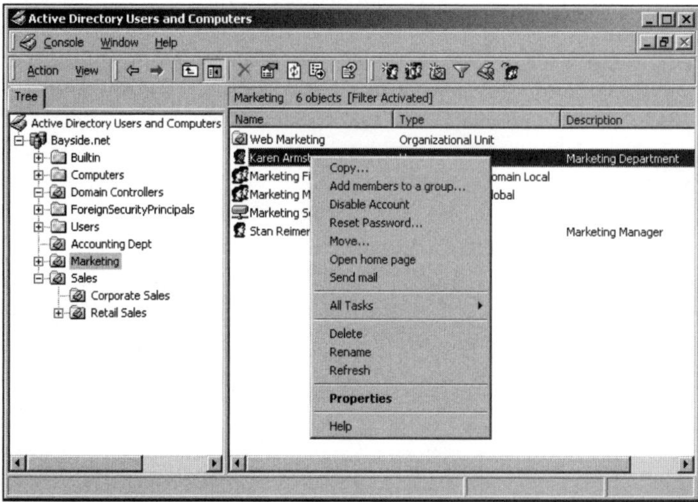

Figure 3-9 Viewing the additional tasks associated with a user object

User account attributes can be viewed and modified by clicking Properties in the context menu. As shown in Figure 3-10, a user account has a number of tabs that allow you to add specific information or enable specific functionality for the user account.

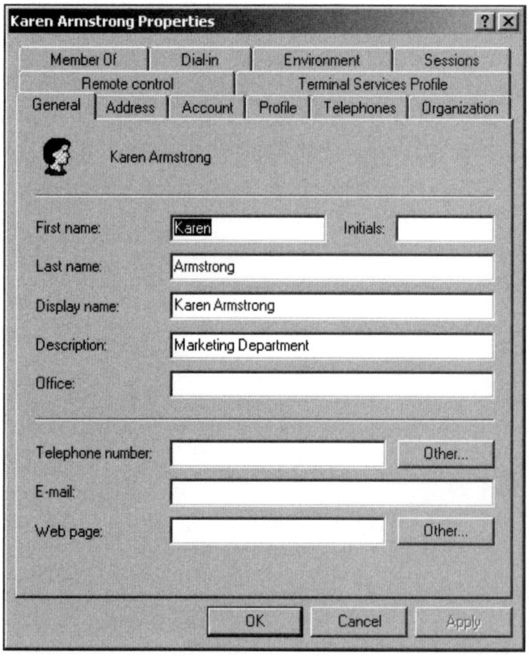

Figure 3-10 Viewing user object attributes

Most of the attributes listed in the properties dialog box of a user account can be used as search criteria within Active Directory. For example, if you wanted to find the address of a specific user, a search for the user name reveals any attributes that the administrator has allowed to be viewed from the user object. For more information on searching the Active Directory, read Chapter 5, "Administering File and Print Resources."

Table 3-4 describes the tabs that are available for the properties of a user account object.

Table 3-4 Properties of a user account object

Tab	Description of Attributes
General	Displays user name, description, office, telephone number, e-mail, and Web page information
Address	Displays fields for the full physical address of the user account
Account	Displays account information such as logon name, logon restrictions, password options, and expiration date options; also accessed to unlock user accounts
Profile	Displays the user profile and logon script paths as well as the user's home folder location
Telephones	Displays fields for various types of telephone numbers such as home, pager, mobile, fax, and IP phone
Organization	Displays information related to the organization such as title, department, and the manager's name
Member Of	Displays all of the user's group memberships
Dial-in	Displays the user's dial-in permissions and configurations
Remote Control, Terminal Services Profile, Environment, Sessions	These tabs relate to the user's terminal services permissions and configurations

Creating Computer Accounts

A **computer account** is an Active Directory object. There are two ways to create a computer account in Active Directory:

- You can create the computer account automatically during the initial installation of the client operating system. The computer object is placed in the Computers container within Active Directory.
- The computer account can be preconfigured in Active Directory before the client installation. The advantage of this method is that you can designate a specific container in which to place the computer object.

To create a computer object in Active Directory:

1. Open Active Directory Users and Computers from the Administrative Tools menu.

2. Choose the container in which the computer object is to be placed. Right-click the container, click **New**, and then click **Computer**. The New Object – Computer dialog box opens, as shown in Figure 3-11.

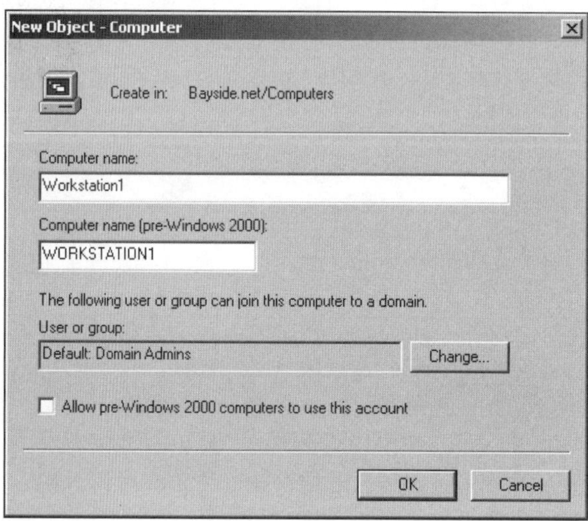

Figure 3-11 Creating a new computer object

3. Type the computer name in the Computer name text box.
4. If the user that is joining the computer to the domain is not an administrator, click the **Change** button, and add the appropriate user or group name. By default, only the Domain Admins group has the rights to add the computer to the domain. Click **OK**.

Moving Active Directory Objects

Objects created within the Active Directory Users and Computers console can be moved between any containers within the same domain. The only containers that cannot be moved are the Builtin, Computers, ForeignSecurityPrincipals, and Users containers. The default local groups found in the Builtin container also cannot be moved because these groups are local and they provide rights to the specific computer itself.

To move an object within an Active Directory domain:

1. Right-click the object to be moved, and click **Move** from the Context menu. The Move dialog box appears, as shown in Figure 3-12.
2. Select the container in which to place the moved object, and click **OK**.

Drag and drop functionality within Active Directory Users and Computers is not available with Windows 2000 Server, but has been added into the next generation of Windows.

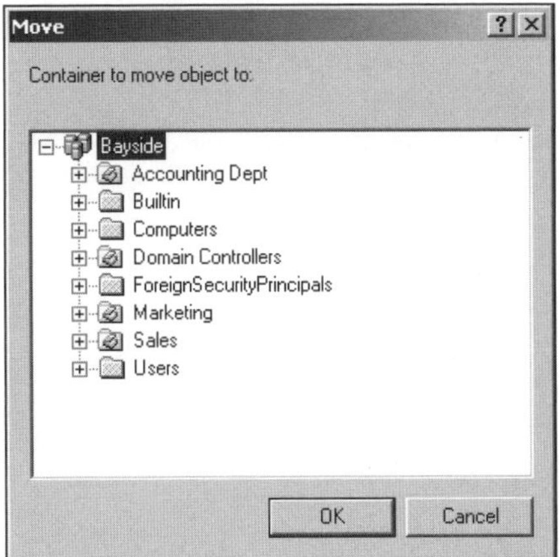

Figure 3-12 Moving an object within the domain

Creating Group Objects

A Windows 2000 **group** is a container object that is used to organize a collection of users, computers, contacts, or other groups into a single security principal. You would use a group object to simplify administration by assigning rights and resource permissions to a group rather than to individual users. Groups sound similar to organizational units in that both organize other objects into logical containers. The main differences between an OU and a group are as follows:

- Organizational units cannot be used as a security principal and cannot be used to define permissions on resources or be assigned rights. Groups have the ability to be a security principal.
- Organizational units can only contain objects from their home domain. Some groups have the ability to contain objects from any domain within the forest

The next few sections introduce you to the different group types and group scopes available in Windows 2000.

Group Types

Windows 2000 allows the creation of two group types:

- *Security group*—A group that can be listed in discretionary access control lists (DACLs) used to define permissions on resources and objects. A security group can also be used as an e-mail entity. Sending an e-mail message to the group sends the message to all the members of the group.
- *Distribution group*—A group that is used solely for e-mail distribution and that is not security enabled. Distribution groups cannot be listed in

discretionary access control lists (DACLs) used to define permissions on resources and objects. Distribution groups can be used only with e-mail applications (such as Microsoft Exchange) to send e-mail to collections of users. If you do not need a group for security purposes, create a distribution group instead of a security group.

Group Scopes

The group scope refers to the logical boundary within which a group can be assigned permissions to a specific resource within the domain or forest. Security and distribution groups can be assigned one of three possible scopes: global, domain local, and universal. The following sections define each scope option.

Global

A **global group** can be assigned permissions to any resource in any domain within the forest. The main limitation of a global group is that it can only contain members of the same domain in which it is created. Global groups are mainly used to organize user objects into logical administrative units. For example, if sales managers from domain A need access to a shared file stored in domain B, you can create a global group in domain A called sales managers, place all individual sales manager user accounts from Domain A into this group, and then assign the sales managers global group to the resource located in Domain B.

Domain Local

A **domain local group** is created on a domain controller and can only be assigned permissions to a resource available in the local domain in which it is created. However, group membership can come from any domain within the forest. Domain local groups are mainly used to assign access permissions to a resource. For example, you may want to add users, global groups, or universal groups to a domain local group and then assign the domain local group the actual permissions to a resource within the domain.

Groups created on Windows 2000 member servers or Windows 2000 Professional clients are called **local groups**. Local groups can only be assigned permissions to a resource available on the local machine in which it is created.

Universal

A **universal group** can be assigned permissions to any resource in any domain within the forest. This seems very similar to a global group, but actually has two main differences. First of all, a universal group can consist of user objects from any domain in the forest; global groups can only consist of user objects from the same domain. Second, universal groups are only available in native mode; if your domain is in mixed mode, this group scope is disabled.

Native mode means that all domain controllers are Windows 2000 servers. In other words, a native mode domain does not contain any Windows NT backup domain controllers (BDCs). **Mixed mode** domains consist of Windows 2000 domain controllers and Window NT BDCs. To change a domain to native mode, open Active Directory Users and Computers, right-click the domain name, click Properties, and then click the Change Mode button.

3

Be sure to only switch to native mode when there is no longer any need for NT 4.0 BDCs. Once you switch to native mode, there is no capability to switch back to mixed mode.

Universal groups should be used with caution. All universal groups along with their memberships are listed in the global catalog. When there is any change to any member of a universal group, this change must be replicated to every global catalog in the forest. Global and domain local groups are also listed in the global catalog, but do not have their memberships listed. A best practice is to place individual members within the global groups, and then place the global groups within universal groups.

Table 3-5 provides a summary of each group type, its use, and its membership options.

Table 3-5 Windows 2000 group summary

Group Type	General Use	Mixed Mode Membership Options	Native Mode Membership Options
Local	Assigned to resources on local computer	User accounts from any domain, global groups from any domain	User accounts from any domain, global groups from any domain
Domain local	Assigned to resources within local domain	User accounts from any domain, global groups from any domain	User accounts, global and universal groups from any domain; other domain local groups from the same domain
Global	Used to organize individual objects such as user accounts into administrative units	User accounts only from the domain in which the group is created	User accounts and other global groups from the same domain in which the group is created
Universal	Used to organize various objects into administrative units	N/A	User accounts, global and universal groups from any domain

Creating a Group Object

To create a group object, follow these steps:

1. Open Active Directory Users and Computers from the Administrative Tools menu.

2. Right-click the container in which the group is to be created, and point to **New**, **Group**. The New Object – Group dialog box opens, as shown in Figure 3-13.

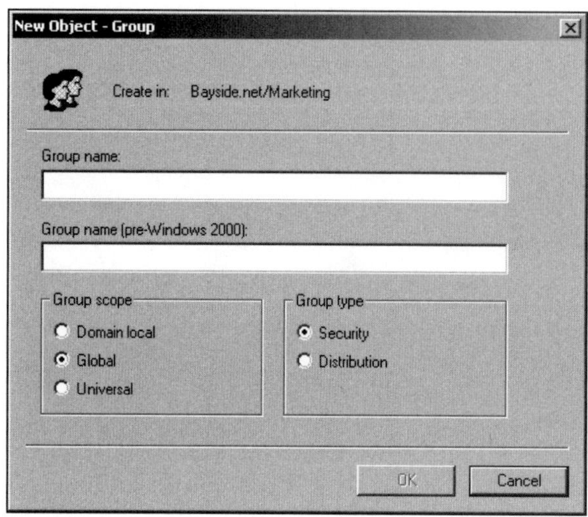

Figure 3-13 Creating a new group object

3. Fill in the group name. The name must be unique within the domain.
4. Choose the Group scope. If your domain is in mixed mode, the Universal scope is grayed out.
5. Select the Group type. You probably want to leave the selection at **Security** for most Windows 2000-based situations. Click **OK**.

Modifying Group Memberships

Once a group object is created, you can then add the membership required. Depending upon which type of group is created, Windows 2000 groups can possibly contain users, contacts, other groups, and computers. To add or modify group memberships follow these steps:

1. Open Active Directory Users and Computers from the Administrative Tools menu.
2. In the console pane, click the container that holds the group to be modified.
3. In the details pane, right-click the group, and click **Properties** on the shortcut menu. The group properties dialog box opens, as shown in Figure 3-14.
4. Click the **Members** tab, and then click **Add**.
5. Choose the accounts that you want to add, and click **Add**. Click **OK** when finished.

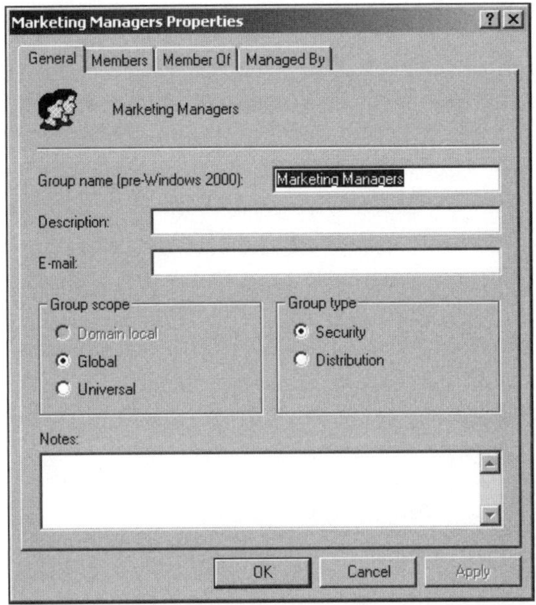

Figure 3-14 Adding or modifying group memberships

6. Click **OK** to return to the Active Directory Users and Computers console.

Changing a Group Scope

Windows 2000 native mode provides the ability to change a group scope, if the need arises. For example, you may want to change a global group to a universal group if you need to add user accounts from another domain. You can change the group scope by accessing the properties of the group and selecting the appropriate group scope that is needed. However, there are a few rules that must be followed:

- A global group can only be changed to a universal group as long as it is not a member of another global group.
- A domain local group can only be changed to a universal group as long as it does not contain any other domain local groups as a member.

To summarize, a group can change its scope as long as the group's membership rules, as stated in Table 3-5, are not violated.

Understanding the Built-in Local Groups

There are a number of built-in, local security groups with various preassigned rights, which you may want to use to allow users to perform certain network tasks. Whenever possible, you should use one of the built-in local groups to assign permissions because this eases the implementation of delegation and security rights throughout the network. For example, rather than creating a special group with permissions to back up and restore servers, you can use the built-in, backup operators group.

Windows 2000 domain controllers have built-in local groups that provide certain rights within the domain. These groups can be found in the Active Directory Users and Computers console in the Builtin container, as shown in Figure 3-15.

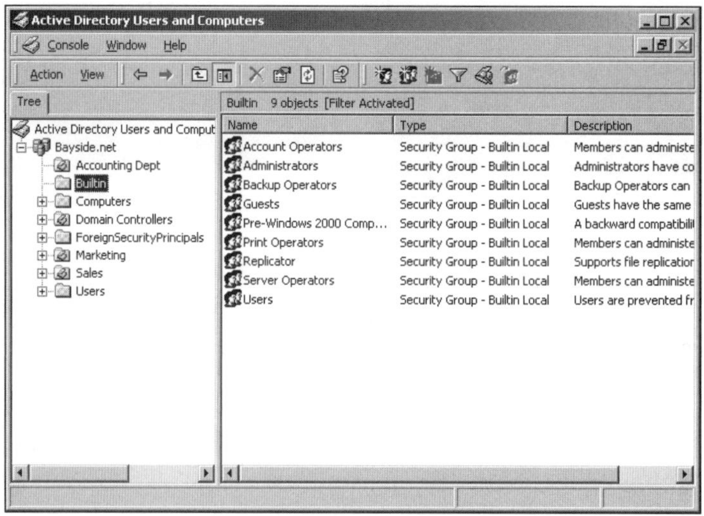

Figure 3-15 Viewing the built-in local groups

Table 3-6 lists the types of local groups available in Active Directory, and the rights assigned to each.

The Users container in Active Directory Users and Computers also contains various global groups that can be used throughout the domain, as shown in Figure 3-16. Notice that some of the global groups, such as Domain Controllers, contain computer objects as opposed to user objects.

Table 3-6 Local groups and their rights

Group Type	Rights
Account Operators	Have the ability to create, delete, and modify user accounts and groups within the domain; they cannot place themselves or anyone else in the administrators group
Administrators	Assigned complete unrestricted access to the local computer and possibly the domain
Backup Operators	Have the ability to override security restrictions for the purpose of backing up or restoring files
Guests	Have no default permissions or rights; the guests group is a member of the special group. Everyone; this means that any access permissions to the Everyone group give permission to the Guests group
PreWindows 2000 Compatible Access	This group is created to support applications that work with Windows NT 4.0, but may have problems with Windows 2000 security. This group has read access on all users and groups within the domain. This is used primarily for Windows NT RAS servers that require access to Active Directory.
Print Operators	Members of this group have all print administration rights
Replicator	Used by the File Replication Service
Server Operators	Members of this group can share disk resources, backup and restore files, and shut down or restart the server
Users	Have no default permissions, except for permissions assigned by the administrator

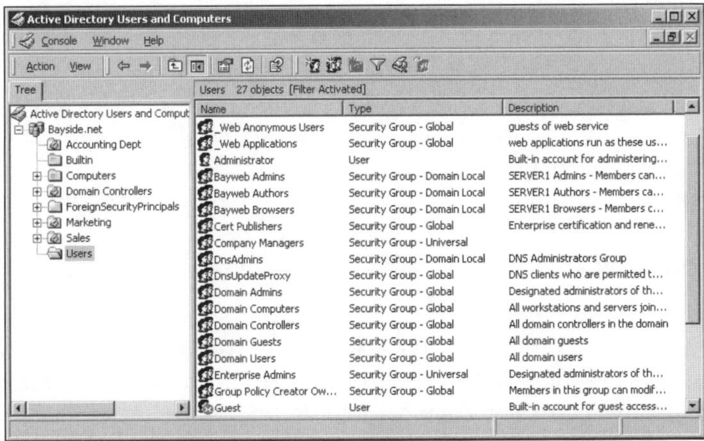

Figure 3-16 Viewing built-in global groups

Managing Security Groups

As you start to implement the use of security groups, a general strategy is to use the acronym A G U DL P. This refers to the following:

1. Create user **A**ccounts, and organize them within **G**lobal groups. Often users are grouped in global groups based on departments in the organization.
2. Optional: Create **U**niversal groups and place global groups from any domain within the universal groups.
3. Create **D**omain **L**ocal groups that represent the resources in which you want to control access, and add the global or universal groups to the domain local groups.
4. Assign **P**ermissions to the domain local groups.

For example, Bayside Detailing has a shared file called Reports. All users in all domains that work in the Marketing Department must have access to the Reports Share. Following the steps previously discussed, this is how you can organize access:

1. In each domain, create a global group called **Marketing Members**, and add any appropriate user account to the group.
2. Optional: Create a universal group called **Bayside Marketing Dept**, and add all global groups created in step 1, from all domains to the universal group.
3. Create a domain local group called **Reports Share**, and add the Bayside Marketing universal group to the local group. (If you skipped step 2, you can add the Marketing Members global group instead.)
4. Assign the Reports Share local group to the access control list of the actual share on the network, and specify the appropriate permissions.

If your domain is running in native mode, you can use the option of nesting groups to simplify administrative tasks. For example, Bayside Detailing may have three global groups called Agents, Marketing, and Distributors. Together, these three groups of users may represent the Customer Service Department of Bayside Detailing. You could create the CustServ global group and put the Agents, Marketing, and Distributors groups into this one group, thus simplifying the assignment of permissions for resources to which all three groups should have access. You do not need to add individuals to the CustServ group. When you are assigning permissions to resources, assign the permissions to domain local groups.

If you are working in a single domain and a single site, you can use global groups or universal groups interchangeably. Choose one of these options to group your users, and then add these groups to the local domain groups.

ADMINISTERING PERMISSIONS IN ACTIVE DIRECTORY

Active Directory is a database that must be protected just like any other network resource. Active Directory uses permissions much like regular NTFS file permissions to protect the creation, deletion, or viewing of objects within the database. By default, administrators have full access to all objects within the domain. Users are given the initial right to read most attributes of the objects stored in the database. As an administrator, you can easily edit the object permissions within the database, although care must be taken not to assign permissions that might make an object inaccessible by everyone including yourself.

Active Directory Object Permissions

Active Directory objects can be assigned permissions at two levels:

- **Object level permissions** define which types of objects a user or group can view, create, delete, or modify within Active Directory.
- **Attribute level permissions** define which attributes of a certain object a user or group can view or modify within Active Directory.

Object-level permissions must be granted for a user to have the right to create or modify an object such as an organizational unit, user, or group account. Attribute level permissions are administered to control which attributes a user or group can view or modify. For example, if you want the address information of user accounts to be viewed only by the Human Resources Department, you would modify the attribute level permissions to apply this restriction.

Object level permissions can be applied according to a preconfigured set of standard permissions. Table 3-7 lists the standard permissions available for most objects in Windows 2000.

Table 3-7 Standard permissions available in Windows 2000 Active Directory

Permission	Gives the Right To
Full control	Perform all standard permissions plus change permissions and take ownership of an Active Directory object
Read	View Active Directory objects and their attributes
Write	Make changes to an Active Directory object's attributes
Create all child objects	Add child objects to an organizational unit
Delete all child objects	Remove child objects from an organizational unit.

For each permission listed in Table 3-7, you can allow, deny, or not specify the permission. If you do not specify a permission by explicitly selecting the allow or deny check boxes, you allow the object to inherit the permission settings from its parent container.

To view the standard permissions for an object follow these steps:

1. Open Active Directory Users and Computers from the Administrative Tools menu.
2. Click the **View** menu, and click **Advanced Features**.

The Advanced Features mode must be turned on to be able to view the Security tab on each object in Active Directory.

3. Right-click the object for which you want to modify the standard permissions, and click **Properties**.
4. Click the **Security** tab. The Access Control List and standard Permissions are illustrated, as shown in Figure 3-17.

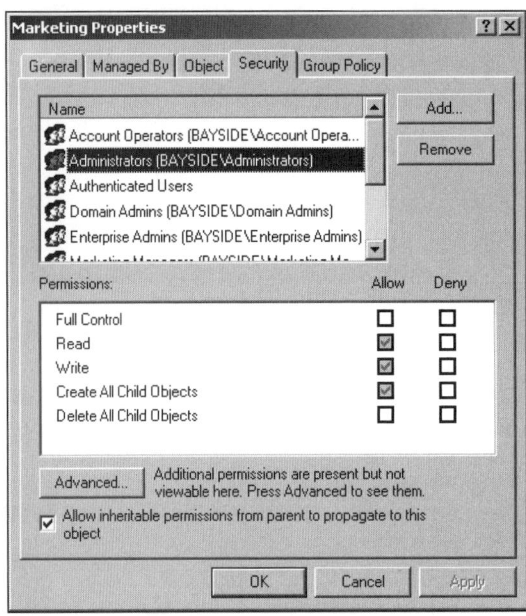

Figure 3-17 Viewing the Security tab of an Active Directory object

5. Click the **Advanced** button on the Security tab of an object to open the Access Control Settings dialog box, which allows you to apply advanced object or attribute permissions, configure auditing, and view or edit ownership, as shown in Figure 3-18.
6. To view attribute level permissions, click the **View/Edit** button within the Access Control Settings dialog box, and then click the **Properties** tab. Figure 3-19 illustrates the attribute level permissions.

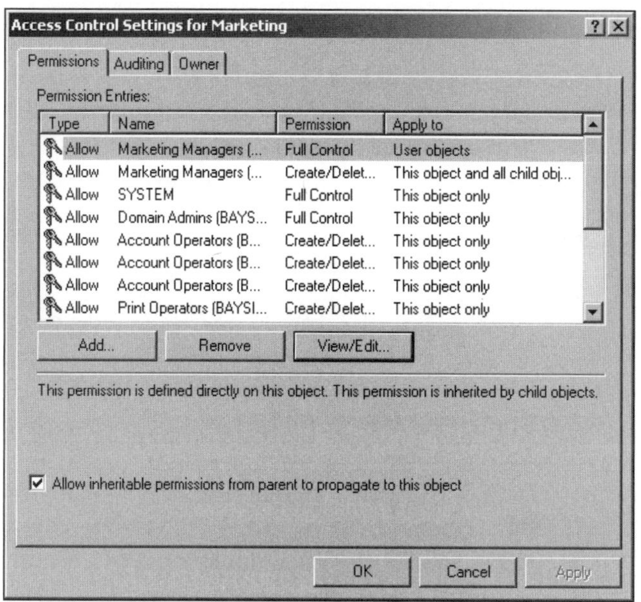

Figure 3-18 Viewing advanced permissions

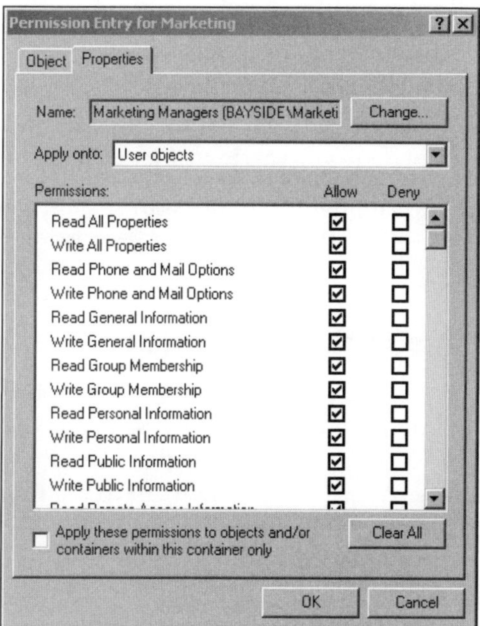

Figure 3-19 Viewing the attribute level permissions

Permission Inheritance

By default, all child objects inside a container object inherit the permissions from the parent object. By using this inheritance and planning carefully, you can eliminate the need to assign permissions to every container object or to every object inside a container. The permissions are inherited from the parent container when the object is created. If the permissions to the parent container are changed after the child object has been created, the permissions can be forced to the child container by making sure that all child objects inherit any change in permissions. You can do this by making sure that "This object and all child objects" is selected under Advanced on the Security tab of the Active Directory parent container.

This default inheritance of permissions can be modified by blocking the inheritance at a container or object level. For example, you may want to have all of the permissions that are set at an upper-level OU inherited by all child OUs except for one particular child OU. You may want to give the help desk personnel the right to reset the passwords for all of the users at the corporate head office OU, except for the executives. In this case, you could put all of the executives in an Executives OU, and then accept the default inheritance for all child OUs, but block the inheritance for the Executives OU. To override the inheritance of permissions at an OU level, follow these steps:

1. Open **Active Directory Users and Computers**.
2. Browse to the OU where you want to override the inherited permissions, right-click it, and then click **Properties**.
3. Click the **Security** tab.
4. To override the inherited permissions, clear the **Allow inheritable permissions from parent to propagate to this object** check box.
5. You are given the choice to copy the inherited permissions and then change them, or to remove all permissions and then assign new permissions, as shown in Figure 3-20.

Delegating Authority Over Active Directory Objects

The delegation of administration allows you to distribute and decentralize the process of administering Active Directory. To accomplish this goal, the first step is to design the OU structure so that the administration work can be distributed. For example, you may want to assign the task of managing one small part of the network to a junior administrator or an administrator in a remote location. Creating an OU and then delegating the administrative control to that person is an ideal solution to accomplish this step.

The second step in delegating the administrative control is to configure the appropriate level of administrative permissions for each administrator. You may want to give another administrator full control of one particular OU, but you may not want that person to have any administrative permissions anywhere else. Again, the option of assigning permissions to specific OUs allows you to achieve this goal.

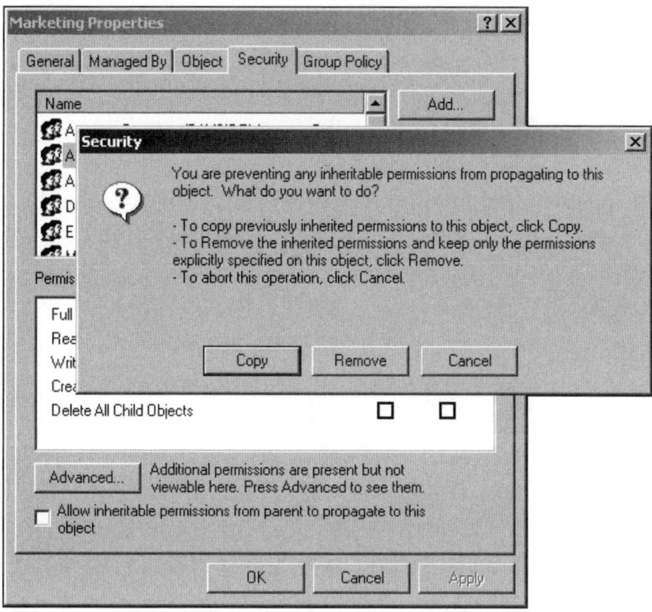

Figure 3-20 Overriding inherited permissions

Implementing Delegation

You can manage the permissions on every Active Directory object by directly viewing and modifying the Security tab on the object. However, this can be a very complicated task, especially if you are delegating a variety of tasks in a complex OU structure.

To make the delegation quicker and easier, Windows 2000 provides the **Delegation of Control Wizard**. This wizard guides you through the process of determining the permissions that you want to delegate, and then configures the permissions for the object and child objects.

To use the Delegation of Control Wizard, follow this procedure:

1. Right-click the container, domain, or OU where you are delegating control, and click **Delegate Control**.
2. The Delegation of Control Wizard starts. Click **Next**.
3. You are given the choice to delegate control to particular users or groups. Click **Add**, choose the user or group, and then click **OK**. Click **Next**.
4. You are now given a list of common tasks to delegate, as shown in Figure 3-21. If the task that you are looking for is not on the common task list, click the **Create a custom task to delegate** option to assign different levels of permission to specific objects in the container or to the container itself. If you are using one or more common tasks, select the task(s), and click **Next**.

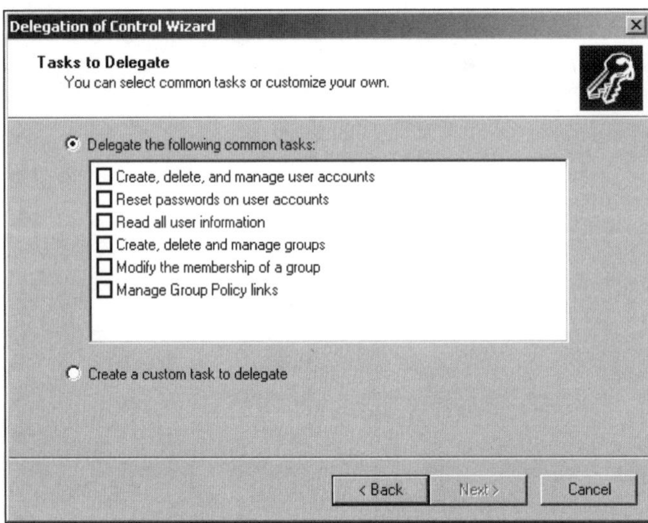

Figure 3-21 Delegating an administrative task in Active Directory

5. Review the information about the delegation that you configured, and click **Finish**.
6. To confirm that the permissions are configured correctly, right-click the container object for which you assigned permissions, and click **Properties**. Click the **Security** tab. The user or group name is listed. To see specific permissions, click **Advanced**. You can modify the permissions here if you wish.

If you decide to change the permissions you have granted to a user, you can run the Delegate Control Wizard again and assign new permissions to the user. The new permissions overwrite or add to all previous permissions.

MANAGING ACTIVE DIRECTORY REPLICATION

Active Directory replication refers to the process of data being synchronized and maintained between domain controllers throughout the domain. As stated previously, Windows 2000 uses a multi-master replication concept, which means that multiple domain controllers have the authority to update and replicate database changes to each domain controller. Multi-master replication also provides a level of fault tolerance because if one domain controller fails, the other domain controllers within the domain can provide the services needed.

Since changes can potentially be made at two domain controllers at the same time, a mechanism must be in place that ensures that all changes are updated correctly, and any conflicting changes can be resolved. For example, if two administrators were to change the telephone number of the same user object at the same time, Active Directory must be able to resolve which change to accept.

Replication Components and Processes

When an object is created, deleted, or modified, replication has to take place among all domain controllers within the domain. The initial modification to the database on a specific domain controller is called the **originating update**. This originating update then needs to be replicated to all other domain controllers. All synchronized copies sent to the other domain controllers are called **replicated updates**. The time that it takes to replicate an update to another domain controller is called **replication latency**.

Each time an originating or replicated update takes place, the domain controller where the change occurred waits five minutes to enable an accumulation of changes. After five minutes, a change notification message is sent to its first replication partner notifying the other domain controller about the change. After a 30-second interval, it then notifies its other replication partners. The replication partners then pull the changed information into their own copies of the database. If no changes occur, replication takes place automatically every hour to ensure that all database information is converged.

Any changes that are considered security sensitive, such as an account lockout, are immediately replicated to all replication partners, and do not wait the 5-minute interval. This process is called **urgent replication**.

To optimize replication traffic, Active Directory sites can be configured between areas connected by slow network connections. For more information on sites, refer to Chapter 1, "Windows 2000 Network Administration."

Identifying Replication Problems

Replication problems can easily arise in multi-master scenarios such as Windows 2000 Active Directory. There are three main areas that can cause potential conflict within the database:

- *Attribute value errors*—These can occur when the same attribute of an object is edited at the same time on two different domain controllers.
- *Placing objects within containers marked for deletion*—This error occurs in a situation where one administrator may delete a container, while another administrator creates an object or moves an object into the deleted container before replication takes place.
- *Sibling name error*—This error can occur if two administrators concurrently create an object with the same relative distinguished name on two different domain controllers.

To help in the resolution of possible conflicts, Active Directory applies unique stamps to every attribute that is replicated. The stamp includes a version number that is increased by one for each originating update. The stamp also includes a time stamp and an indication of the server where the replicated attribute originated.

To resolve attribute value errors, Active Directory uses the highest stamp value as the value to be written to the attribute. Before replication has taken place, if an object has been created or moved into a deleted container, the object is automatically moved into the LostAndFound container within Active Directory after replication takes place. To resolve sibling name errors, the object with the higher time stamp retains the relative distinguished name and the object with the lower time stamp is renamed with its GUID appended to the name.

Three tools can be used to assist you in viewing replication information or diagnosing replication problems:

- *Event Viewer*—If replication problems occur, Windows 2000 will generate errors that can be viewed in the Directory Service or System logs of a domain controller.
- *DCDIAG*—This command line utility can be used to view a variety of information including replication status. To use the utility, type **dcdiag** at the command prompt.
- *Replication Monitor*—This utility is part of the Windows 2000 Support Tools available on the Windows 2000 Server CD in the \Support\Tools folder. This utility can check for replication errors, illustrate the replication topology, and generate replication status reports, as well as other useful information.

CHAPTER SUMMARY

- After installing Active Directory on a Windows 2000 server, management tools are automatically installed to assist in the administration of the directory objects. Some of the new management tools include Active Directory Users and Computers, Active Directory Sites and Services, and Active Directory Domains and Trusts.
- Active Directory Users and Computers is the primary administration tool used to manage users, groups, organizational units, and published information within an Active Directory domain. It is also one of the tools that can be used to create and manage Group Policy objects, which control such elements as user desktop settings, security, logon/logoff scripts, and software deployment.
- When designing an OU structure, the main goal is to create a granular structure that meets the group policy and delegation needs of the organization.
- Some standards that should be considered when creating user accounts include establishing a naming convention, determining password ownership, and determining which attributes are required to be added for each user.
- A computer account can be created automatically during the initial client installation of the operating system, or it can be preconfigured in Active Directory before the initial installation.

- There are two types of groups that can be created in Windows 2000: security groups and distribution groups. Security groups are used for defining permissions on resources. Distribution groups are used only for e-mail distribution lists.
- Groups can be assigned one of three types of scopes: domain local, global, or universal.
- As you start to implement the use of security groups, a general strategy is to use the acronym A G U DL P. This refers to placing user accounts into global groups, global groups into universal groups, universal groups are then assigned to domain local groups, domain local groups are assigned permissions to a resource.
- Active Directory permissions can be assigned at the object level or attribute level.
- The Delegation of Control Wizard can be used to simplify the application and delegation of Active Directory object permissions to departmental network administrators.
- There are three main replication problems that may occur within Active Directory: attribute level conflicts, sibling name conflicts, and the creation or moving of objects to deleted containers.

Key Terms

Active Directory Domains and Trusts — An Active Directory MMC tool that allows you to configure trust relationships between domains as well as the UPN suffix for the forest.

Active Directory Sites and Services — An Active Directory MMC console that allows you to configure site objects and site links, and configure replication costs and times between sites.

Active Directory Users and Computers — An Active Directory MMC console that allows you to create various objects such as organizational units, user accounts, groups, computers, and contacts.

attribute level permissions — Define which attributes of a certain object a user or group can view or modify within Active Directory.

computer account — An Active Directory object that represents a physical computer that is a member of the domain.

container — An object that is used to organize related objects within the Active Directory hierarchy. Container objects can consist of other child containers or leaf objects, such as organizational units.

Delegation of Control Wizard — An Active Directory MMC tool that guides you through the process of determining the permissions that you want to delegate, and then configures the permissions for the object and child objects.

distribution group — A group that is only used for an e-mail distribution list.

domain local group — Can only be assigned permissions to a resource available in the domain in which it is created. However, group membership can come from any domain within the forest. Created on domain controllers within the domain.

global group — A group that is mainly used for organizing other objects into administrative units. A global group has the ability to be assigned permissions to any resource in any domain within the forest. The main limitation of a global group is that it can only contain members of the same domain in which it is created.

group — A container object that is used to organize a collection of users, computers, contacts, or other groups into a single object reference.

leaf — An object that represents resources within a selected domain. Leaf objects are stored within a container, and cannot contain other objects, for example user or group objects.

local group — Can only be assigned permissions to a resource available on the local machine in which it is created.

mixed mode — Domains consisting of Windows 2000 domain controllers and Windows NT backup domain controllers (BDCs).

native mode — Domains consisting of Windows 2000 domain controllers only. No Windows NT BDCs exist in the domain.

object-level permissions — Define which types of objects a user or group can view, create, delete, or modify within Active Directory.

originating update — The initial change to the Active Directory database performed on a specific domain controller, e.g., creating a user.

organizational unit (OU) — A logical container that can contain other objects such as users, groups, computers, published resources, or other OUs.

replicated update — An update to the Active Directory database that has been copied from another domain controller.

replication latency — The time that it takes to replicate an Active Directory update to another domain controller.

script — A file that includes various commands to automate routine operations.

security accounts manager (SAM) database — The local directory service that stores user and group information for standalone Windows NT and 2000 computers.

security group — A group that can be used to define permissions on a resource object.

universal group — Can be assigned permissions to any resource in any domain within the forest. Universal groups can consist of any user or group object except for local groups.

urgent replication — The immediate replication that takes place when any changes that are made to the Active Directory database are considered security sensitive, such as account lockouts.

user account — An object that is stored in Active Directory that represents all of the information that defines a physical user who has access permissions to the network.

user principal name (UPN) — Consists of the user logon name and a domain name identifying the domain in which the user account is located.

Review Questions

3

1. Which type of security group has its entire membership stored in the global catalog?
   a. domain local groups
   b. universal groups
   c. local computer groups
   d. global groups
   e. all of the above
2. Which of the following can be considered a container object in Active Directory?
   a. user
   b. contact
   c. organizational unit
   d. none of the above
3. Which MMC console is the primary administration tool used to create user, group, and computer objects?
   a. Active Directory Domains and Trusts
   b. Active Directory Sites and Services
   c. Active Directory Users and Computers
   d. none of the above
4. Organizational units are security principals that can be assigned permissions to resources. True or False?
5. You would like to allow access to a shared file in your domain to three users from a trusted domain. To what type of group must the users belong in order for you to assign the permission to the group?
   a. global group
   b. domain local group
   c. local computer group
   d. domain local or global group
   e. any of the above
6. Your company is opening an office in a city where you do not currently have an office. You would like to be able to have one of the users in the new office perform some simple user administration tasks and reset passwords, but the user should not be able to do anything else on your network. What would be the most

appropriate configuration option in Active Directory for the users and computers in the new office?

a. Create an OU inside of an existing domain.

b. Create a new domain that is not part of an existing domain tree.

c. Create a new child domain inside an existing domain tree.

d. Create a new domain tree inside an existing forest of domain trees.

7. You want to give the help desk personnel the right to reset passwords for all user accounts in your office except for the user accounts for the executives and managers. The easiest way to do this is:

   a. give the help desk personnel the right to reset user accounts at the domain level

   b. put all the help desk personnel into an OU, and assign the OU the right to reset passwords

   c. put the entire executive and manager accounts into an OU, and assign the help desk personnel the reset password permission at the domain level

   d. put all the nonexecutive and nonmanager user accounts into an OU, and give the help desk personnel the right to reset passwords for the OU

8. You have created a new group in your domain called Managers, and you put all of the appropriate users into the group. You have also just installed a new file and print server on your network, and configured a new Managers share on the server. However, when you try to add the Managers group to the NTFS permission on the folder, you cannot locate the group through the interface. What happened? (Choose all that apply.)

   a. The new server has not been added to your domain.

   b. You created a distribution group rather than a security group.

   c. You created a global group rather than a domain local group.

   d. You did not enable the group.

9. You have just created a Windows 2000 Network with a single domain. You would like to grant the help desk staff the ability to reset user passwords, but not allow them to create and delete user accounts. This cannot be done. True or False

10. Active Directory objects can easily be moved between domains using the Active Directory Users and Computers console. True or False?

11. A universal group can consist of local group memberships. True or False?

12. Bill attempts to create a universal group, but the selection is grayed out. What could be the problem?

    a. He must create a global group first and then convert it to a universal group.

    b. Universal groups can only be created on the first domain controller in the forest.

    c. The domain needs to be converted to native mode.

    d. none of the above

13. You need to convert a domain local group into a universal group. The domain local group has a second domain local group nested within it. You can still convert to a universal group. True or False?
14. An organizational unit can contain other organizational units. True or False?
15. Which built-in local group has the ability to create, delete, and modify user accounts and groups within the domain, but cannot place themselves or anyone else in the Administrators group?
    a. backup operators
    b. guests
    c. account operators
    d. print operators
16. The user principal name (UPN) can be used to log on from any trusted domain within the forest. True or False?
17. You try to modify permissions to various objects using Active Directory Users and Computers, but you notice that the Security tab is missing. You are an administrator of the domain. What is the problem?
    a. You cannot modify AD object permissions using Active Directory Users and Computers.
    b. Advanced features is not selected in the View menu of the console.
    c. Active Directory only allows changes on one domain controller at a time.
    d. none of the above
18. You create a new organizational unit, and then view the access control list. You notice that some of the entries have grey-shaded boxes under Permissions. What does this mean?
    a. Permissions are not applied to the specific user or group.
    b. Permissions are not inherited from a parent container.
    c. Permissions are inherited from a parent container.
    d. Permissions are suggested as indicated by the grey-shaded boxes.
19. Account lockouts are replicated immediately throughout the domain. True or False?
20. An administrator changes the telephone number attribute on a user object. One minute later, a second administrator changes the e-mail address of the same user object from a different domain controller. What will happen when replication occurs?
    a. Only the changes from the last administrator take effect because replication takes place at the object level.
    b. Both changes merge, because replication takes place at the attribute level.
    c. Only the changes from the first administrator take effect.
    d. An error will occur and result in no changes taking effect.

HANDS-ON PROJECTS

For the benefit of this and subsequent projects, you need to grant permission for regular users to be able to log on to the server. **To allow any authenticated user to log on to the server, follow these steps:**

1. Click **Start**, point to **Programs**, point to **Administrative Tools**, and then click **Domain Controller Security Policy**.
2. In the console pane, expand **Security Settings**, expand **Local Policies**, and click **User Rights Assignment**.
3. In the details pane, double-click **Log on locally**.
4. Click **Add**, click **Browse**, and choose the **Authenticated Users group**.
5. Click **Add**, and then click **OK** three times to return to the Domain Controller Security Policy console.
6. Close all windows, and restart your computer.

Project 3-1

In this Hands-on Project, you create two organizational units within Active directory.

To create an organizational unit:

1. Open Active Directory Users and Computers from the Administrative Tools menu.
2. Right-click **Bayside.net**, point to **New**, and click **Organizational Unit**.
3. Name the organizational unit **Winnipeg Dept**, and click **OK**.
4. Repeat steps 2 and 3 to create the **Toronto Dept** organizational unit.

Project 3-2

In this Hands-on Project, you create four new user accounts and create in advance one computer account in Active Directory.

To create a new user account:

1. Right-click the **Winnipeg Dept** organizational unit, click **New**, and click **User**.
2. In the New Object – User dialog box, fill in the appropriate information from the following table:

Text Box	Value
First Name	Bill
Last Name	Meyers
Full Name	Bill Meyers
User logon name	First Name-Last Initial (billm)

3. Click **Next**. Type **password** for the password. Click **Next**, and then click **Finish**.
4. Repeat the above steps for the remaining three users.

Name	Organizational Unit (department)
Tim Vans	Winnipeg Dept
Alan Scone	Toronto Dept
John Riley	Toronto Dept

To create a new computer account:

5. Right-click the **Toronto Dept** organizational unit, point to **New**, and click **Computer**.
6. Type **workstation1** as the Computer name. Click **OK**.
7. Click each OU, and verify that each object was created successfully.

Project 3-3

In this Hands-on Project, you create a new global group object called Executive Managers. You also add members to the Executive Managers global group.

To create a new global group:

1. Choose the **Users** container, right-click it, and point to **New**, **Group**.
2. Name the group **Executive Managers**, and verify that **Global** and **Security** are selected. Click **OK**.

To add members to the new global group:

1. Right-click the **Executive Managers** global group, and click **Properties**.
2. Click the **Members** tab, and click **Add**.
3. Choose **Bill Meyers** and **Alan Scone** from the list, and click **Add**. Click **OK**. (Hold down the **Ctrl** key to invoke multiple selections.)
4. Click **OK** again to return to the Active Directory Users and Computers console.

Project 3-4

In this Hands-on Project, you delegate the ability to create, delete, and manage user accounts of the Winnipeg and Toronto department OUs to the Executive Managers global group.

To delegate control by using the Delegation of Control Wizard:

1. Click the **View** menu in the Active Directory Users and Computers console, and verify that the **Advanced Features** option is checked.
2. Right-click the **Toronto Dept** OU, and click **Delegate Control**. Click **Next** at the Welcome screen.
3. In the Users or Groups dialog box, click **Add**.

4. Scroll and choose the **Executive Managers** group, and click **Add**. Click **OK** to return to the Delegation of Control Wizard. Click **Next**.
5. Check the **Create, delete, and manage user accounts** option. Click **Next**, and then click **Finish**.

To verify that delegation has been successfully completed:

1. Right-click the **Toronto Dept** OU, and click **Properties**.
2. Click the **Security** tab. Verify that the Executive Managers group is listed on the Access Control List.
3. Click the **Executive Managers** group. Notice that there are no check marks listed in the Permissions section.
4. Click the **Advanced** button. Notice that Executive Managers are listed in the Permission Entries list.
5. Close all windows.

Project 3-5

In this Hands-on Project, you experiment with the **dcdiag** utility and the **replication monitor** to diagnose domain controller replication problems.

To experiment with the dcdiag utility:

1. Click **Start**, and then click **Run**. The Run dialog box opens.
2. Type **cmd** in the Open text box, and click **OK**. The command prompt window opens.
3. Type **dcdiag /?** to view the various command line switches that can be used with the utility.
4. Type **dcdiag** at the command prompt, and view the output.
5. Type **dcdiag /test:replications** to view just the replication details.
6. Type **dcdiag /v** to view the extended (verbose) information.

To install and experiment with the Replication Monitor:

1. Install the Windows 2000 Support Tools from the \Support\Tools folder of the CD-ROM or the W2KAS folder on drive D:.
2. Click **Start**, point to **Programs**, point to **Windows 2000 Support Tools**, click **Tools**, and then click **Active Directory Replication Monitor**.
3. In the leftmost pane, right-click **Monitored Servers**, and click **Add Monitored Server**.
4. In the Add Server to Monitor dialog box, click **Next**.
5. Type the name of your server in the text box under Enter the name of the server to monitor explicitly. Click **Finish**.

6. Right-click your server name, and click **Properties**. Browse through the various tabs. Click **OK**.
7. Right-click your server name, and click **Generate Status Report**.
8. Click the desktop icon, and then type **report** as the file name. Click **Save**.
9. In the Report Options dialog box, make sure that all options are checked. Click **OK**. Click **OK** when the report generation is complete.
10. Close the Active Directory Replication Monitor, and then double-click your report that is saved on the desktop. Read the information that can be collected using this report.
11. Close all windows, and log off.

CASE PROJECTS

Case Project 3-1

Bayside Detailing has three main departments in its organization: Marketing, Finance, and Human Resources. Bayside has sold its Montreal division and has decided to only create one domain called *Bayside.net,* which will consist of two locations: Winnipeg and Melfort. The physical network connection between Melfort and Winnipeg is 100 Mbps.

1. Design a possible organizational unit structure for *Bayside.net.* What are the main decision goals in your design?
2. If the connection between Melfort and Winnipeg is slower than initially thought, what can be done to optimize replication traffic?
3. Replication problems are occurring. Which tools can help you troubleshoot the problems?

Case Project 3-2

Bayside Detailing has a folder on a file server that stores all of the human resources information for the entire company. You need to give access to this folder to all members of the Human Resources Department within the domain. Explain how you would complete this task. Do you need universal groups?

CHAPTER

4

MANAGING GROUP POLICY

After reading this chapter and completing the exercises, you will be able to:

- Create and manage Group Policy objects to control user desktop settings, security, scripts, and folder redirection
- Manage and troubleshoot Group Policy inheritance
- Deploy and manage software using Group Policy

An important part of your Windows 2000 management skills is the ability to effectively incorporate Group Policy into your Active Directory structure. **Group Policy** allows you to easily manage and control various configurations such as user desktop settings, desktop and domain security, and the deployment and management of software.

Another important aspect is understanding how to control the inheritance and application of Group Policies throughout the Active Directory hierarchy. The following sections discuss these concepts as well as basic group policy troubleshooting techniques.

INTRODUCTION TO GROUP POLICY

Group Policy enables the centralized management of user and computer configuration settings throughout your network. A **Group Policy object (GPO)** is an Active Directory object that is used to configure and apply policy settings for user and computer objects and perform a variety of administrative tasks, including:

- Configuration of desktop settings through the use of administrative templates
- Control of security settings for users and computers
- Assignment of scripts to run when a user logs on or off, or when a computer is turned on or off
- The redirection of folders, such as the My Documents folder, out of a user's local profile to a physical network location
- The automation of software distribution and maintenance to computers throughout the network

To implement Group Policy, you must first create a GPOs, or use and modify one of the default GPOs to meet the company requirements.

There are two default GPOs created when Active Directory is installed. The first GPO is linked to the domain container and is called the **default domain policy**. The second is linked to the domain controllers OU and is called the **default domain controllers policy**.

Once the GPO is created, you can then link the Group Policy to a site, a domain, or an organizational unit. When you link the Group Policy to one of these container objects, the policy settings are applied to all users, groups, child OUs, and computers in the container.

Group Policy can only be applied to Windows 2000- or Windows XP-based computers. If you still have down-level clients such as Windows NT or Windows 9x, you must use system policies.

Creating a Group Policy Object

A Group Policy object can be created in two different ways: by using the Group Policy stand-alone snap-in or by using the Group Policy extension in Active Directory Users and Computers.

To create a new Group Policy object using the stand-alone snap-in, follow these directions:

1. Create a custom MMC, and add the Group Policy snap-in. When you are loading the snap-in, you can choose the policy you want to administer. Click **Browse**.

2. You can now browse for any existing Group Policy to edit, or you can create a new Group Policy by clicking the **New Policy** icon. Type the name of the Group Policy, and click **OK**.
3. Return to the console root, and you can edit the policy to match your needs.
4. When you have finished editing the policy, you can apply it to any container in Active Directory.

To create a new Group Policy using the Group Policy extension in Active Directory, follow this procedure:

1. Open Active Directory Users and Computers, and right-click the container object in which you want to create and link the new Group Policy object.
2. Click **Properties**, and then click the **Group Policy** tab.
3. Click **New**, and type in the name for the policy.
4. To edit the policy, point to the policy, and click **Edit**. The Group Policy dialog box opens, as shown in Figure 4-1.

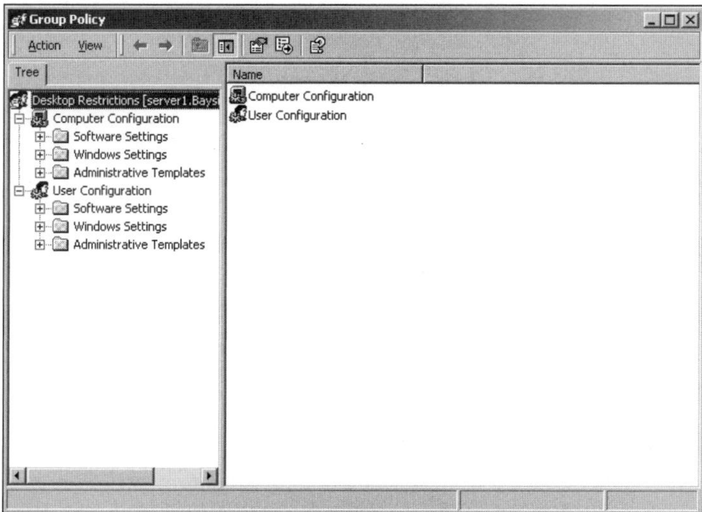

Figure 4-1 Creating a Group Policy object

5. Expand the appropriate container and choose the category to which the policy setting that is to be edited belongs.

Table 4-1 lists the configuration categories available under both computer and user configuration.

Table 4-1 Configuration categories available for Group Policy objects

Configuration Categories	Explanation
Software settings	Used to centralize the management of software installation and maintenance; the installation, upgrading, and removal of applications can be controlled from one central location
Windows settings	Used to manage the deployment and management of scripts, security settings, Internet Explorer settings, and features such as Remote Installation Services and folder redirection
Administrative templates	Used to set registry-based settings to configure application and user desktop settings; this includes access to the operating system components, access to Control Panel settings, and configuration of offline files

As you are creating or editing a Group Policy and want to enable a particular setting, choose the appropriate configuration category in the left console pane, and then, in the details pane, right-click the specific configuration setting, and click Properties.

Figure 4-2 shows the User Configuration\Administrative Templates\Control Panel category selected and the properties of the option to Hide specified control panel applets. The Policy tab allows you to enable or disable the setting, as well as set any parameters that may be needed. The Explain tab provides information on what the effect of applying that setting is.

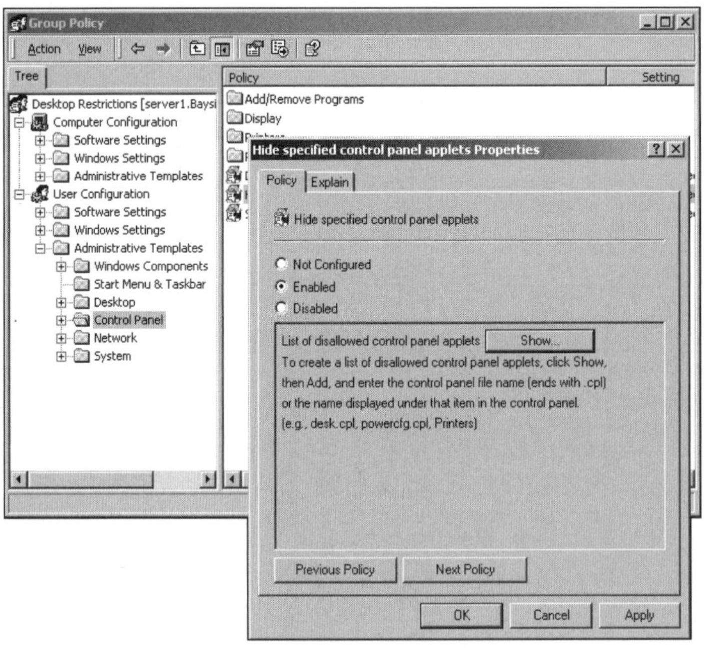

Figure 4-2 Configuring a Group Policy setting

When a Group Policy object is created, the GPO content is stored in two different locations on the server.

- *Group Policy container (GPC)*—An Active Directory container that stores information about the GPO and includes a version number that is used by other domain controllers to ensure that they have the latest information. The version number is also used to make sure that the Group Policy template is synchronized. The GPC is located in Active Directory Users and Computers\System\Policies. Note: The Advanced Features view must be enabled.
- *Group Policy template (GPT)*—Contains the data that makes up the Group Policy. The template includes all the settings, the administrative templates, security settings, software installation settings, scripts, etc. The registry changes are stored in a configuration file named Registry.pol. A configuration file is stored for both the user settings and computer settings. The GPT is stored in the %systemroot%\Sysvol\Sysvol folder.

Both the GPC and the GPT are identified by a **globally unique identifier (GUID)**, which is a unique 128-bit number assigned to the object when it is created. GUIDs are guaranteed to be unique for the entire forest. When a computer accesses the GPO, it uses the GUID to distinguish between group policies.

Application of Group Policy

GPOs can apply a variety of configuration options to the local computer, site, domain, and organizational unit. There are two main categories to a Group Policy:

- *Computer configuration*—Any configuration settings set within the computer category affect computers located in the container to which the GPO is linked.
- *User Configuration*—Any configuration settings set within this category apply to any user objects located in the container.

When a computer is started and a user logs on, the following process takes place:

1. A Windows 2000 client computer in a domain starts up. The client computer queries the domain controller for a list of GPOs that it needs to apply. The domain controller examines all of the GPOs to see which policies apply to the computer. Policies that are executed on the computer include the computer settings and startup scripts.
2. The domain controller presents the client with the list of GPOs that apply to it in the order that the GPOs need to be processed. The computer contacts the domain controller and extracts the Group Policy templates from the Sysvol share and applies the settings and runs the scripts.
3. When the user logs on, the same process happens again, except this time the user settings, logon scripts, software policies, etc., are applied.

Controlling User Desktop Settings

Companies spend a lot of time and money designing standard computer installation configurations, only to have users change settings, thus resulting in nonstandard configurations and increased calls to the help desk. Group Policy helps reduce administrative costs by allowing you to enforce standard computer configurations, limit user access to various areas of the operating system, and ensure that users have their own personal desktop and application settings. Administrative templates consist of a number of administrative configurations, which can be used to apply these settings.

Administrative templates are basically registry settings that can be configured to manage Windows 2000 and user desktop settings. There are seven main categories of configuration settings that can be applied to either the computer or user section of a Group Policy object.

Table 4-2 explains each of the main categories of configuration settings for administrative templates and the section of the Group Policy object to which each can be applied.

Table 4-2 Configuration categories of administrative templates

Configuration Category	Explanation	Configuration
Windows components	Allows the configuration of settings for applications such as Internet Explorer, NetMeeting, Task Scheduler, and the Microsoft Management Console	User and computer
System	Allows the configuration of settings related to Group Policy, disk quotas, logons, and code signing	User and computer
Network	Allows the configuration of offline files and network and dial-up connections	User and computer
Printers	Allows the configuration of settings related to installing, publishing, and maintaining printers	Computer
Start menu and taskbar	Allows configuration settings related to options available on the Start menu and taskbar	User
Desktop	Allows the configuration of user desktop settings such as wallpaper, display of icons, and Active Desktop	User
Control Panel	Allows the restriction of the various icons and applets within the Windows 2000 Control Panel	User

Managing Security with Group Policy

Group Policy can be used to modify and maintain a number of domain-based security configurations in order to comply with organizational security standards. Windows 2000 provides the capability to create security templates based on current security standards. These templates can then be used to continually make certain that the standard is being met.

The most common security setting that you will likely be configuring is the Account Policies section, which allows you to configure settings that are used to control user password, account lockout, and Kerberos configurations.

Configuring Account Policies

One security category that deserves special attention is the Account Policies node. This node includes configuration settings that may be the initial step to securing the computer network. The Account Policies node, as shown in Figure 4-3, can be found under the computer configuration category of a Group Policy object, and includes three subcategories: Password Policy node, Lockout Policy node, and Kerberos Policy node.

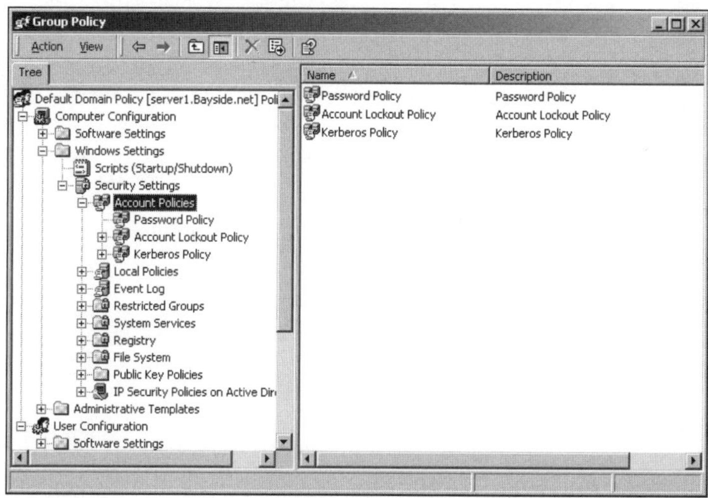

Figure 4-3 Viewing the Account Policies node in a Group Policy object

Password Policy

The Password Policy node contains configuration settings that refer to the password's history, length, and complexity. Table 4-3 describes each setting:

Table 4-3 Password policies in Windows 2000

Configuration Setting	Description
Enforce password history	Defines the number of passwords that have to be unique before a user can reuse an old password
Maximum password age	Defines the number of days that a password can be used before the user is required to change it; if you never want the passwords to expire, set the number of days to 0
Minimum password age	Defines the number of days that a password must be used before a user is allowed to change it
Minimum password length	Defines the least number of characters required in a password (values can be from one to 14 characters); if no password is required, set the value to 0
Passwords must meet complexity requirements	Increases password complexity by enforcing rules that passwords must follow. See the list of complexity requirements following this table.
Store password using reversible encryption for all users in the domain	This setting is the same as storing passwords in clear text; this policy provides support for applications which use protocols that need the passwords in clear text for authentication purposes

If you configure the Password Policy node, Windows 2000 passwords must meet the following complexity requirements:

- They cannot contain any part of the user's account name
- They must be at least six characters in length
- They must contain characters from three of the four categories below:
  - English uppercase letters
  - English lowercase letters
  - Numbers
  - Nonalphanumeric (!, $, #)

Account Lockout Policy

The Account Lockout Policy node contains configuration settings that refer to the password lockout threshold and duration, as well as reset options. Table 4-4 describes each setting.

Table 4-4 Account lockout policies

Configuration Setting	Description
Account lockout threshold	Determines the number of failed logon attempts that results in the user account being locked
Account lockout duration	Determines the number of minutes that a locked account remains locked; after the specified number of minutes, the account automatically becomes unlocked. You can specify that an administrator must unlock the account by setting the value to 0
Reset account lockout counter after	Determines the number of minutes that must elapse after a single failed logon attempt, before the bad logon counter is reset to 0

Kerberos Policy

The Kerberos Policy node contains configuration settings that refer to the Kerberos ticket granting ticket and session ticket lifetimes and time stamp settings. Table 4-5 describes each setting.

Table 4-5 Kerberos policy node configuration

Configuration Setting	Description
Enforce user logon restrictions	Requires the **Key Distribution Center (KDC)**, a service of Kerberos V5, to validate every request for a session ticket against the user rights policy of the target computer; if enforced, there may be performance degradation on network access
Maximum lifetime for service ticket	Determines the maximum amount of time, in minutes, that a service ticket is valid to access a resource; default: 600 minutes (10 hours)
Maximum lifetime for user ticket	Determines the maximum amount of time, in hours, that a **ticket granting ticket (TGT)** may be used; default: 10 hours
Maximum lifetime for user ticket renewal	Determines the amount of time, in days, that a user's TGT may be renewed; default: seven days
Maximum tolerance for computer clock synchronization	Determines the amount of time difference, in minutes, that Kerberos tolerates between the client machine's clock and the time on the server's clock; default: five minutes (used to prevent "replay attacks")

To configure an account policy for the domain, the GPO must be linked at the domain level of Active Directory. Account policy configurations applied at an OU level only affect the local SAM database of the computers within the OU, and do not affect domain logons.

The other nodes under the security settings category can be applied to both the domain and OU levels. Here is a summary of the functions of each node:

- *Local Policies*—This category applies security settings to the local account database of the workstation or server. These may be overwritten at the site, domain, or OU level, but remain in effect if there are no other policies at those levels. There are three subcategories that can be configured:
  - *Audit Policy*—Defines various successful or unsuccessful events that can be audited and recorded in the event logs.
  - *User Rights Assignment*—Controls local computer rights that may be assigned to users or groups. For example, the right to log on locally, or to shut down the computer.
  - *Security Options*—Defines a wide variety of configuration settings that adjust the registry. Some examples include restricting floppy or CD-ROM access, logon banner configurations, and removing the last logged-on user name from the logon screen.
- *Event Log*—Defines configuration settings in relation to event log size, retention period, and access restrictions.
- *Restricted Groups*—This category gives the administrator the ability to control who is a member of any security group. Each time that the policy is refreshed, any users that have been added to the group by any means other than the security template, are removed automatically. This category can also control the other groups to which a particular security group belongs.
- *System Services*—This category allows an administrator control over service startup mode, disabling of a service, permissions to edit the service mode, and auditing of the service.
- *Registry*—This category defines security and auditing ACL settings for Registry keys and subkeys. This allows an administrator to control who has access and the right to change or overwrite registry settings.
- *File System*—This category defines and maintains security permissions (DACL) and auditing permissions (SACL) for any folder or file listed in the policy. Files or folders must reside on an NTFS partition.

Using the Security and Configuration Tool Set with Group Policy

In the past, as network systems increased in size and complexity, administering security across the enterprise also became increasingly complex. Windows NT did not provide adequate tools or utilities to implement and manage an effective network security policy. For example, if an administrator wanted to implement security auditing on a particular group of workstations, either she would have to visit each machine individually, or try to find adequate third-party tools to assist in the configuration.

Another common problem with managing security policies in Windows NT is the maintenance of the configuration. If a company or department has more than one administrator in charge of applying and maintaining the security settings, it can be difficult to keep track of configuration changes to the policy. Without proper documentation and good communication between the administrators, a great deal of time may be spent figuring out which auditing and security settings each administrator has changed.

Windows 2000 makes significant changes to how security configurations can be maintained. One of the sets of tools included with Windows 2000 is called the **Security and Configuration Tool Set**. This tool set, together with Windows 2000 Group Policies, allows an administrator to configure a specific group of security settings to form a **Security Policy Template**. This template can then be administered centrally and applied throughout Active Directory.

To assist with security policy changes, the Security and Configuration Tool Set can also be used to analyze and implement security settings on a computer system. In the analysis, a comparison can be made between a computer system's security settings and a previously defined security template file. Differences between the computer system and the policy template can then be viewed and reported, and action can then be taken to change the settings on the computer to the desired settings.

For example, your security plan may provide detailed information on the security settings for the company's computers. Creating the design is only the first step, however. You also need to implement the design, which could mean making changes to every computer on the network. The Security and Configuration Tool Set is designed to make the implementation of the security policy much easier. When the security policy has been designed and approved, the settings can then be defined in a security template. This template can then be compared to the current settings on the network by using the Security Configuration and Analysis tool. This will show which current settings match the security policy and which ones do not. You can then apply and implement the new settings with a simple command.

The Security and Configuration Tool Set is also useful in maintaining the security settings. Using this tool, it is easy to check the security settings for the network on a regular basis and reapply any settings that have been changed.

The Security and Configuration Tool Set consists of the following components:

- Security templates
- Security settings in Group Policy Objects
- Security Configuration and Analysis tool
- Secedit command line tool

Security Templates

An administrator uses a security template to define, edit, and save baseline security settings to be applied to computers with common security requirements in order to meet organizational security standards. Templates help ensure that a consistent setting can be applied to multiple machines and be easily maintained.

The templates are text-based files that can be read, but should not be changed or edited using any text editor. Be sure to use the Security Templates snap-in to create and edit the templates.

Security settings can be defined by loading the Security Templates snap-in on the Microsoft Management Console (MMC). To load the snap-in, create a new MMC by clicking Start, clicking Run, and then typing mmc in the Run text box. The snap-in can then be added by clicking the Console menu and clicking Add/Remove Snap-in.

Save the new MMC by clicking the File menu and choosing Save As. Choose an appropriate name and location for the MMC console file. An example of the Security Templates console is shown in Figure 4-4.

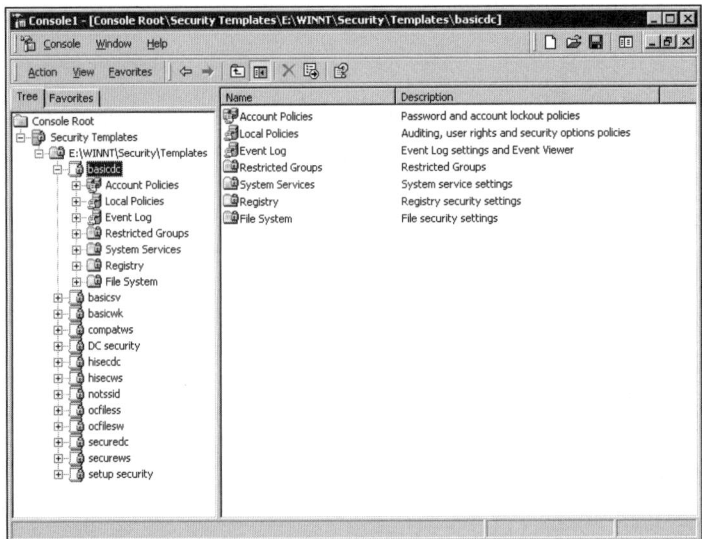

Figure 4-4 Viewing the Security Templates console

Security templates include the same categories as discussed earlier in Tables 4-3, 4-4, and 4-5. You can configure settings such as audit or security policies and then save them as a template to be applied to any number of computers in the domain.

Analyzing the Pre-configured Security Templates

The first step in configuring and implementing security templates is to categorize the network computers into three main categories: **workstations**, **servers**, and **domain controllers**. These three categories relate to the default security templates included with Windows 2000, although an administrator can design a new custom template. Keep in mind that only Windows 2000-based computers can take advantage of security template configurations and deployments.

It is essential to understand the security differences between a newly installed Windows 2000-based computer and one that has been upgraded from Windows 9x or NT. When Windows 2000 is installed as a fresh install on an NTFS partition, a basic template is applied that increases security on specific folders, such as the %systemroot%, and the system registry. Computers upgraded from Windows NT maintain their previous security settings, and do not receive the increased security on the folder's or registry's access control lists.

Windows 9x computers upgraded to Windows 2000 will have the default security settings applied, with the exception that all local user accounts become members of the local administrators group, if the file system is converted to NTFS. Be sure to review and edit the local administrator's group membership after an upgrade.

The Basic Templates

There are three basic security templates that will be applied to a new installation of Windows 2000. The template that is applied depends on the role of the machine itself.

- *Defltwk.inf*—Applied to Windows 2000 Professional workstations
- *Defltsv.inf*—Applied to Windows 2000-based servers
- *Defltdc.inf*—Applied to Windows 2000-based servers that are promoted to domain controllers

These files are stored in the %systemroot%\inf hidden folder. When a template is applied during an installation, the default template is copied, renamed to Setup Security.inf, and placed in the %systemroot%\security\templates folder.

As stated earlier, computers that are upgraded from Windows NT to Windows 2000 do not have any default templates applied. This is to ensure that any previous security configurations are still maintained after the upgrade.

The three following templates can be applied to computers to "harden" the security settings after you have upgraded them from Windows NT. The only settings that are not affected are user rights and group modifications, as some applications may need specific rights or group assignments to function correctly.

- *Basicwk.inf*—Applied to computers upgraded to Windows 2000 Professional

- *Basicsv.inf*—Applied to servers upgraded to any version of Windows 2000 server that are not configured as domain controllers
- *Basicdc.inf*—Applied to domain controllers upgraded to Windows 2000

Incremental Templates

If the basic security settings do not meet your security needs, you can apply various additional security configurations using **incremental templates**. These templates modify security settings incrementally. However, these templates should only be applied to machines already running the default security settings, as they do not include any of the initial configurations that the basic templates apply.

- *Compatws.inf*—This template can be applied to workstations or servers. Windows 2000 has increased the default security considerably over previous versions. In some cases, this increased security brings application compatibility problems, especially for non-certified applications that require user access to the registry. One way to run these applications is to make the user a member of the **Power Users group**, which has a higher level of permissions than a normal user. Another option is for the administrator to increase the security permissions for the Users group. The Compatws.inf template provides a third alternative by weakening the default security to allow legacy applications to run under Windows 2000.

A utility called Apcompat.exe, which is included in the Windows 2000 support tools, can also be used by an administrator to configure legacy applications to run in Windows 2000. This utility can configure Windows 2000 to emulate a particular Windows operating system environment so that the application can run properly.

- *Securews.inf* and *Securedc.inf*—These templates provide increased security for areas such as account policy, auditing, and registry permissions. The securews template is for any workstation or server, while the securedc template should only be applied to domain controllers.
- *Hisecws.inf* and *Hisecdc.inf*—These templates can be incrementally applied after the secure templates have been applied. Security is increased primarily in the areas that affect network communication protocols. These templates should only be applied to pure Windows 2000 environments and should be applied to all machines to ensure proper connectivity. The hisecws template is for any workstation or server, while the hisecdc template should only be applied to domain controllers.
- *DC Security.inf*—This template is applied automatically whenever a Windows 2000 member server is promoted to a domain controller. This is available to give the administrator the option to reapply the initial domain controller security if the need arises.
- *OCFilesw.inf* and *OCFiless.inf*—These two templates increase the local security of optional components such as Internet Explorer, Microsoft NetMeeting, or

Internet Information Services. OCFilesw should only be installed on stand-alone or member servers running Windows 2000, while OCFiless should only be installed on Windows 2000 Professional.

- *Notssid.inf*—This template removes the Terminal Users security group SID from all DACLs. If this is defined, all terminal server users will have their permissions applied through individual user and group memberships rather than the terminal server access account SID.

The security templates provided in Windows 2000 provide the administrator with acceptable security configurations for a variety of situations. If there is a unique situation where a pre-configured template is not suitable, you can create a custom template. To create a new security template, open an MMC with the Security Templates snap-in loaded. You can then right click the %systemroot%\Security\Templates node and choose New Template.

You can also use a pre-configured template as a baseline and save any changes to a new template. To do this, right-click a pre-configured template, and then choose Save As.

Applying Security Templates

Security templates can be applied to either the local machine, or to the domain via Group Policy Objects. To apply a security template to a local machine, open the Local Security Policy from the Administrative Tools menu. Right-click Security Settings in the console pane, and choose Import Policy. You can then select the template file to be imported.

In the Local Security Settings MMC, there are two columns: one that displays local settings and one that displays effective settings, as shown in Figure 4-5. Local settings are the settings that are applied to the local computer. Effective settings indicate that there are domain-level or OU-level security settings applied for that particular policy. The settings that are applied at a domain or OU level will always override the local settings. Domain-level security settings are applied any time the machine is rebooted, and at 90-minute intervals if changes have been made to the policy. If there have been no changes, the domain policy is refreshed every 16 hours.

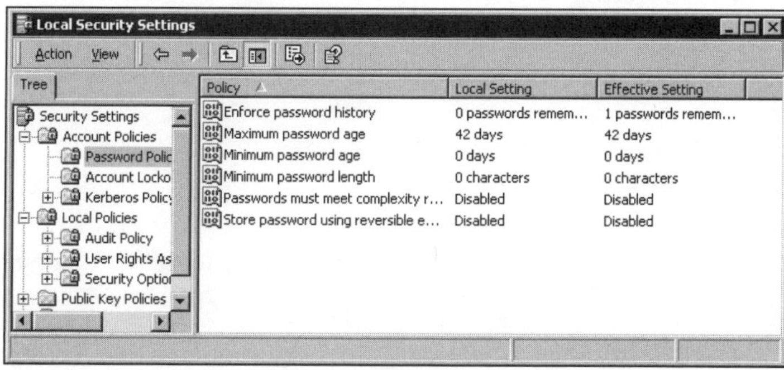

Figure 4-5 Viewing the Local Security Policies

To apply security templates to Active Directory using Group Policy, follow the steps below:

1. Open Active Directory Users and Computers.
2. Right-click the node that is to have the security settings applied and click **Properties**. If the security settings refer to the Account Policies, be sure to apply this template to the Domain Controllers OU.
3. Click the **Group Policy** tab and click **New** or **Edit**, depending on whether there is already a Group Policy that can be edited.
4. Under **Computer Configuration**, click **Windows Settings**, and expand the **Security Settings** node.
5. Right-click the **Security Settings** node and click **Import Policy**.
6. Choose the appropriate policy to import and click **Open**.

Security Configuration and Analysis

The Security Configuration and Analysis utility allows administrators to compare current system settings to a previously configured security template. The comparison identifies any changes to the original security configurations and any possible security weaknesses that may be evident when compared to a stronger security baseline template.

In order to perform a security analysis, the Security Configuration and Analysis snap-in must be loaded into a Microsoft Management Console shell. To load the snap-in, click Start, click Run, and then type mmc in the Open text box. You can then add the snap-in by clicking the Console menu and clicking Add/Remove Snap-in. Figure 4-6 shows an example.

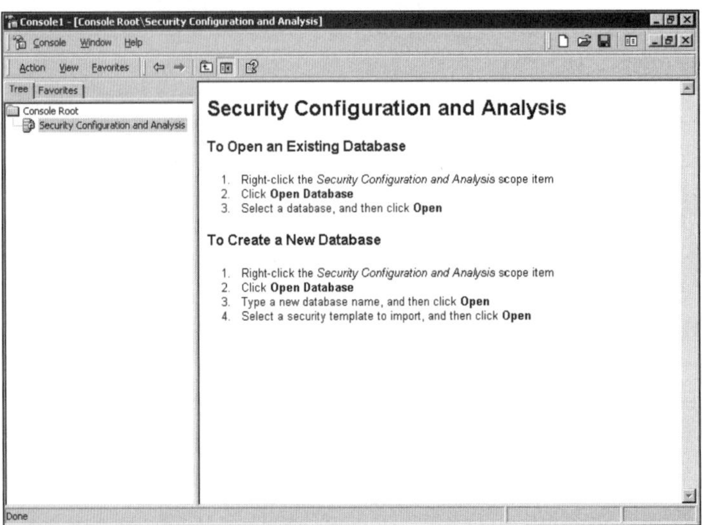

Figure 4-6 Viewing the Security Configuration and Analysis Tool

The Security Configuration and Analysis tool uses a container, called a database, to store the imported templates to be compared to the working system. The administrator imports a template into the database, and then compares the template settings to the actual computer settings. If desired, the administrator can import more than one template to compare the effects of combining templates on the current settings. Once a combined template has been created, it can be saved and exported for future analysis, or it can be used to configure working computer systems.

To create the database and perform the analysis, follow the steps below:

1. In the Security Configuration and Analysis MMC, right-click the **Security Configuration and Analysis** node and click **Open Database**.
2. Type a name for the database and click **Open**.
3. Choose the security template to import into the database. If the database is being reused, click the **Clear This Database Before Importing** check box. Figure 4-7 shows the interface after you have imported the security template.

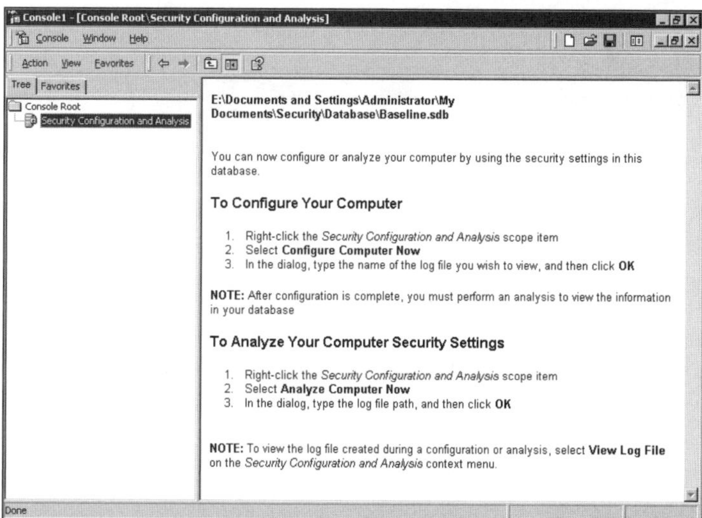

Figure 4-7 Importing a Security Template

4. To compare the security template to the current computer settings, right-click **Security Configuration and Analysis**, and then click **Analyze Computer Now**.
5. An error log path appears to allow an error log to be saved at a particular location on the computer. Specify a path, a name, and then click **OK**.
6. A progress meter will appear as the analysis takes place. See Figure 4-8.

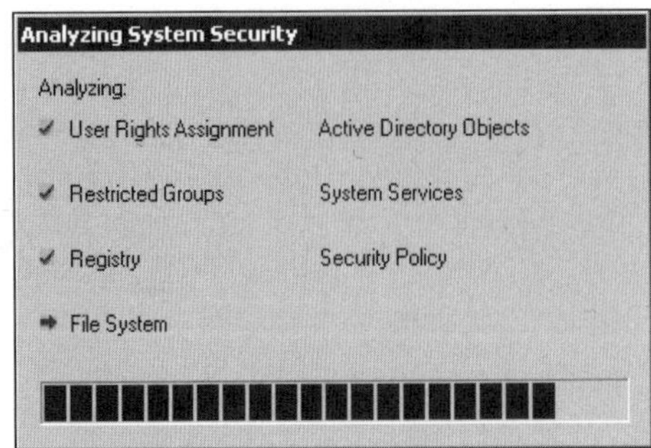

Figure 4-8 Analyzing security on a computer

7. After the analysis, the security categories will appear. As each node is expanded, you can see the comparison between the database (imported templates) and the computer's current configuration. See Figure 4-9. A green check mark indicates that the two settings match; a red X indicates a mismatch. You can make changes by double-clicking any configuration entry and selecting the desired configuration.

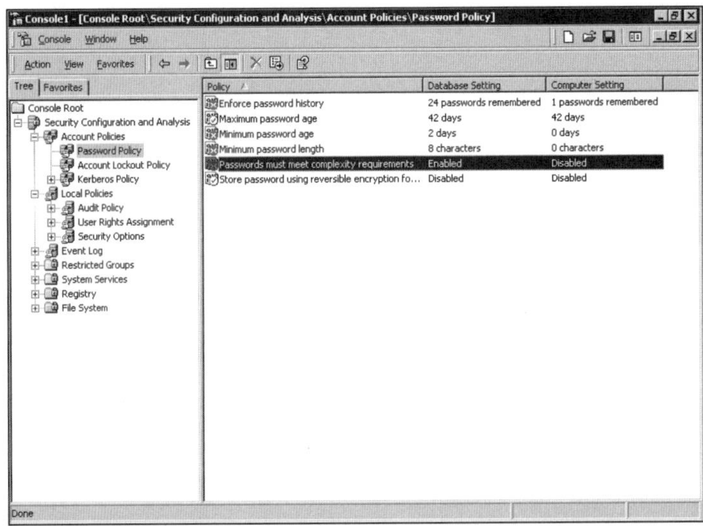

Figure 4-9 Viewing the results of the security analysis

8. If you want to apply the database setting to the computer, right-click **Security Configuration and Analysis** and click **Configure Computer Now**. If you do this, the computer settings will be modified to match the settings in the template.

9. If you want to reuse the template that you have modified, you can export the template by choosing **Export Template** and creating a filename for the new template. The new template can then be deployed using Windows 2000 Group Policy.

Secedit Command Line Tool

Secedit.exe is a command-line tool used to create and apply security templates, as well as analyze security settings. This tool can be used in situations where group policy cannot be applied, such as in workgroup configurations. Secedit.exe, along with the Task Scheduler, can ensure that every computer in the workgroup maintains consistent security policy settings. The secedit.exe command uses five main switches:

- */analyze*—Analyzes database settings and compares them to a computer configuration
- */configure*—Configures a system with database and template settings
- */export*—Exports database information to a template file
- */refreshpolicy*—Triggers group policy propagation
- */validate*—Verifies the syntax of a template

For more information on Secedit.exe, consult Windows help.

Assigning Scripts and Redirecting Folders

Most administrators are familiar with the application of various types of **scripts** or files that incorporate a number of commands used to automate routine operations. Logon scripts have been most popular in the past, and were used to automate tasks such as drive mapping, or application updates.

Windows 2000 can use scripts to perform tasks at various times during the logon or logoff process. Group Policy allows you to configure computer startup and shutdown scripts, which are configured in the computer section of a Group Policy object. User logon and logoff scripts can also be configured by accessing the user section of a Group Policy object. To assign a script using a Group Policy object, obtain or write the script required, and then follow these steps:

1. Open Active Directory Users and Computers, and right-click the container object in which you want to create and link the new Group Policy object.
2. Click **Properties**, and then click the **Group Policy** tab.
3. Click **New**, and type in the name for the policy.
4. To edit the policy, point to the policy, and click **Edit**.
5. To apply a computer-based script, expand the **Computer Configuration\Windows Settings** node, and choose the **Scripts (Startup/Shutdown)** container. To apply a user-based script, expand the **User Configuration\Windows Settings** node, and choose the **Scripts (Logon/Logoff)** container. The script configuration icons are displayed in the details pane, as shown in Figure 4-10.

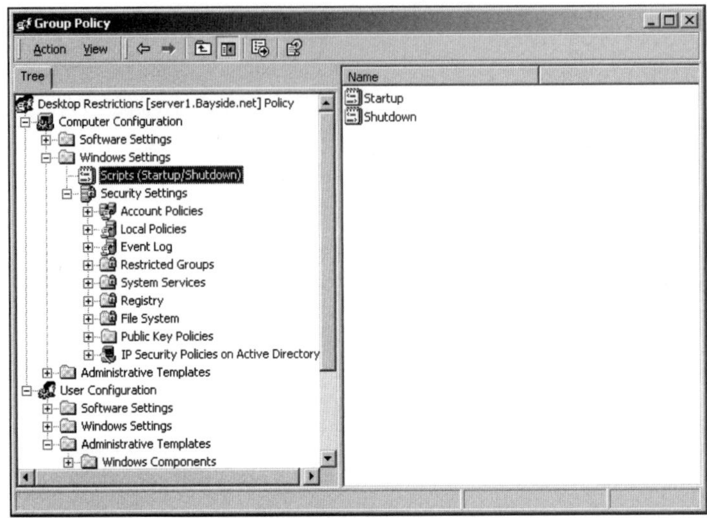

Figure 4-10 Viewing the startup and shutdown configuration icons

6. In the details pane, double-click the type of script you want to assign.
7. In the Startup Properties dialog box, click **Show Files** to open the Group Policy template (GPT) folder. Copy your script into this folder, and close the window. Because you have copied your script into this window, the script automatically replicates to every domain controller throughout the domain. This is done because the scripts are stored in the Winnt\sysvol\sysvol\domain name\ scripts folder on the domain controller.
8. Click **Add**, and enter the script name and path to the GPT folder.
9. Click **OK**. See Figure 4-11.

If you assign multiple logon/logoff or startup/shutdown scripts to the configuration containers, each script is run synchronously in order from top to bottom. You can modify the order by selecting the script and clicking the Up or Down buttons in the Properties dialog box. In addition to modifying the order, other policy settings for groups allow you to specify script time-outs, change the running of the scripts to asynchronous, and specify whether scripts are hidden when they are executed.

Folder redirection is a Group Policy feature that enables you to redirect the following contents of a user's profile to a network location:

- Application data
- Desktop
- My Documents
- My Pictures
- Start menu

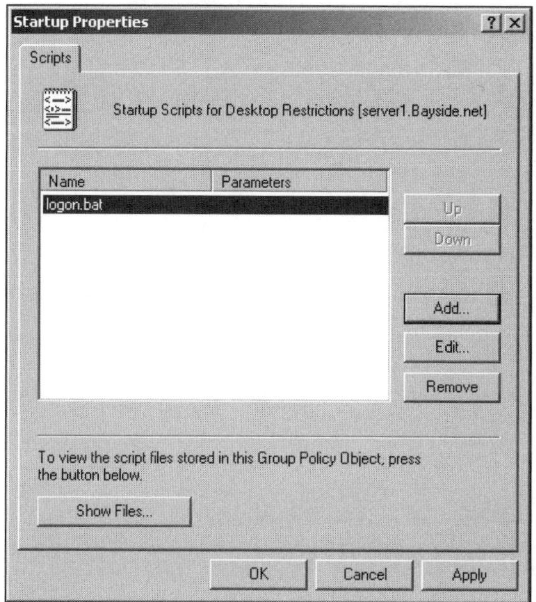

Figure 4-11 Assigning a script to the startup icon in Group Policy

Some of the reasons why you would want to redirect the folders out of a user's profile include the following:

- Storing the folders on the network ensures that user information is backed up at all times, as opposed to being stored on the local workstation.
- User logon time is reduced, as the contents of the folder do not have to be copied from the workstation to the server each time the user logs on or off.
- Folder redirection allows you to create a standard desktop for multiple users.

To implement folder redirection follow these steps:

1. Open Active Directory Users and Computers, and right-click the container object in which you want to create and link the new Group Policy object.
2. Click **Properties**, and then click the **Group Policy** tab.
3. Click **New**, and type in the name for the policy.
4. To edit the policy, point to the policy, and click **Edit**.
5. Expand **User Configuration\Windows Settings\Folder Redirection**, as shown in Figure 4-12.

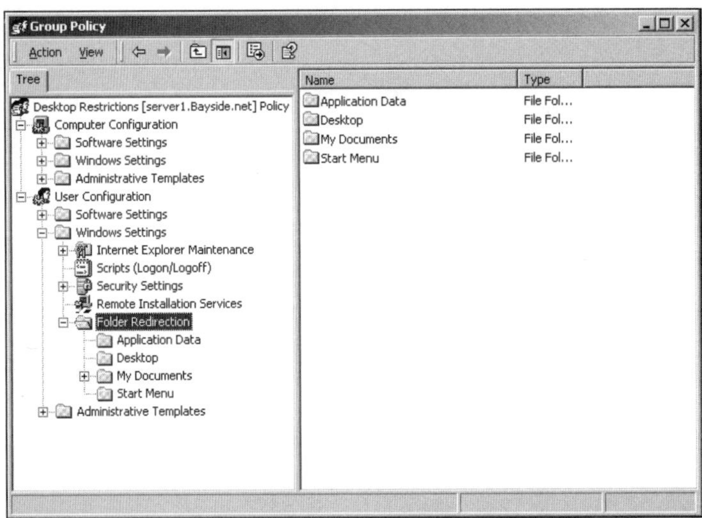

Figure 4-12 Redirecting a folder in Group Policy

6. Right-click the folder that you want to redirect, and then click **Properties**.
7. Choose a setting on the Target tab. The options are:
   a. *Basic*—Redirects all folders to the same location; variables can be used to specify individual subfolders, as shown in Figure 4-13.

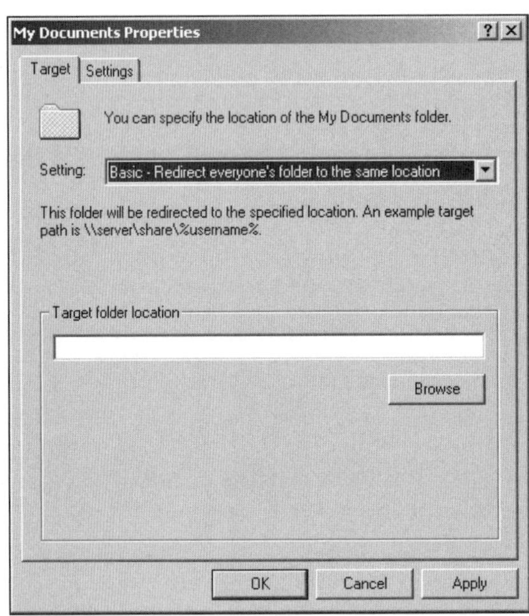

Figure 4-13 Configuring a basic folder redirection

b. *Advanced*—Allows you to specify a location based upon security group membership, as shown in Figure 4-14.

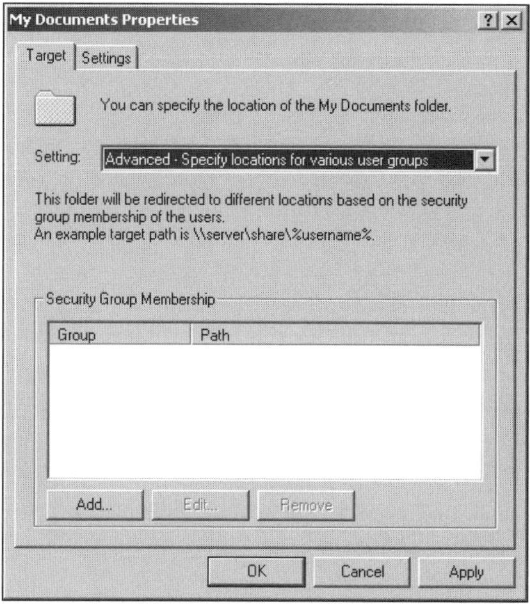
My Documents Properties
Target
Settings
You can specify the location of the My Documents folder.
Setting:
Advanced - Specify locations for various user groups
This folder will be redirected to different locations based on the security group membership of the users.
An example target path is \\server\share\%username%.
Security Group Membership
Group
Path
Add...
Edit...
Remove
OK
Cancel
Apply

Figure 4-14 Configuring advanced folder redirection

c. No administrative policy specified

The Settings tab has a number of options that control the behavior of folder redirection. Table 4-6 describes each setting.

Table 4-6 Folder redirection settings

Configuration Setting	Description
Grant the user exclusive rights to <folder name>	This setting makes sure that only the individual user that owns the folder has access; this is enabled by default.
Move the contents of <folder name> to the new location	This setting moves the contents of the folder to the new location specified; if this check box is cleared, the contents of the folder, before the redirection, are not moved to the new location (this is enabled by default).
Policy removal	When a folder redirection policy is removed, by default the redirected folder remains in the redirected location; you can choose to redirect the folder back to the users profile if the policy is removed.

MANAGING GROUP POLICY INHERITANCE

As a Windows 2000- or XP-based computer starts, multiple Group Policy objects are applied in the following order:

1. Local computer
2. Site
3. Domain
4. Parent OU
5. Child OU

All of the individual Group Policy object settings are inherited. For example, a Group Policy setting on a parent container is also applied to the child containers, and therefore to all the users and computers in the child containers. One computer or user could be processing many policies during startup and logon.

At each level, more than one GPO can be applied. If there is more than one GPO per container, the policies are applied in the order that they appear on the Group Policy tab for the container, starting with the bottom GPO first.

Be careful about the number of Group Policy objects that are to be applied. Computer startup and logon performance may be affected if a large number of GPOs need to be applied to the user or workstation.

Because of the multiple policies that can be applied to a user or computer, there is the chance that there could be a conflict in the settings between policies. The computer uses the following steps to determine which policy to apply:

1. If there is no conflict, then both policies are applied. For example, if a policy at a domain level enables a certain setting and the policy at an OU level has that setting set as "Not Configured," then the domain policy is applied.
2. If there is a conflict, then later settings overwrite earlier settings. If both a domain-level policy and an OU-level policy configure the same setting differently, then the OU-level policy is applied.
3. Computer policies usually overwrite user policies.

After a user has logged on, the computer refreshes its policies every 90 minutes plus a random number of minutes (no more than 30) so that all the computers don't contact the DC to refresh at the same time. If a user does not shut down his computer, or a setting has changed in the Group Policy, then refreshing the policy makes sure that the computer and user settings are up to date. Domain controllers and member servers refresh their policy settings for groups every five minutes.

You can refresh a Group Policy manually by typing:
secedit /refreshpolicy [user_policy or machine_policy] /enforce

As mentioned previously, Group Policy objects can be linked to site, domain, or OU containers in Active Directory. This allows the administrator maximum flexibility when applying Group Policies in the domain. There are a number of possibilities.

- If you have a certain policy that applies to everyone in a site, then apply the policy at that level. You can also configure other settings at a domain level. In fact, policies like the account policy can only be set at the domain level. You can then set very specific policies based on OUs.
- You can have multiple Group Policies assigned to one container. You may want to create several GPOs that define different settings and then link all of them to a specific container. For example, you may want to create a policy that defines security settings, and another that defines user desktop settings, and then link both of them to the same container.
- You can use the same Group Policy, and link it to multiple containers. This allows you to create a policy once and then use that policy for different containers. For example, you may create a policy for software distribution, and then link that policy to the OUs where the policy should be applied.

To link Group Policy objects to Active Directory containers, use the following procedure:

1. Open Active Directory Users and Computers, and right-click the container you want to link to a GPO. (If you are linking a GPO to a site, open Active Directory Sites and Services, and right-click a site.)
2. Click **Properties**, and click the **Group Policies** tab.
3. Click **Add**, and you see all of the possible locations where GPOs can be stored. If you have created that GPO for another container, browse to that container, choose the GPO, and then click **OK**.

To identify all containers linked to a particular GPO:

1. Click the GPO in one of the containers, and click **Properties**.
2. Click the **Links** tab to make sure that you are searching for the right container.
3. Click **Find Now**. The list shows all of the containers with links to the GPO.

Configuring Block Policy Inheritance, No Override, and Filtering

By default, all policy settings for groups are inherited from parent containers. However, there are several ways to change this default behavior:

Blocking Group Policy Inheritance—If you do not want any of the higher-level settings to be applied to a particular child container, then check the Block Policy inheritance option on the Group Policy tab for the container properties. Figure 4-15 shows the interface.

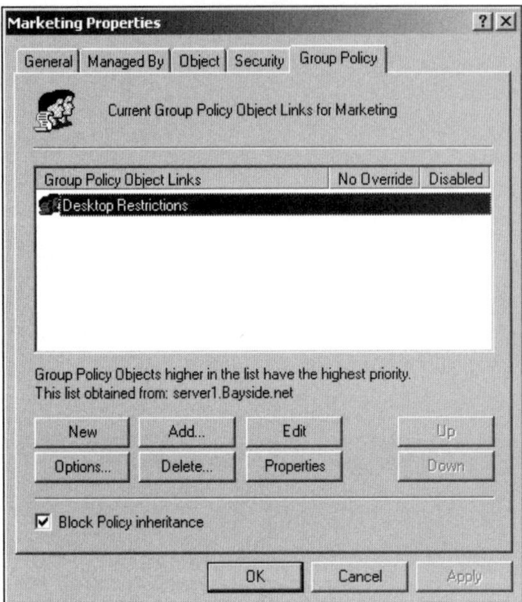

Figure 4-15 Blocking Group Policy inheritance

Checking this option means that all policies from parent containers are blocked. Individual Group Policies from parent containers cannot be blocked; policies that are set to *No override* from a parent container are not blocked.

Blocking Group Policies can be very useful if you have one OU that has very different policy requirements than all of the other OUs, or if the OU must be separately managed.

Configuring No Override—If you want a particular Group Policy to always be enforced, then you can force a Group Policy by choosing Options for a particular Group Policy, and then choosing No Override, as shown in Figure 4-16.

This results in the policy being enforced even if a lower-level policy that is processed later tries to change a setting. The No Override setting also enforces a policy on a container that has Block Policy inheritance set. Use this option if there is a particular group of settings that must be enforced in your entire network and then link this policy to the domain or site level so that it applies to all containers.

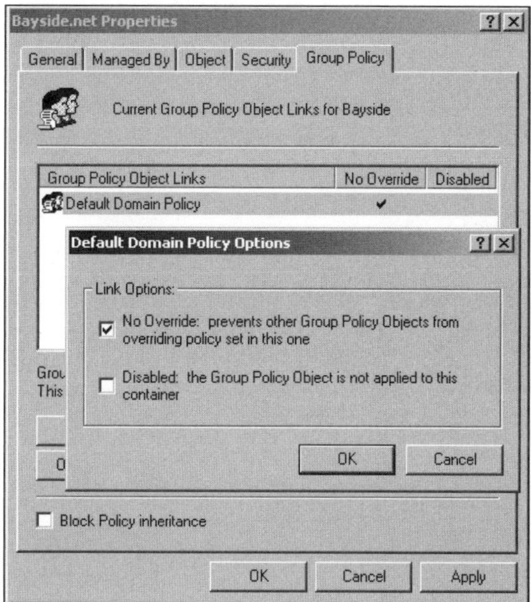

Figure 4-16 Configuring No Override on a Group Policy object

Filtering policy settings for groups—Another way of affecting the inheritance of Group Policies is to prevent policy settings for groups from applying to a particular user, group, or computer within a container. For example, the Managers OU may have a GPO linked to it, but you don't want the settings from the GPO to apply to the General Manager. To filter the General Manager so that he does not have the GPO applied:

1. Click the **Group Policy** tab, click the GPO that you are configuring, and then click **Properties**.
2. Click the **Security** tab. Figure 4-17 shows the interface.
3. Select or add the user, group, or computer that you want to filter out, and then clear the **Apply Group Policy** and **Read** permissions.

This now prevents this Group Policy from being applied to the General Manager, but it still affects all other users within the OU.

Troubleshooting Group Policy Settings

There may be times when a Group Policy does not work as expected. Restrictions may not be enforced as configured or may be too restrictive and interfere with user productivity.

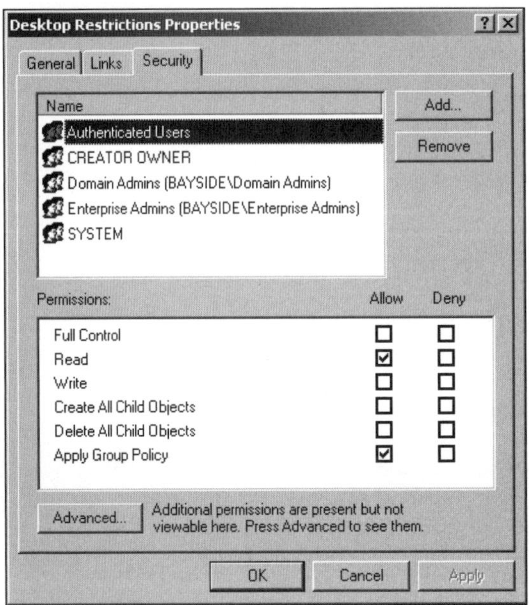

Figure 4-17 Filtering a Group Policy

A careful inspection of the Active Directory hierarchy could possibly uncover the reasons for a Group Policy not working the way it should. Do not forget the order of Group Policy processing: local computer, site, domain, and OU. Be sure to inspect all containers above and below the OU that is causing the problem. In some cases, improper use of No Override or Block Policy inheritance settings can cause problems. Another area to be aware of is the Group Policy's Security tab. Make sure that the user or group has been assigned the Read and Apply Group Policy permissions.

You can also use a utility from the Windows 2000 Resource Kit called **Gpresult**. This utility is useful because it can be used to discover Group Policy-related problems and to illustrate which Group Policy objects were applied to a user or computer. Gpresult also lists all group memberships of the user or computer being analyzed.

You must run Gpresult at a command prompt on the computer where the user logs on. Gpresult uses the following common syntax switches:

```
Gpresult [/V] [/S] [/C] [/U] [/USER <TargetUserName>]
/V–verbose mode
/S–super verbose mode
/C–shows only Group Policy objects applied to the computer
/U–shows only Group Policy objects applied to the user
/USER TargetUserName – Specifies the user name of the user
 whose RSOP data is to be displayed.
```

For a full list of switches, type /? at the command prompt.

If you are experiencing performance problems that you can relate to the processing of Group Policy objects, you may want to disable the unused portion of the computer or user section of the policy. To disable an unused portion of a policy follow these steps:

1. Right-click the OU that has the policy that you want to edit, and click **Properties**.
2. Click the **Group Policy** tab, click the GPO that you are editing, and then click **Properties**.
3. In the Disable section, choose to disable either the unused computer or user configuration settings as shown in Figure 4-18. Click **OK**.

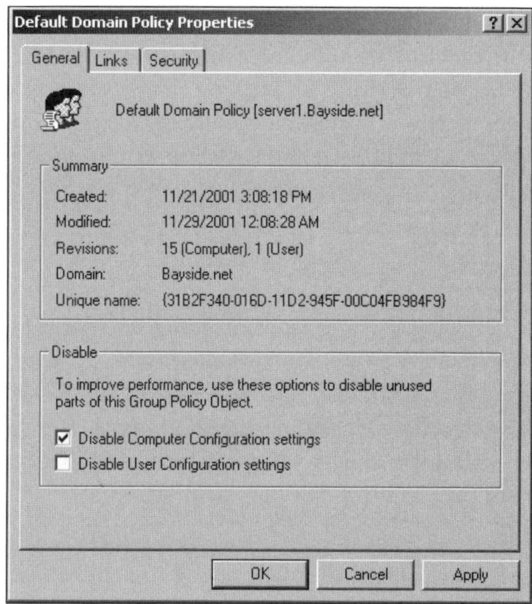

Figure 4-18 Disabling a section of a Group Policy object

Deploying Software Using Group Policy

In addition to managing user desktops, maintaining security, applying scripts and redirecting folders, Group Policy also has the ability to assist you in deploying and maintaining software installations throughout the domain. There are a variety of applications that can be deployed using Group Policy, including business applications such as Microsoft Office, utilities such as anti-virus software, and software updates such as service packs.

When a company rolls out a new software application, there are four main phases that are addressed:

- Software preparation
- Deployment
- Software maintenance
- Software removal

Software Preparation

The first phase of software deployment is to prepare the software for distribution. Windows 2000 Group Policy uses a special installation file called a Microsoft **Windows installer package (MSI)**. An MSI file contains all of the information needed to install an application in a variety of configurations. Many software vendors are starting to include preconfigured MSI packages with their applications to enable administrators to take advantage of the features provided by Windows 2000 Group Policy. For older applications, you can create your own MSI packages by using third-party utilities such as a program called WinINSTALL LE from VERITAS.

WinINSTALL LE is included on the Windows 2000 CD in the ValueAdd\3rdparty\mgmt folder.

After you obtain or create an MSI package file, place the file, along with any related software installation files, in a shared folder on the network. You configure Group Policy to access this shared folder so that a successful installation is ensured.

If an MSI package is not available for an application, and you cannot repackage the application using WinINSTALL LE, you have an option to use another file type called a ZAP file. A **ZAP file** is a text file that can be used by Group Policy to deploy an application. However, the following limitations apply to applications deployed by using the ZAP file:

- Can only be published.
- Are not resilient and do not repair themselves automatically.
- Usually require user intervention and require the user to have the proper permissions to install applications on their local computer.

For more information on creating a ZAP file, consult KB article Q231747 on the Microsoft Web site.

Deployment

Using Windows 2000 Group Policy, applications can be deployed in one of two ways:

- Assigning applications
- Publishing applications

Assigning Applications

When you create a policy to assign an application, any user that receives the policy has a shortcut to the application advertised on the Start menu. The application is installed when a user clicks the shortcut for the first time or double-clicks a document that is associated with the application. If the user does not click the shortcut, the application is not installed, which saves space on the hard drive.

If the policy was configured in the computer section of the Group Policy, any computer that receives the policy has the application automatically installed the next time that the computer is started.

One other advantage to assigned applications is that applications are resilient, meaning that if a user deletes the application or if files become corrupt, the application automatically reinstalls itself.

Publishing Applications

When a policy is created to publish an application, the application is not advertised on the Start menu. Users install published applications by accessing the Add/Remove Programs applet in the Control Panel, or by double-clicking a document associated with the application. Applications cannot be published to the computer section of Group Policy.

One other caution about publishing applications is that if a user deletes an application, or if the application becomes corrupt, it does not reinstall itself. Only assigned applications are resilient.

Configuring the Deployment

Configuring the deployment of the software package involves creating or editing a Group Policy object and specifying the deployment options. To configure a Group Policy object to deploy an application, follow this procedure:

1. Open Active Directory Users and Computers from the Administrative Tools menu.
2. Right-click the root or OU container to which the policy is being applied, and click **Properties**.
3. Click the **Group Policy** tab, and then click the **New** button to create a new GPO, or click **Edit** to edit an existing GPO.

4. If you are creating a new GPO, choose the new GPO, and click **Edit**.
5. In the Group Policy window, expand either the **Computer Configuration** or the **User Configuration** section. This depends on whether you are assigning the application to the computers or to the users of the OU.
6. Expand **Software Settings**, and right-click **Software installation**.
7. Point to **New**, **Package**, as shown in Figure 4-19.

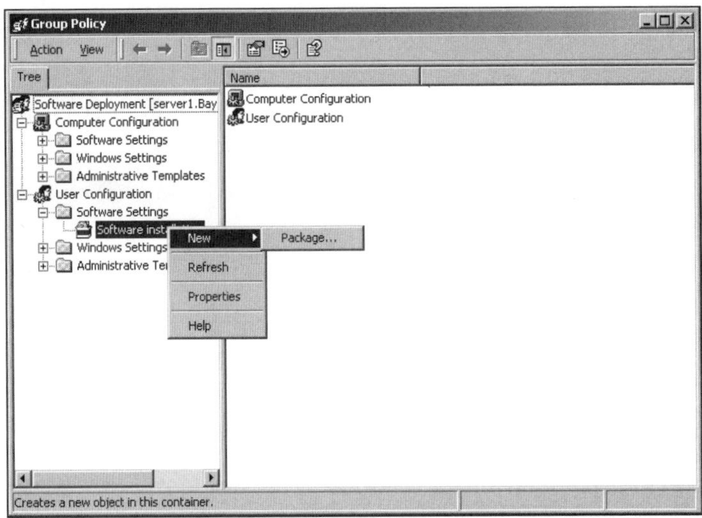

Figure 4-19 Configuring software deployment using Group Policy

8. In the Open dialog box, type or browse to the shared network location of the application's installation files. Choose the MSI file, and then click **Open**.
9. In the Deploy Software dialog box, choose the deployment method, and then click **OK**. After a minute, the application appears in the details pane, as shown in Figure 4-20.

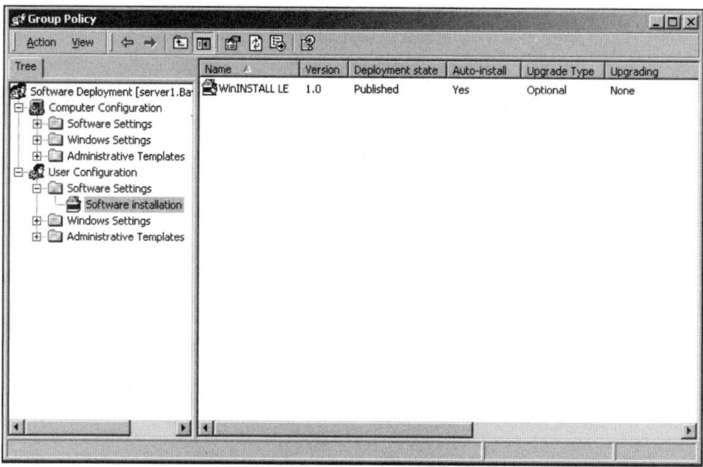

Figure 4-20 Viewing a published application

Software Maintenance

After an application has been deployed, there are various types of maintenance tasks that usually need to be performed. Most vendors provide periodic updates and service patches to fix reported problems with their applications. You have the task of keeping the deployed software updated with the latest service releases. If vendors release new versions of the software, your users may want to transition slowly to the new version. You may want to allow the users to use both the old and new versions of the software.

When deploying application patches or upgrades, you have three choices for how the deployment is performed:

- A mandatory upgrade
- An optional upgrade
- Redeploying an application

A mandatory upgrade automatically replaces the old version of the software with the new version that is being deployed. To perform a mandatory upgrade of an application, take the following steps:

1. Publish or assign the software upgrade as stated previously in the chapter.
2. Right-click the newly deployed software update, and then click **Properties**.
3. Click the **Upgrades** tab.
4. In the Packages that this package will upgrade, click **Add**. Choose the old version of the application, and click **OK**.

5. To specify this as a mandatory upgrade, check the **Required upgrade for existing packages** option, as shown in Figure 4-21.

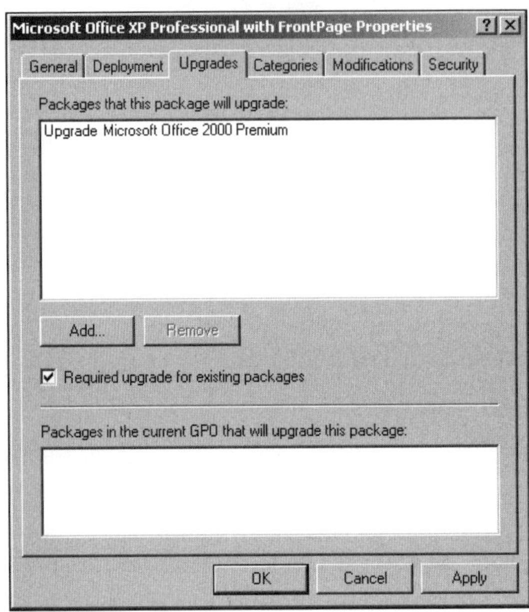

Figure 4-21 Configuring a mandatory upgrade

If the original package and the updated package are both native Windows installer files, the update automatically knows that it is to replace the original package; you just have to configure the mandatory selection box.

To perform an optional upgrade, do not check the Required upgrade for existing packages option. If the user has installed the original application, all shortcuts still open the first version of the program. To install the upgrade, the user has to access Add/Remove Programs from the Control Panel, and choose to install the upgrade. If the original version was never installed, clicking the advertised icons invokes an installation of the updated version.

Redeployment of a package means to force an application to reinstall itself everywhere that it is already installed. You may have to do this if you need to deploy an application service pack or hot fix. The main requirement for redeployment is that the patch has to come with an MSI file. To configure redeployment, place the update in the same installation folder as the original application. Open the original GPO that deployed the package, right-click the application, and click All Tasks, Redeploy application.

Software Removal

The final phase of an application life cycle is the removal process. When you need to remove an application that you no longer want to deploy in the organization, Group Policy can save a great amount of time and money. The only caution is that the application must have been installed using a Windows installer package.

When you remove an application you are given two choices of how the removal process takes place:

- A forced removal
- An optional removal

A forced removal automatically uninstalls the application from all computers and prevents the software from being reinstalled. The removal takes place either the next time the computer restarts (for computer-based policies) or when the user logs on (for user-based policies).

An optional removal does not remove any of the installed copies of the software, but does prevent any future installations from taking place. If users remove the application, they are not able to reinstall it.

CHAPTER SUMMARY

- Group Policy enables the centralized management of user and computer settings throughout your network. Group Policy objects can be used to perform a variety of administrative tasks, including configuration of desktop settings, control of security settings for users and computers, assignment of scripts, the redirection of folders, and the automation of software distribution on computers throughout the network.
- Group Policy is applied in the following order: local computer, site, domain, OU, child OU.
- The Configuration and Analysis tool can be used to analyze, modify, and apply security templates to objects within Active Directory.
- Group Policy is automatically inherited from parent containers to child containers. This can be modified by applying Block Policy Inheritance, No Override, or by filtering the policy for specific users.
- When deploying software, Group Policy uses a Windows installer package (MSI) file to determine the installation options.
- Applications can either be assigned or published within a Group Policy object. Assigned applications are advertised for users and automatically installed for computers. Published applications appear in the Add/Remove Programs applet for users. Computers cannot have applications published.

Key Terms

default domain controllers policy — The name of the default Group Policy object that is linked to the domain controllers organizational unit. Used primarily for configuration of policy settings that are only to be applied to the domain controllers in the domain (i.e., auditing).

default domain policy — The name of the Group Policy object that is linked to the domain container in Active Directory; used primarily for configuration of domain-wide password policies.

Folder redirection — A Group Policy feature that enables you to redirect the contents of the Application Data, Desktop, My Documents, My Pictures, and Start menu folders from a user's profile to a network location.

globally unique identifier (GUID) — A unique 128-bit number assigned to the object when it is created.

Gpresult — This utility can be used to discover Group Policy-related problems and to illustrate which Group Policy objects were applied to a user or computer. Gpresult also lists all group memberships of the user or computer being analyzed.

Group Policy — Enables the centralized management of user desktop settings, desktop and domain security, and the deployment and management of software throughout your network.

Group Policy object (GPO) — An Active Directory object that is configured to apply Group Policy and linked to either the site, domain, or organizational unit level.

incremental templates — A set of text-based security template files that you can use to apply uniform security settings on computers within an enterprise. The templates modify security settings incrementally and do not include the default security settings.

Key Distribution Center (KDC) — A Kerberos version service that runs on a domain controller. It issues ticket-granting tickets (TGTs) and service tickets for obtaining network authentication in a domain.

Power Users group — Power Users have less system access than adminstrators but more than users. By default, members of this group have Read/Write permissions to other parts of the system in addition to their own profile. Power Users can perform many system-wide operations, such as changing system time and display settings, and creating user accounts and shares.

script — A file that includes various commands to automate routine operations.

secedit.exe — A command-line tool that allows you to perform security configuration and analysis. The secedit.exe command-line tool allows the following high-level operations: analyze, configure, export, and validate.

Security and Configuration Tool Set — A security toolset consisting of security templates that can be used to analyze and apply security configurations.

Security Policy template — A template used to apply various security settings to an Active Directory container or object.

ticket-granting ticket (TGT) — A ticket issued by the Kerberos version Key Distribution Center (KDC) for purposes of obtaining a service ticket from the ticket-granting service (TGS).

Windows installer package (MSI) — A file that contains all of the information needed to install an application in a variety of configurations.

ZAP file — A text file that can be used by Group Policy to deploy an application; it has a number of limitations compared to an MSI file.

Review Questions

1. Joe attempts to publish an application to a computer, but the publish setting is disabled. What is wrong?
   a. Joe has wrong permissions on the installation share.
   b. The computer is turned off.
   c. The GPO has not replicated to all domain controllers.
   d. You cannot publish applications to computers.
2. What is the order in which Group Policy objects are applied?
   a. OU, domain, site, local computer
   b. local computer, site, domain, OU
   c. site, local computer, domain, OU
   d. domain, site, local computer, OU
3. You configure a GPO to apply a password policy to a particular organizational unit, but you notice that the GPO has not been applied. What is wrong?
   a. The GPO has not replicated correctly.
   b. It takes 90 minutes to update the GPO settings.
   c. You have to click the Save button in the policy window.
   d. Password policies must be configured at the domain level.
4. You need to configure two user accounts in a certain OU to not have any GPO applied to them, while ensuring that the other users still get the restrictions. What can be done to accomplish this?
   a. Configure a block inheritance.
   b. Create a GPO filter.
   c. Configure No Override.
   d. None of the above
5. Published applications are resilient in that they reinstall automatically if any files become corrupt. True or False?
6. Assigned applications are advertised on the Start menu of any user that receives the Group Policy deployment object. True or False?

7. What type of file is used to deploy applications with Windows 2000 Group Policy?
   a. .msc
   b. .mcs
   c. .msi
   d. .csi
8. When a Group Policy object is created, the GPO content is actually stored in which two locations on the server? (Choose two.)
   a. the Group Policy container within the Active Directory database
   b. the Group Policy container in the Sysvol folder
   c. the Group Policy template within the Active Directory database
   d. the Group Policy template in the Sysvol folder
9. You have created a GPO that removes the run command, and have linked it to the domain level. At the OU level, you have created a GPO to enable the run command. Which GPO takes effect?
   a. the OU level
   b. the domain level
   c. The GPO settings cancel each other out and have no effect.
10. An account policy GPO must be linked to which container within the domain to take effect?
    a. the domain controllers OU
    b. a departmental OU
    c. a site object
    d. the domain container
11. By default, if a folder redirection policy is removed, the folder contents remain in the redirected location. True or False?
12. You have just made a change to the computer portion of a Group Policy object and want to manually refresh the policy settings. Which command accomplishes this?
    a. secedit /refreshpolicy
    b. secedit /refreshpolicy user_policy
    c. secedit /refreshpolicy machine_policy /enforce
    d. All of the above
13. A ZAP file can be used by a Group Policy object to assign applications to any OU in the domain. True or False?

14. If an application has been assigned to a computer using Group Policy, when is the application installed?
    a. when a user accesses Add/Remove Programs and starts the installation
    b. when a user logs on to the computer
    c. when the computer is restarted
    d. when the computer is about to shut down
15. A user has accidentally deleted a required file on his local machine for an application that you had previously assigned to the domain using an MSI file and Group Policy. What must you do to make sure that the application continues to function?
    a. Redeploy the application using the original GPO and MSI file.
    b. Do nothing; the application automatically fixes itself.
    c. Publish the application to the domain.
    d. Reinstall the application locally on the user's machine using a CD-ROM or the installation point.
16. Which removal option allows users to continue to work with an installed application, but prevents any new installations?
    a. forced removal
    b. optional removal
    c. installation removal
    d. None of the above
17. In which folder do scripts have to be stored to ensure proper functioning and replication to all DCs?
    a. the temp folder
    b. the sysvol folder
    c. the replication folder
    d. the system 32 folder
18. Redirecting folders may decrease a user's logon and logoff time. True or False?
19. You need to redirect the My Documents folder to a server location based upon security group memberships. Which setting do you choose?
    a. basic
    b. advanced
    c. None of the above
20. When a folder redirection policy is put into effect, the contents of the folder are automatically moved to the new location by default. True or False?

HANDS-ON PROJECTS

Project 4-1

In this Hands-on Project you create a new security policy and configure an account policy by editing the default domain policy.

1. Open Active Directory Users and Computers from the Administrative Tools menu.
2. Right-click **Bayside.net**, and click **Properties**.
3. Click the **Group Policy** tab. Notice the Default Domain Policy.
4. Click **Edit** to open the Group Policy window.
5. Under the Computer Configuration section, expand **Windows Settings**.
6. Expand the **Security Settings** node.
7. Expand the **Account Policies** node. Configure the following settings:

Enforce password history	Four passwords must be remembered
Maximum password age	30 days
Minimum password length	Seven characters
Account lockout duration	Administrator must unlock account
Account lockout threshold	Account locks out after four attempts
Reset account lockout counter after	30 minutes

8. Close all windows.
9. Restart your computer.

Project 4-2

In this Hands-on Project you will create a custom Microsoft Management Console and add the Security Templates snap-in.

1. With an administrator account, log on to your Windows 2000 computer.
2. Click **Start**, click **Run**, and type **mmc** at the command line. Click **OK**.
3. In the Console window, click **Console**, and click **Add/Remove Snap-in**.
4. Click **Add** and scroll down to choose the **Security Templates** snap-in.
5. Click **Add** and then click **Close** to return to the custom MMC dialog box. Then click **OK**.
6. Maximize the Console Root window.
7. Click **Console** and then click **Save As**. Name the console **Security Templates** and then click **Save**.
8. Close the **Security Templates** console.

9. Click **Start**, point to **Programs**, and point to **Administrative Tools**. You should see your newly created **Security Templates** console.
10. Close all windows and log off.

Project 4-3

In this Hands-on Project you will create a new security template that will set account policy configurations for the domain.

1. Log on to your Windows 2000 computer with an administrator account.
2. Click **Start**, point to **Programs**, and then point to **Administrative Tools**. Click **Security Templates**.
3. Expand the **Security Templates** node. Notice the physical path to the location of the actual template files.
4. Expand the template path node to view the various pre-configured templates.
5. Right-click the template path node, and choose **New Template**. Name the new template **Account Template**. Click **OK**.
6. Expand the **Account Template** node to view the configuration categories.
7. Expand the **Account Policies** node. Configure the following settings:

Password History	4 passwords must be remembered
Maximum Password Age	30 days
Minimum Password Length	7 characters
Account Lockout Duration	Administrator must unlock account
Account Lockout Threshold	Account locks out after 4 attempts
Account Lockout Counter	30 Minutes

8. Right-click **Account Template** and click **Save**.
9. Close all windows. Click **Yes** to save the console settings.
10. Log off.

Project 4-4

In this Hands-on Project you will create another new MMC console with the Security Configuration and Analysis snap-in added. You will then use the console to analyze and compare the Account Template configurations to the local computer.

To create a new MMC console:

1. With an administrator account, log on to your Windows 2000 computer.
2. Create another MMC console with the Security Configuration and Analysis snap-in added. (If you forget how to create an MMC console, refer to Project 4-2.)
3. Save the new console with the name **Security Analysis**.

To analyze a security template:

1. In the left pane, expand the Security Configuration and Analysis node. Read the instructions that appear in the details pane.
2. Right-click **Security Configuration and Analysis** and choose **Open Database**.
3. In the filename box type **Policy** and then click **Open**.
4. On the Import Template screen select the **Account Template** file and then click **Open**. Again read the directions that appear in the details pane.
5. Right-click **Security Configuration and Analysis** and click **Analyze Computer Now**.
6. Click **OK** to accept the log file path.
7. Expand the **Account Policies** node. Click the **Password Policy and Account Lockout Policy** to view the configuration differences between the local computer and the Account Template file. All differences will have a red X indicating that the template and computer settings are not the same.

Project 4-5

In this Hands-on Project, you create a Group Policy object that removes the run command from all users in the Toronto Dept OU. The Executive Managers group should not have this policy applied.

To create the Group Policy object:

1. Log on to your Windows 2000 computer with an administrator account.
2. Click **Start**, point to **Programs**, point to **Administrative Tools**, and then click **Active Directory Users and Computers**.
3. Right-click the **Toronto Dept** OU, and click **Properties**.
4. Click the **Group Policy** tab, and click the **New** button.
5. Name the new Group Policy object **Remove Run Command**.
6. Click the Remove Run Command object, and click **Edit**.
7. Under the **User Configuration** container, expand **Administrative Templates**.
8. Click the **Start Menu & Taskbar** node.
9. In the details pane, double-click **Remove Run menu from Start Menu**.
10. Click the **Enabled** radio button, and click **OK**.
11. Close the Group Policy window.

To filter the Executive Managers from getting the policy:

1. Click the **Remove run command** Group Policy, and click **Properties**.
2. Click the **Security** tab. Click **Add**.
3. Double-click the **Executive Managers** group, and click **OK**.

4. Click **Executive Managers**, then set the Apply Group Policy permission to **Deny**. Click **OK** and click **Yes** at the Security warning.
5. Close all windows, and log off.

To test the policy settings for groups:

1. Log on as John Riley (with **johnr** as the password). Notice that the Run command is not available.
2. Log on as Alan Scone (with **alans** as the password). Notice that the Run command is available, because Alan is a member of the Executive Admins group.
3. Close all windows, and log off.

Project 4-6

In this Hands-on Project you experiment with software deployment. All users require the WinINSTALL LE program to be advertised in their Programs menu. The Windows 2000 Support Tools installation is to be listed in Add/Remove Programs. The Toronto Dept OU must not have the WinINSTALL LE program advertised, but they do require the Windows 2000 Support Tools to be available.

To create the software installation GPO:

1. Log on to the computer as the administrator.
2. Click **Start**, point to **Programs**, point to **Administrative Tools**, and then click **Active Directory Users and Computers**.
3. In the console pane, right-click **Bayside.net**, and click **Properties**.
4. In the domain properties dialog box, click the **Group Policy** tab.
5. Click **New**, type **WinINSTALL LE App**, and then press **Enter**.
6. Click **New** again, type **Support Tools App**, and then press **Enter**.

To assign the WinINSTALL LE program:

1. Double-click **WinINSTALL LE App**. Under the User Configuration section, expand **Software Settings**. Click **Software installation**.
2. Right-click **Software installation**, and then click **New**, and click **Package**.
3. Click **My Network Places** in the shortcut bar.
4. Double-click **Entire Network\Microsoft Windows Network\Bayside\Server1\W2KAS.**
5. Double-click **\VALUEADD\3RDPARTY\MGMT\WINSTLE**.
6. Click **SWIADMLE**, and click **Open**.
7. Click **Assigned**, and then click **OK**.
8. Close the Group Policy window.

To publish the Windows 2000 Support Tools:

1. Double-click **Support Tools App**. Under the User Configuration section, expand **Software Settings**. Click **Software installation**.
2. Right-click **Software installation**, click **New**, and then click **Package**.
3. Click **My Network Places** in the shortcut bar.
4. Double-click **Entire Network\Microsoft Windows Network\Bayside\Server1\W2KAS.**
5. Double-click **\Support\Tools**.
6. Point to **2000RKST**, and click **Open**.
7. Point to **Published**, and click **OK**.
8. Close the Group Policy window.

To ensure that the Windows 2000 Support Tools are always available:

1. Right-click **Support Tools App**, and click **No Override**.
2. Click **Close**.

To block the inherited policy for the Toronto Dept OU:

1. Right-click the **Toronto Dept** OU, and click **Properties**.
2. Click the **Group Policy** tab.
3. Place a check mark next to **Block Policy Inheritance**. Click **OK**.
4. Close all windows, and log off.

To test the software deployment policy:

1. Log on to your computer as Tim Vans (using **timv** as the username) with the password of **password**.
2. Click **Start**, point to **Programs**, click **Veritas Software**, and then click **Veritas Discover**. The application should install and then run. Close the application.
3. Log off and log back on as Alan Scone (using **alans** as the username) with the password of **password**.
4. Click **Start,** and point to **Programs**. Notice that you do not have the Veritas Software link.
5. Click **Start**, point to **Settings**, and click **Control Panel**.
6. Double-click **Add/Remove Programs**.
7. Click **Add New Programs**. Notice that Windows 2000 Support Tools is listed. Close all windows, and log off.

To remove all policy settings for groups:

1. Log on again as the administrator.
2. Click **Start**, point to **Programs**, point to **Administrative Tools**, and then click **Active Directory Users and Computers**.

3. In the console pane, right-click **Bayside.net**, and click **Properties**.
4. In the domain properties dialog box, click the **Group Policy** tab.
5. Right-click **WinINSTALL LE App**, and click **Delete**. Click **Remove the link from the list**. Click **OK**.
6. Repeat Step 5 to remove the **Support Tools APP** GPO.

Do NOT remove the default domain policy.

7. Close all windows, and log off.

CASE PROJECTS

Case Project 4-1

One of the Bayside Detailing user accounts is located in the Managers OU. The Managers OU is a child OU of the Administration OU. The Administration OU is in the Bayside.net domain, which is in the Default-First-Site-Name site. The following table lists the GPO settings for the domain.

Container	GPO Setting
Default-First-Site-Name	Restricts the user from using author mode when using customized MMCs
Bayside.net	Password length must be at least eight characters; removes the Run command from the Start menu
Administration OU	Disables Control Panel; adds the Run command to the Start menu
Managers OU	Allows the user to use author mode in MMC; password length must be at least 10 characters

What effective settings are applied to the user account located in the Managers OU?

Case Project 4-2

A fellow administrator is having problems with Group Policy objects not being applied as expected. List five troubleshooting methods that you would use to diagnose problems with Group Policy objects.

CHAPTER

5

ADMINISTERING FILE AND PRINT RESOURCES

After reading this chapter and completing the exercises, you will be able to:

- Create and manage shared folders using Windows Explorer and the Microsoft Management Console
- Manage shared folder permissions
- Integrate shared folder and NTFS permissions
- Monitor access to shared folders
- Create and modify Web folders
- Configure and manage DFS
- Create and modify shared printer resources
- Set up and manage published resources in Active Directory
- Audit access to shared resources
- Manage data storage

Two common functions of a computer network are to provide client access to shared file storage locations and print access to shared printers. Windows 2000 includes many new and improved methods to create, configure, and manage shared file and print resources. New features, such as Web folder sharing and the distributed file system, can be used to simplify the sharing of information in an organization. This chapter discusses these various methods and how they are used to share files and printers throughout your networking environment.

The combination of NTFS and shared file permissions has often been the basis of intensive troubleshooting tasks for administrators. It is important to understand how permissions are applied to ensure that clients obtain appropriate access to resources. To ensure an understanding of this concept, NTFS and shared file integration are discussed later in the chapter, as well as monitoring access to folders that are shared on the network. You are also introduced to file encryption, which provides another level of security in addition to the regular permissions used to protect folders and files.

Once you have created and shared the file and print resources, your users may need a simple and effective way to search for these objects throughout the network. Publishing resources into Active Directory allows any Active Directory-aware client the ability to perform a simple search on the network. This chapter illustrates how to configure resource publishing and perform Active Directory searches.

Once resources have been shared throughout the network, it is important to be able to audit client access in order to discover security problems that may occur. You might also need to perform disk management tasks such as configuring volumes, controlling the amount of disk space that a typical client may use to store data on a shared network location, or enabling compression. The final sections of this chapter help you understand how to manage disk resources, configure security auditing, and control access to shared data.

Creating and Managing Shared Folders

To permit general user access to data on a network system, you are often required to configure shared folders with the proper access control permissions. A **shared folder** is a data resource container that has been made available over the network to authorized network clients. These clients can then view or modify the shared information within the folder, depending upon the level of permissions granted to the user.

To create these shared folders, you are required to have the appropriate rights. A domain administrator or server operator has the default rights to create shared folders within a domain. There are several ways to create shared folders; two of the more popular ones include the Windows Explorer interface and the Computer Management console.

Using Windows Explorer to Create a Shared Folder

Windows Explorer is the standard method used to create and share folders for all versions of Windows NT 4.0 and Windows 2000. It can be used to create, maintain, and share folders on any drive connected to the computer. There are many ways to open Windows Explorer. For example, you can click the Windows Explorer icon on the Accessories menu, or you can right-click almost any drive-related object, and click the Explore command on the shortcut menu. Figure 5-1 illustrates Windows Explorer, which has been opened by right-clicking My Computer, and selecting Explore.

If you do not have an existing folder that you want to share, the first step in sharing a folder is to select a drive, and create a new folder. To create a new folder, click File, point to New, and then click Folder. You can then name the folder with an appropriate name.

The next step to sharing a folder is to right-click the new or existing folder, and click the Sharing command on the shortcut menu. In the properties box that opens, you can then click the Sharing tab, and configure the sharing options as needed. Figure 5-2 shows an example of sharing an application folder on a Windows 2000 server.

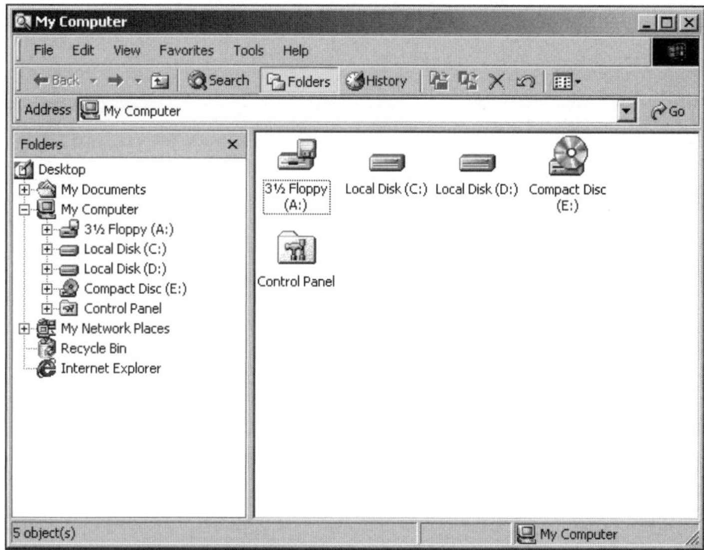

Figure 5-1 Windows Explorer

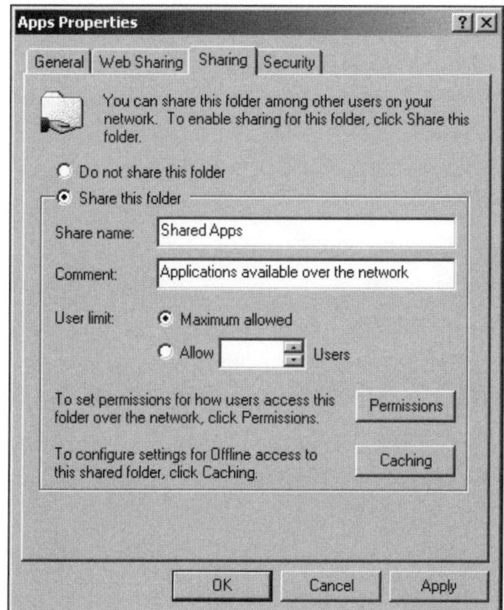

Figure 5-2 Sharing a folder using Windows Explorer

By default, the folder name appears as the share name. It is important to provide a useful share name, as this is how your users find this share. Be careful of any share names that are longer than eight characters if you have any legacy clients that cannot handle long names.

Windows Explorer indicates a shared folder by placing a hand icon under the folder, as shown in Figure 5-3.

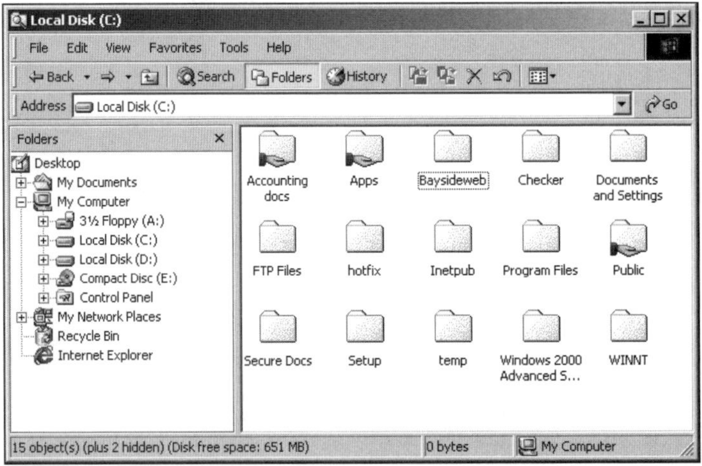

Figure 5-3 Shared folders in Windows Explorer

There may be times when you would like to create a shared folder, but not have it listed in My Network Places or Network Neighborhood. To hide a share, place a dollar sign ($) just after its name. For example, if you create a share called Salary, you can hide the share by actually naming it Salary$. To map or connect to the hidden share, a user needs to manually type the share name, including the dollar sign.

The final step in creating a shared folder is to secure the share by modifying user and group permissions on the resource. By default, initially the Everyone group has Full Control of this share. This permission should be modified, or NTFS permissions should also be incorporated, to further control user access. This concept is covered later in the chapter.

Using Computer Management to Create a Shared Folder

A new method for creating and managing shared folders in Windows 2000 is through the use of the Computer Management console. **Computer Management console** is a predefined Microsoft Management Console (MMC) application that allows you to perform a variety of administrative tasks from a local or remote computer.

To open the Computer Management console, right-click My Computer, and click the Manage command on the shortcut menu. The Computer Management console opens, as shown in Figure 5-4

When you expand the Shared Folders container and then click the Shares node, you can view all of the shared folders that are located on the local computer, as shown in Figure 5-5.

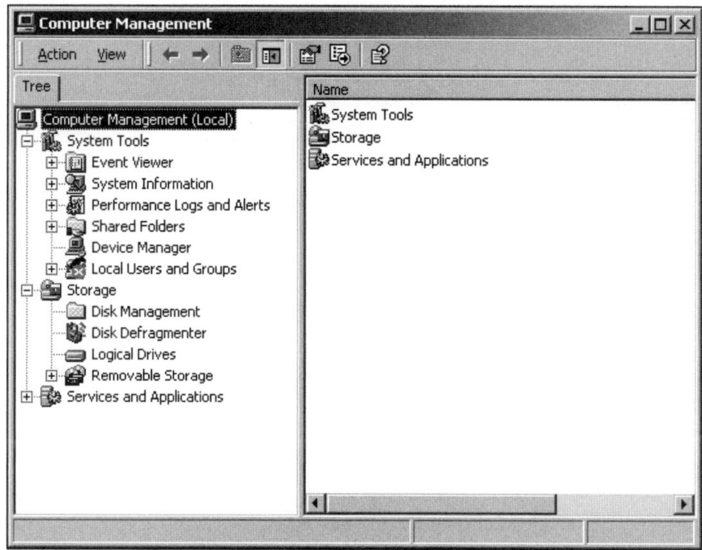

Figure 5-4 The Computer Management console

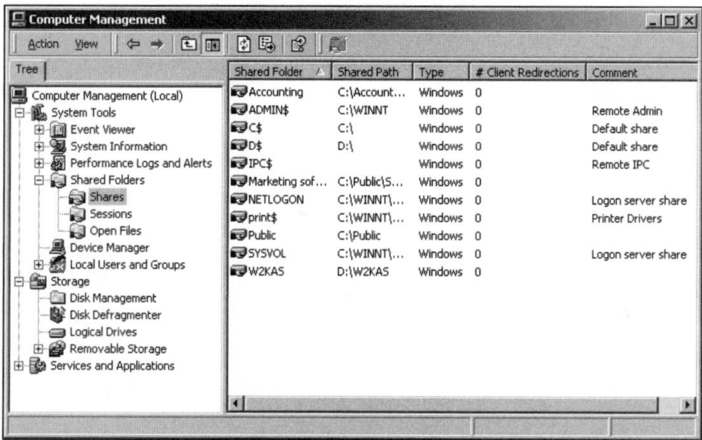

Figure 5-5 Shared folders on the local computer

To create a new shared folder, you can either click the Action button on the menu, or right-click Shares, and then click New File Share. A wizard-like dialog box opens, as shown in Figure 5-6, which allows you to input all of the information needed to create the new, shared folder.

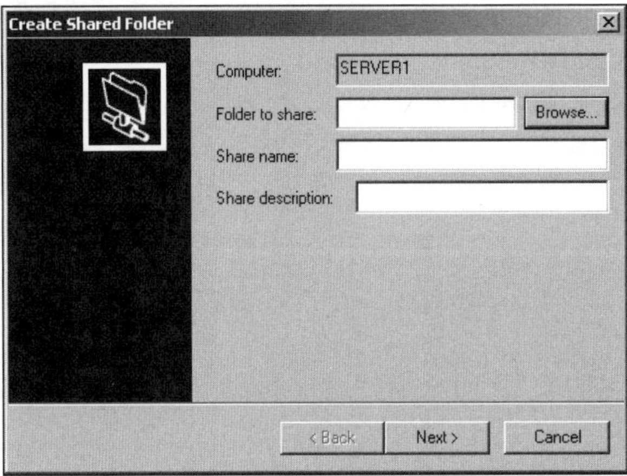

Figure 5-6 Creating a new shared folder using the Computer Management console

As you make your way though the wizard, you are asked to either choose an existing folder to share, or create a new folder that is to be shared on the network. Figure 5-7 illustrates the dialog box that appears to allow you to select or create the folder that is to be shared.

Figure 5-7 Selecting or creating a new folder

The final step in the wizard is to define the share permissions for the folder. Three of the choices are preconfigured. These include:

- *All users have full control*—Grants Full Control to the Everyone group
- *Administrators have full control; other users have read-only access*—Grants Full Control to the local Administrators group, and Read to the Everyone group

- *Administrators have full control; other users have no access*—Grants Full Control to the local Administrators group
- *Customize share and folder permissions*—Allows you to define both share and NTFS permissions manually; manual assignment of permissions is dealt with later in the chapter.

When specifying permissions in the Create Shared Folder Wizard, a best practice is to choose Administrators have full control; other users have no access. This ensures that all other users, other than ones that you explicitly define manually, do not have any access. Figure 5-8 illustrates the permissions step of the Create Shared Folder Wizard.

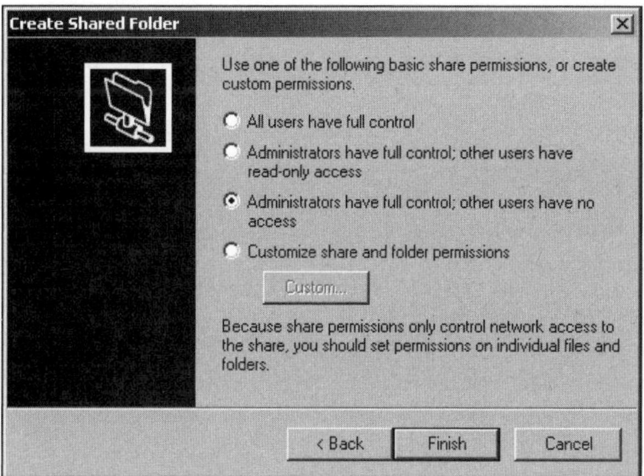

Figure 5-8 Configuring permissions on a shared folder using the Create Shared Folder Wizard

If you want to stop the sharing of a folder resource, the easiest way to do this is to choose the Shares container in the Computer Management console. The list of shares appears in the details pane of the console. There are two ways to stop sharing a folder. The first method is to right-click the share that is to be discontinued, and click Stop Sharing on the shortcut menu. The second method is to click the share, and then click Stop Sharing on the Action menu.

MANAGING SHARED FOLDER PERMISSIONS

Each share that is created has a **discretionary access control list (DACL)**. A DACL is a part of an object's security descriptor that contains a list of user or group references that have been allowed or denied permissions to the resource. Each user or group name listed in the DACL is referred to as an **access control entry (ACE)**. The DACL is accessed by clicking the Permissions button on the Sharing tab of a folder's Properties dialog box. It can also be accessed by clicking the Custom button, when using the Create Shared Folder Wizard. Figure 5-9 illustrates the DACL for a shared folder called Apps.

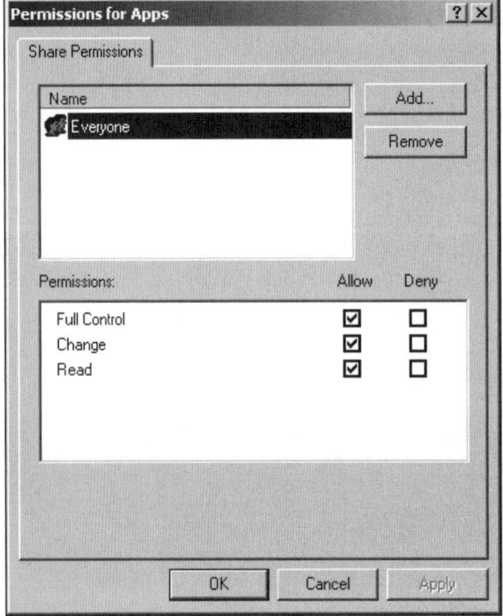

Figure 5-9 The DACL of the Apps shared folder

Windows 2000 supports three share permissions, as explained in Table 5-1.

Table 5-1 Share permissions in Windows 2000

Windows 2000 Permission	Permissions Granted
Read	Allows the user to browse the file and folder names (including subfolders), read the data in a file, and execute programs
Change	Includes the Read permission, plus permission to add and delete files and subfolders, and change the data in the files
Full Control	Includes the Read and Change permission, plus the right (on an NTFS partition) to change permissions on a folder or file and to take ownership of a folder or file

Notice that Windows 2000 does not have a No Access share permission as Windows NT did in the past. Instead, to deny a user or group access to a shared folder, an administrator must explicitly deny the user permission, as shown in Figure 5-10.

As discussed previously, when a new share is created, the default permission on the share gives the Everyone group full access. One of the first steps an administrator should perform after creating a share is to remove this permission and substitute more appropriate permissions or incorporate NTFS permissions.

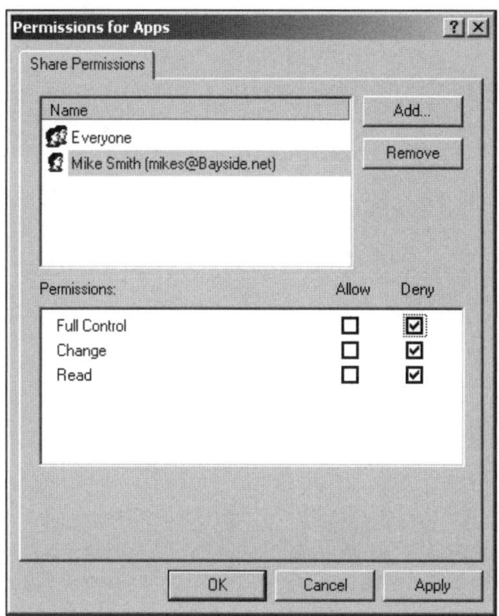

Figure 5-10 Denying Full Control to the Apps shared folder

The Everyone group includes all users who have access to the computer, whether or not they are members of the domain.

When a share is created and a user is assigned permission to that share, the user also has the same level of permissions to all subfolders inside that share. In other words, permissions are inherited by subfolders.

Shared permissions are cumulative for the user. All the permissions assigned to the user and any group of which the user is a member are combined and the least restrictive of all the permissions applies. For example, a user named Jill is a member of the Sales group, as well as a member of the Managers group. If the Sales group is assigned Read permission to a share, the Managers group is assigned Full Control, and Jill is assigned Change permission, Jill has Full Control of the share.

INTEGRATING SHARED FOLDERS WITH NTFS PERMISSIONS

Shared folder permissions can only protect folders that are accessed over the network. When permissions are set on a shared folder, the permissions determine what restrictions apply to the folder when it is accessed from another computer across a network connection. These restrictions do not apply if the user were to log on locally to the computer. This is where NTFS file and directory permissions can assist in your security plan.

NTFS permissions are applied whenever a file or folder is accessed, whether the person is logged on to the computer where the file is located or the person is accessing the file across a network connection. To assist in troubleshooting file access problems, it is essential to understand how NTFS file and directory permissions protect the resource, and how these permissions work with share-level permissions. The next section discusses NTFS file and directory permissions in greater detail.

NTFS File and Directory Permissions Concepts and Rules

It is important to understand NTFS file and directory permissions and how they are applied.

- NTFS permissions are set on the Security tab, which may be accessed by right-clicking any file or folder and clicking Properties.
- NTFS permissions are cumulative. If a user is a member of multiple groups that have different permissions, the final permission is the sum of all permissions. For example, a user named Jim may be a member of a group called Marketing, as well as a group called Sales. If Marketing is given Read permission to the folder, and Sales is given Full Control, then Jim has full access to the folder.
- The Deny Access file permission overrides all other permissions. In this example, if Jim is explicitly denied Full Control rights to the folder through an individual assignment or through a different group assignment, this overrides any permission Jim may have. Deny Access overrides all other permissions because of the way the ACEs are evaluated by the security subsystem. When a user tries to access a folder, all of the ACEs that deny access are evaluated first. If the Security ID (SID) on any of the ACEs that deny access matches the SIDs in the user's access token, then access is denied and no more ACEs are evaluated.
- NTFS folder permissions are inherited by child folders and files, unless otherwise specified. Clearing the Allow inheritable permissions from parent to propagate to this object option on the Security property sheet can prevent inheritance of NTFS permissions.
- NTFS permissions can be set at a file level, as well as at a folder level.
- Unless explicitly specified, Full Control for the Everyone group is the default NTFS permission for all files.
- Windows 2000 has a set of standard NTFS permissions, as well as special permissions.

Table 5-2 lists the standard NTFS permissions.

Table 5-2 Standard NTFS permissions

Windows 2000 Permissions	Permissions Granted
Full Control	The user can make any changes to the file or folder; the detailed permissions are listed in Table 5-3
Modify	Gives full permissions except the permission to delete subfolders and files, change permissions, and take ownership
Read and Execute	Gives permissions to traverse folders, list folders, read attributes and extended attributes, read permissions, and synchronize; these permissions are inherited by both files and folders
List Folder Contents	Same as Read and Execute permissions, except that the permissions are inherited only by folders and not by files; visible only on folders
Read	Same as Read and Execute, except without the permission to traverse folders; inherited by files and folders
Write	Gives permissions to create files and folders, write attributes and extended attributes, read permissions, and synchronize

Special NTFS Permissions

Windows 2000 uses 13 individual NTFS permissions to specify the level of access provided to a given resource. Occasionally one of the standard permissions may not provide detailed enough control. To access the special permissions, click the Advanced button in the Security dialog box on the Properties tab for the folder or file. The resulting Access Control Settings dialog box allows you to assign special permissions to existing accounts. To view or edit the special NTFS permissions for a specific user or group, click the user or group, and then click the View/Edit button. The Permission Entry dialog box opens, as shown in Figure 5-11.

The Permission Entry dialog box provides for the selection of special permissions, as well as the rules for their application. Special permissions can be applied at the following levels:

- This folder only
- This folder, subfolders, and files (default)
- This folder and subfolders
- This folder and files
- Subfolders and files only
- Subfolders only
- Files only

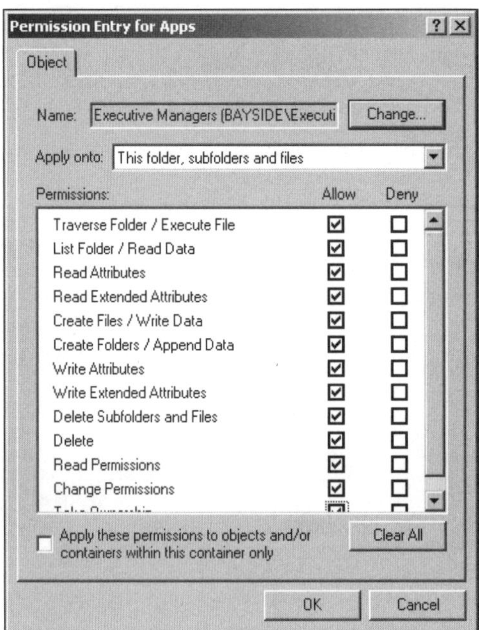

Figure 5-11 Advanced NTFS permissions

Table 5-3 shows the special access permissions that can be applied and their function.

Table 5-3 Special access permissions

Special Permission	Function
Traverse Folder/Execute File	Supports or cancels passing through folders that the user does not have explicit permission to enter, in order to get to an intended folder. For example, a user may not have permission to read the Salesdata folder, but may have Read permission to JuneSales.doc in the Salesdata folder. If the user has traverse folder permissions, the user would be able to open the JuneSales.doc file by typing in the full path to the file.
List Folder/Read Data	Supports or cancels viewing of file names and subfolder names within the folder
Read Attributes	Supports or cancels ability to read attributes of a file or folder
Read Extended Attributes	Supports or cancels viewing of extended attributes of a file or folder; extended attributes are additional information attached to a file, as defined by an application
Create Files/Write Data	Supports or cancels the creation of files within the folder (applies to folders only); supports or cancels the making of changes to the file and overwriting existing content (applies to files only)

Table 5-3 Special access permissions (continued)

Special Permission	Function
Create Folders/Append Data	Supports or cancels the creation of folders within a folder (applies to folders only). Supports or cancels the making of changes to the end of the file, but not changing, deleting, or overwriting existing data (applies to files only)
Write Attributes	Supports or cancels changing the attributes of a file or folder, such as read-only or hidden; attributes are defined by NTFS
Write Extended Attributes	Supports or cancels changing the extended attributes of a file or folder; extended attributes are defined by programs and can vary
Delete Subfolders and Files	Supports or cancels the deletion of subfolders and files, even if the delete permission has not been granted on the subfolder or file
Delete	Supports or cancels the deletion of the file or folder
Read Permissions	Supports or cancels the reading of permissions for the file or folder
Change Permissions	Supports or cancels the changing of permissions for the file or folder
Take Ownership	Supports or cancels the taking of ownership of the file or folder

Combining Share and NTFS Permissions

NTFS permissions are often combined with share permissions to provide a strong combination of local and remote security for files and directories. When share and NTFS permissions are combined, the following rules apply:

- When a user is accessing a share across a network and the NTFS and share permissions are combined, the most restrictive permission is the overriding permission. For example, if the share-level access is Full Control, but the NTFS permissions are set at Read, then the user has Read permission.
- When a user accesses a file locally, only NTFS permissions apply.

Encrypting File System

Another option available for securing files and folders is to implement encryption. This adds another level of protection on top of setting share or NTFS permissions. The **encrypting file system (EFS)** uses public keys to transparently encrypt folders and files. A user's public key is used to encrypt the data. The data cannot be decrypted without the corresponding private key. Therefore, only the user who encrypts the data can decrypt it.

Encryption is only available on partitions formatted with NTFS version 5.0.

File and folder encryption is implemented using encryption keys. When data is marked to be encrypted, the EFS encrypts the data using a file encryption key (FEK). The FEK is added to a header attached to the encrypted data known as the data decryption field (DDF). The DDF is encrypted using the user's public key so only they can decrypt it using their private key.

The only problem with EFS is that if someone were to leave the company, all data that has been encrypted with their key would be inaccessible from any other user account. For data recovery purposes you can configure a **data recovery agent**. In the event that a user encrypts data and leaves the company or loses their private key, the data recovery agent can recover the encrypted data. When the data is encrypted, the FEK of the data recovery agent is also stored in a second header called the data recovery field. It is encrypted so only the data recovery agent can decrypt it and recover the data. By default, the local administrator of a stand-alone workstation or member server is the recovery agent. Any computer that is a member of a domain uses the domain administrator as the recovery agent. Additional recovery agents can be designated using Certificate Services and Group Policy.

A folder or file can be encrypted through Windows Explorer by setting the encryption attribute. Right-click the folder or file you want to encrypt and click Properties. Click the Advanced button and click the Encrypt contents to secure data check box, as shown in Figure 5-12.

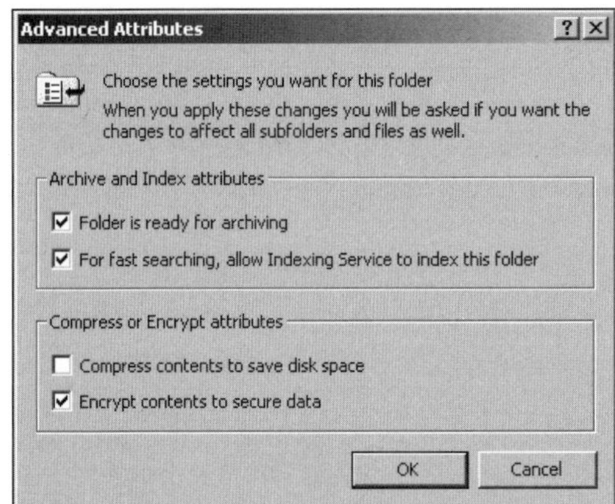

Figure 5-12 Setting the encryption attribute

Before encrypting data keep the following points in mind:

- If you set the encryption attribute on a folder, the folder itself is not actually encrypted, only the contents of the folder.
- Once a folder is encrypted, any data saved in the folder, or copied or moved into the folder, is encrypted.

- If an encrypted file is copied or moved into a folder that is not encrypted, the file retains its encryption attribute as long as the file system is an NTFS partition.
- You cannot encrypt and compress data at the same time.

MONITORING ACCESS TO SHARED FOLDERS

To assist in maintaining network security and statistics, you may need to periodically monitor shared folder and open file access. Keeping track of the number of users actually connected to a specific network share can help you plan for future capacity requirements and fine-tuning of performance levels. In Windows 2000, you are able to see how many people are connected to a share, who they are, and what files are actually open at any given time. If necessary, you can also disconnect users from a specific share, as well as send network messages to alert users of changes in server or share status.

As mentioned earlier, the Computer Management console can be used to create, share, and assign permissions to folders on the network. This utility can also be used to perform the folder monitoring tasks that may be required within the network. The Computer Management console allows monitoring of local or remote computers on the network. To monitor computers in a domain environment, you need to be a member of the Administrators or Server Operators groups. Stand-alone servers and even Windows 2000 Professional workstations can also be monitored as long as you are at least an administrator or member of the Power Users group on the computer.

To monitor a shared folder, open the Computer Management console, expand the Shared Folders container, and click the Sessions node. This node allows you to view a list of users that have network connections to the computer that you are monitoring. As shown in Figure 5-13, the Administrator and Karena user accounts have connections to the local server

To manage a different computer, right-click Computer Management (Local), and click Connect to another computer. Click the computer to manage, and then click OK.

To view all of the files that are open by network clients, click the Open Files node. This information is useful if you need to troubleshoot file access problems, or need to verify which files are open by specific users.

If you need to disconnect a session or open file connection, right-click the entry in the details pane, and click Close Session or Close Open File on the shortcut menu. This can assist you in situations where you have changed permissions on a folder or file, and you want the new permissions to take effect immediately.

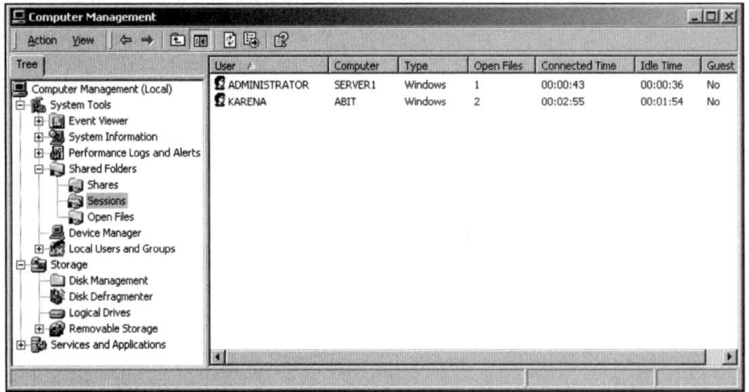

Figure 5-13 Monitoring the number of sessions connected to the local computer

If the user has gained access to the share using a Windows-based computer, the client computer automatically attempts to reconnect to the folder if you disconnect the connection. To prevent this from happening, you have to modify the share permissions to deny access to the folder.

To prevent data loss, it is always a best practice to notify the user in advance before disconnecting a user from a session or open file. This can be done by right-clicking the Shared Folders node. On the shortcut menu that appears, click All Tasks, and then click Send Console Message. Figure 5-14 shows the Send Console Message dialog box.

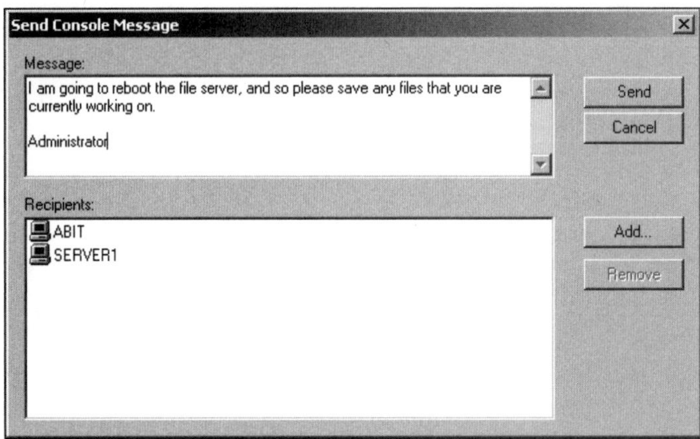

Figure 5-14 Sending a console message to connected users

Creating and Modifying Web Folders

Your organization may have data that is intended to be shared via HTTP or FTP access by clients. For example, your company may want its yearly financial reports to be publicly available on the Internet. To allow files and folders to be accessed from the Internet or an intranet, **Internet Information Services (IIS)** needs to be installed and configured in Windows 2000. IIS is Microsoft's implementation of a Web server, which is used to provide access to file resources utilizing a number of protocols such as Hypertext Transfer Protocol (HTTP), File Transfer Protocol (FTP), Network News Transfer Protocol (NNTP), and Simple Mail Transfer Protocol (SMTP). Chapter Six, "Administering Web Resources in Windows 2000," discusses Internet Information Services in greater detail.

Windows 2000 includes a new feature that allows you to create and share files on a Web server using a **Web folder**. A Web folder is a folder designed to be accessed from the Internet or an internal intranet using the HTTP or FTP protocols. Clients can then use any application that can integrate with the Web server to save or delete files like a regular shared folder. Some common applications that can use Web folders include Microsoft Office XP and Internet Explorer.

Configuring a folder to be shared over the Web is very similar to regular folder sharing in that you right-click the folder, click Properties, and then click the Web Sharing tab. If the IIS Web server is configured properly, you can choose the specific Web site from which you want this folder to be available. Figure 5-15 shows the administrator choosing the Bayside Detailing Web site in which to link a shared Web folder.

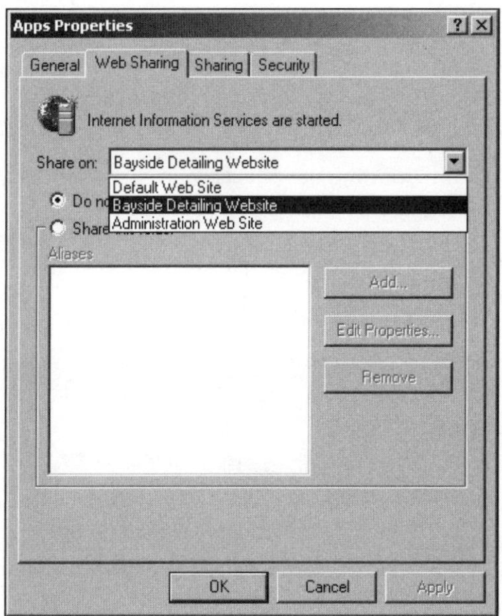

Figure 5-15 Selecting a Web site on which to share a Web folder

Shared Web folders do not have to use the actual folder name to be referenced. Web folders can instead use an alias name to which you want your Web clients to refer when accessing the shared resource. Figure 5-16 illustrates the Edit Alias dialog box.

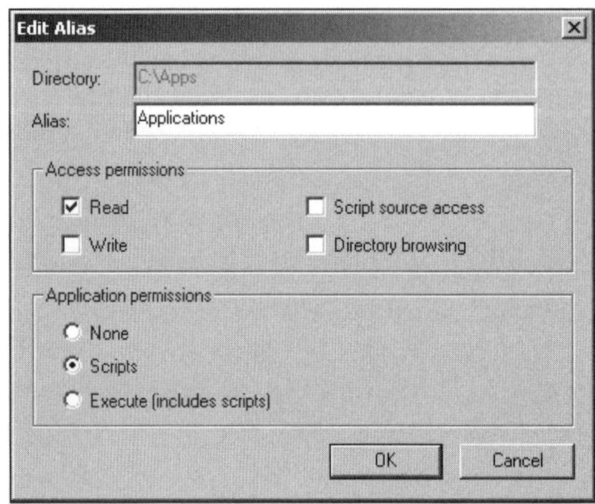

Figure 5-16 Editing the alias name and permissions of a Web folder

In the Edit Alias dialog box, you should also configure the access permissions and application permissions that you would like Web clients to have for the data within the shared resource. Tables 5-4 and 5-5 explain the various Web folder access permissions.

Table 5-4 Web folder access permissions

Access Permission	Description
Read	Allows users to read and view Web-based information
Write	Allows users to modify the contents of the shared Web folder
Script source access	Allows users to view the contents of Web-based scripts
Directory browsing	Allows users to browse the actual folder structure of the shared resource; FTP access usually has this enabled

Table 5-5 Application permissions

Application Permission	Description
None	Provides no permissions to execute script or application commands
Scripts	Allows the user to run scripts to perform Web-based functions
Execute (includes scripts)	Allows users to run scripts or applications over the Web-based connection

Network clients can open a Web-based file share using one of three main methods:

- *Internet Explorer*—To open a Web folder using Internet Explorer, click the File menu, and then click Open. Type the URL of the folder share (http://*webserver/share*) in the Open text box, and then click the check box next to Open as a Web Folder.
- *My Network Places*—Open My Network Places, and double-click the Add Network Place Wizard. You can then type the URL of the Web folder in the form of http://*webserver/share*.
- *Microsoft Office XP*—In a Microsoft Office application, click File, click Open, and then type the URL of the Web folder in the File name text box.

Configuring and Managing A Distributed File System

The **distributed file system (DFS)** allows administrators to simplify access to multiple shared file resources by making it appear as though multiple shared file resources are stored in one location. For example, if the network has eight Windows 2000 servers that provide a variety of shared folders to network users, DFS can be set up so that users do not have to know which specific server offers which shared folder. All of the folders can be set up to appear as though they are on one server and under a single folder structure. This eliminates the need for users to have to browse the network looking for shared resources. DFS also makes managing folder access easier for server administrators.

To access Windows 2000 DFS resources, clients must be running DFS client software. All previous versions of Windows must have the Active Directory client extensions installed in order to access a DFS. You can download the Active Directory extensions from the Microsoft Web site.

DFS is configured using the Distributed File System console in the Administrative Tools menu (accessed by clicking Start, pointing to Programs, and pointing to Administrative Tools) or using the Distributed File System MMC snap-in.

A DFS share resembles a tree structure and consists of a root and DFS links. When configuring DFS, the root is configured first, then the DFS links. The DFS root is at the top of the tree structure and is the container for DFS links. The DFS links point to shared folders and files on the network. A DFS share can have multiple DFS links.

DFS Models

There are two models for implementing DFS: the stand-alone model and the domain-based model. The stand-alone DFS model offers limited capabilities compared to the domain-based model. Table 5-6 summarizes the difference between the two models.

Table 5-6 Difference between stand-alone DFS and domain DFS

DFS Model	Description
Stand-alone DFS	DFS information is stored in the local registry. Only a single level of DFS links is permitted. This model offers no fault tolerance.
Domain DFS	DFS information is stored within Active Directory. Multiple levels of DFS links can be configured. Links can be configured to point to multiple copies of a share for fault tolerance. DFS root must be on an NTFS partition.

The hierarchical structure of DFS in the domain-based model is called the **DFS topology** or logical structure. There are three elements to the DFS topology:

- The DFS root
- The DFS links
- Servers on which the DFS shared folders are replicated as replica sets

A **DFS root** is a main container that holds links to shared folders that can be accessed from the root. The server that hosts the DFS root is called the host server. When a network client views the shared folders under the DFS root, all of the folders appear as though they were physically located in one main folder on the DFS root computer, even though the folders may actually reside on many different computers in the domain.

A **DFS link** is a pointer to the physical location of shared folders that are defined in the root. DFS links can also be made to another DFS root on a different computer or to an entire shared volume on a server.

A **replica set** is a set of shared folders that is replicated or copied to one or more servers in a domain. Configuring a replication set includes establishing links to each server that participates in the replication as well as setting up synchronization so that replication takes place among all servers at a specified interval, such as every 15 minutes.

The first step in creating a DFS is to configure a DFS root. To configure a DFS root, click Start, point to Programs, point to Administrative Tools, and click Distributed File System. Click New DFS Root from the Action menu to launch the New DFS Root Wizard. The first option that appears allows you to choose whether you want to create a stand-alone or domain DFS.

Once the root is configured you can create DFS links that point to the actual physical location of the shared files and folders. From within the Distributed File System console, click the DFS root and click New DFS Link on the Action menu. Once you have entered the required information into the Create a new DFS Link dialog box, the link appears under the DFS root.

Managing DFS

After the DFS root system is set up, there are several tasks involved in managing the root, which can include:

- Deleting a DFS root
- Removing a DFS link
- Adding root and link replica sets
- Checking the status of a root or link

Each of these tasks is described in the following sections.

After a DFS root is created, it is possible to delete it—when you want to configure it differently, for example. To delete a DFS root, open the Distributed File System console, and right-click the root you want to delete. You can then click Delete DFS Root on the shortcut menu.

A link is removed from the DFS root by right-clicking the link in the details pane on the right and then clicking Remove DFS Link on the shortcut menu.

One of the features of a domain-based DFS is that an entire DFS root or specific DFS links in a root can be replicated on servers other than the one that contains the master folder. The replication capability is what enables you to provide fault tolerance and to create load balancing. On a network in which there are multiple servers, replication can prove to be a vital service to provide uninterrupted access for users, in case the computer with the master folder is inaccessible. Load balancing also is vital as a way to provide users with faster service and better network performance by enabling users to access the nearest server containing the DFS shared folders. You can set up a DFS link for replication by right-clicking the link and selecting the New Replica option.

To set up replication of a designated link:

1. Right-click the **DFS link** in the Distributed File System tool, and click **New Replica**.
2. Enter the computer name and shared folder on the computer to use for the replica, or use the browse button to locate the computer and shared folder in the domain. The computer name and shared folder are specified in UNC format.
3. Click **Manual replication** or **Automatic replication**, and then click **OK**.
4. If you selected Automatic replication in Step 3, set the replication policy, which enables you to change the master folder and designate which replicas are enabled for automatic replication. Click **OK**.
5. The replica computer and folder path is added under the Replica(s) column in the DFS tree for the designated link.

You can configure replication to occur manually or automatically. If you choose automatic make sure the File Replication Service is started and set to start automatically.

The most common problem associated with DFS shared folders is that one or more DFS links are inaccessible because a particular server is disconnected from the network or has failed. You can quickly check the status of a DFS root, DFS link, or replica by right-clicking it in the Replica(s) column of the Distributed File System management tool, and then clicking Check Status. A DFS root, link, or replica that is working and fully connected has a green check mark in a white circle through its folder icon. One that is disconnected has a white "x" in a red circle through its folder icon.

Creating and Modifying Shared Printer Resources

Managing a Windows 2000 network includes configuring and maintaining an efficient network of shared printers. You need to know how to install and configure these printers to ensure that users have the appropriate access when needed. One of the most common troubleshooting tasks of any network administrator is ensuring the continued availability of the shared network printers.

To successfully configure and troubleshoot Windows 2000-based printing, you should be aware of very specific terms used to define the components of the printing system. The following list defines these terms:

- ***Print device***—The actual hardware device that produces the printed document. There are two main types of print devices: a local print device and a network print device. Local print devices are connected directly to a port on the print server or workstation. A network print device connects to a print server through its own network adapter and connection to the network.
- ***Printer***—A configuration object in Windows 2000 that controls the connection to the print device
- ***Print driver***—Files that contain information that Windows 2000 uses to convert raw print commands to a language that the printer understands. A specific print driver is needed for each print device model used and for each type of operating system in place.
- ***Print server***—The computer in which the printers and print drivers are located. This is usually where you set up and configure the shared printing system.

To set up an efficient printing environment, it is also important to make sure that your network meets the following hardware requirements:

- One or more computers to act as a print server. Both Windows 2000 Server and Professional can be used as a print server, although Professional is only recommended for networks with 10 or fewer concurrent client connections.

- Sufficient space on the hard drive for the print server. This is very important because Windows 2000 uses space on the hard drive to queue and buffer documents as they are being directed to the print device.
- Sufficient RAM beyond that of the minimum Windows 2000 requirements. This is critical if you expect to have a large number of print jobs and still require acceptable performance.

Adding a Printer as a Local Print Device

Smaller networks may have workstations or servers that share print devices connected directly to a local port on the computer. To add and share a local print device, you need to have administrator privileges on the computer that acts as the print server. The Add Printer Wizard can be used to install and configure the printer. This wizard can be found by clicking the Start menu, clicking Settings, and then clicking Printers. The Printers window opens, as shown in Figure 5-17

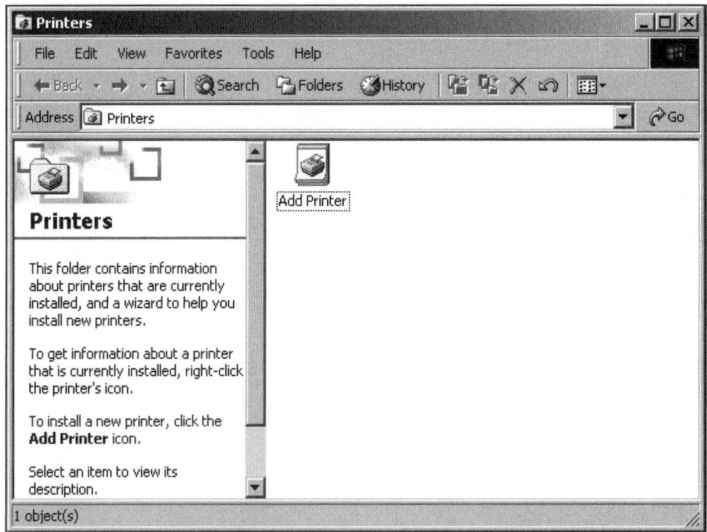

Figure 5-17 The Printers folder

When you double-click the Add Printer icon, the Add Printer Wizard starts. Make sure that Local printer is chosen in the Local or Network Printer dialog box. If you have a plug and play printer, you can also click the check box next to Automatically detect and install my Plug and Play printer, as shown in Figure 5-18.

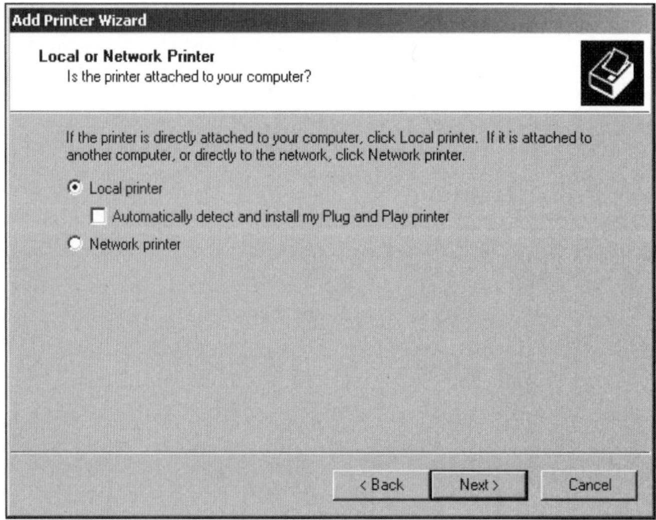

Figure 5-18 Adding a local printer

As the wizard continues, you are able to choose the port to which the local print device is connected. In the Select the printer port dialog box, make sure that Use the following port is chosen, and that LPT1 is the chosen port, as shown in Figure 5-19.

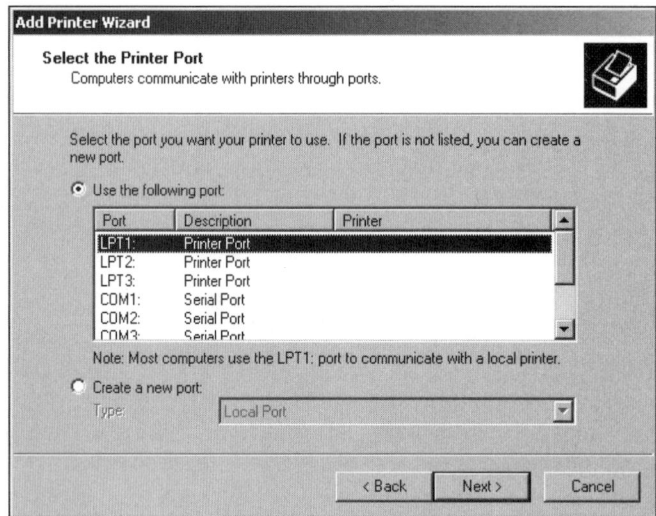

Figure 5-19 Configuring the local port

The Add Printer Wizard also allows you to choose the print driver. Make sure that you choose the correct printer driver for your local print device. If your print device is not on the list, you can download the newest drivers from the manufacturer's Web site or provide drivers from an alternate location. The final steps of the Add Printer Wizard have you configure printer sharing and locations, and ask you if you want to print a test page.

Adding a Printer as a Network Print Device

Many corporate print devices have direct connections to the network and are not required to be attached to a host computer through the parallel port. These network print devices are equipped with network adapters that access an IP address to allow communication over the network.

You can use the Add Printer Wizard to add network print devices to your network. The only difference is that on the Select printer port dialog box, you need to create a new TCP/IP port to be able to communicate directly over the network. To create this new TCP/IP port, click the Create a new port option button, and then click Standard TCP/IP port. When you click Next, the Add Standard TCP/IP Printer Port Wizard starts. Clicking Next then opens the Add Port dialog box, as illustrated in Figure 5-20. You then complete the remainder of the wizard, as previously explained.

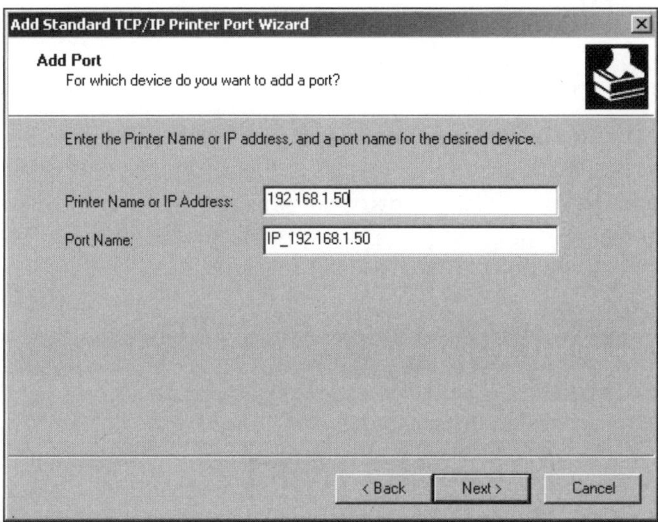

Figure 5-20 Configuring a network printer

Configuring an Existing Printer

Once you have a printer set up, you may want to modify some of the configuration options such as sharing, permissions, and other advanced settings. To modify these options you can access the properties of the printer by right-clicking the printer icon and clicking Properties. Figure 5-21 illustrates the configuration options that can be modified.

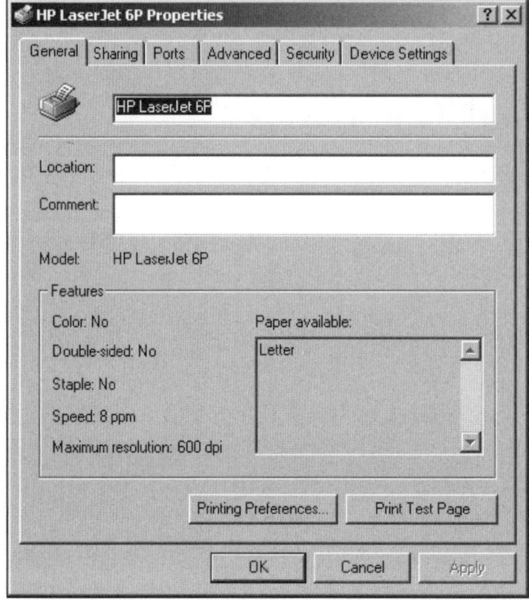

Figure 5-21 Modifying printer properties

Two of the most important configuration options are the Sharing and Security tabs. The Sharing tab allows you to enable or disable print sharing and Active Directory publishing, and install additional drivers. The Security tab allows you to control printer permissions. There are three levels of print permissions, as illustrated in Table 5-7.

Table 5-7 Printer permissions

Permission	Description
Print	Allows users to connect to a printer, print documents, and edit the user's own print jobs; by default, the Everyone group has this permission
Manage Documents	Allows all of the Print permissions except users having the right to control the document print jobs of all users; by default, the Creator Owner special group has permission to control document print jobs of all users
Manage Printers	Allows all of the Print and Manage Documents permissions, and also allows the user to share, modify, or delete printers and their properties; by default, administrators, print operators, and server operators have this permission

Some advanced features of Windows 2000 printing include setting up a printer pool and configuring printer priorities.

A **printer pool** consists of a single printer that is connected to a number of print devices. You can configure a printer pool by configuring multiple ports to be connected to different print devices. One caution is that all print devices must use the same print driver. The advantage of setting up a printer pool is that in a high-volume print environment, documents can be quickly printed and available to the users. A printer pool is configured by selecting the Ports tab and then placing a check mark in the box next to the Enable printer pooling command, as shown in Figure 5-22.

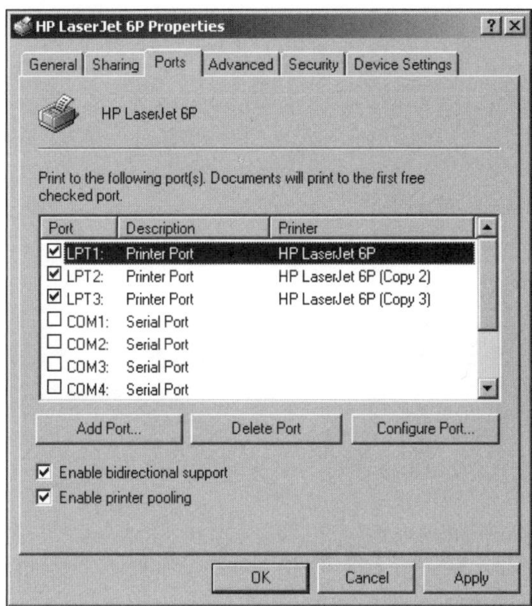

Figure 5-22 Enabling the printer pooling feature

There may be times that you need to set **printer priorities** for different groups of documents. For example, you may want to configure your print environment to treat any printouts from the CEO of the company to print first, even if there are other documents in the print queue.

To configure printer priorities, install two printers on the print server and connect them both to the same print device. You can then configure the priority of each printer by clicking the Advanced tab and then adjusting the Priority to a number between 1 and 99, with 1 being the lowest priority and 99 being the highest priority, as shown in Figure 5-23. Again, higher priority printers print first.

The next step in configuring print priorities is to only allow specific users to print to a specific printer. For example, if you want the CEO to always be able to have first priority at printing, only allow the CEO to print to the printer with the higher priority setting. All other users print to the printer with the lower priority setting. This can be done by configuring the printer security settings, as discussed earlier in this section.

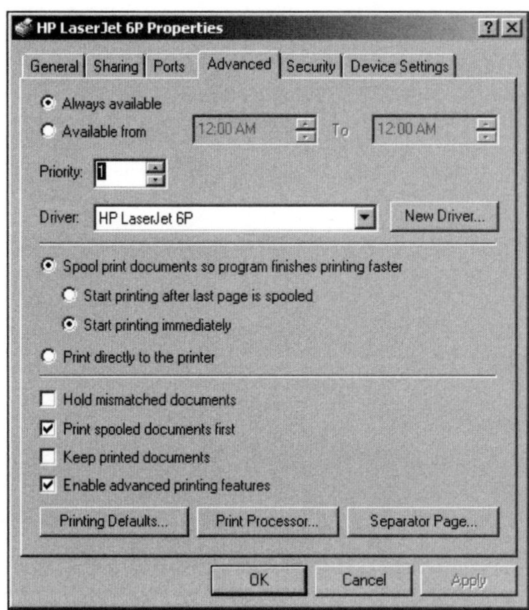

Figure 5-23 Configuring printer priority

Setting Up and Updating Client Computers

Once the printer is added and configured, you must next set up the client computers to be able to print to the print server. If there is a mix of client operating systems throughout the network, a different version of the print driver is needed for each operating system that is connected to the print server.

Any client computers that run Windows 2000 or Windows XP automatically download the print driver when they are initially connected to the printer. Windows 95, Windows 98, Windows ME, and Windows NT 4.0 clients automatically download the appropriate print driver as long as there is a copy of the driver on the print server. To install print drivers to be available to other operating systems, perform the following steps:

1. Click **Start**, point to **Settings**, and then click **Printers**. The Printers window opens.
2. Right-click the printer in which you want to install additional print drivers, and click **Properties**.
3. Click the **Sharing** tab.
4. Click the **Additional Drivers** button. The Additional Drivers dialog box opens.
5. Under the Environment column, click the check box next to the Windows version that you want your print server to support, as shown in Figure 5-24. Click **OK**.

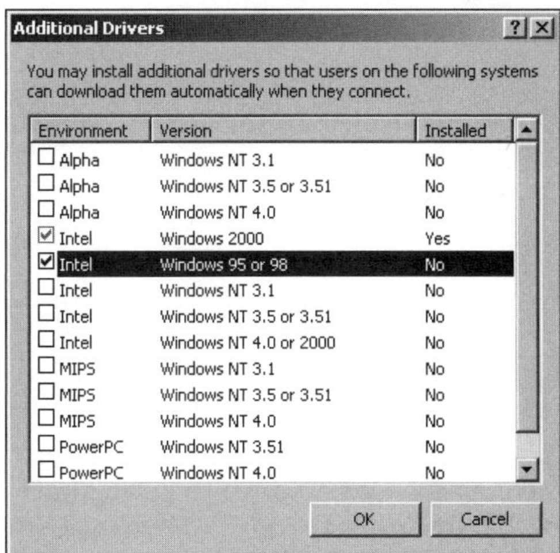

Figure 5-24 Installing additional print drivers

6. You are prompted to browse to or insert the Windows 2000 source files or CD.

If you have any older Windows clients such as Windows 3.x, or non-Microsoft clients such as Macintosh or UNIX clients, you are required to manually install the print driver. Non-Microsoft clients may also require additional print services to be installed on the print server.

You can also add, remove, and update additional print drivers by clicking the Server Properties command on the File menu of the Printers folder. The Drivers Tab lists all installed printer drivers, as shown in Figure 5-25.

Troubleshooting Printers

The two printing problems that you often encounter are:

- *Print jobs that become stuck in the print queue*—Some documents may appear in the print queue, but they do not print, and they cannot be deleted. To fix this problem, on the print server, open the Services console on the Administrative Tools menu, right-click the Print Spooler service, and then click Restart. Note that any print jobs that are in the queue are deleted.
- *Failure of a print device*—A print device may fail because of a paper jam, hardware failure, or a stuck print job. Any documents that are behind the current document in the queue can be redirected to a new print device. To redirect the print jobs, access the properties of the printer that is connected to the failed print device. Click the Ports tab, and then click the port to another printer assigned on the print server. If you need to redirect to another print server, click the Add Port button to add a local port that is directed to the IP address and share name of the of the other print server.

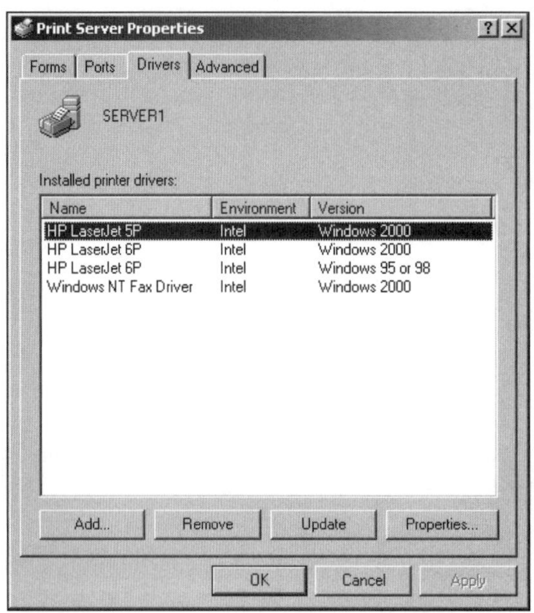

Figure 5-25 The installed printer drivers

PUBLISHING RESOURCES IN ACTIVE DIRECTORY

Windows 2000 Active Directory provides a mechanism that can assist network clients in effectively searching for frequently accessed network resources such as shared folders and printers. A shared resource can be **published** into Active Directory, which means that Active Directory contains an object that represents a link or direct information on how to use or connect to the shared resource. Network users can then query Active Directory to find these published resources. In order to publish resources into Active Directory, you must be logged in with administrative rights.

To query the Active Directory database, client computers must be installed with a Windows 2000 or XP Professional operating system. Windows 9x- and NT-based computers must have the **Active Directory client extensions** installed to be able to interact with Active Directory. As discussed previously, the Active Directory client extensions allow legacy operating systems to perform searches in Active Directory. Plus, the client extensions provide site awareness and access to Windows 2000 distributed file systems.

You can download the client extensions by accessing *www.microsoft.com* and performing a search for Active Directory client extensions.

Publishing Shared Folders into Active Directory

In the past, whenever a user required access to a shared folder, the user needed to know exactly which server the share resided upon. Administrators attempted to fix this problem by creating logon scripts that mapped the required shares to the user account during logon. Logon scripts that map folder shares are quite effective, but may not map to every share that a client needs to access. An extensive amount of time can be wasted searching for files, especially if there are a number of file servers in the organization.

In an attempt to solve this problem, Windows 2000 introduced the concept of a published folder. A **published folder** is an Active Directory object that points to a related folder share on a file server. Clients can then search for the folder by the share name or by preconfigured keywords.

Publishing a shared folder into Active Directory does not actually create the physical share on the file server. Creating the actual shared folder and configuring permissions has to be done before attempting to publish the resource into Active Directory. Refer back to the beginning of this chapter for more information on creating and configuring shared folders.

Once the physical share has been created, you can publish a link to the shared folder by following these steps:

1. Open Active Directory Users and Computers on the Administrative Tools menu.
2. Right-click the root or OU container in which you want to place the shared folder object.
3. Point to **New**, and then click **Shared Folder**. The New Object – Shared Folder dialog box opens.
4. Type a name for the shared folder in the Name text box. Keep the name simple and intuitive so users can easily remember what the share is called.
5. Type the physical network path to the shared folder in the Network path text box. The completed dialog box is illustrated in Figure 5-26. Click **OK**.
6. An icon appears that represents a shared network drive, as shown in Figure 5-27.

To assist users in searching for the published folder, administrators can add a number of keywords that represent the folder object. For example, if you have published a folder called Applications, you may want to add keywords such as "programs," "software," "Microsoft," or "Excel." The keywords could be any common phrases that users might use to attempt to find the resource.

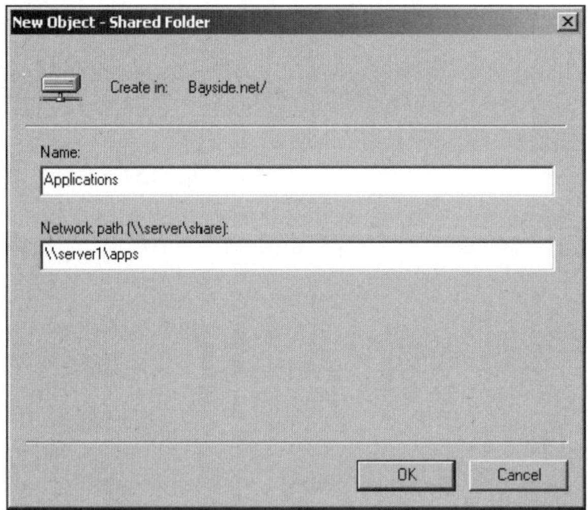

Figure 5-26 Configuring a published folder in Active Directory

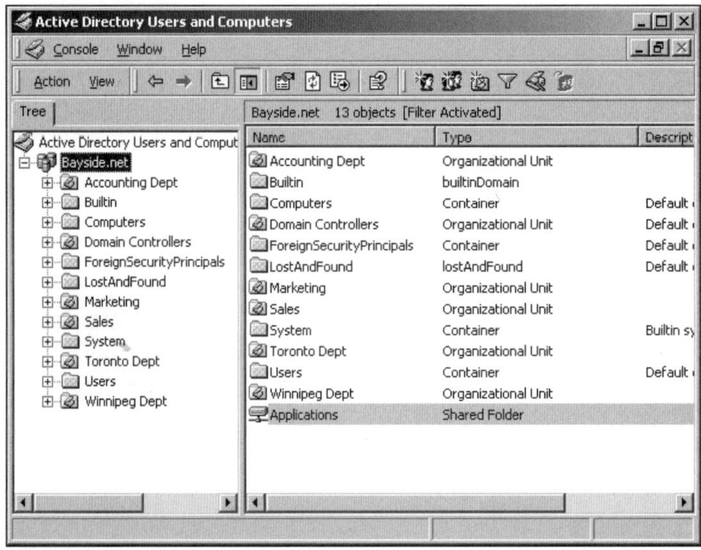

Figure 5-27 A published folder in Active Directory

To add keywords to a published shared folder object, right-click the folder object, and click Properties. Notice the button labeled Keywords, as shown in Figure 5-28.

Click the Keywords button, and then add or remove keywords, as shown in Figure 5-29.

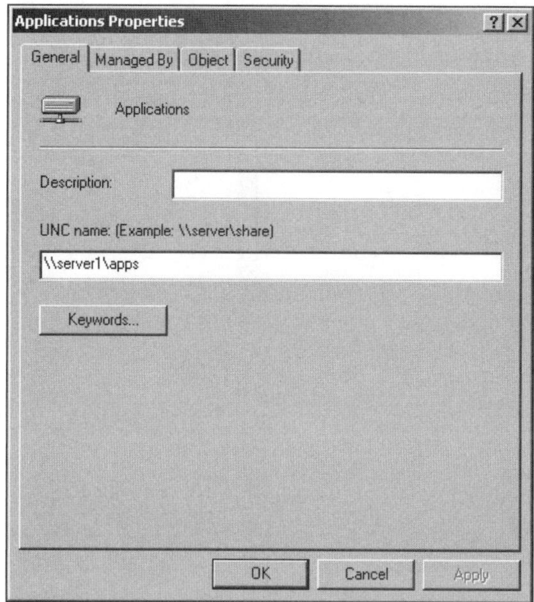

Figure 5-28 The published shared folder properties dialog box

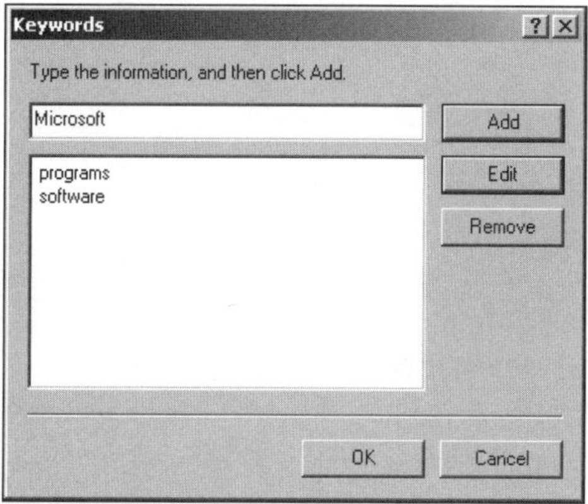

Figure 5-29 Configuring key words for a published folder share

Publishing Printers into Active Directory

To help users find printer resources, shared printers can also be published into Active Directory. In fact, any Windows 2000 compatible printer that is installed on a print server is automatically published into Active Directory during installation. By default, published printer objects are hidden in Active Directory.

To view the published printers in Active Directory, click the View menu, and click Users, Groups, and Computers as containers. This option modifies the view to show objects that are associated with a user, group, or a computer object. Printer objects are associated with the computer object that represents the print server. You can then expand the container that contains the computer object representing the print server. When you click the print server's computer object, notice the Printer object in the details pane, as shown in Figure 5-30.

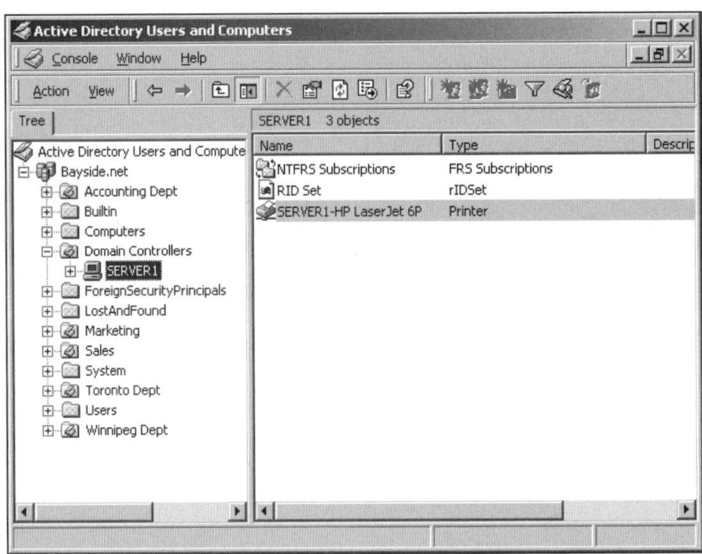

Figure 5-30 A published printer object in Active Directory

Print shares that are created on pre-Windows 2000 print servers can also be published into Active Directory by creating a new printer object. A new printer object can be created when you right-click a container, and click New, and then click Printer. The New Object – Printer dialog box then opens, as shown in Figure 5-31. The next step is to type a network path to the print server and share, and then click OK.

Managing Published Printers

When a print server is removed from the network, its Active Directory object is automatically removed from the database. This prevents users from trying to connect to print servers that are not actually running on the network. Active Directory removes the orphaned printer objects through a process called the **orphan pruner**. The orphan pruner verifies that all printer objects are still valid in Active Directory. If the orphan pruner cannot find a print server, it checks again in eight hours. This goes on for a total of three 8-hour intervals. If the print server is not located after the last interval, the orphan pruner removes the published printer object.

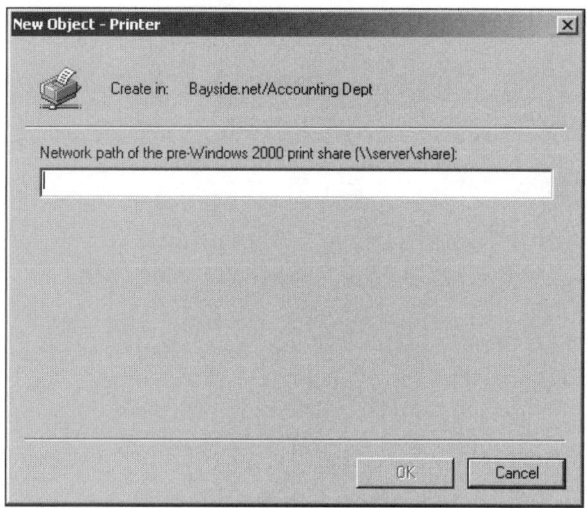

Figure 5-31 Configuring a pre-Windows 2000 published printer share

There may be some printers that you do not want to have published in Active Directory. For example, you may only want specific people to be able to find and print to an expensive, color laser printer. To turn off printer publishing, access the Printers folder and right-click the printer that you do not want to be published in Active Directory. Click Properties, and then click the Sharing tab. You can then clear the check box next to List in the Directory, as shown in Figure 5-32.

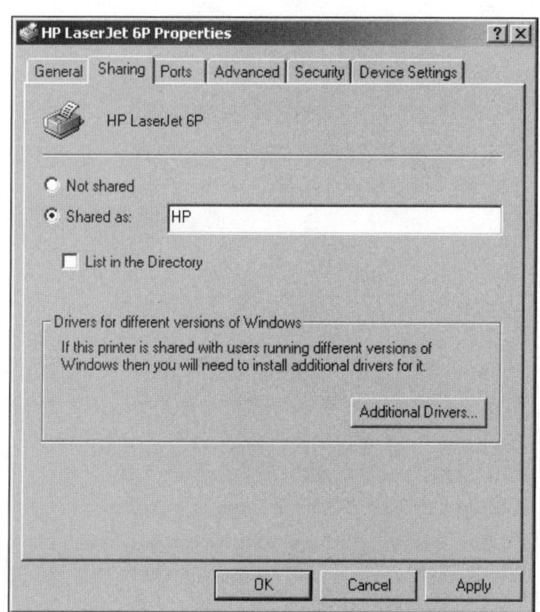

Figure 5-32 Turning off printer publishing

Searching for Objects in Active Directory

Once objects are published in Active Directory, users can easily perform searches to find the objects. The objects and attributes that users can find, and the tasks that can be performed on the objects, depend on the Active Directory permissions you have assigned for the objects. To perform an Active Directory search, follow these steps:

1. Click **Start**, point to **Search**, and then click **For Files and Folders**.
2. In the Search Results window, click the list arrow under **Look in**, and click **browse**.
3. In the Browse For Folder dialog box, browse to **My Network Places*Entire Network\Directory\<domain name>***.
4. Right-click the domain name, and click **Find**. The Find Users, Contacts, and Groups dialog box opens, as shown in Figure 5-33.

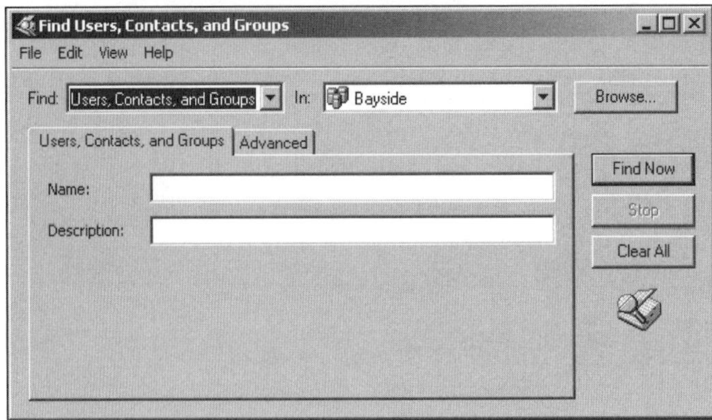

Figure 5-33 Searching Active Directory

5. Click the list arrow next to Find, and click the type of object that you are searching for. For example, if you are searching for a published folder, click the **Shared Folders** item.
6. Click **Find Now**.

Another common way in which you can browse for objects in Active Directory is by using the My Network Places icon found on the Windows 2000 desktop. If you double-click My Network Places, you notice an icon named Entire Network. Double-click this icon, and then click the entire contents link found at the bottom of the window. As shown in Figure 5-34, you see the Directory icon that represents Active Directory. When you access this directory, you are able to right-click your domain and click the Find menu, as previously discussed in Steps 4-6.

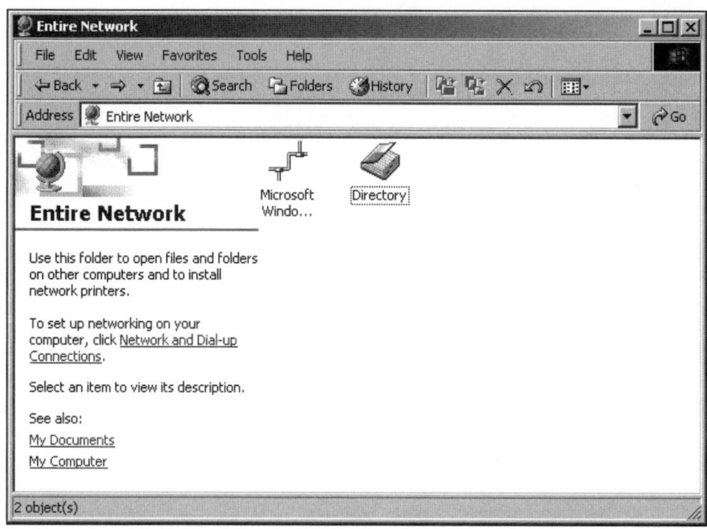

Figure 5-34 The directory icon

Remember that you can use the Find feature to search for a variety of information such as users, computers, printers, shared folders, and information about organizational units.

You can also search for objects in Active Directory using the Active Directory Users and Computers snap-in. Because the global catalog maintains a partial replica of all objects in a domain or forest, you can easily search for objects regardless of the domain in which they are located.

To locate an object, click Start, point to Programs, point to Administrative Tools, and click Active Directory Users and Computers. Right-click the domain or OU in which you want to search for an object, and click Find. The Find Users, Contacts and Groups dialog box appears, as shown in Figure 5-35. Use the Find list arrow to select the types of objects to include in your search. The In list arrow allows you to specify the location in which you want to search for an object. The Users, Contacts and Groups tab allows you to enter in a name or a description of the object, and the Advanced tab allows you to enter more specific search criteria. Once you click the Find Now tab, the results are displayed in the bottom pane.

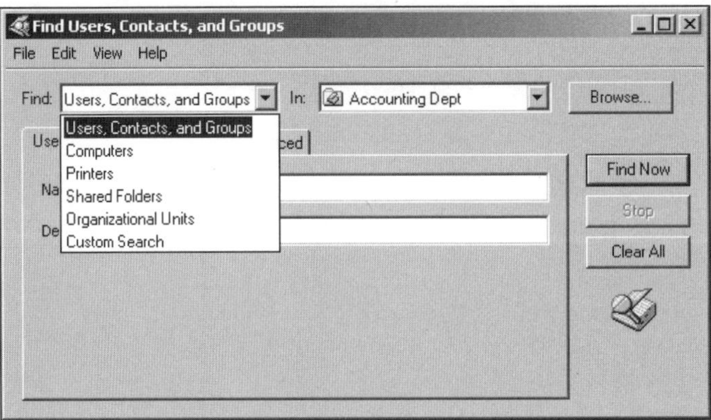

Figure 5-35 Using Active Directory Users and Computers to locate objects

AUDITING ACCESS TO SHARED RESOURCES

Monitoring events as they occur on a network is an important facet of security. Monitoring helps detect potential security threats, increases user accountability, and provides evidence of security breaches if they do occur. Monitoring can also be used for resource planning. Auditing specific resources such as printer and file shares can tell you how often they are being accessed by users. For example, if you determine through auditing that a specific share is heavily used by users on the network, you may need to create another instance of the share on another server or physically move it to a server that is more capable of handling the workload.

Auditing in Windows 2000 is used to monitor and track activities on a network. You can specify which events to monitor based on your security requirements. When an event does occur, a record of it is written to the **security log**. The audit entry in the security log provides you with such information as the user who performed the action, the specific action that was performed (for example, a logon attempt), and whether it was a success or failure. You can use **Event Viewer** to view the audit entries in the security log.

Before you can begin monitoring activities, you must set up an audit policy. The **audit policy** defines the events on the network that Windows 2000 records in the security log as they occur. For example, if you choose to monitor failed logon attempts, when a user attempts to log on with an invalid username and/or password, an event is written to the security log. Keep in mind that an event is not written to the security log on the local computer; rather, the event is written to the security log on the domain controller that attempted to validate the user. In other words, events are stored in the security log on the computer on which they occur.

When implementing an audit policy, you need to determine those events you wish to track and whether to track the successes and/or failures. See Figure 5-36 for an example. Table 5-8 outlines the different events that can be monitored.

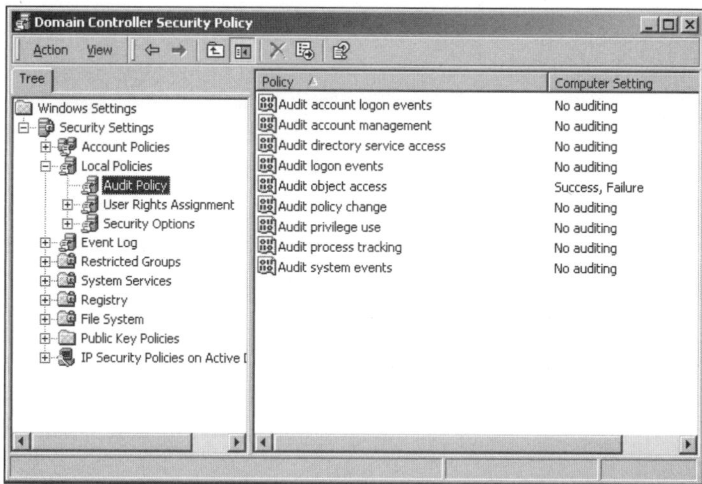

Figure 5-36 Audit events

Table 5-8 Events that can be monitored

Event Category	Explanation of Event
Audit account logon events	Activated when a user logs on to a computer. If the logon occurs on the local computer, the event is recorded on the local computer's event log. If the logon is on a domain controller, the DC records the event. This includes issuing Kerberos tickets for resource access.
Audit account management	Activated whenever a user or group is created, deleted, or modified; also tracks successful or unsuccessful password changes
Audit directory service access	Activated when an Active Directory object is accessed; the specific Active Directory object that is to be audited must also have auditing enabled
Audit logon events	Activated when a user logs on or off a local computer or Active Directory; audits logon failures to find out if password hacking is taking place
Audit object access	Activated when an object such as a folder or printer is accessed; the administrator must also configure the specific object for audit successes and failures
Audit policy change	Activated when a policy that affects security, user rights, or auditing is changed
Audit privilege use	Activated whenever a user uses an assigned right, such as changing the system time, or taking ownership of a file
Audit process tracking	Activated any time an application process takes place; can assist developers in discovering which files or registry settings an application accesses when executing a command
Audit system events	Activated when a system event takes place, such as the computer restarting

Configuring Auditing

Once you have determined the events that need to be audited based on the security requirements of your network, you are ready to configure an audit policy. The following section outlines the requirements of which you should be aware, the steps in configuring an audit policy, and some general guidelines.

How you configure an audit policy is determined by the role of the computer on the network. If the computer is a member server or a stand-alone server, an audit policy is implemented on a computer-by-computer basis using the local Group Policy. For domain controllers, an audit policy can be implemented through a Group Policy object and applied to the domain controllers OU within Active Directory.

Requirements

The following requirements must be met in order to configure an audit policy:

- You must be a member of the Administrators group or be assigned the Manage Auditing and Security Log user right.
- If you are auditing files and folders, they must be on an NTFS volume (auditing is not available on FAT volumes).

Setting Up an Audit Policy

Setting up an audit policy involves choosing the events you want to monitor and deciding whether to monitor the successes and/or failures. If you are auditing access to files, folders, printers, and active directory objects, you need to specify those particular resources for which you want to monitor access.

To set up auditing on a domain controller:

1. Open Active Directory Users and Computers.
2. Right-click the **Domain Controllers OU**, and click **Properties.**
3. Click the **Group Policy** tab. Click the policy you want to use to configure the auditing, and click **Edit**, or create a new policy by clicking **New**.
4. The Group Policy snap-in window opens. In the console tree, expand **Computer Configuration\Window Settings\Security Settings\Local Policies**, and then click **Audit Policy**.
5. Right-click an event you wish to audit, and click **Security**. The Security Policy Setting dialog box opens, as shown in Figure 5-37.
6. Check the **Define these policy settings** option to enable auditing for this event. Check the **Success** option and/or **Failure** option. Click **OK**.
7. Repeat Steps 5 and 6 for each event you want to configure.

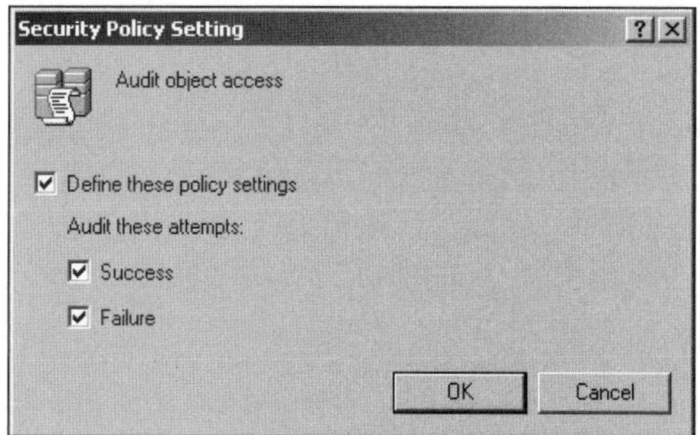

Figure 5-37 Configuring an audit policy

Windows 2000 uses automatic propagation to apply changes made to any audit policy settings. This means that you can make policy changes and they eventually are applied. The default propagation time is eight hours. If you want to apply the changes immediately, you can do one of the following:

- Restart the computer.
- At the command prompt, type the following command
  `secedit /refreshpolicy machine_policy`

Use the following steps to configure auditing on a stand-alone server:

1. Click **Start**, point to **Programs**, point to **Administrative tools**, and click **Local Security Policy**.
2. In the Local Security Policy Settings console, expand **Local Policies**, and click **Audit Policy**.
3. Right-click the event you want to audit, and click **Security**.
4. The Security Policy Setting dialog box appears. Check the **Success** option and/or **Failure** option for the event you want to audit. Click **OK**.
5. To apply the policy settings immediately, you can use one of the methods listed above or wait for propagation to occur.

The effective policy setting tells you the current value for the event that is currently applied to the system. Remember, any policy settings applied at the domain or organizational unit level override those applied through the local policy.

Auditing Object Access

If your files and folders are on an NTFS volume, you can set up auditing to monitor user access. For example, some information such as employee records or financial data may be confidential. To maintain a high level of security for this information you need to enable auditing to detect any security breaches.

Enabling auditing for objects is a two-step process. The first step entails enabling auditing for object access through an audit policy. (These steps are outlined above.) The second step is to enable auditing on specific resources and to specify the type of actions you want to monitor, as well as which users and groups to monitor.

Use the following steps to enable auditing on files and folders:

1. From within Windows Explorer, right-click the folder or file you want to audit, and click **Properties**.
2. Click the **Security** tab, and then click the **Advanced** button. From the Access Control Settings window, click the **Auditing** tab, as shown in Figure 5-38.

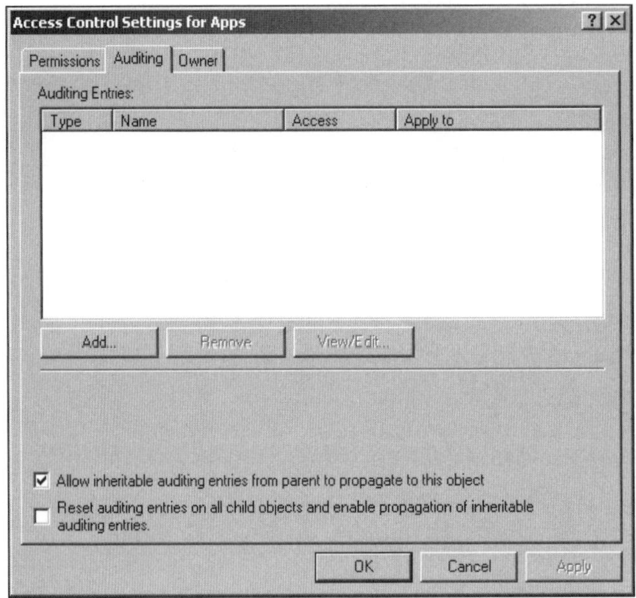

Figure 5-38 Configuring auditing on a shared folder

3. Click **Add** to choose the users and groups for which you want to audit access. Click **OK**.
4. The Auditing Entry for Apps window appears, as shown in Figure 5-39. Check the **Successful** and/or the **Failed** check boxes for those events you want to audit.
5. If you are configuring auditing on a folder, you have the option to specify to what you want the auditing settings to apply. The default is to apply the settings to This folder, subfolders and files. To change the default, click the **Apply onto** list arrow, and make your selection. Click **OK** to return to the Access Control Settings window.

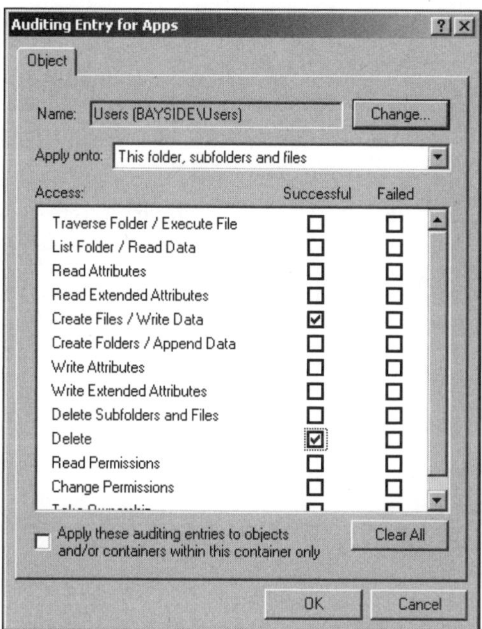

Figure 5-39 The Auditing Entry window

When the Apply these auditing entries to objects and/or containers within this container only check box is chosen, the auditing settings you configure are applied to your selection within the Apply on to box and any child objects.

6. If you do not want auditing settings that are applied to a parent folder to be inherited by the currently selected folder, clear the Allow inheritable auditing entries from parent to propagate to this object check box. Refer to Figure 5-38 for an illustration. Click **OK**.

Auditing can also be configured for objects that are stored within Active Directory. The process is very similar in that the audit policy is first configured, then auditing is enabled for individual objects within Active Directory, including computers, users, groups, and OUs.

Best Practices

To implement an audit policy that is effective in terms of meeting security requirements, it is a good idea to take some time to plan. Planning includes determining the computers for which auditing should be configured, what objects need to be audited, the type of events to audit, and whether to audit the successes, failures, or both. An audit policy can quickly become unmanageable and provide you with information that is of no use. Only choose to audit those events that are going to provide you with valuable information about your network. Also keep in mind that auditing events does create overhead on your server, so auditing all events is generally not recommended. Here are some general guidelines that should be followed when you are planning your audit policy:

- Only enable auditing for those events that can provide you with useful information. Auditing unnecessary events increases overhead and fills up the security log with information that is not useful.
- Review the audit entries in the security log on a regular basis so you are aware of any security issues.
- Enable auditing for sensitive and confidential information.
- Audit the Everyone group instead of the Users group because the Everyone group includes the guest account.
- Audit the use of user rights assignment so users are more accountable.
- Always audit the Administrators group so you can track changes made by users who are members of this group.

Analyzing Security Logs

Once an audit policy has been created, each time an event occurs that is defined within the policy, an entry is written to the security log. For example, if you enable auditing for object access and audit all successful and failed read attempts on a folder called Accounting Docs, when a user opens the folder or attempts to open it, an entry is written to the security log. You can then use Event Viewer to examine the contents of the log. All information that is written to the log is a result of the audit policy that you configure.

For security purposes, only the administrators and those users assigned the Manage Auditing and Security Log user right can view the contents of the security log.

To open Event Viewer and view the contents of the security log, access Event Viewer from the Administrative Tools menu. The contents of the security log are displayed in the details pane, providing a summary of each audit entry, including the date and time that the event occurred and the user who performed the action. Successful events are represented by a key icon, and unsuccessful events (failures to perform a specific action) are represented by a lock icon, as shown in Figure 5-40. You can then double-click an audit entry to view more detailed information.

By default, the security log shows events that occurred on the local computer. You can also use Event Viewer to view the security log on a remote computer by right-clicking Event Viewer (Local), and clicking Connect To Another Computer.

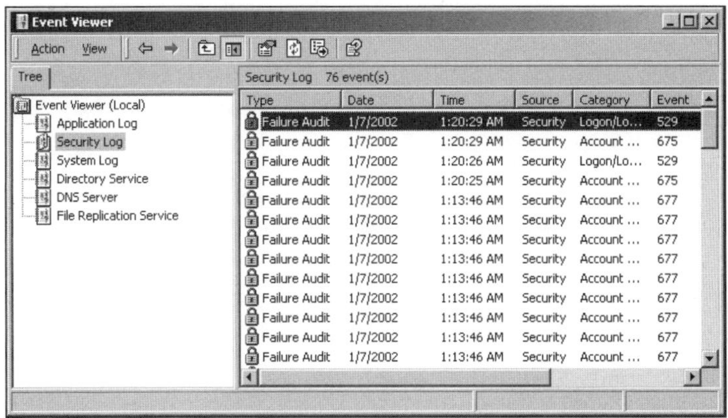

Figure 5-40 The Security Log

5

Depending on the number and type of events you choose to audit, the security log can quickly grow in size, making it difficult to pick out certain events. Fortunately, Event Viewer has a Find option that allows you to search through the security log to locate specific events. You can search for specific event types such as successful events or unsuccessful events. You can also do a more detailed search by providing an event ID, category of event, or even a user logon name. To use the Find option, click the Security Log within the Event Viewer console, click the View menu, and click the Find option. The Find in local security log window appears, as shown in Figure 5-41.

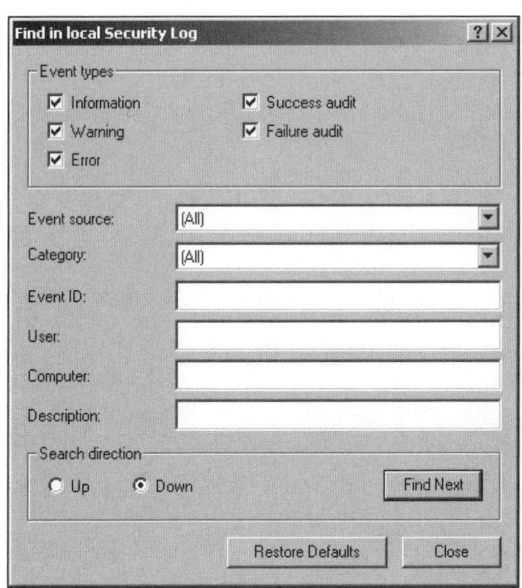

Figure 5-41 Finding information in the Security Log

Events in the security log can also be filtered so only those events matching your criteria are displayed in the details pane. This is useful if you have a large number of audit entries in the log and want to view entries based on event type or entries that occurred during a specific date and time. Similar to the Find option, you can also filter events based on event ID, category, user logon name, and computer name. To use the filter command, click the security log within the Event Viewer console, and click the Filter option located under the View menu, as shown in Figure 5-42.

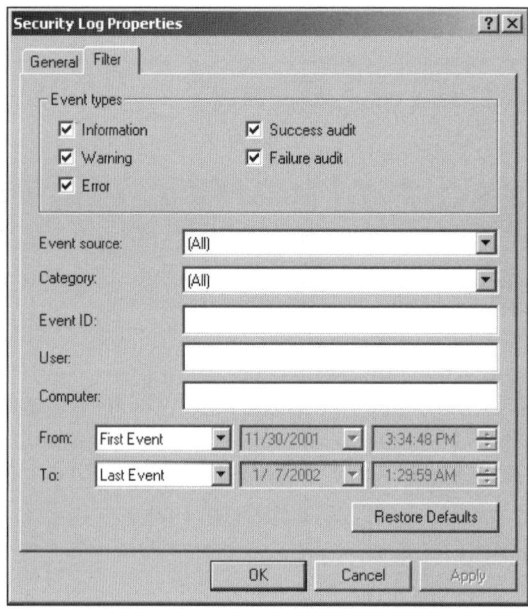

Figure 5-42 Filtering information in the Security Log

You may have noticed two other logs available within Event Viewer. The application log and the system log. The application log contains information such as warnings and error messages generated by any programs. The system log contains information such as warning and error messages that are generated by the operating system.

Domain controllers also have three more logs that refer to Active Directory and DNS events. These are the Directory Service, DNS Server, and File Replication Service logs.

Configuring the Event Viewer

One of the problems with auditing a large number of events is that the security log becomes full very quickly. By default, the security log is limited to 512 KB and once it reaches this size, logging stops. If you check and clear your security log on a regular basis, then this is not much of a concern. If the log does become full, however, and logging stops, you may not be aware of security issues occurring on the network. One way to avoid this problem, which was already mentioned, is to audit only those events that are essential. Another way is to change the default settings or properties of the security log.

To configure the properties of the security log, right-click the Security Log and click Properties. The Security Log Properties window appears, as illustrated in Figure 5-43. From the General tab you can configure the properties of the log. Table 5-9 summarizes the configuration options available.

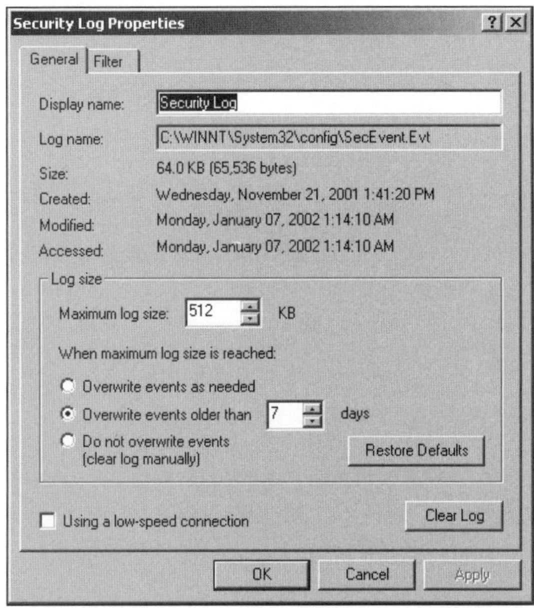

Figure 5-43 Configuring Security Log properties

Table 5-9 Security log configuration options

Option	Description
Display name	Allows you to change the name of the log view; this is useful for distinguishing between different views of the same log or for distinguishing between logs on different computers
Log name	Allows you to change the name and location of the log
Size	Specifies the size of the log file; the default is 512 KB
Overwrite events as needed	If you choose this option, all new events overwrite the oldest events when the log file becomes full; if you plan to use this option, check the log file at regular intervals

Table 5-9 Security log configuration options (continued)

Option	Description
Overwrite events older than *X* days	Allows you to set the number of days before a log is overwritten (between 1 and 365)
Do not overwrite events (clear log manually)	Events in the log are not overwritten and new events are discarded when the log becomes full until the log is manually cleared
Using a low-speed connection	Specifies whether the log is located on another computer and whether you are connected using a low-speed device (such as a modem)

MANAGING DATA STORAGE

Windows 2000 introduces many new features for managing data storage that provide more functionality and capabilities than previous versions of Windows. One of the new features, known as a dynamic disk, overcomes many of the limitations and restrictions imposed by the traditional basic disk. Disk quotas have also been introduced in Windows 2000 to provide administrators with a way to track and limit the amount of disk space available to users. Both of these management features are discussed in the following section.

Basic vs. Dynamic Disks

Windows 2000 supports two types of disks for storage: basic and dynamic. Basic disks are the traditional storage type and use primary partitions, extended partitions, and logical drives. Dynamic disks are a new storage type introduced with Windows 2000 that includes many new enhancements over basic disks, as you see in the following section.

A computer can be configured with both basic and dynamic disks. In addition, a single disk can be either basic or dynamic, and if a volume, such as a mirrored volume, contains partitions from multiple physical disks, all disks must be initialized as the same type.

Basic Disks

A **basic disk** is divided into primary and extended partitions where each partition acts as a separate storage unit. A basic disk can be configured with a maximum of four primary partitions, or three primary partitions and one extended partition.

Primary partitions are used to start a computer running Windows 2000. Each primary partition must be formatted with FAT, FAT32, or NTFS, and assigned a drive letter. Of the primary partitions that are configured, one (and only one) must be marked as the Active partition, also known as the system partition containing the hardware-specific files required to start the operating system.

The boot partition is where the operating system files are installed. Unlike the system partition, the boot partition can be located on a primary or an extended partition.

To overcome the limitation of only being able to create four primary partitions, you can create three primary and a single extended partition. An extended partition can be created using free hard disk space. Extended partitions are not formatted or assigned a drive letter. The extended partition is further divided into logical drives. Each logical drive within the extended partition is formatted and assigned a drive letter.

When you install Windows 2000, all disks are automatically initialized as basic. Disks can be converted from basic to dynamic after the installation, or they can remain as basic.

Dynamic Disks

A **dynamic disk** does not use traditional partitioning, thus making it possible to set up a large number of volumes on one disk and provide the ability to extend volumes on to additional physical disks. Some of the reasons why you may opt to implement dynamic disks include the following:

- Volumes can be extended.
- RAID volumes can be configured.
- Missing or offline disks can be reactivated.
- Changes to disks can be made without having to restart the computer.
- Mirrored and RAID-5 volumes can be applied.

Dynamic disks do not contain primary and extended partitions, but are instead configured with volumes. There are different types of volumes that can be created depending on your requirements. The different types of volumes that can be configured on a dynamic disk are discussed in the following section.

Configuring Volumes

The Disk Management snap-in is the tool used to centrally configure and manage volumes. To open Disk Management, click Start, point to Programs, point to Administrative Tools, and click Computer Management. Within the Computer Management console, click Disk Management. The details pane displays the physical drives and volumes in a graphical view, as shown in Figure 5-44.

Before you can create any new volumes, you must convert your disk or disks from basic to dynamic. A basic disk can be converted to dynamic using the Disk Management snap-in by simply right-clicking the disk you want to convert, and clicking Upgrade to dynamic disk, as shown in Figure 5-45.

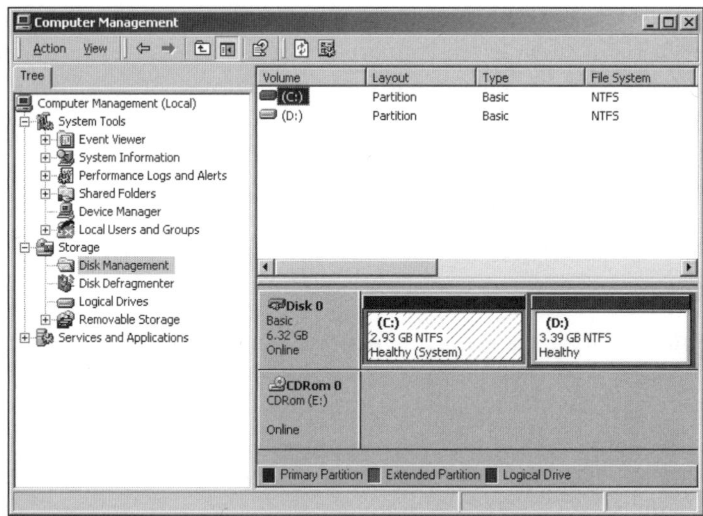

Figure 5-44 Graphical view within Disk Management

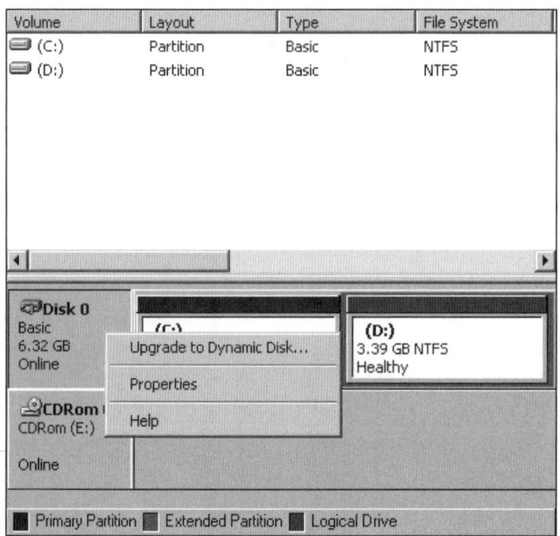

Figure 5-45 Converting to a dynamic disk

Keep the following key points in mind before you upgrade:

- You must have administrative privileges in order to perform the upgrade.
- The disk must contain at least 1 MB of free space for the upgrade to succeed.
- No data is lost when you upgrade from basic to dynamic. To revert back to a basic disk, however, all volumes must first be deleted. Data is restored from backup once the disk has been reverted to basic.

- Once upgraded, the disk can only be accessed by Windows 2000.
- Once upgraded, the primary and extended partitions become simple volumes.

In order to create any new fault tolerant volumes under Windows 2000, such as a mirrored volume or a RAID-5 volume, the disks must be converted to dynamic.

Once you have converted to dynamic, you can create any of the following Windows 2000 volumes, depending on the number of physical disks in your computer:

- Simple volume
- Spanned volume
- Striped volume
- RAID-5 volume
- Mirrored volume

A simple volume is created from free space on a single disk. It can consist of a single area of free space or multiple areas of free space on the same disk. A simple volume can be extended to include an area of free space on the same disk or another physical disk. Once a simple volume is extended to include free space from another physical disk, it becomes a spanned volume. A simple volume can be created within Disk Management by right-clicking an area of free space on the disk where the volume is to reside and clicking Create Volume.

A spanned volume consists of free space from multiple physical disks. It can include space from up to a maximum of 32 disks. When data is written to a spanned volume, it is written to the free space on the first disk (filling all available space), then written to the free space on the next physical disk. A spanned volume does not offer any fault tolerance. If any disk within the spanned volume fails, data within the entire volume is lost and must be restored from backup. You can create a spanned volume by right-clicking an area of free space and clicking the Create Volume option.

The areas of free space included in a spanned volume do not have to be the same size.

Free space can be added to a simple or spanned volume that is formatted for NTFS by extending it in Disk Management as long as the volume does not contain the system or boot volume. To do so, right-click the simple or extended volume, and click the Extend Volume option.

A striped volume writes data across two or more physical disks (up to 32) and is sometimes referred to as RAID-0. Data is written evenly across all disks in the volume in 65 KB blocks.

For example, if you save a 320 KB file to a striped volume, the first 64 KB is written to disk one, the next 64 KB is written to disk two, and so on. Striped volumes offer high performance, but no fault tolerance. If one disk in the striped volume fails, data must be restored from backup. Right-clicking an area of free space, and clicking Create Volume can create a striped volume. Click Next at the Create Volume Wizard screen, and click the striped volume option.

A RAID-5 volume is similar to a striped volume only it offers fault tolerance. It requires a minimum of three physical disks and can include space from up to 32 disks. Data is written evenly across the disks in 64 KB blocks. Parity information is added to reconstruct the data in the event that a physical disk in the volume fails. In terms of performance, a RAID 5 volume offers faster read performance but slower write performance.

A mirrored volume offers fault tolerance by duplicating data from one physical disk onto another one. Should one of the physical disks fail, data is still available from the mirrored copy. In terms of performance, a mirrored volume is slower in read performance than a RAID-5 volume, but provides faster write performance.

Disk Quotas

In a server environment, at some point in time disk space usually becomes an issue. Often users are storing their data on network servers instead of on their local computers. Depending on the number of users on the network and the amount of data they are storing, disk space can soon become scarce.

Windows 2000 uses disk quotas as a means of monitoring and controlling the amount of disk space available to users. Administrators can use disk quotas as a capacity-planning tool or as a way of managing data storage.

Using disk quotas has the following advantages:

- Prevents users from consuming all available disk space
- Encourages users to delete old files as they reach their disk quota
- Allows an administrator to track disk usage for future planning
- Allows administrators to track when users are reaching their available limit.

Disk quotas can be enabled on any NTFS volume. By default, disk quotas are disabled. By enabling disk quotas on a volume, you can see the amount of disk space that is being consumed by users. This allows you to use disk quotas as a capacity-planning tool. To use it as a management tool, you can set default quotas for all users. This is particularly useful for volumes hosting home folders which tend to consume a lot of disk space. For example, many organizations establish a default quota of 10 to 100 MB per user on home folder volumes. The default quota prevents a few users from occupying disk space that is needed for all users, while also encouraging users to save only essential information and delete files and folders that are no longer needed.

Disk quotas can be implemented only on NTFS volumes, and they are set on a per-user/per-volume basis.

To configure disk quotas:

1. Double-click the **My Computer** icon on the desktop.
2. Right-click the volume for which you want to configure a disk quota, and click **Properties**.
3. In the Properties dialog box, click the **Quota** tab.
4. To enable disk quotas for the volume, click **Enable quota management**, as shown in Figure 5-46. Removing this check mark at any time disables disk quotas for the chosen volume. Table 5-10 summarizes the available configuration options.

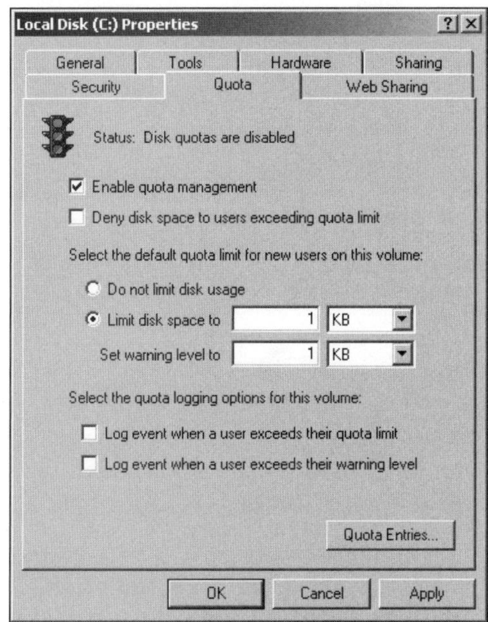

Figure 5-46 Configuring disk quotas

5. Click **Deny disk space to users exceeding quota limit**.
6. Click the radio button for **Limit disk space to**, and enter a numeric value, such as 100 MB.
7. Enter values in the Set warning level boxes, such as 90 and MB. This means when a user reaches 90 MB, they receive a warning that they are reaching their quota limit.

8. Click **Log event when a user exceeds their quota limit** if you want to be notified when a user does exceed their available limit.
9. Click **Log event when a user exceeds their warning level** if you want to be notified when a user exceeds the configured warning level.
10. Click **OK**.
11. If you see a warning that you are about to enable the disk quota system, click **OK**.

Table 5-10 Disk quota configuration parameters

Parameter	Description
Enable quota management	Tracks disk space on the volume and allows for the configuration of disk quotas
Deny disk space to users exceeding quota limit	Once users reach their quota limit they are denied any more disk space
Do not limit disk usage	Tracks disk usage, but does not limit disk space to users
Limit disk space to	Sets the default amount of disk space that is available to users
Set warning level to	Sets the default amount of disk space that a user can consume before a warning message is sent to the user stating the quota is being reached.
Log event when a user exceeds their quota limit	Causes an event to be entered in the system log to notify the administrator that the user has reached their quota
Log event when a user exceeds their warning level	Causes an event to be entered in the system log to notify the administrator that the user is approaching their quota

Exceptions can be created for users requiring more disk space than others. Disk quotas for specific user accounts can be set by clicking the Quota Entries button on the Quota tab, and then clicking New Quota Entry from the Quota menu. You can then choose the user account for which you want to establish a quota and configure the quota limits. The Quota Entries dialog box is updated to reflect the quota for that user account, as shown in Figure 5-47.

The disk quota configuration for a specific account can be modified by clicking the Quota Entries button again to open the Quota Entries dialog box. Double-click the account you want to modify, and then change the values in the Quota Settings dialog box. To delete a quota associated with an account, right-click the account in the Quota Entries dialog box, and click Delete.

Keep in mind that the amount of disk space a user is currently occupying can change when ownership of files transfers from one user account to another. For example, Conan Kezema creates a database called Clients.mdb that occupies 1022 KB on a volume that contains a shared folder. After Conan creates and saves the database, his available disk space is decreased by 1022 KB. If Conan changes job roles within the company and Mike takes ownership of the database, Conan's available disk space goes up by 1022 KB and Mike's is decreased by the same amount.

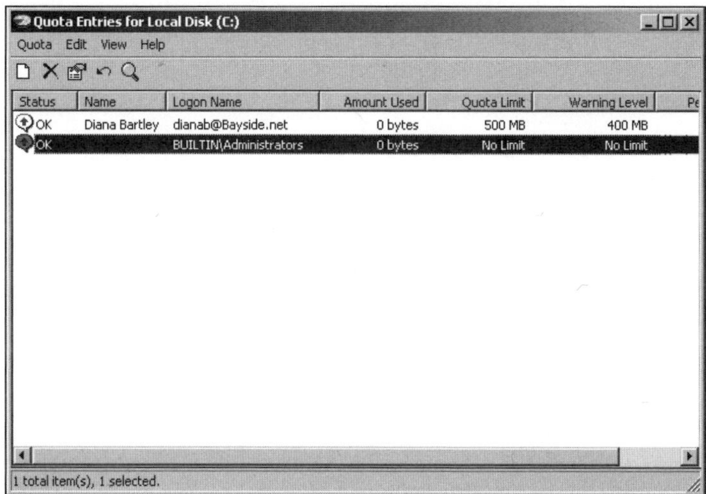

Figure 5-47 Configuring individual disk quotas

At any time, you can click the Quote Entries button to view the disk quota limit and warning level configured for any account and the amount of disk space used by an account.

Managing File and Folder Compression

On volumes that are formatted with NTFS, data **compression** can be enabled to reduce the amount of disk space that folders and files take up, thus allowing you to save more data on a volume. Once a volume, folder, or file is compressed you do not need a third-party product to uncompress it. When a user accesses the file it is automatically uncompressed and transparent to the user.

Configuring compression is as simple as enabling or disabling the compression attribute within Windows Explorer. To enable compression, right-click the folder or file you want to compress, and click Properties. Click the Advanced button, and click the Compress contents to save disk space option, as shown in Figure 5-48.

Notice that you can choose either compression or encryption, but both attributes cannot be configured at the same time. To compress an entire drive, right-click the drive and click Properties. Click the General tab, and then click the Compress drive to save disk space option. Once the compression attribute is set and you click OK, you have the option of specifying to what the changes apply. If you select the Apply changes to the folder only option, only the files within that folder are compressed. If you choose the Apply changes to this folder, subfolders and files option, all files and subfolders within the folder are compressed.

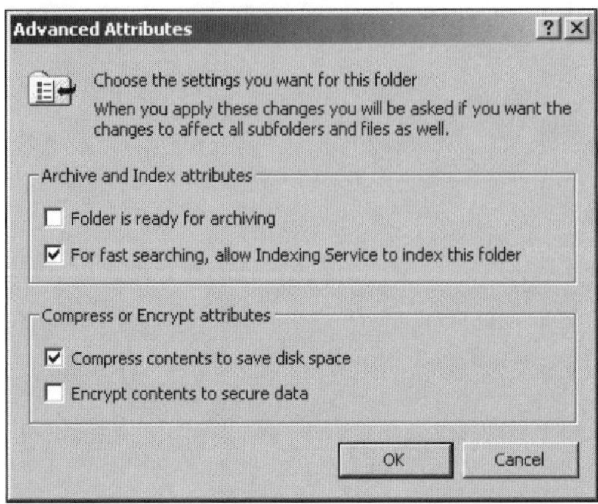

Figure 5-48 Setting the compression attribute

After a folder or file has been compressed, it is displayed in a different color within Windows Explorer (making it easy for an administrator to identify what is and what isn't compressed). Compressed folders and files are displayed in blue, by default. To change the default color, click Folder Options from the Tools menu. Click the View tab, and click the Display compressed files and folders with alternate color.

As with permissions and encryption, the compression attribute can be affected when copying and moving files. Keep the following points in mind when using the compression attribute:

- If a file is *copied* to another folder within the same NTFS volume, it automatically inherits the compression attribute of the destination folder.

- If a file or folder is *moved* within the same NTFS volume, it retains its compression attribute.
- If a file or folder is *copied* between NTFS volumes, the file or folder inherits the compression attribute of the destination folder.
- If a file or folder is *moved* between NTFS volumes, the file or folder inherits the compression attribute of the destination folder.

Because compression is only available on NTFS volumes, if a folder or file is copied or moved to a FAT volume, the compression attribute is not retained.

CHAPTER SUMMARY

- To create a shared folder, you are required to have the appropriate rights. A domain administrator or server operator has the default rights to create shared folders within a domain.
- Windows 2000 supports three share permissions: Read, Change, and Full Control. Share permissions are cumulative. If a user is a member of multiple groups that have different permissions, the final permission is the sum of all permissions.
- NTFS permissions are cumulative. If a user is a member of multiple groups that have different permissions, the final permission is the sum of all permissions.
- When Share and NTFS permissions are combined, the most restrictive applies.
- The Deny permissions override all other permissions.
- Files and folders can be encrypted using the encrypted file system.
- The distributed file system can be used to logically group network resources in a single tree structure.
- Two kinds of printer devices can be shared: a local print device, which is a print device connected to a port on a print server, or a network print device, in which the print device has its own network connection and IP address.
- Both printer and folder shares can be published into Active Directory to make it easy for clients to find the shared resources.
- Auditing in Windows 2000 is used to monitor and track activities on a network. You can specify which events to monitor based on your security requirements. When an event does occur, a record of it is written to the security log.
- Windows 2000 supports basic and dynamic disks.
- Basic disks can be converted to dynamic disks without losing any data. To revert back to a basic disk, all volumes must be deleted and data restored from backup.
- Depending on the number of users on the network and the amount of data they are storing, disk space can soon become scarce. Windows 2000 uses disk quotas as a way of managing data storage. Disk quotas are configured on a per-user/per-volume basis.

KEY TERMS

access control entry (ACE) — An entry in an object's discretionary access control list (DACL) that grants permissions to a user or group. An ACE is also an entry in an object's system access control list (SACL) that specifies the security events to be audited for a user or group.

Active Directory client extensions — These allow legacy operating systems to perform searches in Active Directory; they also provide site awareness and access to Windows 2000 distributed file systems.

audit policy — Defines the events on the network that Windows 2000 records in the security log as they occur.

auditing — The process that tracks the activities of users by recording selected types of events in the security log of a server or a workstation.

basic disk — The traditional storage type that divides physical disk space into primary partitions, extended partitions, and logical drives.

compression — Data is stored in a format that takes up less disk space enabling you to store more data.

Computer Management console — A predefined Microsoft Management Console (MMC) application that allows you to administer a variety of computer-related tasks on the local computer or a remote computer.

data recovery agent — Individual responsible for recovering encrypted data in the event a user's private key is lost.

discretionary access control list (DACL) — A part of the security descriptor of an object that contains a list of user or group references that have been allowed or denied permissions to the resource.

disk quotas — A Windows 2000 feature that is used as a means of monitoring and controlling the amount of disk space available to users.

distributed file system (DFS)— A file system that organizes shared folders located throughout a local or wide area network into a single logical tree structure.

DFS topology — The logical structure of a distributed file system, which includes the DFS root and DFS link.

DFS root — The top level of a DFS tree structure that contains links to the shared folders on the network.

DFS link — A pointer to the physical location of a share on the network.

dynamic disk — A new storage system supported by Windows 2000 that divides physical disk space into volumes.

encrypting file system (EFS) — The Windows 2000 file system that enables you to encrypt files and folders on NTFS volumes for security purposes.

Event Viewer — A component you can use to view and manage event logs, gather information about hardware and software problems, and monitor security events. Event Viewer maintains logs about program, security, and system events.

Internet Information Services (IIS) — Is used to provide access utilizing a number of protocols such as Hypertext Transfer Protocol (HTTP), File Transfer Protocol (FTP), Network News Transfer Protocol (NNTP), and Simple Mail Transfer Protocol (SMTP).

orphan pruner — A process that removes orphaned printer objects from the Active Directory. The orphan pruner verifies that all printer objects are still valid in Active Directory.

print device — The actual hardware device that produces the printed document. A local print device connects directly to a port on the print server. A network print device connects to a print server through its own network adapter and connection to the network.

print driver — Files that contain information that Windows 2000 uses to convert raw print commands to a language that the printer understands.

print server — The computer in which the printers and print drivers are located. This is usually where you set up and configure the shared printing system.

printer — A configuration object in Windows 2000 that controls the connection to the print device.

printer pool — Consists of a single printer that is connected to a number of print devices.

printer priorities — Configuring multiple printers to print to the same print device. One printer is then configured to print before any of the other printers by adjusting the priority setting from one (lowest priority) to 99 (highest priority).

published — An Active Directory object that represents a link or direct information on how to use or connect to the shared resource.

published folder — An Active Directory object that points to a related shared folder on a file server.

replica set — A set of shared folders that is replicated or copied to one or more servers in a domain.

security log — A Windows 2000 event log used to record security events such as auditing information.

shared folder — A data resource container that has been made available over the network to authorized network clients.

Web folder — A folder that is intended to be accessed from the Internet or an internal intranet using the HTTP or FTP protocols.

Review Questions

1. Your organization requires that all users be limited to 10 MB of disk storage space on each volume in which they store data, including the volume hosting home folders. How should you proceed?
   a. Configure a disk quota of 10 MB for each disk.
   b. Configure a warning level of 10 MB.
   c. Configure a disk quota of 10 MB for each volume.
   d. Limiting disk space is not possible in Windows 2000.
2. By default, disk quotas are enabled for each NTFS volume. True or False?

3. Mike and Conan both have a disk quota of 4 MB. Conan creates an employee database that is 600 KB in size. A change in job roles later requires Mike to take ownership of the database. How does this affect their available storage space?
   a. Both users' available storage space is decreased by 600 KB.
   b. Conan's available space remains the same. Mike's is decreased by 600 KB.
   c. Both users' available storage space is increased by 600 KB.
   d. Conan's available space is increased by 600 KB. Mike's is decreased by 600 KB.
4. The hard drive on a server is partitioned into four separate volumes. Users store data on volumes E, F, and G. E is formatted with FAT, and F and G are both NTFS volumes. You attempt to enable disk quotas on volume E through the properties of the volume, but cannot find the quota tab. What is the problem?
   a. The volume is currently in use.
   b. The volume must be formatted with NTFS.
   c. Disk quotas are enabled through Active Directory Users and Computers.
   d. You must use the Quotas command at the command prompt to enable disk quotas.
5. By default, auditing on all domain controllers is turned on. True or False?
6. Your company decides to audit access to confidential folders and files stored on all domain controllers. You are responsible for implementing the required audit policy. Through Windows Explorer, you attempt to configure the auditing settings on the Accounting Docs folder using the Auditing tab, but you are unsuccessful. What must be done first?
   a. Format the volume hosting the Accounting Docs folder with NTFS.
   b. Enable auditing for object access in the audit policy through Active Directory Users and Computers.
   c. Enable auditing for object access through the local security policy.
   d. Publish the share in Active Directory.
7. Which tool can be used to view the audit entries within the security log?
   a. Security Viewer
   b. Performance Monitor
   c. Event Monitor
   d. Event Viewer
8. The security log on your server is checked every other day for any new audit entries. How can you ensure that no entries are overwritten until it is checked by a member of the Administrators group or by a user with the appropriate user rights?
   a. Under the properties for the security log, click the option to Overwrite events as needed.
   b. Under the properties for the security log, click the option to Overwrite events older than *X* days, and set the value to 2.

c. Under the Properties of the security log, set the default log size to 1 MB.

d. Under the properties for the security log, click the option Do not overwrite events (clear the log manually).

9. What two ways can you give a user the right to view the security log? (Choose two answers.)

a. Add them to the Administrators group.

b. Add them to the Security group.

c. Assign them the right to view the security log.

d. Assign them the right to manage auditing and security log.

10. Which two of the following allow you to create a shared folder? (Choose two answers.)

a. Active Directory Users and Computers

b. Windows Explorer

c. Computer Management console

d. Performance Monitor

11. How can you create a shared folder, but make it hidden so it is not visible through My Network Places or Network Neighborhood?

a. Right-click the shared folder, and click the Hide Share option.

b. Place a $ at the end of the share name.

c. Place a $ at the beginning of the share name.

d. A shared folder cannot be hidden.

12. Bob is a member of the following groups that have been assigned different permissions for the Accounting Docs folder:

Accountants	Change
Managers	Full Control
Users	Read

What is Bob's effective permission to the Accounting Docs folder?

a. Change

b. Full Control

c. Read

d. No Access

13. Robert is a member of the Sales group and the Managers group. Each group has been assigned the following share permissions and NTFS permissions to the Accounting Docs folder.

Group	Share Permission	NTFS Permission
Managers	Full Control	Modify
Sales	Read	Write

What is Robert's effective permission for the Accounting Docs folder when he accesses it from across the network?

a. Full Control

b. Modify

c. Read

d. Write

14. Using the example in question 13, what is Robert's effective permission when he accesses the Accounting Docs folder locally?

a. Full Control

b. Modify

c. Read

d. Write

15. Which of the following utilities allows you to create a new share on a domain controller from your workstation running Windows 2000 Professional?

a. Windows Explorer

b. Active Directory Users and Computers

c. Server Manager

d. Computer Management

16. Your Windows 2000 Server has an HP Laser Jet printer attached to it and is acting as a print server. A new driver has recently been released for Windows 2000 Professional clients. What must be done to distribute the updated drivers to the clients?

a. Install the updated driver on the printer server, and manually update the driver on the Windows 2000 clients.

b. Install the updated driver on the print server, and do nothing more.

c. Install the updated driver on the print server, and instruct users to manually download the new driver.

d. Install the updated driver on the client workstations only.

17. You recently installed a new printer on your print server. Users are now reporting that their documents are not printing, and they cannot delete their documents

from the print queue. You open up the print queue, see the documents listed, and discover that you cannot delete the entries. What is causing the problem?

a. The print spooler is stalled.

b. The incorrect driver is installed.

c. There is not sufficient space on the hard disk for spooling.

d. Users do not have the correct protocol installed.

18. The default permission for a shared folder is the Users group receives Full Control. True or False?

19. You want to configure an audit policy to track any changes that are made to user accounts. Which of the following options should you enable in your audit policy?

    a. Audit object access

    b. Audit directory service access

    c. Audit account management

    d. Audit privilege use

20. When a user has been assigned multiple share permissions through group membership, the user's effective permission is the most restrictive. True or False?

21. You attempt to create a mirrored volume using Disk Management, but are not given the option. You have not made any configuration changes since installing Windows 2000. What must be done?

    a. Format the partitions with NTFS.

    b. Convert the disks to basic.

    c. Convert the disks to dynamic.

    d. Reinstall Windows 2000.

22. You set permissions on your shared resources stored on your file server. Some of the information is high security. You are concerned about the possibility of someone taking the drive and being able to access the files. What technology can you implement to add another level of file and folder security?

    a. compression

    b. encrypting file system

    c. distributed file system

    d. file protection system

23. Which of the following offer fault tolerance? (Choose all that apply.)

    a. spanned volumes

    b. mirrored volumes

    c. striped volumes

    d. RAID-5 volumes

24. You can either enable the compression attribute or the encryption attribute for a folder or file, but not both. True or False?
25. You enable compression on a shared folder. You move the folder from an NTFS volume to a FAT volume. What happens to the compression attribute?
    a. The compression attribute is lost.
    b. The compression attribute is retained.
    c. The compressions attribute is inherited from the target folder.
    d. Nothing. You cannot copy folders between an NTFS and a FAT volume.

Hands-on Projects

Project 5-1

In this Hands-on Project, you create a shared folder using the Computer Management console:

1. Right-click **My Computer**, and click **Manage**.
2. In the console pane, expand the **Shared Folders** node, and click **Shares**.
3. Right-click **Shares**, and click **New File Share**.
4. In the Create Shared Folder dialog box, click the **Browse** button.
5. Click drive **C:**, and then click the **New Folder** button. Name the new folder **Clients**.
6. Click the new **Clients** folder. Make sure that the folder name is listed in the Folder text box. Click **OK**.
7. In the Share name text box, type **Clients**.
8. In the Share description, type **Client information folder**. Click **Next**.
9. For the Share permissions, click **Administrators have full control; other users have read-only access**. Click **Finish**. Click **No** at the prompt.
10. Verify that the Clients shared folder is listed in the details pane of the Shares node.
11. Close all windows.

Project 5-2

In this Hands-on Project, you create and test a shared Web folder.

To create a shared Web folder:

1. Right-click **My Computer**, and click **Explore**.
2. Click drive **C:**, right-click the **Clients** folder, and click **Properties**.
3. Click the **Web Sharing** tab.

4. Click **Share this folder**, and then make sure that Read, Write, and Directory browsing is selected for permissions. Click **OK**, and then click **Yes** at the prompt.
5. Click **OK**.

To test the shared Web folder:

1. Double-click **Internet Explorer** on the desktop.
2. Click **File**, and click **Open,** and then type **http://<*servername*>/clients** in the Address bar (*servername* represents the name of your server).
3. Check the **Open as Web folder** option. Click **OK**.
4. The Server1/clients/ Web folder opens.
5. Close all windows.

Project 5-3

In this Hands-on Project, you create a shared printer.

1. Click **Start**, point to **Settings**, and then click the **Printers** folder.
2. Double-click the **Add Printer** icon. Click **Next** when the wizard opens.
3. Click **Local Printer**. Do not check the option Automatically detect my Plug and Play printer. Click **Next**.
4. Click **LPT1** as the Printer Port, and click **Next**.
5. Click **HP** as the Manufacturer and **HP LaserJet 6P** as the Printer. Click **Next**.
6. In the Name your Printer dialog box, leave all default settings, and click **Next**.
7. On the Printer Sharing tab, click **Share as** and name the share **HP**. Click **Next**.
8. Click **Next** in the Location and Comment dialog box.
9. Click **No** to print a test page. Click **Next**, and then click **Finish**.
10. Close all windows.

Project 5-4

In this Hands-on Project, you publish a shared folder into Active Directory, and verify that your printer is published into Active Directory.

To publish a shared folder into Active Directory:

1. Click **Start**, point to **Programs**, point to **Administrative Tools**, and then click **Active Directory Users and Computers**.
2. Right-click the **Toronto Dept OU**, point to **New**, and click **Shared Folder**.
3. Type **Clients** in the Name text box.
4. In the Network path text box, type **\\<*servername*>\clients**, (where *servername* is the name of your server). Click **OK**.

To add key words to the published folder:

1. Right-click the **Clients share** in the Toronto Dept OU, and click **Properties**.
2. Click the **Keywords** button.
3. Add the following keywords: **customers**, **accounts**. Click **OK**.
4. Click **OK** to return to Active Directory Users and Computers.

To verify that your printer is published in Active Directory:

1. Click the **View** menu, and click **Users, Groups, and Computers** as containers.
2. Expand the OU in which your server is placed. (It should be found under domain controllers.)
3. Click your server name, and verify that a printer object appears in the details pane.
4. Click the **View** menu, and uncheck **Users**, **Groups, and Computers** as containers.
5. Click **Start**, point to **Settings**, and then click **Printers**.
6. Right-click **HP LaserJet 6P**, and then click **Properties**.
7. Click the **Sharing** tab. Verify that the List in Directory option is checked. Click **OK**.
8. Close all windows.

Project 5-5

In this Hands-on Project, you perform a search for a published folder and a published printer.

To search for a published folder in Active Directory:

1. Click **Start**, point to **Search**, and then click **For Files or Folders**.
2. Click the list arrow under the Look in command, and click **Browse**.
3. Expand **My Network Places\Entire Network\Directory**.
4. Right-click your domain name, and click **Find**.
5. Click the **Find list** arrow, and click **Shared Folders**.
6. In the Keywords text box, type **customers**, and click **Find Now**. Verify that the Clients share is listed in the details pane.

To search for a published printer in Active Directory:

1. Click the Find list arrow, click **Printers**, and click **OK** to clear the search results.
2. Type **HP** in the Name text box, and click **Find Now**. Verify that your printer object appears in the details pane.
3. Close all windows.

Project 5-6

In this Hands-on Project, you configure disk quotas on your D drive.

To configure disk quotas on drive D:

1. Double-click **My Computer**.
2. Right-click drive **D:**, and click **Properties**.
3. Click the **Quota** tab, and click the option **Enable quota management**.
4. Click the option **Deny disk space to users exceeding quota limit**.
5. In the text box next to Limit disk space to, type **500** and then choose **MB** from the drop down menu.
6. In the text box next to Set warning level to, type **400** and then choose **MB** from the drop down menu.
7. Click the check box next to both quota-logging options at the bottom of the dialog box.

To configure an exception to the quota limit:

1. Click the **Quota Entries** button.
2. In the Quota Entries for Local Disk dialog box, click the **Quota** menu, and click **New Quota Entry**.
3. Click **John Riley**, and click **Add**. Click **OK**.
4. Click **Limit disk space to**, and set the entry to **1 GB**. Set the warning level to **800 MB**.
5. Click **OK**. Verify that John Riley is listed in the Quota Entries dialog box. Close the window.
6. Click **OK** twice, and then close all remaining windows.

Project 5-7

In this Hands-on Project, you enable auditing for all failed logons and any access to the Notepad application. Any time a domain user fails to log on or when a user runs NOTEPAD.EXE, events are logged to the appropriate event log.

1. Click **Start**, point to **Programs**, point to **Administrative Tools**, and click **Domain Controller Security Policy**.
2. Expand the **Security Settings** node in the left pane.
3. Expand the **Local Policies** node.
4. Click the **Audit Policy** node. The details pane lists the various auditing configuration selections.
5. Double-click **Audit logon events**.
6. Click the check box to define this policy, and choose to audit the failed logons. Click **OK**.

7. Double-click **Audit object access**.
8. Click the check box to define this policy, and choose to audit all successes. Click **OK**. Close the Domain controller security policy console.
9. Right-click **My Computer**, and click **Explore**.
10. Browse to **C:\Winnt\System32**. Click **Show Files** to view the details pane.
11. Right-click **NOTEPAD.EXE,** and click **Properties**.
12. Click the **Security** tab, and then click the **Advanced** button.
13. Click the **Auditing** tab, and then click **Add**.
14. Double-click the **Domain Users** group.
15. Click the **Successful** check box for List Folder/Read Data and Read Permissions. Click **OK** four times.
16. Close all windows and log off.

Project 5-8

In this Hands-on Project, you attempt to log on with an invalid password and then successfully log on and run the Notepad application. You then view the results of the audit.

1. At the Logon prompt, press **Ctrl+Alt+Delete**. Type **administrator** as the user name and **1234** as the password.
2. Click **OK** at the logon message. Repeat Steps 1 and 2 two more times.
3. Log on as the administrator with the proper password.
4. Click **Start**, point to **Programs**, point to **Accessories**, and open the **Notepad** application.
5. Close **Notepad**.
6. Click **Start**, point to **Programs**, point to **Administrative Tools**, and click **Event Viewer**.
7. Click **Security Log**.
8. Double-click the various events to view the details. Note the information that the audit provides.
9. Close all windows and log off.

Project 5-9

In this Hands-on Project, you encrypt and compress two new folders on drive C:.

1. Log on as the administrator.
2. Right-click **My Computer**, and click **Explore**.
3. Click drive **C:**.
4. Click **File**, click **New**, and then click **Folder**. Name the new folder **compress**.
5. Click drive **C:** and then click **File**, click **New**, and then click **Folder**.

6. Name the new folder **encrypt**.
7. Right-click the **compress** folder and click **Properties**.
8. Click the **Advanced** button.
9. Click the **Compress contents to save disk space** option. Click **OK**. Click **OK** again to return to Windows Explorer.
10. Right-click the **encrypt** folder and click **Properties**.
11. Click the **Advanced** button.
12. Click the **Encrypt contents to secure data** option. Click **OK**. Click **OK** again to return to Windows Explorer.
13. Close all windows and log off.

Case Projects

Case Project 5-1

This case project involves configuring permissions, auditing, and disk quotas. Bayside is in the process of reviewing their current structure and practices. There has been talk of minor security breaches occurring in which users are able to gain access to information they should not be permitted to view. Management would like you to make some recommendations on how permissions can be changed on specific folders. They also want to know if there is a way to track user access so that, if a security breach does occur, there is a record of it. Management has also expressed a concern over the amount of disk space users are consuming, and you need to come up with a solution to address this.

1. Two network servers maintain confidential information pertaining to financial data and employee data. Users access the folders both locally and on the network. Only members of the Managers group, Human Resources group, and Accountants group should have access to these folders. Explain how permissions can be implemented, including a short description of how share permissions and NTFS permissions work together.
2. Bayside has recently hired a new server administrator to assist you. He has worked with Windows NT 4.0 in the past and is unfamiliar with Windows 2000. Prepare a brief explanation for the new administrator about how to configure share permissions and NTFS permissions.
3. Once the appropriate permissions have been established, you want to be able to track user access to these folders. Explain how you can use auditing, and the general steps that you need to complete in order to implement an audit policy.
4. Management has expressed a concern over disk usage because of the number of support calls indicating that server volumes are full. To date, all you have been doing is sending out memos asking users to delete any temporary or old files. Discuss how Bayside can use disk quotas to limit usage and plan for future storage capacity requirements.

Case Project 5-2

Bayside is in the process of adding two new print devices on the network. One is for the Managers group and the other is for the Sales and Accountants groups. Both printers are identical and are connected to two separate servers. Bayside has asked you to advise them about how to set up the printers.

1. Bayside has asked you to briefly outline how to set up these two print devices and make them accessible on the network. Keep in mind that all workstations that are using the print devices are running Windows 2000 Professional.
2. In your documentation, include a description of the permissions assigned to those users responsible for managing the printers.
3. Explain how the printer permissions are configured so the appropriate groups have access to the printers.

Case Project 5-3

To understand how NTFS and share permissions work together, consider the following example and answer the questions below.

Table 5-11 Permissions example

Users:	Group Membership:
User1	Sales, Marketing, domain users
User2	Managers, domain users

Directory Structure:	Share Permissions	NTFS Permissions
SalesData	Sales – Full Control	Sales – Modify
	Managers – Read	Marketing – Full Control
CompanyData	domain users – Change	default
HRData	Managers – deny Full Control	default

1. What permissions would User1 have for the SalesData folder if the user were accessing the folder across a network connection?
2. What permissions would User1 have for the SalesData folder if the user were logged on to the computer where the folder was located?
3. What permissions would User 2 have for the CompanyData folder if accessing the folder across the network?
4. What permissions would User 2 have for the HRData folder if accessing the folder across the network?
5. What permissions would User 2 have for the HRData folder if accessing the folder on the computer in which it is located?

CHAPTER

6

ADMINISTERING WEB RESOURCES IN WINDOWS 2000

After reading this chapter and completing the exercises, you will be able to:

- Install and configure Internet Information Services (IIS)
- Create and configure Web site virtual servers and virtual directories
- Configure Web site authentication
- Configure and maintain FTP virtual servers
- Update and maintain security for an IIS server
- Troubleshoot Web client browser connectivity

Windows 2000 includes a variety of Internet-related services that can assist a company in developing an effective online Internet or intranet presence. Companies are beginning to realize the potential and importance of Web-based services to provide employees and customers efficient and alternative ways of interacting with the organization.

To help develop and host these services, Microsoft has included an application called **Internet Information Services (IIS)** within Windows 2000. IIS provides the foundation for the Web-related services that an organization needs to create an effective and secure Internet or intranet presence. In this chapter, you learn how to install, configure, maintain, and secure a Windows 2000 Internet Information Services server. You also learn how to configure each of the components that IIS has to offer an organization, such as Web and FTP services. The final section of this chapter discusses client connectivity troubleshooting issues that you may face as users attempt to access the Internet or your internal intranet.

Installing and Configuring Internet Information Services

Internet Information Services (IIS) 5.0 is a Windows 2000 application that provides Web-related services to an organization. IIS consists of four main components:

- *World Wide Web (HTTP) services*—Provides the capability of hosting multiple Web sites accessible from the Internet or an intranet
- *File Transfer Protocol (FTP) services*—Can be installed and configured to have the ability to copy files between the server and a remote location
- *Network News Transfer Protocol (NNTP) services*—Used to provide a means of maintaining a list of topics and threaded conversations between users, such as a corporate discussion newsgroup in which employees can post messages and read replies related to various company matters.
- *Simple Mail Transfer Protocol (SMTP) services*—This service is included in IIS to provide e-mail capabilities to the other services, such as HTTP or NNTP. For example, you might create a Web form that requires the response to be e-mailed to another location. This service is also used extensively when Microsoft Exchange 2000 is installed.

These services can be implemented to host a corporate intranet or Internet presence. An organization that hosts a corporate intranet can provide employees with:

- Interactive online company resources, such as employee handbook information, employee news, or department meeting minutes
- Team collaboration using various applications, such as Office XP
- Web-based applications to assist employees in filling out forms or other internal business processes

An Internet presence for an organization can provide customers with:

- Additional customer service, such as online manuals or frequently asked questions about products or services
- The ability to order products online and track shipping progress
- Dynamic company information and news bulletins

To make these services available to your employees and customers, it is important that you understand how to configure, maintain, and secure Internet Information Services. These concepts are discussed in the sections that follow.

Installing Internet Information Services

IIS 5.0 is automatically installed during a standard installation of Windows 2000. If you have performed a custom Windows 2000 installation and removed the IIS components, they can be reinstalled by accessing the Add/Remove Programs applet in Control

Panel. Next, click the Add/Remove Windows Components button, which opens the Windows Components Wizard. This wizard is used to add or remove specific components, such as Internet Information Services.

Figure 6-1 illustrates the Internet Information Services (IIS) option in the Windows Components Wizard dialog box.

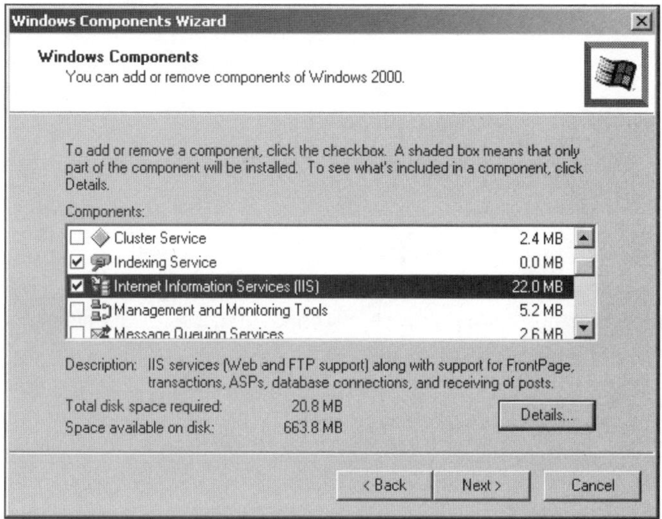

Figure 6-1 Installing Internet Information Services

When you click the Details button in the Windows Components Wizard dialog box, you notice that IIS consists of a number of individual components that can be selectively installed or removed, as shown in Figure 6-2.

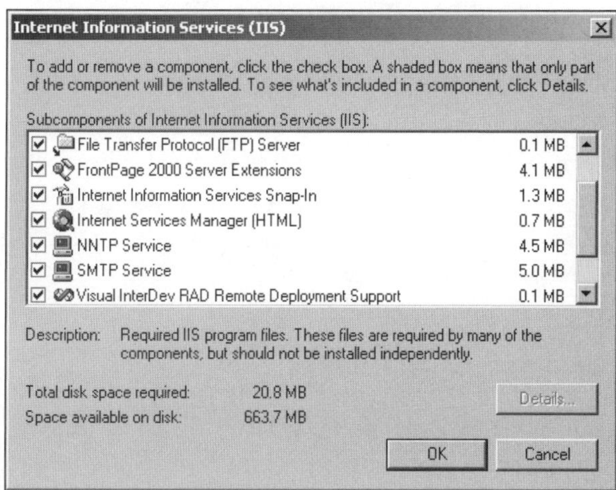

Figure 6-2 Viewing additional IIS applications and components

Table 6-1 lists and explains each of the individual components that can be installed as part of Internet Information Services.

Table 6-1 Internet Information Services components

IIS Component	Purpose
Common files	These are the required IIS program files
Documentation	Information on administering Web and FTP servers
File Transfer Protocol (FTP) server	Used to install the components to set up an FTP server which can allow you to upload and download files to and from the server
FrontPage 2000 server extensions	Enables creating, developing, and maintaining Web-based material using Microsoft FrontPage, SharePoint Portal Server, or Visual InterDev
Internet Information Services snap-in	Installs the Microsoft Management Console snap-in to allow management of an IIS server
Internet Services Manager (HTML)	Allows Web browser or HTML-based administration of an IIS server
NNTP service	Installs the capability for an IIS server to function as a Network News Transfer Protocol server; this can be used to provide newsgroup subscriptions to clients
SMTP service	Installs the capability for an IIS server to function as a Simple Mail Transfer Protocol Server; this gives the ability to provide support for e-mail on a network or the Internet
Visual InterDev RAD Remote Deployment Support	Used to remotely deploy applications developed with the Visual InterDev Rapid Applications Development tool
World Wide Web server	Installs the capability for an IIS server to function as a Web server on an intranet or the Internet; this provides access to custom-designed Web sites

After a successful installation of IIS, you notice a number of changes on the server. Some of these changes include additional folders on the hard drive, additional user objects in Active Directory, and additional services installed within the operating system.

It is important to understand the location and purpose of the folders that are created by IIS during installation. By default, it is in these folders that the IIS system files and the physical files for your Default Web or FTP site are located. Table 6-2 explains these folders in greater detail.

Initially, the Everyone group is assigned Full Control of the ftproot and mailroot folders. This should be modified with tighter permissions, depending upon the level of functionality that you are providing to your users. When you open Active Directory Users and Computers and click the Users container, you notice the addition of two new user objects. The first object is ISUSR_*servername,* which is an account that IIS uses to provide anonymous access to the server. The second object is IWAM_*servername,* which is an account used to allow IIS to start out-of-process applications.

Table 6-2 IIS folder structure

IIS Folder	Purpose
%systemroot%\System32\inetsrv	Contains all of the program files and .dll files needed for IIS to function
%systemroot%\System32\inetsrv\iisadmin	Contains the files necessary to access the administration Web site which can be used to administer IIS functions with a Web browser
C:\inetpub	Contains various subfolders such as ftproot, wwwroot, and mailroot, which store all of the source content for the FTP, Web, and SMTP services provided by the server
C:\Winnt\help\iishelp	Contains the IIS documentation

Figure 6-3 highlights these new user accounts created in Active Directory after IIS is successfully installed.

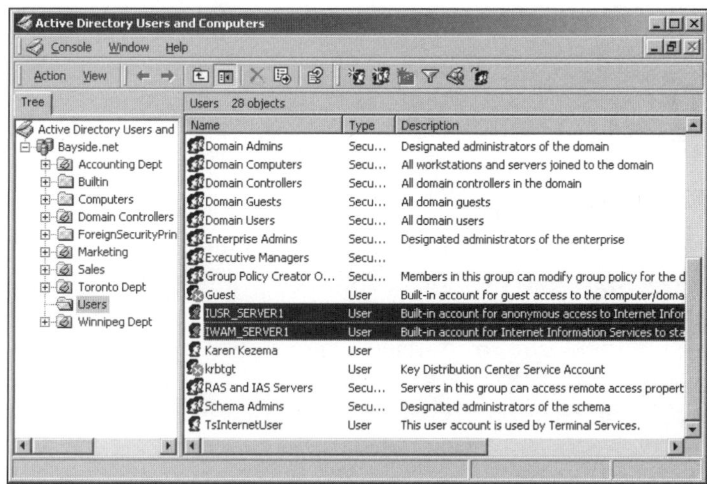

Figure 6-3 Viewing the IIS user accounts

The final change that you notice after an IIS installation is the addition of several operating system services to Windows 2000. To view the additional services, you can access the Services console on the Administrative Tools menu. The new IIS-based services include:

- *FTP Publishing Service*—Provides the FTP connectivity and administration functions for the Web server
- *IIS Admin Service*—Allows the administration of Web- and FTP-related services through the Internet Information Services snap-in

- *Simple Mail Transport Protocol (SMTP)*—Provides the function of transporting electronic mail throughout the network
- *World Wide Web Publishing Service*—Provides Web connectivity to allow administration and posting of various types of Web content

Figure 6-4 shows the Services console open with the FTP Publishing Service highlighted and the IIS Admin Service located below the highlight.

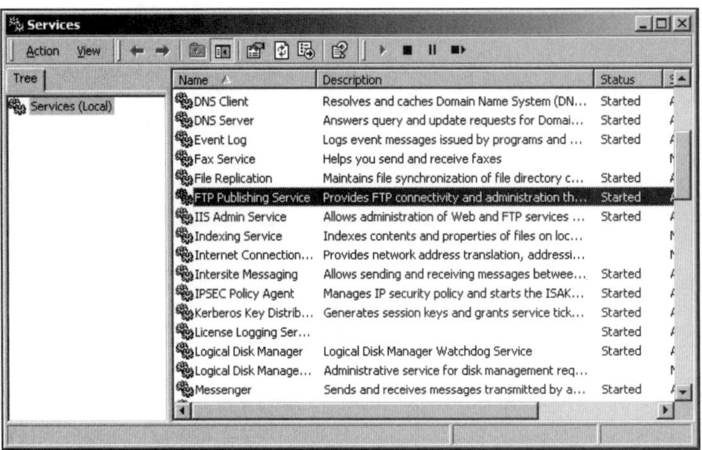

Figure 6-4 Viewing the various Internet Information Services

Configuring Web Server Properties

After installing the IIS components, you can manage IIS by using an administrative tool called the **Internet Services Manager**. This tool can be accessed by clicking Start, pointing to Programs, and then clicking Administrative Tools. When you click the Internet Services Manager icon, the Internet Information Services console opens, as shown in Figure 6-5.

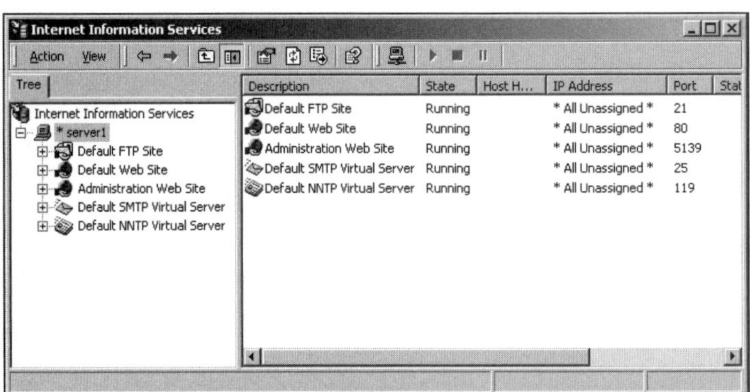

Figure 6-5 The Internet Information Services console

As illustrated in Figure 6-5, the IIS console displays the default sites and services that are initially installed and that can be managed with this utility. These default sites and services are described in the following list:

- ***Default FTP site***—An FTP server that responds to TCP/IP port 21 on all configured IP addresses of the server that are not assigned to another site.
- ***Default Web site***—A Web site configured with FrontPage extensions that responds to TCP/IP port 80 on all unassigned IP addresses of the server. This Web site is initially empty and may be used to create a custom Web site for your organization.
- ***Administration Web site***—A Web site that is configured to allow administrators to manage the Web server from a remote location using a Web browser. During installation, this site is assigned a random port number and is configured with a restriction that only allows access from the 127.0.0.1 IP address. This IP address is actually the local server itself. To allow remote administration, this restriction would have to be modified.
- ***Default SMTP virtual server***—An e-mail component server that responds to port 25 on all IP addresses of the server that have not been assigned to another site
- ***Default NNTP virtual server***—A newsgroup server that responds to port 119 on all configured IP addresses of the server that have not been assigned to another site

As you create new Web or FTP sites, each has its own icon listed in the left details pane of the console. The creation of new Web and FTP sites is discussed in greater detail later in the chapter.

To increase security, it is recommended to stop any IIS site or service that you are not using in your organization. To stop a specific component, right-click the icon and click Stop on the shortcut menu, or you can click the component and click the Stop Item button in the toolbar menu.

The first step in configuring IIS is to understand how the **master properties** affect the overall Web server. The master properties are IIS parameters that can be configured on the server and inherited by all Web and FTP sites hosted on the server. If your IIS server hosts a large number of Web sites, the master properties feature is convenient because you can quickly set various configurations, such as security and performance tuning, on all Web or FTP sites hosted on your server.

If a specific site requires its own individual settings, parameters can be set that apply only at that individual site and override the master properties settings.

To set master properties for your server, right-click your server name in the left scope pane of the console, and then click Properties. The server properties dialog box opens, as shown in Figure 6-6.

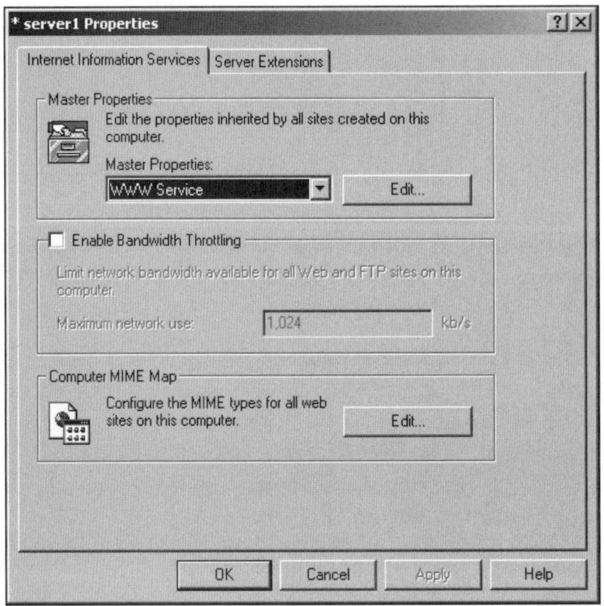

Figure 6-6 Configuring the properties of an IIS server

The server properties dialog box allows you to configure a number of server-specific settings such as bandwidth throttling, and modification of the server extensions. **Bandwidth throttling** allows you to limit the network bandwidth that is available for Web and FTP connections to the server.

On the Internet Information Services tab is the Master Properties section. If you click the drop-down menu under Master Properties, you notice there are two choices: WWW Service and FTP Service. Choose the service that you want to globally modify, and then click the Edit button. Figure 6-7 illustrates the master properties for the WWW Service.

Any property that is not specific to an individual site can be set as a master property. For example, you cannot set the TCP port at the master level, because each Web site likely has different port numbers. However, if you want to limit all Web sites on your server to a specific number of connections, you are able to configure this as a master property and have it be inherited by all sites on the server.

If an individual site has its own configuration settings, and you decide to change the Master Properties, IIS gives you the option of whether or not to apply the changes to the preconfigured site. For example, you have configured the default Web site to only allow 500 connections. You then set the master WWW service to allow 1000 connections. You are prompted on whether or not the new setting should apply to the default Web site, as shown in Figure 6-8.

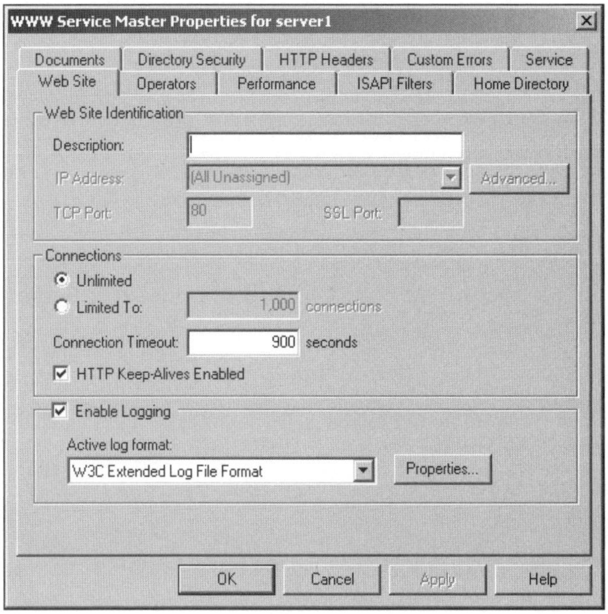

Figure 6-7 Viewing the Master Properties of the WWW service

Any configuration settings that are changed at the site, folder, or file level override the Master Properties and allow you to determine how inheritance takes place for any objects below the level that you are modifying.

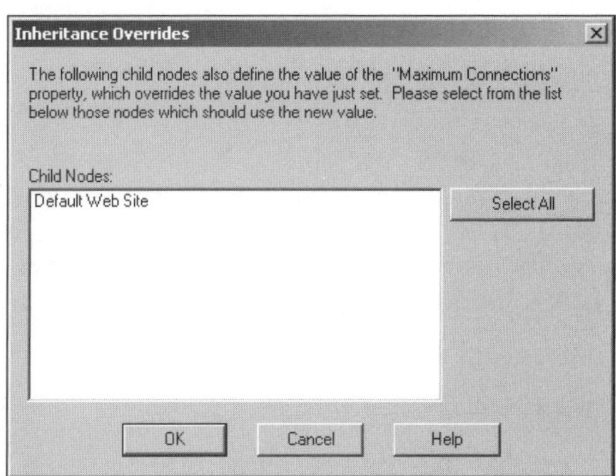

Figure 6-8 Configuring inheritance overrides

CREATING AND CONFIGURING WEB SITE VIRTUAL SERVERS

Internet Information Services has the ability to host a large number of Web site virtual servers on a single server. To make certain that no configuration conflicts take place between sites, the following information issues should be decided before creating a new site:

- Indentify the IP address to which the Web site responds.
- Identify the TCP/IP port to which the Web site responds.
- If you have multiple Web site virtual servers responding to the same IP address, identify the host header name to which your new Web site responds.

Each Web site on your server must have a way of being uniquely identified. There are three ways that you can be sure that each Web site is unique:

- Use a separate IP address to distinguish each Web site.
- Use a single IP address with a specific port number for each Web site. For example, you might have a Web site at 192.168.1.100 with a host name of *www.washex.com* that uses the default port 80, and another Web site using the same IP address, but with the host name *www.bayside.com*, which uses port 8000. The client would then have to append a colon and the port number to the IP or host name in order to access the second site, as in 192.168.1.100:8000 or *www.bayside.com:8000.*
- Use a single IP address with multiple host headers representing each Web site. A **host header** is the fully qualified DNS name that clients type in the browser to access multiple Web sites. For example, if you host two Web sites on your server, you may create *www.bayside.net* and *www.washex.net* as host headers for the single IP address 192.168.1.100.

To enable the use of host names, proper DNS entries would also have to be configured for each of the preceding points. DNS resolves host names to IP addresses. For example, you could type a host name such as *www.bayside.net* instead of having to remember the IP address associated with the Web site. More information on DNS is discussed in Chapter 7, "Administering the Network Infrastructure."

To create a new Web site, follow these steps:

1. Open the Internet Services Manager on the Administrative Tools menu.
2. Right-click your server name, and then click **New**, and click **Web Site**. The Web Site Creation Wizard opens. Click **Next**.
3. In the Web Site Description dialog box, type a short description stating the purpose of the Web site. Click **Next**.

4. In the IP Address and Port Settings dialog box, choose the IP address that responds to client requests. "All Unassigned" means to respond to all IP addresses configured on the server that are not assigned to another site.
5. Type the TCP port number that responds to client requests. HTTP usually uses port 80, but if you already have a Web site using port 80, you need to choose an alternate port. Figure 6-9 illustrates the default settings for the new Web site.

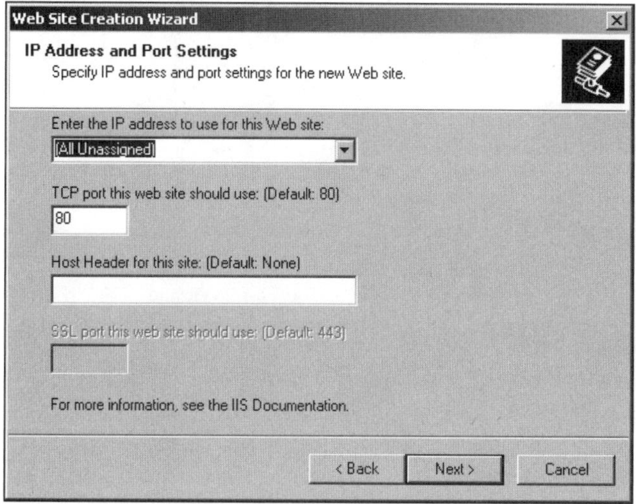

Figure 6-9 Assigning an IP address and port number to a new Web site

6. If you have decided to use host headers to distinguish multiple sites on one IP address, type the host header name in the indicated text box. Click **Next**.
7. In the Web Site Home Directory dialog box, enter the path to the physical location of your Web content. If you want to allow regular client access to this Web site, leave the check box selected next to Allow anonymous access to the Web site. Click **Next**.
8. As shown in Figure 6-10, the final step is to configure access permissions to be used for this site. The permissions configured here start at the root of the site and are inherited by all subfolders below the site. These permissions can be modified after the creation of the site. Click **Next**, and then click **Finish**.

Initially, the new Web site appears in the console, indicating that it is stopped. To start the new Web site, right-click the icon, and click Start on the shortcut menu. If you are using the default settings, be sure to stop the default Web site first, so as not to conflict with the IP address or port settings of the new Web site, as shown in Figure 6-11.

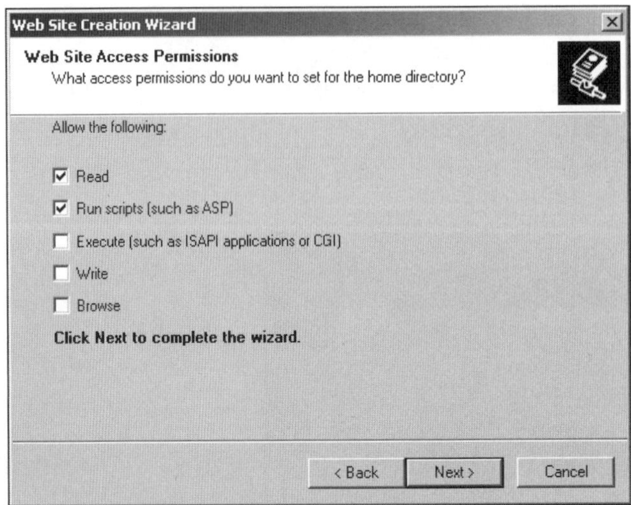

Figure 6-10 Configuring Web site access permissions

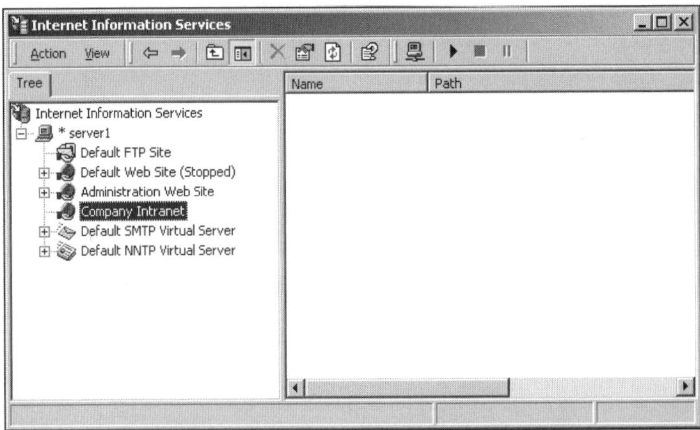

Figure 6-11 Viewing the new Web site

Modifying Web Site Properties

Once your Web site has been created, you can then modify a number of properties to fine-tune some of the parameters of the site. To access the properties of your new site, right-click your Web site, and click Properties. The Web site properties dialog box opens, as shown in Figure 6-12.

You notice that the Properties dialog box is very similar to the master properties dialog box discussed earlier in the chapter. It is important to remember that any parameters configured at the site level override the master properties that have been set at the server level.

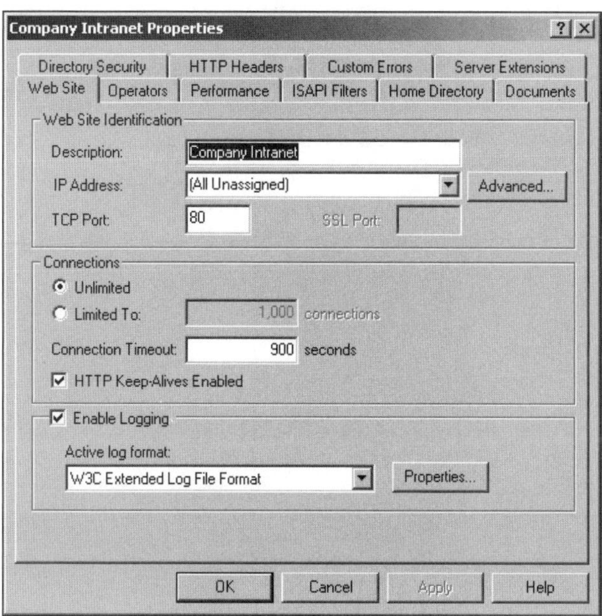

Figure 6-12 Configuring the new Web site properties

Table 6-3 explains each of the tabs on the Properties dialog box.

Table 6-3 Web site properties tabs

Properties Tab	Purpose
Web Site	Used to configure the IP address, TCP port, number of connections and logging; host header names can be configured by clicking the Advanced button on this page
Operators	Used to grant operator privileges to user accounts or groups that permit Web site management; click the Add or Remove button to edit this list
Performance	Used to modify performance-based parameters such as daily hits, bandwidth throttling, and process (CPU) throttling
ISAPI Filters	Used to set up Internet Server Application Programming Interface (ISAPI) filters that respond to events that occur on the server during the processing of an HTTP request
Home Directory	Used to control where the Web site looks for Web content and to set security on that specific folder
Documents	Used to define a default Web page for the Web site and enable a common footer to be placed at the bottom of each Web page

Table 6-3 Web site properties tabs (continued)

Properties Tab	Purpose
Directory Security	Used to configure security for the Web site, such as authentication control, IP address or domain name restrictions, and SSL certificate configurations
HTTP Headers	Used to configure expiration dates on Web site content, custom HTTP headers, and content ratings; content expiration is effective when you want to control the amount of time that your Web site material is to be cached in a client's Web browser cache folder
Custom Errors	Used to customize common Web browser error messages that may be displayed to users who experience an error
Server Extensions	Used to establish security and authoring control for the Web server. For new Web sites, there is nothing on this tab until you configure the server extensions. To configure the server extensions, right-click your Web site, and then click All Tasks, Configure Server Extensions. A wizard appears to guide you through the task.

CREATING VIRTUAL DIRECTORIES

You may have information that is stored on multiple servers throughout your organization. If you want any of this information to be included in your Web site, you can create a **virtual directory** that points specifically to the shared folder that stores the data. Clients would then access the information by appending the alias name of the virtual directory to the Web site host name. An **alias** is used to hide the real directory name, and to simplify the name that would be used to access the information. For example, Bayside Detailing may have a shared folder called Company Customers. For your intranet site, you might create a virtual directory that has an alias name of Customers. Your employees would then type *www.bayside.net/customers* to access the virtual directory. Your employees will not be able to tell that the information has come from a different server and folder.

To create a virtual directory, follow these steps:

1. Right-click your Web site, and then click **New**, **Virtual Directory**. The Virtual Directory Creation Wizard opens. Click **Next**.
2. In the Virtual Directory Alias dialog box, type a name that clients can easily remember. Click **Next**.
3. In the Web Site Content Directory dialog box, enter the physical location of the content that is to become the virtual directory. Click **Next**.
4. The final step is to configure access permissions for the virtual directory. Configure the appropriate permissions, click **Next**, and then click **Finish**. Figure 6-13 illustrates the Customers virtual directory.

You can modify the virtual directory parameters by accessing the Properties dialog box for the virtual directory. To access this dialog box, right-click the virtual directory, and then click Properties. The Properties dialog box appears, as shown in Figure 6-14.

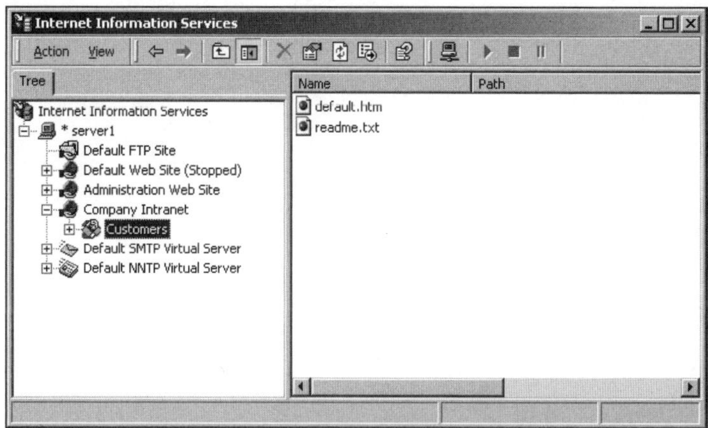

Figure 6-13 Viewing the Customers virtual directory

The Virtual Directory tab allows you to choose the path to the content's location and the security settings that should be used for the link. The rest of the tabs are the same as previously described in Table 6-3.

You can also create a virtual directory by creating a Web share. To do this, right-click a folder, click the Web Sharing tab, and configure the folder so that it can be shared on the Web site.

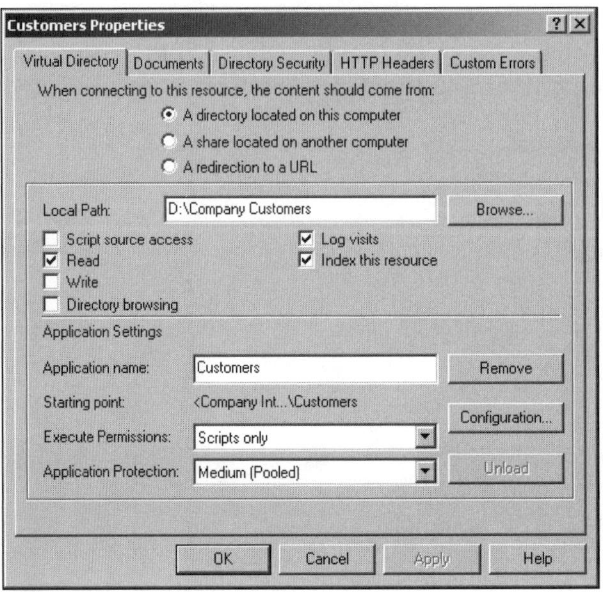

Figure 6-14 Configuring a virtual directory

CONFIGURING AUTHENTICATION FOR WEB SITES

All Windows 2000 servers require that any user who tries to access the server be authenticated to a valid user account. **Authentication** refers to determining whether a user has a valid user account with the proper permissions to access a resource such as a shared folder or Web site. After a user account has been validated, it is given access to all resources to which it has the proper permissions. Windows 2000 Web servers are no exception to this rule. Proper authentication and permissions have to be in place before a client can access a Web site on the server.

IIS provides four levels of authentication that can be used to validate users that are trying to access a Web site stored on the server:

- Anonymous access
- Basic authentication
- Digest authentication
- Integrated Windows authentication

To configure the authentication settings, right-click your Web site, and click Properties. In the Properties dialog box, click the Directory Security tab, and then click Edit in the Anonymous access and authentication control section. The Authentication methods dialog box opens, as shown in Figure 6-15.

Anonymous Access

Anonymous access allows users to access a Web site without having to provide a username and password. When a user attempts to access your Web site, IIS uses the ISUR_*servername* user account to provide the required authentication credentials. To configure an alternative user account for Anonymous access, open the Authentication Methods dialog box, and then click the Edit button next to Account used for anonymous access. The Anonymous User Account settings are illustrated in Figure 6-16.

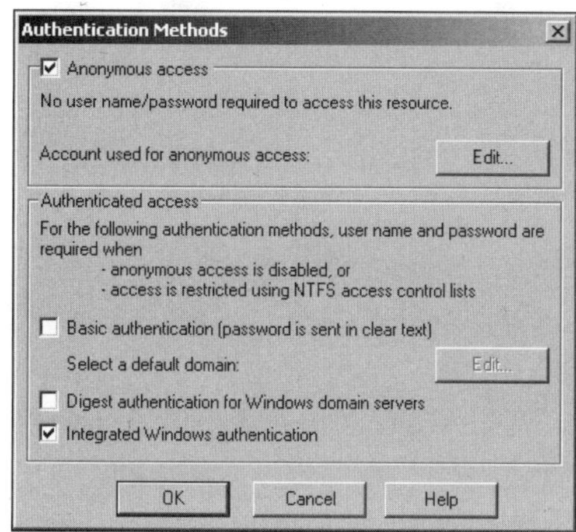

Figure 6-15 Configuring authentication on the Web site

Figure 6-16 Modifying the Anonymous User Account

Basic Authentication

Basic authentication prompts users for a username and password to be able to access the Web resource. The user needs to have a valid Windows 2000 user account to be able to gain access to the Web site. One problem with Basic authentication is that the username and password are transmitted in clear text, and can easily be captured and read by hackers.

Digest Authentication

This is a new authentication method in IIS 5.0. **Digest authentication** works the same way as Basic authentication, except that the username and password are hashed to prevent hackers from obtaining the information. This option requires Windows 2000 servers with Active Directory and Internet Explorer 5.0 or higher.

Integrated Windows Authentication

Integrated Windows authentication does not ask the user for a password, but rather uses the client's currently logged-on credentials to supply a challenge/response to the Web server. This option is primarily used on internal intranets. Once this choice has been enabled, it can only be used if anonymous access is disabled on the Website, and Windows file permissions have been set, requiring users to provide authentication to access the resources.

Note that if multiple authentication methods are configured, the following rules apply:

- If Anonymous authentication and one other method are selected, the other method only applies if Anonymous authentication fails.
- FTP sites cannot use Digest or Integrated Windows authentication.
- Both Digest and Integrated Windows authentication take precedence over Basic authentication.

Configuring Server Certificates and SSL

The Directory Security tab also allows you to configure secure Web communications by implementing **Secure Socket Layer (SSL)** protocol. This protocol is used to encrypt Web traffic between a client and the Web server. Clients can access a secure server using SSL by using URLs that begin with https:// instead of the common http:// prefix. SSL communication is established by default over port 443.

The first step in using SSL on a Web server is to obtain and install a server certificate from a certificate authority such as Verisign, Inc., or you can install certificate services on the server in your organization that is used to dispense certificates. The certificate can then be installed by clicking the Server Certificate button on the Directory Security tab of the Web site, as shown in Figure 6-17.

After obtaining a certificate, SSL can be enabled by clicking the Edit button on the Directory Security tab. Make sure to click the Require secure channel (SSL) check box, as shown in Figure 6-18.

The final step is to configure an SSL port for the Web site. To do this, click the Web site tab, and type the appropriate port number in the SSL text box. Port 443 is the default SSL port number typically used.

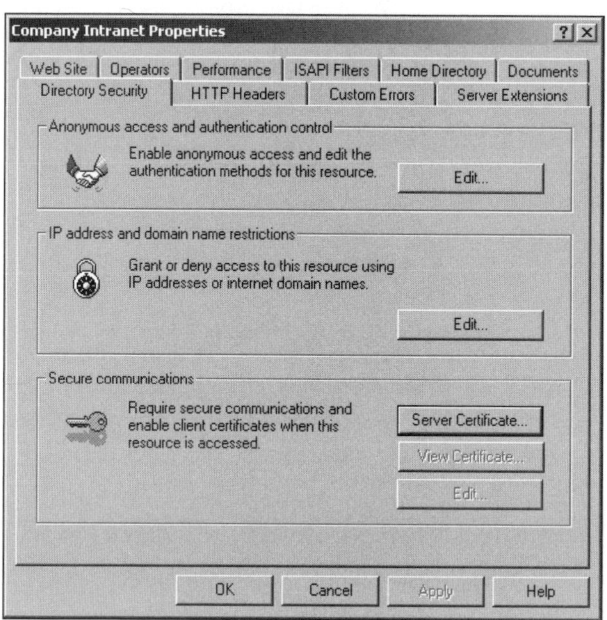

Figure 6-17 Viewing the Directory Security tab of a Web site

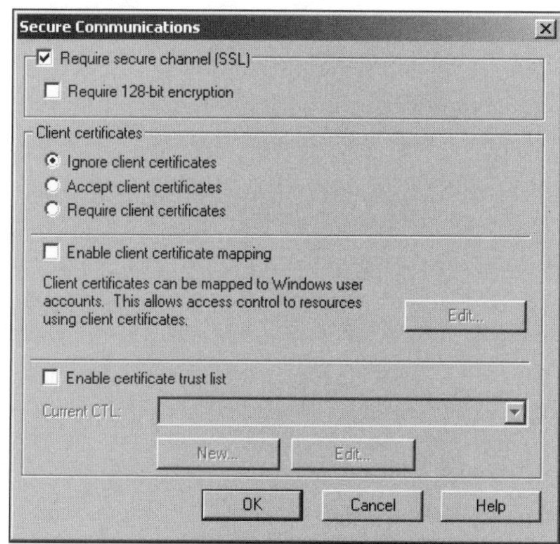

Figure 6-18 Requiring secure channel communication

CONFIGURING FTP VIRTUAL SERVERS

File Transfer Protocol (FTP) is used to transfer files between two computers that are both running TCP/IP. The FTP service included with IIS 5.0 supports FTP and enables users to transfer files between the Internet and a private network. The following section looks at some of the basic concepts behind FTP, how to configure the FTP properties, as well as how to create and manage an FTP site.

File Transfer Protocol

The File Transfer Protocol is an industry-standard, and is used to transfer files between two hosts running TCP/IP. FTP has pretty much been replaced by HTTP for many functions, but is still a useful protocol for file transfers. FTP is a more efficient protocol for file transfers because it uses two ports; ports 20 and 21, whereas HTTP uses only port 80 for transmissions.

FTP uses the **Transmission Control Protocol (TCP)** for file transfers. TCP is a connection-based protocol, which means a session is established between the two hosts before any data is transferred.

Some of the important features of TCP include the following:

- The sending computer waits for an acknowledgment from the receiving computer before sending any more packets. If the sending computer does not receive an acknowledgement, it retransmits the original data.
- All packets at the sending computer are assigned a sequence number so their data can be reorganized at the receiving computer.
- Each packet also contains a checksum for ensuring the integrity of the data.

To use FTP to transfer files between two computers, one machine must be configured as the client and the other configured as the host. The server would be running FTP server software such as IIS 5.0 and the client would be running a Web browser such as Internet Explorer or using the FTP command line utility included with Windows 2000. To access this utility, open a command prompt, and type FTP. You can then type a question mark (?) to view the commands that are available.

There are a number of easy–to-use, graphic-based FTP utilities that can be downloaded from the Internet. Perform a search for FTP using your favorite search engine to find a list of available downloads.

With this configuration, files can be uploaded and downloaded between the client and the server.

Configuring FTP Properties

When you are configuring the properties for FTP, they can be configured at one of three different levels:

- You can configure Master Properties for all FTP sites running on an IIS server, just as you can for a Web site. The settings are inherited by all FTP sites.
- You can configure properties for each individual FTP site by right-clicking the appropriate site in the Internet Information Services console, and clicking Properties, as shown in Figure 6-19.
- You can configure properties at the virtual directory level by expanding the appropriate FTP site, right-clicking the virtual directory, and clicking Properties, as shown in Figure 6-20.

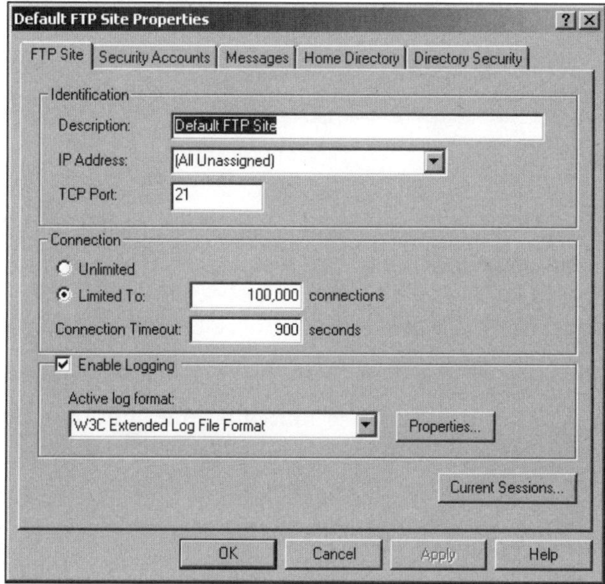

Figure 6-19 The default FTP site properties

Like the WWW service, you can configure multiple FTP sites running on a single IIS 5.0 server. Each site behaves and operates independently and, to a client, it appears as though they are running on separate Web servers. Each site has its own set of property sheets allowing you to customize settings on a site-by-site basis. There are five tabs available from the site properties sheet that are shown on Figure 6-19 and summarized in Table 6-4.

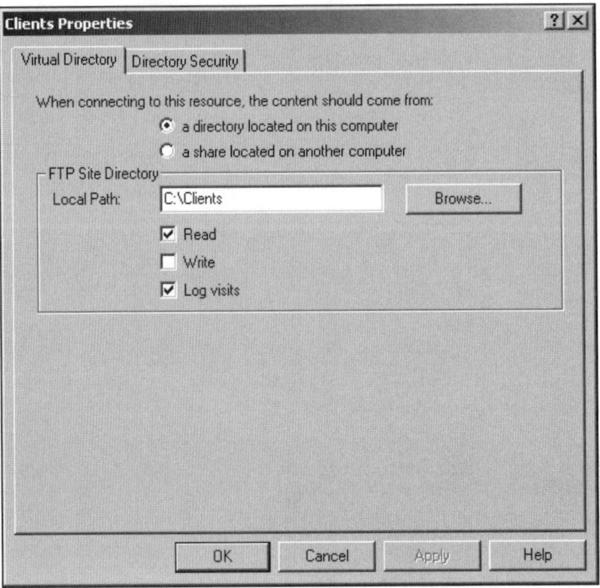

Figure 6-20 Viewing FTP virtual directory properties

Now that you are familiar with the different configuration settings associated with an FTP site, look at how to create a new FTP virtual server using the Internet Services Manager.

Creating an FTP Site Virtual Server

FTP sites can be created using one of three tools: the Internet Services Manager, the administration Web site, or through scripting. The following steps outline how to create an FTP site using the Internet Services Manager.

To create a new FTP site:

1. From within the Internet Services Manager console, right-click your IIS server, click **New**, and click **FTP site**. This launches the FTP Site Creation Wizard. Click **Next**.
2. Enter a name for the new site, and click **Next**.
3. The next dialog box allows you to select an IP address for the new site and a port number. (The default port is 21.) Click **Next**.
4. Specify a location for the FTP home directory. This can be a local directory or network location. Click **Next**.
5. Specify the access permissions for the directory by clicking the Read and/or Write check boxes. (Usually, only Read permission is assigned to the home directory.) Click **Next**.
6. Click **Finish** to complete the wizard.

Table 6-4 FTP site property tabs

Tab	Description
FTP Site	Used to configure site identification, configure connection limits, and enable FTP logging
Security Accounts	The Security Accounts tab allows you to configure which account is used for anonymous access to the FTP site. You can also disable anonymous access requiring all users to have a user account and password to access the site. From this tab you can also grant users site operator privileges, enabling those users to administer the FTP site.
Messages	The Messages property tab allows you to configure both the welcome and exit messages that are displayed to users that connect to and disconnect from the FTP site. The Maximum Connections box lets you type in a message that is displayed to users who attempt to connect to the FTP site when the maximum connection has been met.
Home Directory	The home directory is where the files published through your FTP site are stored. Using this tab, you can change the default home directory location to another directory on the server or to a directory located on another server. You can also set the type of access allowed to the folder (read and/or write). The directory style listing lets you select the folder style listing that is displayed to FTP users.
Directory Security	The Directory Security tab allows you to grant or deny access to the FTP site based on IP addresses, as shown in Figure 6-21. You can grant access to all computers except those listed in the exception box, or you can deny access to all computers except the ones listed. Access can be configured based on individual IP addresses, network addresses, or fully qualified domain names.

6

An FTP site may contain files that are located in another directory other than the root or on another server. To include those files in the FTP site, you must create a virtual directory. Similar to a Web site virtual directory, an FTP virtual directory appears to the clients as if it were located in the home directory, but is physically located elsewhere.

To create an FTP virtual directory:

1. Right-click the FTP site for which you want to create a virtual directory, click **New**, and click **Virtual Directory**. This launches the Virtual Directory Creation Wizard. Click **Next**.
2. Enter an alias name for the virtual directory. Click **Next**.
3. Enter the physical path to the data being published in the directory. Click **Next**.
4. Assign permissions to the virtual directory by clicking the Read and/or Write check boxes. Click **Next**.
5. Click **Finish**.

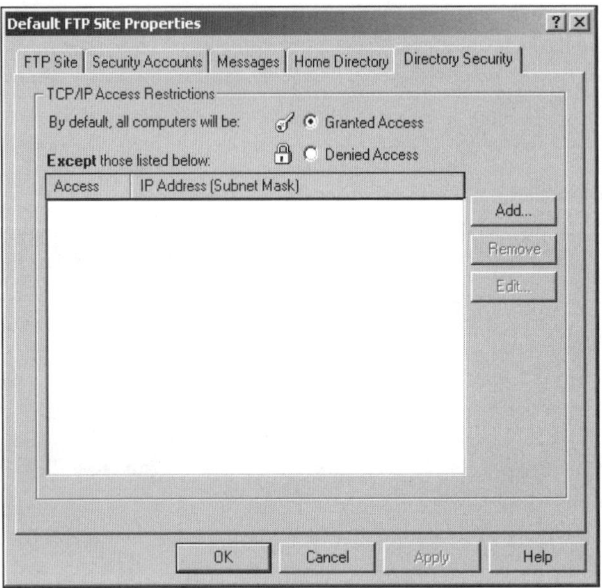

Figure 6-21 Viewing TCP/IP access restrictions

The new virtual directory is now listed under the FTP site. To view the contents of the virtual directory, right-click and then click either the Open or Explore options.

Now that you are familiar with creating and configuring Web sites and FTP sites, look at how to update and maintain security for your IIS server.

Updating and Maintaining Security for an IIS Server

Whenever information is published to users on the Internet, the topic of security arises. You want to be able to provide users access to certain information on your Web servers while restricting access to all other information and the rest of the network. There are several ways an administrator can secure access to information on a Web server. These alternatives are discussed in the following section.

As with any other type of server, once it is installed and configured, an IIS server still needs to be maintained and updated. This usually includes performing regular backups, stopping and starting IIS-related services, and applying updates. These topics are discussed in the next few sections.

Resource Permissions

One of the first ways to control access to information is to set permissions specifying the types of access users are granted. When securing Web content, there are two types of permissions that you can apply to secure resources: NTFS permissions and IIS permissions. To provide the most security for your Web content, you should take advantage of both Windows 2000 security and IIS security.

NTFS Permissions

Access to resources stored on an NTFS volume can be controlled through the use of NTFS permissions. NTFS permissions should be applied to any Web pages and virtual directories published to your Web server.

The first thing you should do when configuring NTFS permissions is remove the default permission that assigns the Everyone group Full Control access. The Authenticated Users group should then be assigned Read permission to any directories. Permissions can then be further broadened or restricted for individual users and groups, based on their access requirements.

One of the differences between NTFS permissions and IIS permissions is that different NTFS permissions can be assigned to users and groups whereas IIS permissions are global.

IIS Permissions

Combining NTFS permissions and IIS permissions provides the most security for your Web content. IIS permissions can be configured for any of the following:

- Web sites and FTP virtual servers
- virtual directories
- physical directories
- files

When restricting access to virtual directories, physical directories, and files, there are two types of permissions that can be set: the Read permission and/or Write permission. The Read permission allows users to view the contents and the Write permission allows users to add content to virtual directories and folders and change the content of a file.

If the directory contains any scripts or executables, you can also configure the Execute permission by choosing None, Scripts, or Scripts and Executables.

When combining NTFS permissions and IIS permissions, the most restrictive permission is the effective permission.

One method that can be used to quickly configure NTFS and IIS permissions is to use the Permissions Wizard. To access the Permissions Wizard, right-click any Web or FTP site, click All Tasks, and then click Permissions Wizard. You are asked how you want to configure folder and file permissions (NTFS) and whether you would like to inherit the IIS permissions from a parent folder or create new security settings from a preconfigured scenario. Hands-on Project 6-6 illustrates the detailed steps in configuring the Permissions Wizard.

IP Address and Domain Name Security

Web content can be secured by granting or denying access to users based on their IP address or domain name. Access can be granted or denied to an individual IP address or to a particular address range. To configure IP address and domain name security for a virtual directory or physical directory, click the component from within the Internet Information Services console, click Properties, click the Directory Security tab, and click Edit under the IP Address and Domain Name Restrictions. To apply IP address and domain name security to a file, right-click the file, choose Properties, click the File Security tab, and click Edit under the IP Address and Domain Name Restrictions.

Here is an example of how an administrator might use IP address and domain name security. Suppose your company provides Web content to another business such as a business partner or a client. The administrator can deny access to all IP addresses except those on the business partner's or client's network.

Starting and Stopping Services

At some point, for administrative purposes, you may need to stop and restart services related to IIS. In previous versions of IIS, stopping and restarting services meant stopping and restarting each individual service, such as the FTP service and the WWW service. IIS 5.0 now makes it simpler to stop and restart your Web services. All of the IIS services can now be stopped and restarted through the Internet Information Services console.

To stop or restart IIS services:

1. From within the IIS console, right-click the IIS server on which you wish to stop the services.
2. Click the **Restart IIS** option. A dialog box appears from which you can stop, start, and restart the services or reboot the server, as shown in Figure 6-22.

There may be instances where you only need to stop and restart an individual Web site or FTP site. This can be done by selecting the site from within the IIS console, and choosing the Stop or Start button in the toolbar or by right-clicking the component and clicking Stop or Start on the shortcut menu.

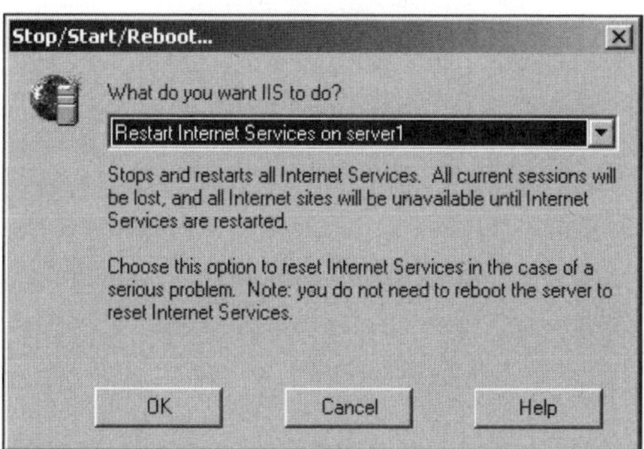

Figure 6-22 Restarting the IIS services

Backing Up the IIS Configuration

It is generally a good idea to periodically back up the configuration settings of your IIS Server. IIS 5.0 stores its configuration settings in a database referred to as the **IIS metabase** that can be backed up separately. This is useful in the event that you have to restore your IIS Server settings.

The default location for backups is the systemroot%\system32\Inetsrv\Metaback directory. The metabase can be backed up using one of four methods:

- Use the Backup utility in the IIS console to back up the database.
- The contents of the backup directory can be copied to another folder to provide redundancy after an initial backup has been performed.
- Use the metabase editor tool to export the contents of the database to a text file.
- Use the scripting tool provided with the IIS software development kit.

The easiest way to back up the metabase is to use the Internet Service Manager. To back up the metabase:

1. From within the IIS console, right-click your IIS Server, and click **Backup/Restore Configuration**.
2. Click **Create backup** in the Configuration/Restore dialog box.
3. Type a name for the backup in the Configuration Backup dialog box.

Verify that the backup was successful by checking for the file using Windows Explorer. The configuration file can then be backed up using your regular server backups.

Updating IIS 5.0

As with most software that you install on your server, updates are released to fix any known bugs and security issues that are reported. The two common types of updates that you apply to your IIS Server are service packs and hot fixes. Hot fixes are usually released to fix a certain component and are usually released between service packs. They are small software fixes designed to solve a known security issue. Service packs are usually an accumulation of software patches and fixes that fix bugs that have been discovered. Service packs are more significant upgrades than hot fixes.

Before you apply any patch, hot fix, or service pack, make sure you perform a full backup of your server before proceeding.

Security is one of the most important aspects of running a Web server. Often hot fixes and patches are released to fix a known security issue. Therefore it's crucial that network administrators know which hot fixes have been applied to a Web server and, more importantly, which hot fixes haven't been applied. One of the tools you can use to determine what hot fixes need to be installed on a server is the Network Hotfix Checking tool (HFNetChk). You can use this tool to determine which IIS hot fixes are currently installed on your Web server. Information about the HFNetChk tool is available at the following URL: *http://www.microsoft.com/technet/itsolutions/security/tools/hfnetchk.asp*

Another interesting utility is the IIS lockdown tool. The IIS lockdown tool is a wizard-based utility that provides security configuration templates based upon the major IIS-dependant Microsoft products like Microsoft Exchange. The wizard turns off unnecessary features, removes unnecessary virtual directories, and sets secure file and IIS permissions based upon the security best practices for the Microsoft product being locked down. The utility can be downloaded by going to *http://www.microsoft.com/security,* and then clicking the Tools & Checklists link.

Troubleshooting Web Client Connectivity Problems

A major part of any administrator's job is troubleshooting network problems. One of the most common problems that may occur when running an IIS server is clients not being able to access one of the sites. The following section looks at some of the common client connectivity problems that can occur and how you can troubleshoot the different problems.

Client connectivity problems usually occur because of access or authentication problems.

Client Access Problems

If users are unable to gain access to an IIS Server, there are several configuration settings that you can verify to troubleshoot the problem.

- Verify the TCP/IP configuration settings that have been configured on the client. Use the IPCONFIG command on Windows NT, 2000, or XP machines to verify the correct IP settings have been assigned. WINIPCFG can be used to verify IP settings on Windows 9x machines. Use the PING command to verify connectivity with remote computers.
- Check the proxy settings that have been configured through the client's Web browser. To be able to access intranet Web sites, be sure to click **Bypass proxy server for local addresses** in the proxy server configuration settings of your Web browser.
- Check for obvious problems such as whether the proxy server is available and online and whether the client is connected to the network.

If users complain that they are unable to gain access to a Web site or FTP site configured on an IIS server, check any one of the following:

- Check the permissions assigned to the site. Make sure that the Users group has been assigned the NTFS Read permission to the directory. Make sure the IIS Read permission has been assigned to the site's home directory.
- Check to see which authentication method has been configured for the site.
- Check to see what IP address and domain name restrictions have been applied to the site.
- If there is a connection limit set for the site, make sure this limit has not been exceeded.
- If the service has been configured to use a port other than the default, make sure the client is specifying the correct port number.
- If you have not enabled anonymous access, make sure the client has a valid user account.
- Client computers may contain invalid cached DNS information about a specific Internet location. From the command prompt, type **ipconfig /flushdns** to clear the DNS cache.

Chapter Summary

- Internet Information Services includes four main components that include the World Wide Web (HTTP) services, File Transfer Protocol (FTP) services, Network News Transfer Protocol (NNTP) services, and Simple Mail Transfer Protocol (SMTP) services.

- The first step to configuring IIS is to understand how the master properties affect the overall Web server. The master properties are IIS parameters that can be configured on the server and inherited by all Web and FTP sites hosted on the server. If an individual site has its own configuration settings and you decide to change the Master Properties, IIS gives you the option of whether or not to apply the changes to the preconfigured site.
- Multiple Web sites can be distinguished on a single Web server by either configuring individual IP addresses for each site, configuring individual port numbers for each site, or by configuring a host header for each site.
- A virtual directory can be used to include information that may be stored on a different server from the one on which the Web site home directory is located.
- By default, anonymous access is used to allow public access to a Web site.
- Four main authentication methods used in IIS are Anonymous, Basic, Digest, and Integrated Windows authentication.
- Regular IIS maintenance tasks include backing up the IIS configuration, starting or stopping services, and installing of hot fixes or service packs.
- The HFNetChk tool can be used to determine which IIS hot fixes are currently installed on your Web server.

Key Terms

administration Web site — A Web site that is configured to allow administrators to manage the Web server from a remote location using a Web browser. During installation, this site is assigned a random port number and is configured with a restriction that only allows access from the 127.0.0.1 IP address. This IP address is actually the local server itself. To allow remote administration, this restriction would have to be modified.

alias — A name used to hide the real name of a directory and to simplify the directory name that would be used to access the information.

anonymous access — Allows users to access a Web site without having to provide a username and password.

authentication — Refers to determining whether a user has a valid user account with the proper permissions to access a resource such as a shared folder or Web site.

bandwidth throttling — Allows you to limit the network bandwidth that is available for Web and FTP connections to the server.

Basic authentication — Prompts users for a username and password to be able to access the Web resource. The username and password are then transmitted as clear text.

Digest authentication — Prompts users for a username and password to be able to access the Web resource. The username and password are hashed to prevent hackers from obtaining the information.

default FTP site — An FTP server that responds to TCP/IP port 21 on all configured IP addresses of the server that are not assigned to another site.

default NNTP virtual server — A newsgroup server that responds to port 119 on all configured IP addresses of the server that have not been assigned to another site.

default SMTP virtual server — An e-mail component server that responds to port 25 on all IP addresses of the server that have not been assigned to another site.

default Web site — A Web site configured with FrontPage extensions that responds to TCP/IP port 80 on all unassigned IP addresses of the server. This Web site is initially empty and may be used to create a custom Web site for your organization.

File Transfer Protocol (FTP) — Used to transfer files between two computers that are both running TCP/IP.

host header — The fully qualified DNS name that is used to access a Web site on an IIS Server.

Integrated Windows authentication — Does not ask the user for a password, but rather uses the clients currently logged-on credentials to supply a challenge/response to the Web server.

Internet Information Services (IIS) — A Windows 2000 component that provides Web-related services to an organization.

Internet Services Manager — The administrative tool used to manage the Internet Information Services server components.

master properties — IIS parameters that are configured on the server and inherited by all Web and FTP sites hosted on the server.

metabase — IIS 5.0 stores its configuration settings in a database referred to as the IIS metabase.

Secure Socket Layer (SSL) — This protocol is used to encrypt Web traffic between a client and the Web server.

Transmission Control Protocol (TCP) — A connection-based protocol, which means a session is established between the two hosts before any data is transferred.

virtual directory — A mapping to a physical directory containing content to be included on a Web site.

Review Questions

1. You are planning to install Exchange Server 2000 in your organization. Which IIS service is used in conjunction with Exchange to enable the sending of e-mail messages?
   a. NNTP
   b. SMTP
   c. HTTP
   d. FTP
2. IIS is automatically installed during a standard installation of Windows 2000. True or False?

3. Which of the following are the two user accounts automatically created during an installation of IIS? (Choose two.)
   a. IWAM_*servername*
   b. Anonymous_*user*
   c. WEBUser_*servername*
   d. ISUSR_*servername*
4. Master properties can be configured to set the IP address and TCP port for all sites located on the server. True or False?
5. Individual site properties override master properties by default. True or False?
6. You are a network administrator responsible for maintaining your company's Web servers. There have recently been several hot fixes released for IIS 5.0. What tool can you use to determine the hot fixes currently installed on your Web servers?
   a. NHNetChk utility
   b. Windows update
   c. HFNetChk utility
   d. System Information
7. A client is reporting that he is unable to connect to your server running IIS. Which of the following should you check first to troubleshoot the problem?
   a. permissions assigned to the Web and FTP sites
   b. TCP/IP parameters assigned to the client
   c. any IP address and domain name restrictions applied
   d. whether anonymous access has been disabled
8. Which of the following IIS permissions can be assigned to a virtual directory? (Choose all that apply.)
   a. Full Control
   b. Read
   c. Write
   d. Delete
9. You have configured a new FTP site on your Web server. The site has been configured to only allow Read access. You have also enabled anonymous access using the IUSR_Server1 account. In addition, you also notice that the following NTFS permissions are in place.

   Users: Full Control

   IUSR_Server1: Change

   Guests: Change

What type of permission do users have to your new FTP site?

a. Full Control

b. Change

c. Read

d. No Access

10. You are the administrator of your company's Web server. You changed the FTP port from 21 to 1223. Clients report that they are not able to access the FTP server. What is most likely causing the problem?

a. You have configured clients with incorrect permissions.

b. There are IP address restrictions in place.

c. Clients are connecting to the default port.

d. There are domain name restrictions in place.

11. Directory security can be configured using which of the following? (Choose all that apply.)

a. IP address

b. Network address

c. Username

d. Domain name

12. You are configuring directory security for your FTP site. You select the granted access option and add the following IP network group address: 129.10.0.0. You also add the following single computer IP address: 135.15.121.10. Which of the following statements are true?

a. All computers on the 129.10.0.0 network are granted access to your FTP site.

b. The IP address 135.15.121.10 is not granted access to your FTP site.

c. All computers on the 129.10.0.0 network are granted access to your FTP site.

d. The IP address 135.15.121.10 is granted access to your FTP site.

13. What protocol does FTP use to establish a session?

a. TCP

b. HTTP

c. UDP

d. POP3

14. When you are creating a virtual directory, which of the following are possible options for the location of the directory? (Choose all that apply.)

a. a directory other than the home directory

b. a URL

c. a directory in a remote computer

d. none of the above

15. Which of the following options can be used to back up the configuration settings of your IIS Server? (Choose all that apply.)
    a. Use the backup program included with Windows.
    b. Use a scripting tool.
    c. Use the back up program within the IIS console.
    d. Use third-party backup software.
16. Which port number does HTTP use?
    a. 21
    b. 80
    c. 443
    d. 119
17. You want to allow one of your users to administer his department's Web site. What is the best way to give the user the necessary privileges to do this?
    a. Grant the user site operator privileges in the IIS console.
    b. Add the user to the Administrators group.
    c. Add the user to the Server Operators group.
    d. Grant the user the administer Web services right.
18. You are configuring authentication for your IIS server. You want all users to provide their Windows 2000 user name and password before gaining access to the Web resources. You also do not want the user names and passwords sent in clear text. Which authentication method should you configure?
    a. Anonymous authentication
    b. Basic authentication
    c. Digest authentication
    d. Integrated Windows authentication
19. You want to configure a maximum connection limit for all sites configured on your Web server. At what level should you make the configuration change?
    a. master
    b. site
    c. folder
    d. file
20. All Web content published through your IIS server must be stored locally. True or False?

HANDS-ON PROJECTS

Project 6-1

In this Hands-on Project, you verify that the required Internet Information Services components have been installed:

1. Log on to your computer with the administrator account.
2. Click **Start**, point to **Settings**, and click **Control Panel**.
3. Double-click **Add/Remove Programs**.
4. Click **Add/Remove Windows Components**.
5. In the Windows Components Wizard, scroll down, and click **Internet Information Services (IIS)**. Click **Details**.
6. Verify that all of the components are selected except for the Visual InterDev RAD Remote Deployment Support, and then click **OK**.
7. In the Windows Components Wizard dialog box, click **Next**.
8. Click **Next** at any other steps that appear in the wizard, and then click **Finish**.
9. Close all windows.
10. To verify that IIS has been installed, click **Start**, click **Run**, and then type **http://localhost** in the Open: text box. Click **OK**. The IIS 5.0 Documentation should appear in the Internet Explorer Web browser.
11. Close all windows

Project 6-2

In this Hands-on Project, you create a virtual directory within the default Web site.

1. Create a new folder on drive C: called **OnlineDocs**.
2. Click **Start**, point to **Programs**, point to **Administrative Tools**, and then click **Internet Services Manager**.
3. Double-click your server name to expand all nodes on the Web server.
4. Right-click the **Default Web Site**, click **New**, and then click **Virtual Directory**. Click **Next** at the Welcome Screen.
5. In the Virtual Directory Alias dialog box, type **Docs**, and then click **Next**.
6. In the Web Site Content Directory dialog box, type the path to the OnlineDocs folder, (e.g., C:\OnlineDocs). Click **Next**.
7. In the Access Permissions dialog box, make sure that the **Read**, **Run scripts**, and **Browse** options are checked. Click **Next**, and then click **Finish**.
8. To verify that the virtual folder is accessible, click **Start**, click **Run**, and then type **http://localhost/docs** in the Open: text box. Click **OK**.

9. The localhost/docs/ Web folder opens.
10. Close all windows.

Project 6-3

In this Hands-on Project, you configure master properties for the Web server and stop all unnecessary components.

1. Click **Start**, point to **Programs**, point to **Administrative Tools**, and then click **Internet Services Manager**.
2. Right-click your server name, and then click **Properties**.
3. In the Master Properties drop down list, click **WWW Service**, and then click **Edit**.
4. In the Connections section, click the **Limited To** option button, and then configure the limit to **500** connections. Click **OK** twice to return to the console.
5. Double-click your server name to expand the IIS components.
6. Right-click **Default SMTP Virtual Server**, and then click **Stop**.
7. Right-click **Default NNTP Virtual Server**, and then click **Stop**.
8. Close all windows.

Project 6-4

In this Hands-on Project, you configure the default FTP site to allow anonymous access.

1. Click **Start**, point to **Programs**, point to **Administrative Tools**, and then click **Internet Services Manager**.
2. Double-click your server name to expand all nodes on the Web server.
3. Right-click the **Default FTP Site**, and then click **Properties**.
4. Click the **Security Accounts** tab, and verify that the **Allow Anonymous Connections** check box is selected.
5. Click the **Messages** tab.
6. In the Welcome Text box, type **Welcome to my FTP Server.**
7. In the Exit Text box, type **Thank you for visiting my FTP Server.** Click **OK**.
8. To test the FTP site, click **Start**, click **Run**, and then type **ftp <*servername*>**, where <*servername*> is the name of your server.
9. Type **anonymous** for the user, and then press **Enter** at the password prompt. Notice the welcome message.
10. Type **Bye**, and then close all windows.
11. At the FTP prompt, type **?** to view the various FTP commands available.

Project 6-5

In this Hands-on Project you back up the IIS configuration, restore the IIS configuration, and then restart the IIS services.

1. Click **Start**, point to **Programs**, point to **Administrative Tools**, and then click **Internet Services Manager**.
2. Double-click your server name to expand all nodes on the Web server.
3. Right-click your server name, and then click **Backup/Restore Configuration**.
4. Click the **Create backup** button.
5. In the Configuration backup name text box, type ***<current date>* backup**, where *<current date>* is today's date. Click **OK**, and then click **Close**.
6. Click the plus sign next to the Default Web Site, and delete the Docs and IISSamples virtual directories.
7. Right-click your server name, and then click **Backup/Restore Configuration**.
8. Click the ***<current date>*** backup entry, and then click the **Restore** button. Click **Yes** at the prompt.
9. After a few minutes, click **OK** at the Operation Completed Successfully message.
10. Close the Configuration Backup/Restore Window.
11. Expand the **Default Web Site**, and verify that the IISSamples and Docs virtual directories are restored.
12. Right-click your server name, and click **Restart IIS**.
13. In the Stop/Start/Reboot dialog box, click the drop-down menu to view the choices available.
14. Click **Restart Internet Services** on *<servername>*, and then click **OK**.
15. Close all windows.

Project 6-6

In this Hands-on Project, you use the permissions wizard to configure security on the default Web site.

1. Click **Start**, point to **Programs**, point to **Administrative Tools**, and then click **Internet Services Manager**.
2. Double-click your server name to expand all nodes on the Web server.
3. Right-click the **Default Web Site**, click **All Tasks**, and then click the **Permissions Wizard**. Click **Next** at the Welcome screen.
4. In the Security Settings dialog box, click **Select new security settings from a template**. Click **Next**.
5. In the Site Scenario dialog box, click **Public Web Site**, and then click **Next**.

6

6. In the Windows Directory and File Permissions dialog box, click **Replace all directory and file permissions (recommended)**, and then click **Next**.
7. Read the final summary screen, and take note of the Authentication methods, Access Permissions, and IP Address Restrictions. Click **Next**, and then click **Finish**.
8. Close all windows.

CASE PROJECTS

Case Project 6-1

Bayside is planning to install a Web server on their corporate network. In a planning session, managers and representatives from each department raise several concerns. You have been asked to address these concerns in the next planning session.

1. Managers are unsure of the different authentication methods available. List the different methods of authentication and the differences between them.
2. Each department will have their own Web site. There will be one user from each department responsible for administering their department's site. How can you allow a user privileges to administer one site without giving them privileges to another?
3. If the Web server will host multiple sites, what methods can be used to uniquely identify each one?

Case Project 6-2

You are configuring a new FTP site for Bayside's Web server. The managers would prefer the information to be physically stored on another server. The site will be used to provide access to some of your company's Web content to network users and an external customer. Your managers are concerned about security because no other external clients or business partners should be allowed to access this content. You have been asked to create a document addressing some of the issues and concerns

1. Outline each of the steps in creating and configuring the new FTP site.
2. Security is a major issue and has been emphasized by your managers. Include in your document the different options you will use to secure the new FTP site so that only the appropriate users have access.
3. Include in your document how NTFS and IIS permissions can be used together to provide the most security.
4. Your managers are also concerned with the security of IIS 5.0 and want to make sure that the latest service packs and hot fixes are always applied. How will you track what hot fixes and patches need to be installed on your server?

CHAPTER

7

ADMINISTERING THE NETWORK INFRASTRUCTURE

After reading this chapter and completing the exercises, you will be able to:

- Understand basic concepts about TCP/IP
- Configure TCP/IP on Windows 2000 Servers and workstations
- Troubleshoot TCP/IP and network connectivity using various utilities
- Administer DHCP in Windows 2000
- Administer the DNS in Windows 2000
- Troubleshoot name resolution problems in Windows 2000

Administering Windows 2000 includes the implementation and management of a variety of networking protocols and services. Windows 2000 has been designed so that many of its main features, such as Active Directory, require the use of TCP/IP. This is a vital component that all network administrators need to understand and master to successfully manage and troubleshoot a Windows 2000 network environment. The first few sections of this chapter introduce you to TCP/IP concepts, as well as the methods used to configure TCP/IP on Windows 2000 servers and workstations. Utilities used to validate and troubleshoot local computer configurations and network connectivity are also discussed.

TCP/IP works with related services such as DHCP and DNS. Knowledge of DHCP and its new integration features with DNS greatly increases the ease of network TCP/IP configuration and management. DNS is another requirement of Active Directory, which makes it essential for administrators to master this service. This chapter discusses the concepts and procedures involved in configuring, managing, and troubleshooting DHCP and DNS within the network.

The final sections of this chapter discuss methods and best practices in troubleshooting name resolution problems within the local network or the Internet.

UNDERSTANDING TCP/IP

Transmission Control Protocol/Internet Protocol (TCP/IP) consists of a suite of protocols and utilities that are used for network communication and troubleshooting on local networks and the Internet. TCP/IP has become one of the most popular network protocols in use. One of the main reasons for this is that TCP/IP is the protocol used for Internet communication. As the Internet becomes essential for many businesses to interact with customers, it makes sense to implement TCP/IP as the primary network protocol. Another advantage of using TCP/IP is that it is an open standard, vendor-independent protocol. It can be used to provide network communication between computers running different operating systems throughout the organization.

Windows 2000 Active Directory's dependence on TCP/IP requires that you understand the various components included with TCP/IP and their function. The following topics are reviewed in later sections to assist you in understanding the fundamentals of TCP/IP.

- TCP/IP architecture
- TCP/IP protocol stack
- TCP/IP installation

TCP/IP Architecture

TCP/IP maps to a four-layer model described in Table 7-1.

Table 7-1 The four layers of TCP/IP

Layer	Description
Application	Identifies which applications use TCP/IP and how they interact with the lower-level protocols
Transport	Protocols at this layer provide communication sessions between hosts
Internet	Responsible for the addressing of packets and determining the routing of packets on the network
Network Interface	Determines how data is transmitted on the physical medium

The TCP/IP Protocol Stack

TCP/IP is a group of protocols, each operating at one of the four layers described in Table 7-1, and each providing a specific function. The following protocols are discussed in this section:

- Transmission Control Protocol
- User Datagram Protocol

- Address Resolution Protocol
- Internet Control Message Protocol
- Internet Group Management Protocol
- Internet Protocol

Transmission Control Protocol

The **Transmission Control Protocol (TCP)** operates at the transport layer and is responsible for the reliable transmission of data on a TCP/IP network. TCP is a connection-based protocol, which means all packets sent using TCP are verified and delivered in the correct order. TCP is also responsible for breaking up large blocks of data into packets and then reassembling those packets when they arrive at the destination. The packets are assigned sequence numbers that tell the destination host how to reassemble them. TCP also provides reliable delivery of packets using acknowledgements.

User Datagram Protocol

The **User Datagram Protocol (UDP)** is another protocol that functions at the transport layer. Unlike TCP, UDP is a connectionless protocol and provides no guarantee of packet delivery. No acknowledgements, sequencing, or session establishment occurs between hosts using UDP.

Address Resolution Protocol

The **Address Resolution Protocol (ARP)** works at the Internet layer and is responsible for mapping IP addresses to hardware media access control (MAC) addresses. Each network interface card has a hard-coded address called a MAC address. Before two computers can communicate, they must know the MAC address of each other's network card.

Every Windows 2000 computer has an ARP cache that stores recent mappings between IP addresses and MAC addresses, as well as any static entries that have been configured. The entries in the cache can be viewed using the arp –a command at the command prompt, as shown in Figure 7-1.

The ARP cache can contain both dynamic and static entries. The dynamic entries are stored in the ARP cache for two minutes, unless the entry is used during those two minutes. If the entry is used within two minutes, then the entry is stored for 10 minutes. The static entries stay in the ARP cache until the computer is restarted or until the entry is removed using the arp –d command.

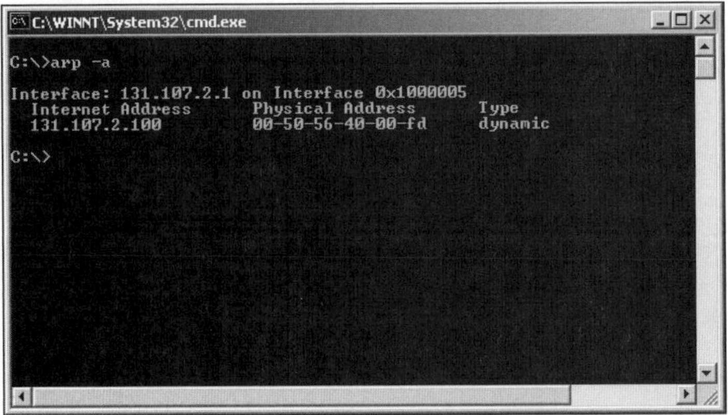

Figure 7-1 Viewing the results of the arp -a command

Internet Control Message Protocol

The **Internet Control Message Protocol (ICMP)** operates at the network layer and is used between two hosts to exchange status and error information. For example, the **ping** command uses ICMP to test for connectivity between hosts. Both the **pathping** and the **tracert** commands also use ICMP packets to check for network connectivity. If the two hosts can communicate, you receive a reply; if there is a problem with connectivity between the hosts, you receive a destination host unreachable message. ICMP is also used to slow down the transmission of data from one host to another if the receiving host cannot accept the data at the rate the sending host is transmitting it.

Internet Group Management Protocol

The **Internet Group Management Protocol (IGMP)** operates at the network layer and is used to manage network and host information when multicasting is used. It informs routers and multicast devices of the multicast group membership.

Internet Protocol

Internet Protocol (IP) is the Internet layer protocol responsible for the addressing and routing of packets so that they are delivered to the correct host on the local network or across routers to a host on another subnet. IP is a connectionless protocol, which means that it does not guarantee the delivery of the packets. Ensuring that the packets arrive is the responsibility of the higher-level protocols, such as TCP.

Now that you are familiar with the protocols that make up the TCP/IP protocol suite, you need to know how to install and configure TCP/IP.

Installing TCP/IP

If your network adapter is automatically detected during the installation of Windows 2000, TCP/IP is the default protocol that is installed. If TCP/IP is not installed during setup, it can be added afterwards.

To install TCP/IP in Windows 2000 you can right-click My Network Places, and click Properties. The Network and Dial-Up Connections dialog box opens. You can then right-click the adapter in which you want to configure TCP/IP, and click Properties. The final step is to click the Install button, and add the Internet Protocol (TCP/IP) selection.

Once TCP/IP has been installed, you can either manually configure the addressing parameters or you can implement dynamic addressing. Configuring TCP/IP using both methods is discussed in the next section.

Configuring TCP/IP on Windows 2000 Computers

All hosts on a TCP/IP network require, at a minimum, an **IP address** and a **subnet mask**. Depending on the complexity of the network, other IP parameters may also need to be assigned, such as a **default gateway** or the IP addresses of DNS name servers.

See Table 7-2 for a description of each of these options.

You have two options when determining how to configure IP addresses on workstations and servers. You can configure each one manually with a static IP address, meaning an IP address that is permanently assigned to the computer until it is manually changed, or you can configure the computers to obtain an IP address automatically. This requires a DHCP server on the network, which is discussed later in the chapter.

Configuring Static IP Addresses

Depending on the size of your network, from an administrative perspective it may be more cost effective or easier to assign IP addresses manually. Even in an environment that does use DHCP for automatic IP address assignment, there may be servers and workstations that require static IP addresses. An example of this would be your DHCP server. The DHCP server requires a static IP address to ensure that clients can find the correct server during lease renewals. This means you have to manually configure the IP address settings.

By default, Windows 2000 is configured to obtain an IP address automatically, but you can still manually assign one by modifying the Internet Protocol (TCP/IP) properties.

For each network card configured to use TCP/IP, you need to configure an IP address and a subnet mask. This can be done by double-clicking the Network and Dial-up Connections icon in Control Panel, opening the Properties dialog box for the appropriate LAN connection, and opening the Properties dialog box for TCP/IP, as shown in Figure 7-2. In the TCP/IP Properties dialog box, click the Use the following IP address option. The options available when configuring a static IP address are summarized in Table 7-2.

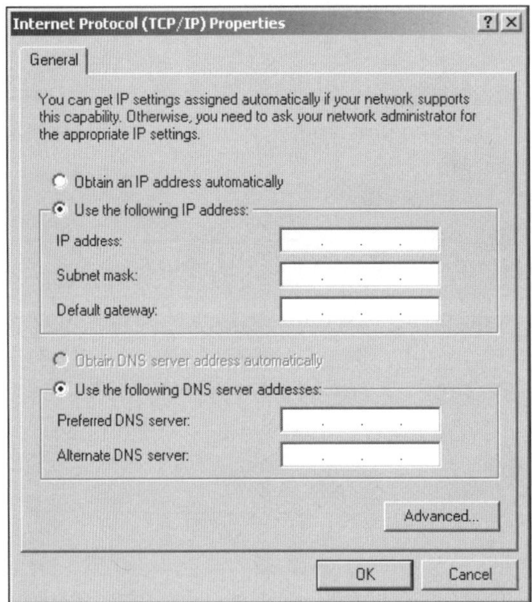

Figure 7-2 Configuring TCP/IP properties on a computer

Table 7-2 TCP/IP options

Option	Description
IP address	This is the 32-bit number that uniquely identifies a host; each host on a given network requires a unique IP address.
Subnet mask	This is the 32-bit number that identifies the network to which the host belongs.
Default gateway	This is the 32-bit number of the router on the local network.

Configuring Automatic IP Addresses

If there is a server on the network running DHCP, you can configure computers on the network to receive IP addresses automatically. Automatic IP addressing can eliminate some of the administrative problems associated with configuring static IP addresses, such as the chance of human error (incorrectly typing an IP address) or IP address duplication, which occurs when a single IP address is assigned to multiple hosts. Both of these problems typically cause an IP communication failure.

A DHCP server is configured with a range of IP addresses that are assigned to clients on the network, ensuring no duplicate addresses exist and that clients receive the correct configuration. The clients on the network are then configured to obtain an IP address automatically. This can be configured by opening the properties dialog box for TCP/IP, as discussed in the previous section, and clicking the Obtain an IP address automatically option button. This option is shown in Figure 7-2.

Automatic Private IP Addressing

Consider the following scenario. You install DHCP on one of your servers on the network, and configure all clients to obtain an IP address automatically. Then, for some reason, the DHCP server goes offline, and clients are unable to lease an IP address.

Windows 2000 implements a technology known as automatic IP addressing that allows DHCP-enabled clients to assign themselves an IP address and subnet mask in the event that a DHCP server is unavailable. The client generates an IP address in the range of 169.254.0.1 to 169.254.255.254. (The Internet Assigned Numbers Authority has reserved the range of IP addresses for this purpose.)

Once the client generates an IP address within this range, it sends out a broadcast on the network to make sure the address isn't already being used. The client continues to use the IP address until it detects a DHCP server online.

Keep in mind that automatic IP addressing provides a client with limited functionality on the network. The only parameters that are assigned are an IP address and a subnet mask. The client is only able to communicate with those computers also using this range of IP addresses and is only able to communicate with computers on the same network or subnet.

TROUBLESHOOTING TCP/IP AND NETWORK CONNECTIVITY

Once TCP/IP is installed and configured, it is a good idea to test connectivity to make sure the computer can communicate over the network. There may also be times that you have to troubleshoot network connectivity problems between computers. TCP/IP comes with several command line utilities that can be used to verify and troubleshoot network connectivity.

Verifying TCP/IP Configurations

The first step in troubleshooting network connectivity is to verify the TCP/IP configuration settings on the computer with the problem. On computers installed with Windows NT, 2000, or XP, you can use the **ipconfig** command to verify the addressing parameters assigned to a computer. There are several parameters that can be used with this command. For example, using the **ipconfig /all** command produces a full display of assigned parameters, as shown in Figure 7-3. Table 7-3 summarizes the parameters.

```
C:\WINNT\System32\cmd.exe
C:\>ipconfig /all

Windows 2000 IP Configuration

        Host Name . . . . . . . . . . . . : server1
        Primary DNS Suffix  . . . . . . . : Bayside.net
        Node Type . . . . . . . . . . . . : Broadcast
        IP Routing Enabled. . . . . . . . : No
        WINS Proxy Enabled. . . . . . . . : No
        DNS Suffix Search List. . . . . . : Bayside.net

Ethernet adapter Local Area Connection:

        Connection-specific DNS Suffix  . :
        Description . . . . . . . . . . . : Allied Telesyn AT-2400 PCI Ethernet
Adapter
        Physical Address. . . . . . . . . : 00-A0-D2-F0-1D-7C
        DHCP Enabled. . . . . . . . . . . : No
        IP Address. . . . . . . . . . . . : 131.107.2.1
        Subnet Mask . . . . . . . . . . . : 255.255.255.0
        Default Gateway . . . . . . . . . :
        DNS Servers . . . . . . . . . . . : 127.0.0.1

C:\>_
```

Figure 7-3 Viewing the results of the ipconfig/all command

Table 7-3 Ipconfig parameters

Parameter	Description
/all	Displays the full TCP/IP parameters assigned to all network adapters
/release	Sends a message to the DHCP server to release the IP address that has been assigned to the network adapter
/renew	Renews the IP configuration information from a DHCP server
/flushdns	Used to purge the DNS resolver cache; this switch can be used in an attempt to troubleshoot DNS name resolution problems
/registerdns	Used to renew all DHCP leases and to reregister dynamic DNS information

Windows 9x machines use the **winipcfg** command to display the TCP/IP configuration settings. This command is very similar to the ipconfig utility used in Windows NT/2000.

The information that is displayed using ipconfig or winipcfg can assist you in determining if the computer is using a correct IP address, subnet mask, or default gateway configuration. If local configuration settings are correct, then the next step is to test network connectivity using tools described in the section that follows.

Verifying Network Connectivity

As an administrator, you may have to troubleshoot a loss of client network connectivity. As discussed in the previous section, one of the first things you need to do is verify the local IP settings to eliminate this as the source of the problem. Next you can look at the network to determine where the loss of connectivity is occurring.

TCP/IP supports a variety of utilities that can be used to troubleshoot connectivity problems, including the following:

- Ping
- Tracert
- Pathping
- Arp
- Route
- Netdiag

Once you've verified the addressing parameters assigned to the computer, you can use the ping command to test for network connectivity. The ping command tests network connectivity with other hosts on the network by sending ICMP packets to a remote computer and listening for an echo reply from the remote host.

To test the TCP/IP configuration using the ping command:

1. Ping the loopback address by typing **ping 127.0.0.1** at the command prompt. This verifies that TCP/IP is installed and initialized on the local computer.
2. Ping the IP address of a local computer (a computer on the same subnet).
3. If successful, ping the IP address of the computer's default gateway. If this fails, verify that you have correctly entered the IP address of the default gateway and that the default gateway is online.
4. Ping the IP address of a remote host (a host on another subnet). If this fails, confirm that the IP address assigned to the remote host is valid, that the remote host is online, and that all routers between the local and remote host are operational.

If you can successfully ping the IP address of a remote host, this verifies the actions taken in Steps 1 and 2.

A screen capture of the ping command is shown in Figure 7-4.

Some of the more common switches that can be used with the ping command are described in Table 7-4.

If you can ping the default gateway, but cannot ping the IP address of a remote host, you need to verify that the routers between the local host and the remote host are operational. This can be done using the tracert command. This TCP/IP utility traces the route a packet takes to reach a destination host. It displays all the routers a packet must pass through to reach the remote host. If packets are unable to reach the remote host, you can use the tracert command to see the last router through which the packet successfully passed, giving you an idea of which one may not be operational.

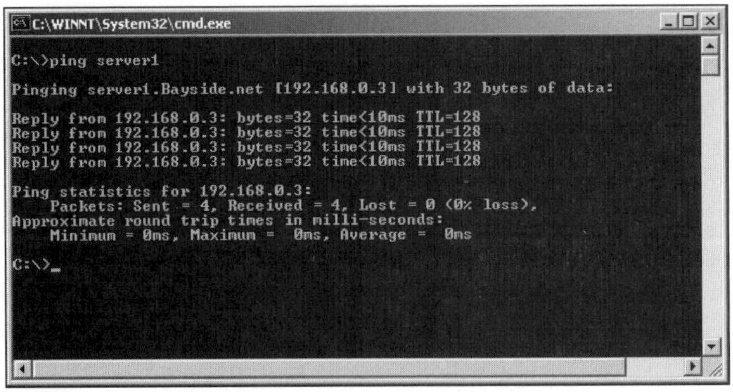

```
C:\WINNT\System32\cmd.exe

C:\>ping server1

Pinging server1.Bayside.net [192.168.0.3] with 32 bytes of data:

Reply from 192.168.0.3: bytes=32 time<10ms TTL=128
Reply from 192.168.0.3: bytes=32 time<10ms TTL=128
Reply from 192.168.0.3: bytes=32 time<10ms TTL=128
Reply from 192.168.0.3: bytes=32 time<10ms TTL=128

Ping statistics for 192.168.0.3:
    Packets: Sent = 4, Received = 4, Lost = 0 (0% loss),
Approximate round trip times in milli-seconds:
    Minimum = 0ms, Maximum =  0ms, Average =  0ms

C:\>_
```

Figure 7-4 Viewing the results of a ping command

Table 7-4 Ping parameters

Parameter	Description
-t	Pings the specified host until stopped. To stop the ping, press Ctrl+C. To pause and view statistics, press Ctrl+Break.
-a	Resolves the IP address to a host name
-n <*count*>	Specifies the number of echo requests to send, e.g., ping –n 10 <*target IP address*>

To run the tracert command, open a command prompt and type tracert <*TargetName*>.

An example of the tracert command is shown in Figure 7-5.

Some of the more common switches that can be used with the tracert command are described in Table 7-5.

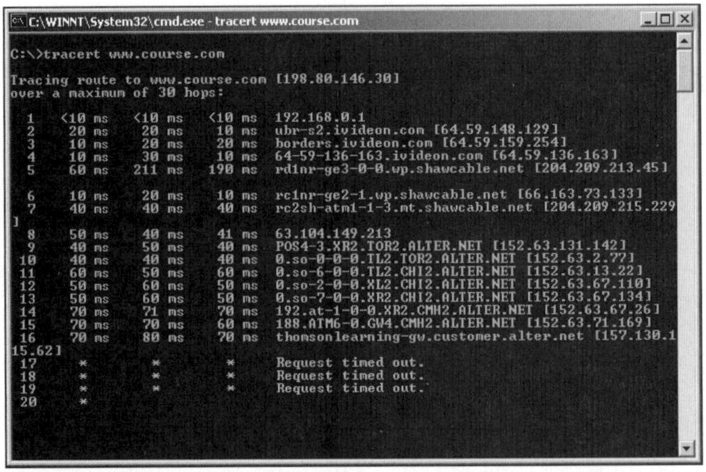

```
C:\WINNT\System32\cmd.exe - tracert www.course.com

C:\>tracert www.course.com

Tracing route to www.course.com [198.80.146.30]
over a maximum of 30 hops:

  1   <10 ms   <10 ms   <10 ms  192.168.0.1
  2    20 ms    20 ms    10 ms  ubr-s2.ivideon.com [64.59.148.129]
  3    10 ms    20 ms    20 ms  borders.ivideon.com [64.59.159.254]
  4    10 ms    30 ms    10 ms  64-59-136-163.ivideon.com [64.59.136.163]
  5    60 ms   211 ms   190 ms  rd1nr-ge3-0-0.wp.shawcable.net [204.209.213.45]

  6    10 ms    20 ms    10 ms  rc1nr-ge2-1.wp.shawcable.net [66.163.73.133]
  7    40 ms    40 ms    40 ms  rc2sh-atm1-1-3.mt.shawcable.net [204.209.215.229
]
  8    50 ms    40 ms    41 ms  63.104.149.213
  9    40 ms    50 ms    40 ms  POS4-3.XR2.TOR2.ALTER.NET [152.63.131.142]
 10    40 ms    40 ms    40 ms  0.so-0-0-0.TL2.TOR2.ALTER.NET [152.63.2.77]
 11    60 ms    50 ms    60 ms  0.so-6-0-0.TL2.CHI2.ALTER.NET [152.63.13.22]
 12    50 ms    60 ms    50 ms  0.so-2-0-0.XL2.CHI2.ALTER.NET [152.63.67.110]
 13    50 ms    60 ms    50 ms  0.so-7-0-0.XR2.CHI2.ALTER.NET [152.63.67.134]
 14    70 ms    71 ms    70 ms  192.at-1-0-0.XR2.CMH2.ALTER.NET [152.63.67.26]
 15    70 ms    70 ms    60 ms  188.ATM6-0.GW4.CMH2.ALTER.NET [152.63.71.169]
 16    70 ms    80 ms    70 ms  thomsonlearning-gw.customer.alter.net [157.130.1
15.62]
 17     *        *        *     Request timed out.
 18     *        *        *     Request timed out.
 19     *        *        *     Request timed out.
 20     *
```

Figure 7-5 Viewing the results of the tracert command

Table 7-5 Tracert parameters

Parameter	Description
-h	Maximum number of hops used to search for the client
-w <timeout>	The amount of time in milliseconds to wait before timing out

Another utility that can be used to troubleshoot routing problems is pathping, which combines the functions of both the ping and tracert commands. The pathping command sends echo request messages to each router between a source and destination host. It then computes the results based on the packets returned from each router displaying the degree of packet loss at each router. This can help you determine which routers are experiencing network problems. To use the pathping command, open a command prompt, and type pathping *<parameter> TargetName*. Figure 7-6 shows an example of the pathping command configured to show a maximum of five hops.

Table 7-6 lists some of the parameters that can be used with this command.

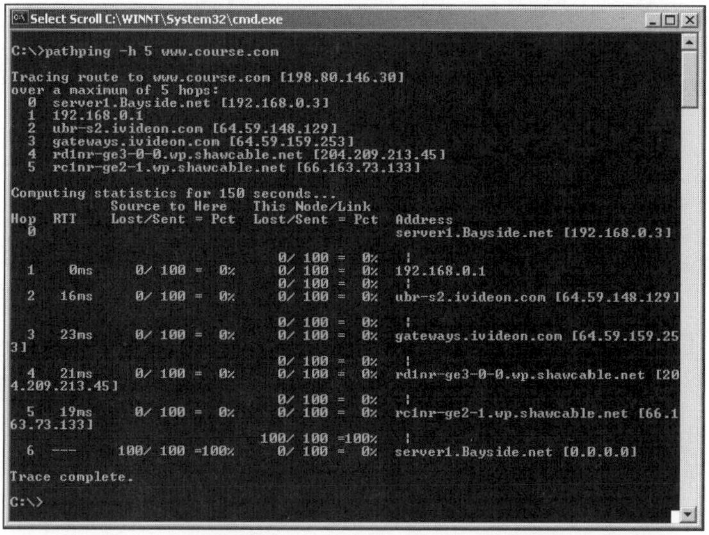

```
Select Scroll C:\WINNT\System32\cmd.exe

C:\>pathping -h 5 www.course.com

Tracing route to www.course.com [198.80.146.30]
over a maximum of 5 hops:
  0  server1.Bayside.net [192.168.0.3]
  1  192.168.0.1
  2  ubr-s2.ivideon.com [64.59.148.129]
  3  gateways.ivideon.com [64.59.159.253]
  4  rd1nr-ge3-0-0.wp.shawcable.net [204.209.213.45]
  5  rc1nr-ge2-1.wp.shawcable.net [66.163.73.133]

Computing statistics for 150 seconds...
            Source to Here   This Node/Link
Hop  RTT    Lost/Sent = Pct  Lost/Sent = Pct  Address
  0                                           server1.Bayside.net [192.168.0.3]
                                0/ 100 =  0%   |
  1    0ms     0/ 100 =  0%     0/ 100 =  0%  192.168.0.1
                                0/ 100 =  0%   |
  2   16ms     0/ 100 =  0%     0/ 100 =  0%  ubr-s2.ivideon.com [64.59.148.129]

                                0/ 100 =  0%   |
  3   23ms     0/ 100 =  0%     0/ 100 =  0%  gateways.ivideon.com [64.59.159.25
3]
                                0/ 100 =  0%   |
  4   21ms     0/ 100 =  0%     0/ 100 =  0%  rd1nr-ge3-0-0.wp.shawcable.net [20
4.209.213.45]
                                0/ 100 =  0%   |
  5   19ms     0/ 100 =  0%     0/ 100 =  0%  rc1nr-ge2-1.wp.shawcable.net [66.1
63.73.133]
                              100/ 100 =100%   |
  6  ---     100/ 100 =100%     0/ 100 =  0%  server1.Bayside.net [0.0.0.0]

Trace complete.

C:\>
```

Figure 7-6 Viewing the results of the pathping command

Table 7-6 Pathping parameters

Parameter	Description
-n	Prevents the command from resolving IP addresses of routers to their host names
-h	Specifies the maximum number of hops required to search for the destination host (the default is 30)
-p	Specifies the number of milliseconds to wait between consecutive pings
-w	Specifies the number of milliseconds to wait for each reply
TargetName	Specifies the destination host either by IP address or host name

As discussed previously, ARP is used to resolve IP addresses to the physical MAC address of a network adapter. Your computer contains an ARP cache of the most recently resolved entries. To view the most recent ARP cache you can type arp –a at a command prompt. You can then verify that the correct IP address is mapped to the appropriate MAC address.

If a client is having connectivity problems with a remote host, you can also use the route command to verify the correct route to the destination host. This command is used to view and modify the contents of the local routing table. The routing table contains entries called routes that are used to locate subnets on an internetwork. Each entry in the routing table consists of a network ID, a forwarding address, the interface used to forward packets to a destination, and a metric. The entry tells the local computer where to forward packets to reach the destination host. Figure 7-7 shows an example of the local routing table that was accessed by typing "route print"at a command prompt.

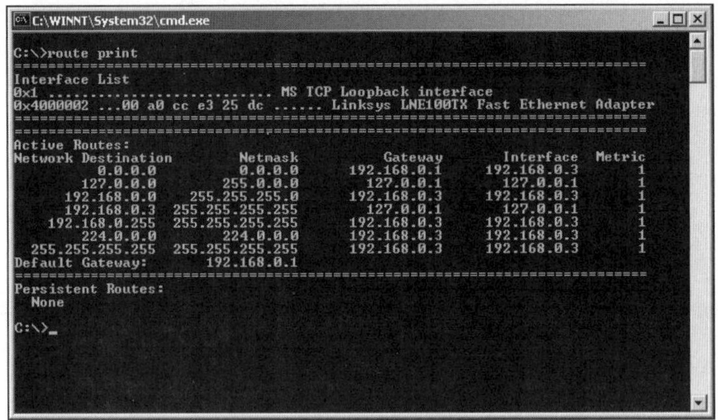

Figure 7-7 Viewing the local routing table

The following switches in Table 7-7 can be used with the route utility.

Table 7-7 Route Parameters

Command	Description
add	Adds a route to the routing table
change	Modifies an existing entry
delete	Deletes an existing route
print	Prints the route or routes

The final utility that you can use to troubleshoot IP configuration and network connectivity is the netdiag command. This utility can be used to diagnose and troubleshoot a variety of network connectivity problems. Some of the useful information that can be tested and displayed includes a list of installed hotfixes, IP configuration, DNS, and host name resolution and domain configuration information. To run netdiag, open a command prompt, and type netdiag. The output appears as shown in Figure 7-8.

The following switches in Table 7-8 can be used with the netdiag utility.

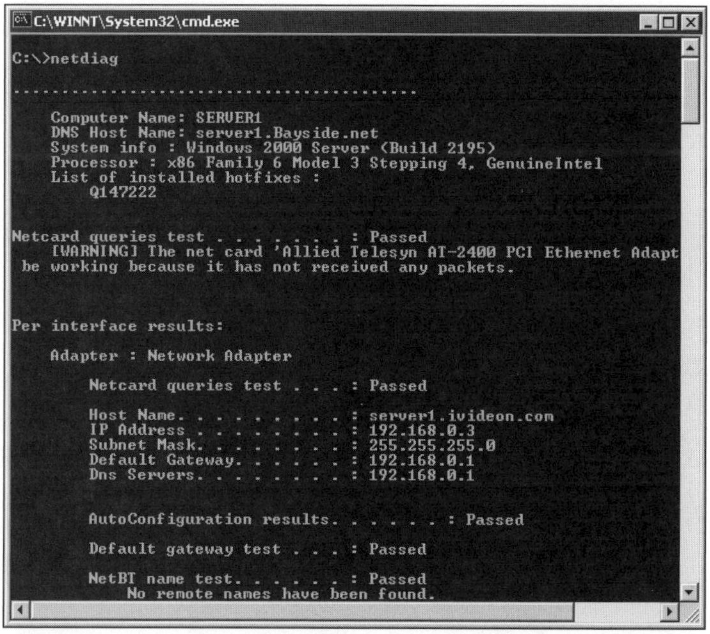

```
C:\WINNT\System32\cmd.exe

C:\>netdiag

..........................................

    Computer Name: SERVER1
    DNS Host Name: server1.Bayside.net
    System info : Windows 2000 Server (Build 2195)
    Processor : x86 Family 6 Model 3 Stepping 4, GenuineIntel
    List of installed hotfixes :
        Q147222


Netcard queries test . . . . . . . : Passed
    [WARNING] The net card 'Allied Telesyn AT-2400 PCI Ethernet Adapt
 be working because it has not received any packets.


Per interface results:

    Adapter : Network Adapter

        Netcard queries test . . . : Passed

        Host Name. . . . . . . . . : server1.ivideon.com
        IP Address . . . . . . . . : 192.168.0.3
        Subnet Mask. . . . . . . . : 255.255.255.0
        Default Gateway. . . . . . : 192.168.0.1
        Dns Servers. . . . . . . . : 192.168.0.1

        AutoConfiguration results. . . . . . : Passed

        Default gateway test . . . : Passed

        NetBT name test. . . . . . : Passed
            No remote names have been found.
```

Figure 7-8 Viewing the results of netdiag

Table 7-8 Netdiag Parameters

Command	Description
/v	Verbose mode
/q	Quiet output; only errors will be reported
/l	Log output to Netdiag.log
/fix	Fix trivial problems

You should now be familiar with how to install, configure, and verify TCP/IP connectivity. If you choose to implement dynamic IP addressing, you also need to know how to install and configure a DHCP server, which is discussed in the following section.

Administering DHCP in Windows 2000

In order to implement automatic IP addressing, the DHCP service has to be installed on at least one server on your network. The **Dynamic Host Configuration Protocol (DHCP)** is used to centralize the administration of IP addresses and various options and eliminate the administrative overhead of statically assigning the information to each network host.

When the DHCP service is installed, it is configured with a range of IP addresses to lease to clients. This range is called a DHCP **scope**. When a client is configured to use DHCP, it receives an IP address and a subnet mask, plus any options that have been configured within the scope. The options that a DHCP server can assign to clients include IP addresses for a default gateway, a WINS server, and a DNS server.

An IP address that is assigned to a client from a DHCP server is known as a DHCP lease. The client essentially leases the address from the DHCP server for a period of time before it must be renewed, which is eight days, by default. A DHCP client attempts to lease an IP address in one of the following situations:

- TCP/IP is installed and started for the first time.
- The client releases its IP address and attempts to renew another one.
- The client attempts to release a specific IP address and is denied.

An IP address can be released using the ipconfig /release command, and a new IP address can be leased using the ipconfig /renew command.

The following process occurs when a DHCP client attempts to lease an IP address from a DHCP Server.

1. The DHCP client begins by broadcasting a DHCPDISCOVER message to locate the DHCP servers on the network. Because the client does not yet have an IP address, it uses the source address of 0.0.0.0 and a destination address of 255.255.255.255. The broadcast also includes the client's computer name and MAC address.
2. All DHCP servers on the network that receive the DHCPDISCOVER message respond with a DCHPOFFER message. If there is more than one DHCP server on the network, the client accepts the first offer it receives. The offer contains the IP address being offered, a subnet mask, the duration of the lease, and the IP address of the DHCP server offering the IP address.
3. Once the client has received a DHCPOFFER message, it broadcasts a DCHPREQUEST to all DHCP servers informing them that it has received an IP address and the IP address of the server from which it has leased the address. All other DHCP servers retract their offer making the IP addresses available for other clients on the network.

4. During the final step of the lease process, the DHCP server sends a DHCPACK message to the client indicating the lease process was successful. If optional components are configured on the DHCP server (such as the IP address of the gateway) this information is included in the DHCPACK message.

A DHCP client periodically attempts to renew its lease to ensure that it has the most up-to-date configuration settings for the network. When 50 percent of the configured lease duration expires, the DHCP client sends a DHCPREQUEST message to the original DHCP server that offered the address. If the server is available, the IP address is renewed with a new lease duration and an update of any changed configuration settings. If the original DHCP server is unavailable, the client continues to use its current IP configuration until 87.5 percent of the lease duration expires. At this point, the client sends out a DHCPDISCOVER message to any DHCP server that is available on the network.

If you restart a DHCP client, it automatically attempts to renew the IP address that it had when it shut down. If it cannot contact the original DHCP server, the client computer attempts to contact its default gateway. If the default gateway responds, and there is still time left on the lease, it continues to use the same IP configurations. If the client cannot find the DHCP server or the default gateway, it stops using its leased IP address and assigns itself an address from the 169.254.0.1 to 169.254.255.254 range. The client computer then attempts to contact a DHCP server every five minutes in an attempt to obtain valid IP configurations.

Now that you are familiar with how a DHCP server provides DHCP clients with IP addressing information, you need to know how to install, configure, and administer the DHCP service on a network.

Installing a DHCP server includes the following steps, each of which are discussed in their respective sections:

- Install the DHCP service.
- Configure the DHCP server with at least one scope.
- Activate the new scope.
- Authorize the DHCP server.

Installing a DHCP Server

Installing the DHCP service is a relatively simple process. Because the DHCP server cannot be a DHCP client, make sure it has been statically assigned an IP address, subnet mask, and default gateway (if required on the network) before installing the service.

The DHCP service can be installed using the Add/Remove Programs icon within Control Panel. In the Add/Remove Programs dialog box, click Add/Remove Windows Components. The DHCP service can be found in the details of the Networking Services section, as shown in Figure 7-9.

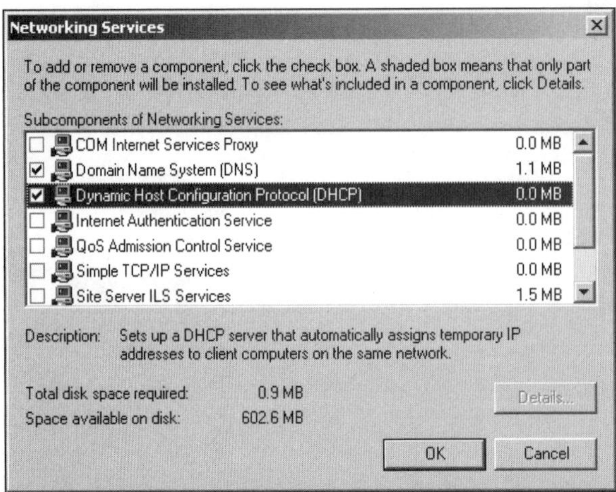

Figure 7-9 Installing the DHCP service

Once the service is installed, it can be configured and maintained using the DHCP console found by clicking Start, clicking Programs, and then clicking the Administrative Tools menu. The DHCP console is illustrated in Figure 7-10.

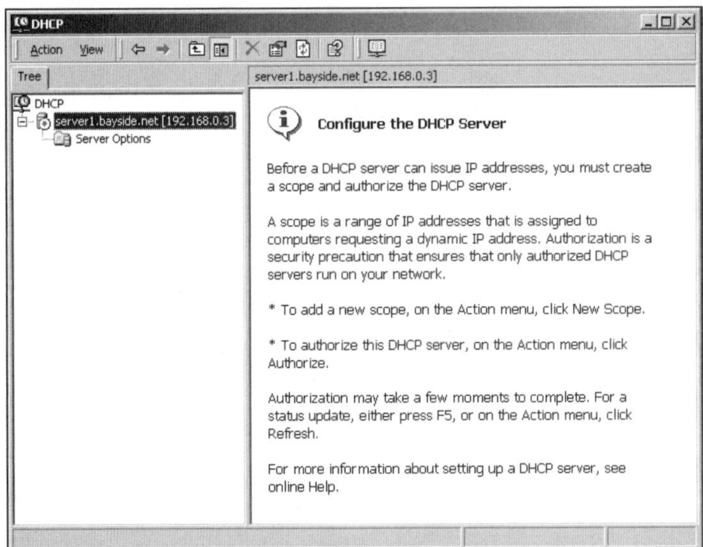

Figure 7-10 The DHCP console

Once the service has been installed, the next step is to configure the DHCP server with a scope of IP addresses. The following section looks at how to create scopes using the DCHP console.

Configuring DHCP Scopes

Each DHCP server needs to be configured with at least one scope. As defined earlier, a scope is a range of IP addresses that can be handed out to network clients. When creating a scope, keep the following points in mind:

- Each DHCP server requires a unique scope to avoid duplicate IP addresses on the network. (DCHP servers do not share scope information.)
- IP addresses that have been statically assigned to clients should be excluded from the scope.
- DHCP servers can be configured with multiple scopes to assign IP addresses to hosts on different subnets.

If you have multiple DHCP servers on your network, it is essential that you plan your scopes. DHCP servers do not inform each other about what IP addresses they have assigned to clients and, if you configure two DHCP servers with the same scope, there is a good chance that there will be duplicate IP addresses on the network. Therefore, when configuring the scopes, make sure that the IP addresses between DHCP servers do not overlap.

DCHP scopes are configured through the DHCP console. Use the following steps to create a new scope:

1. Click **Start**, point to **Programs**, point to **Administrative Tools**, and then click **DHCP**.
2. Double-click your DHCP server listed in the console. On the Action menu, click **New Scope**. This launches the New Scope Wizard. Click **Next**.
3. Type a name for the new scope and an optional description. If your DHCP server is providing IP addresses to multiple subnets, consider using descriptive names so each scope is easily recognizable. Click **Next**.
4. In the IP address Range window, type the range of IP addresses available to DHCP clients, as shown in Figure 7-11. The subnet mask is automatically generated based on the address class, but can be changed if needed. Click **Next**.
5. In the Add Exclusions window, you can exclude any IP addresses from the scope. Once an address has been excluded, it is not leased to any DHCP client. Click **Next**.
6. In the Lease Duration window you can configure how long a client can use an IP address before it must be renewed. The default is eight days. Consider shortening the lease time if the number of IP addresses in the scope is close to the number of DHCP clients. Click **Next**.
7. The Configure DHCP Options window allows you to configure any optional parameters the DHCP server assigns to clients, as shown in Figure 7-12. If you wish to configure DHCP scope options at a later time, click the **No, I Will Configure These Options Later** option. Click **Next**.

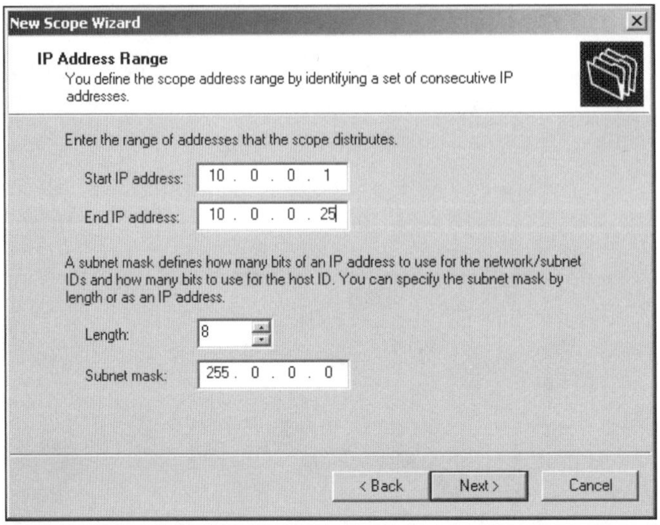

Figure 7-11 Creating a DHCP scope

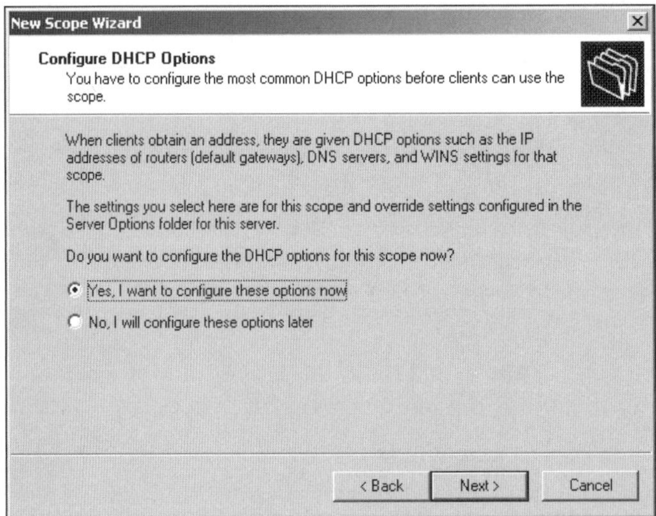

Figure 7-12 Choosing whether to configure the DHCP options

8. Click **Finish**.

The new scope now appears within the DCHP console with a red arrow beside it, meaning the scope has been created but has not yet been activated or authorized, as shown in Figure 7-13.

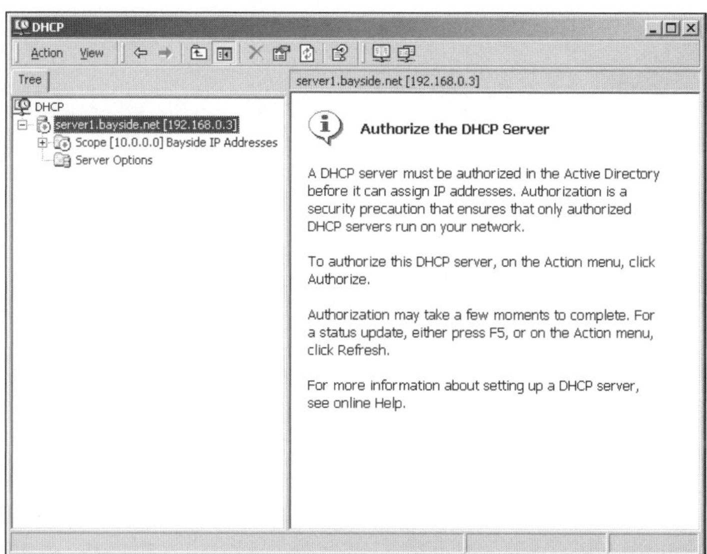

Figure 7-13 The completed DHCP scope

If you need to configure such scope options as a default gateway or DNS server, make sure this is done prior to activating the scope. To activate the scope, click the scope from within the console and, on the Action menu, click Activate. Once the scope is activated, the red arrow disappears. The final step is to authorize the DHCP server, which is discussed later in this section.

Client Reservations

There may be instances where a client on the network requires the same IP address to be assigned at all times. For example, if you are running Cluster service, you can convert the nodes within the clusters into DHCP clients, but they must be reassigned the same IP address. You can assign static IP addresses to the clients or you can configure them to be DHCP clients and create client reservations. A client reservation reserves an IP within the scope for a particular client so it is always reassigned the same IP address. The DHCP server uses the clients MAC address to determine if it has an IP address reserved and which IP address should be reassigned to it.

To create a client reservation:

1. From within the DHCP console, click the scope containing the IP address you want to reserve for a particular client.
2. Click **Reservations** in the scope pane, and click **New Reservation** on the Action menu, as shown in Figure 7-14.
3. Type a name for the reservation (such as the name of the computer for which the reservation is being created).

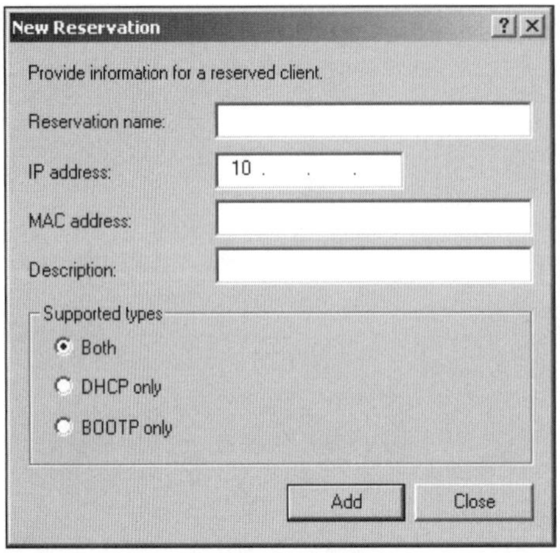

Figure 7-14 Creating a client reservation

4. In the IP address box, type the host ID that is reserved for the client. (The network portion of the IP address is already filled in based on the scope.)
5. Type the MAC address in the MAC Address box. (If you do not know the MAC address of the client, you can use the ipconfig /all command to determine what it is.) When typing in the MAC address, make sure it is entered without the dashes.
6. Type an optional description for the client reservation.
7. Under the supported types, choose one of Both, DHCP only, or BOOTP only.
8. Once all the parameters have been supplied, click **Add**.
9. Click **Close** to exit the New Reservation dialog box.

Superscopes

Many networks today consist of multiple subnets (or segments) either for security reasons or for routing reasons. Each of the segments has its own network address uniquely identifying it on the network. Superscopes (which were introduced in Windows NT 4.0 service pack 2) are included with Windows 2000 DHCP to support these types of subnetted environments.

A **superscope** is a grouping of scopes created for multiple subnets on a physical network. Superscopes are usually created to make the administration of multiple scopes simpler. Scopes created for subnets on a specific network can be grouped together so they are easier to identify. For example, consider a business spanning multiple floors within a single building. Each floor has multiple subnets. For ease of administration, you could create a superscope for each floor and group the scopes accordingly.

To create a superscope, right-click your server name in the scope pane of the DHCP console, and click New Superscope. The New Superscope Wizard opens to guide you through the creation of the combined scope.

Multicast Scopes

Before looking at multicast scopes in DHCP, it is necessary that you have a general idea of what **multicasting** is. Multicasting is the sending of a message to multiple clients or a group of clients. It is not the same as a broadcast message that is sent to every host on a network. With multicasting, the message is intended for a specific group of recipients.

With DHCP in Windows 2000, DHCP servers can now assign multicast addresses to clients as well as the standard unicast address. DHCP clients are assigned their single IP address and are assigned a multicast address as well if they join a multicast group (such as a group of users conferencing using Microsoft NetMeeting). Those clients that are configured with static IP addresses can also receive multicast configuration information from a DHCP server. Multicast scopes are configured with class D IP addresses and provide users with multicast addresses, thus making the administration and configuration of multicast groups simpler. The New Multicast Scope Wizard can be accessed by right-clicking your server name in the scope pane of the DHCP console and clicking New Multicast Scope.

Authorizing a DHCP Server

Now that the service is installed and the scopes are configured and activated, the last step is to authorize the DHCP server in Active Directory. This is a new feature in Windows 2000 designed to increase security on a network. It eliminates the possibility of the DHCP service mistakenly or maliciously being installed on a server and leasing IP addresses to clients. Only those servers that have been authorized by an administrator are permitted to lease IP addresses.

Whenever a Windows 2000 DHCP server is installed, it sends out a DHCPINFORM broadcast to all other DHCP servers. Any other Windows 2000 DHCP server on the network replies with a DHCPACK message that contains information about the Active Directory and the location of the domain controllers. The server that is attempting to start its DHCP services queries Active Directory to see if it is on the list of authorized servers. If the server is on the list, the DHCP services start as usual. If the server is not found on the list, the DHCP services start, log an error in the event log, but do not answer client requests. Only Windows 2000 DCHP servers check for authorization; DHCP servers created on other platforms, including Windows NT, still operate.

The Windows 2000 Resource Kit provides a tool for discovering unauthorized DHCP servers on the network. The utility is called the DHCP Locator utility (Dhcploc.exe), and it alerts administrators about any unauthorized DCHP servers detected.

To authorize a DHCP server:

1. From within the DHCP console, click the DHCP server.
2. On the Action menu, click **Authorize**. A green arrow should appear next to the DHCP server in the console indicating that it has been authorized within Active Directory.

To manage your authorized servers, you can also right-click the DHCP node in the scope pane of the DHCP console, and click Manage Authorized Servers. This dialog box, shown in Figure 7-15, allows you to authorize and unauthorize servers throughout the network.

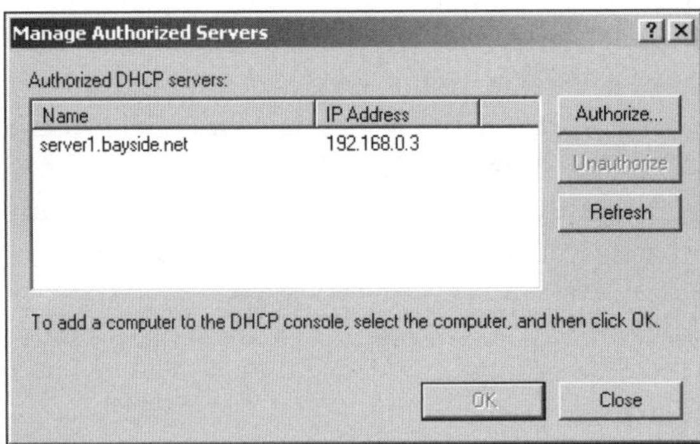

Figure 7-15 Managing server authorization

To be able to authorize servers on a Windows 2000 network you must belong to the Enterprise Admins group.

Using DHCP Options

As mentioned previously, during the creation of a new scope, not only can a DHCP server assign to clients the required TCP/IP parameters (an IP address and a subnet mask), it can also assign optional parameters to clients. Table 7-9 summarizes the most commonly used options.

Table 7-9 Commonly used DCHP options

Option	Description
044 WINS/NBNS Servers	List of IP addresses for NETBIOS name servers
046 WINS/NBT Node Type	The type of name resolution clients use; the following options are available: 1=B-node (broadcast), 2=P-node (peer), 4= M-node (mixed), and 8=H-node (hybrid)
006 DNS Server	List of IP addresses for DNS name servers
003 Router	The default gateway

There are different levels at which scope options can be configured. For example, some options you may want to apply to all clients on the network and other options, such as the default gateway, may be scope specific. The level at which you create the DCHP options determines which scopes or clients are affected. The three levels of scope options that can be configured are server, scope, and client.

- *Server options*—Server options apply to all scopes configured on the DHCP server. Server options are used when all clients require the same configuration information regardless of the subnet they are on.
- *Scope options*—Scope options only apply to a specific scope and the clients that lease an IP address from that scope. For example, if there are different scopes configured for different subnets, the appropriate default gateway can be configured for each scope. Keep in mind that scope options override server options.
- *Client options*—Client options apply to the specified client reservation. Any options applied at the client level override options configured at the server and scope level.

7

Configuring DHCP in a Routed Network

If your network contains multiple subnets connected via routers, you need to spend some time planning your DHCP implementation. When a client attempts to lease an IP address, the client sends out a broadcast message to locate the DHCP servers on the network. The problem in a subnetted environment is that, by default, routers do not pass broadcasts. One of the reasons why networks are subnetted is to cut down on broadcast traffic.

In a routed network, you have three options for implementing DHCP. Your first option is to install and configure a DHCP server on each subnet. If you have a small number of subnets, this may be feasible, but in large networks the resources may not be available for multiple DHCP servers. Your second option is to configure the routers to forward the broadcasts. In a smaller network, this may be a suitable option, but in larger networks it increases network traffic because the broadcasts are then forwarded to all subnets on the network. The third option is to configure a DHCP relay agent on each of the subnets.

The DHCP relay agent included with Windows 2000 relays the DHCP messages between DHCP clients and DHCP servers over routers that separate the subnets. For each IP subnet containing DHCP clients, a DHCP relay agent needs to be configured.

A server that is running the DHCP service cannot be configured as a DHCP relay agent.

A server is configured as a DHCP relay agent through Routing and Remote Access. Expand your server from within the Routing and Remote Access console, expand IP routing, right-click General, and click New Routing Protocol. In the New Routing Protocol window, choose DHCP Relay Agent. The DHCP relay agent is illustrated in Figure 7-16.

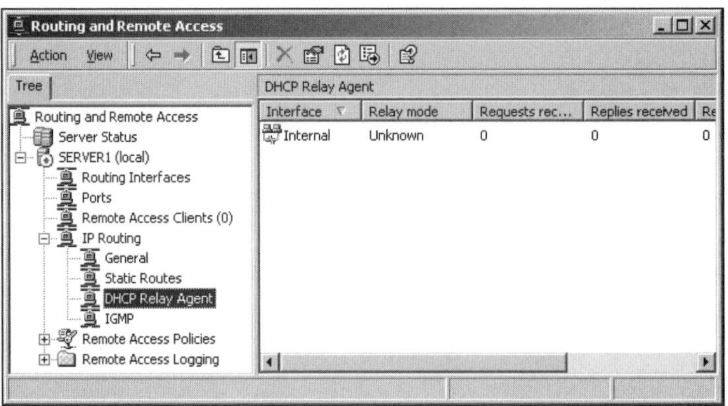

Figure 7-16 Configuring a DHCP relay agent

Once the DHCP relay agent is installed, it needs to be enabled. This can be accomplished by right-clicking the DHCP relay Agent and clicking the New Interface option. Click the LAN interface that will be configured to use the relay agent and click OK. You also need to specify the DHCP server or servers to which the relay agent will forward the DHCP messages. This can be configured by right-clicking the DHCP relay agent within the Routing and Remote Access console and clicking Properties, as shown in Figure 7-17. The window that appears allows you to provide the IP addresses of the DHCP servers on the network.

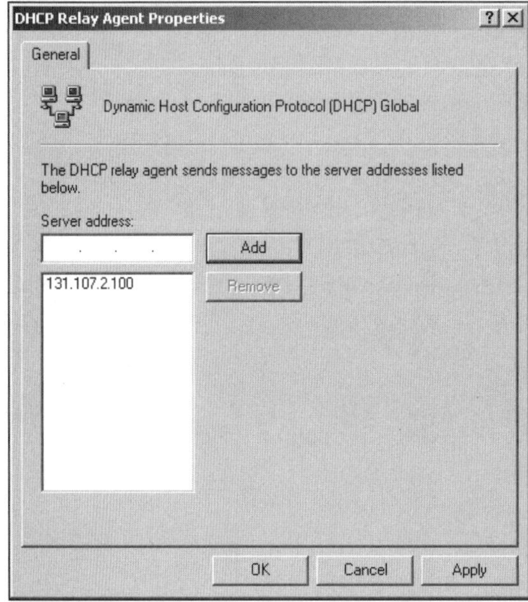

Figure 7-17 Enabling a DHCP relay agent

Once the relay agent is configured, any DHCP broadcast messages sent out by clients on the local subnet are picked up by the relay agent and forwarded directly to a DHCP server.

DHCP and DNS Integration

One of the new features of Windows 2000 is the integration of DHCP and DNS. Dynamic DNS (DDNS) allows name servers and clients to automatically update the DNS database, eliminating the need for an administrator to have to manually update the zone file each time a change is made (such as a client leasing a new IP address). DNS is discussed in greater detail later in this chapter.

By default, the DHCP service automatically registers any PTR records with the DNS server and allows the DHCP clients to register their own A (host) records. To configure DHCP for DNS integration, right-click the DHCP server within the DHCP console, click Properties, and click the DNS tab, as shown in Figure 7-18.

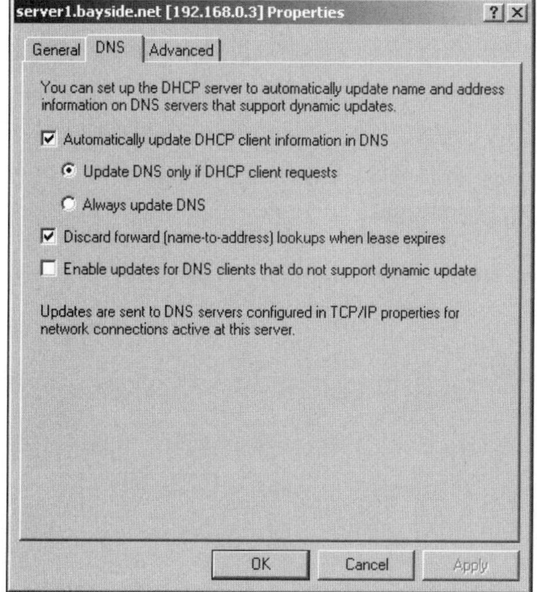

Figure 7-18 Configuring DHCP and DNS integration

The following options are available on the DNS tab:

- *Automatically update DHCP client information in DNS*—This option is selected by default. If requested by the client, the DHCP server updates both the A record and PTR record with the DNS server. Windows 2000 clients, however, are capable of updating their own records with a DNS server, so in an environment with only Windows 2000 clients this option is sufficient.

- *Always update DNS*—This option forces the DHCP server to always update records on behalf of the client.
- *Discard forward (name-to-address) lookups when lease expires*—This option is enabled by default. This option forces the DHCP server to send a request to the DNS server to remove a client's record when their IP address lease expires.
- *Enable updates for DNS clients that do not support dynamic update*—This option forces the DHCP server to update the DNS zone file for clients that do not support dynamic DNS (such as non-Microsoft clients or older Microsoft clients).

Make sure that the DHCP server's TCP/IP client settings include the IP address of the DNS server to which it will be sending automatic updates.

Maintaining DHCP Services

DHCP servers should be monitored to discover or prevent future problems with the DHCP service. There are two ways that DHCP servers can be monitored:

- Periodically look at the Windows System log for any DHCP-related events.
- Enable detailed event audit logging by opening the DHCP console, right-clicking the server, clicking Properties, and then ensuring that the check box next to Enable DHCP audit logging is selected. The server then places detailed event logs in the DHCP database directory (%systemroot%\system32\dhcp). The file name takes the form of DhcpSrvLog.*xxx* (where x represents the first three letters of the day of the week).

Administering DNS in Windows 2000

The **Domain Name System (DNS)** is one of the most important network services that a network based on TCP/IP and Active Directory can use. Windows 2000 uses DNS for two essential tasks: resolution of domain names to IP addresses and location of network services, such as domain controllers that provide user authentication. This section discusses the basics of DNS, and how to configure and manage a DNS server.

Basics of DNS

DNS was invented in 1984 to assist in resolution of host names to IP addresses on the Internet. DNS enables users to type a user-friendly name, such as *www.microsoft.com*, which, when resolved by a DNS server, is automatically converted to its proper IP address, thus facilitating communication over the network. Users do not have to remember the IP address of a Web site because the DNS server converts the name to the proper IP address as needed.

To understand DNS, it is important to understand its three main components:

- *Domain namespace*—The DNS hierarchical structure
- *DNS zones*—One or more DNS domains grouped together for administrative purposes
- *Name servers*—A DNS server that holds all of the host records for a specific zone

The DNS namespace uses a hierarchical structure. At the top of the DNS structure is the root domain, which is represented by a period. Below the root domain are the first-level domains. On the Internet, the first-level domains are represented by specific organizational types, such as .com or .org, or geographical representations such as .ca, which represents Canada.

Below the first-level domains are the second-level domains. The second-level domains usually represent an organization's name, such as Microsoft or Bayside. Beneath the second-level domains, there may be a number of subdomains that divide a second-level domain into logical separations. For example, Bayside may want to divide their domain into two subdomains: sales and marketing.

Within a specific domain, there are a number of host computers. A **host** is any computer that is a member of a specific DNS domain within the network structure. A host is referred to by its **fully qualified domain name (FQDN)**, which describes the location of the host in relation to the DNS namespace. For example, a computer named "Web server" in the marketing domain of Bayside.com would have the FQDN of *webserver.marketing.bayside.com*. Figure 7-19 illustrates an example of the domain namespace of DNS.

DNS zones are one or more domains that are grouped together for administrative purposes. For example, Bayside could create two zones to enable different administrators to manage the marketing and sales domains separately, or you can create one zone that would incorporate all of the three domains of Bayside. There are two types of zones that can be configured: forward lookup zones and reverse lookup zones. A **forward lookup zone** is the most common type of zone, and is used to perform the standard forward lookup queries for host name to IP address. A **reverse lookup zone** is a specific type of zone that performs reverse queries for resolution of IP addresses to host names queries. This is most commonly used if you, or an application, have an IP address and need to find the domain name associated with the address. To keep the number of DNS servers to a minimum, multiple zones can be configured on a single DNS server if needed.

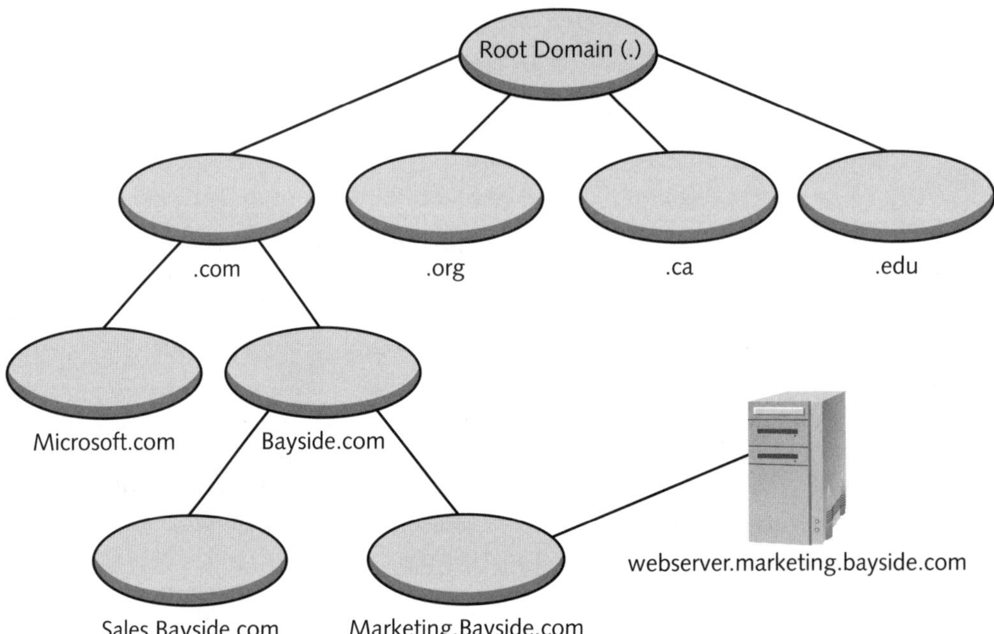

Figure 7-19 The DNS namespace

The information that is used to resolve computer names to IP addresses is stored in a zone database file on a DNS name server. The main DNS name server that contains all of the records for a specific DNS zone is called the primary DNS server. The primary DNS server is also said to be authoritative for the zone, meaning that if this server does not know the IP address about which a machine is being queried, then the machine does not exist in this zone. For example, Bayside could have an authoritative DNS server with a zone that incorporated the DNS domain called Bayside.com. This **zone file** would hold all of the resource records for the domain, such as computer name records, mail exchanger records, and service records. If a client needs to resolve the IP address for any computer or service in the Bayside.com domain, the authoritative primary DNS server provides the information from the zone files.

To assist with redundancy, primary DNS servers can also be connected to one or more secondary DNS servers. A secondary DNS server contains information that is copied from the primary DNS servers, or other secondary servers. Secondary servers can be used as a backup in case the primary server fails. Secondary servers can also be used over a WAN connection to reduce the bandwidth that would otherwise be needed to query the primary server over the link.

To ensure that both the primary server and the secondary server have the same information, you must configure a zone transfer between the servers. The copying of the DNS database information between the primary and secondary servers is called a **zone transfer**.

The Name Resolution Process

When a client needs to communicate to a computer on the network or the Internet, the host name or FQDN is usually supplied. Each client is configured to contact a specific DNS name server whenever it needs to resolve an FQDN to an IP address. The following steps illustrate an example of a client wanting to connect to *www.bayside.com*:

1. The client computer generates a request to resolve *www.bayside.com* to an IP address and sends a recursive query to the DNS name server that the client is configured to use. A **recursive query** is a command that specifies the return of a complete and full answer to the query, not a pointer to another DNS server.
2. The DNS server that received the recursive query checks its zone database for the *www.bayside.com* entry. Because it is not in its database, the DNS server sends an **iterative query** to a DNS server that is authoritative for the root domain. An iterative query means that if the DNS server cannot resolve the name, it gives the requester a pointer to another DNS server that is authoritative for the next level of the FQDN supplied.
3. Because the entry is not listed in the root domain, the DNS server that is authoritative for the root domain sends a reply to the querying client's DNS server with the IP addresses of servers authoritative for the *.com* domain.
4. The client's DNS server then sends an iterative query to a DNS server that is authoritative for the .com domain.
5. The DNS server that is authoritative for the .com domain cannot find the entry, and so then sends the client's DNS server the IP address of a different name server that is authoritative for the bayside.com domain.
6. Again the client's DNS server sends an iterative query to the DNS server that is authoritative for the bayside.com domain.
7. The DNS server that is authoritative for the bayside.com domain finds the record that represents *www.bayside.com,* and then sends the IP address back to the client's DNS server.
8. The client's DNS server now has the information that is needed, and completes the client's original recursive query by supplying the correct resolution for *www.bayside.com.*

When the client's DNS server successfully resolves the query, the query remains in the DNS system cache for one hour. This saves time and bandwidth in the event that the client needs to resolve the same name again.

Installing DNS

Windows 2000 DNS is installed by accessing the Add/Remove Programs applet in Control Panel. After clicking the Add/Remove Windows Components button, you see a section called Networking Services. You have the option to install or uninstall the DNS service, as shown in Figure 7-20.

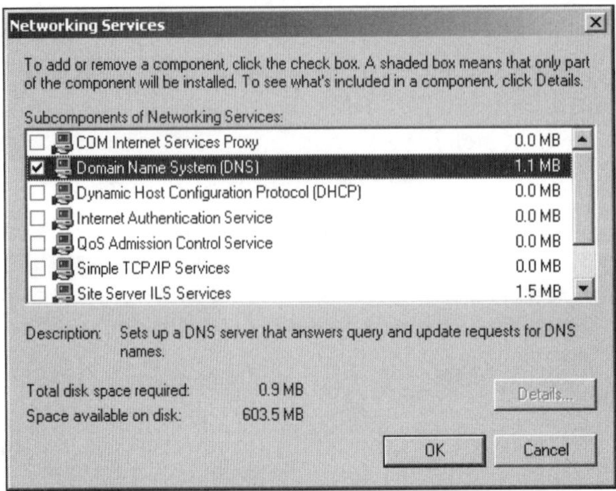

Figure 7-20 Installing DNS

When you are promoting a Windows 2000 server to Active Directory, if a valid DNS server is not detected on the network, the Active Directory Installation Wizard offers to automatically install and configure DNS during the promotion.

Once DNS has been installed, you can access the Administrative Tools menu to open the DNS console.The DNS console is used to configure the forward and reverse lookup zones and to configure the DNS server properties, as shown in Figure 7-21.

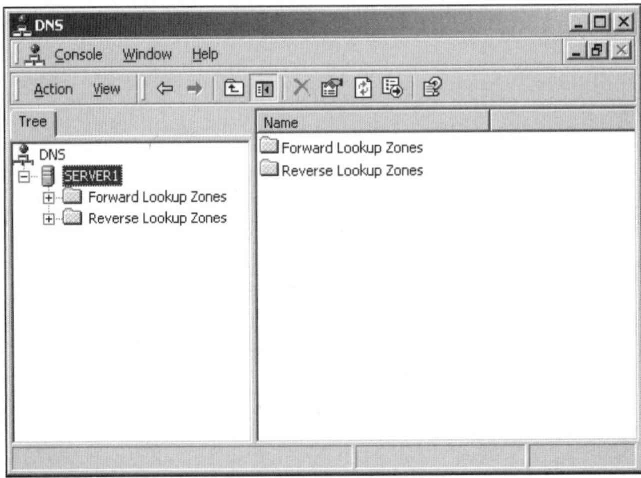

Figure 7-21 The DNS console

Creating and Configuring DNS Zones

In order to create and configure a forward or reverse lookup zone, you must be a member of the Administrators group on the server. If the server is a domain controller, you need to be a member of at least one of the following global groups: Domain Admins, Enterprise Admins, or DNS Admins.

Windows 2000 DNS allows you to configure three types of forward or reverse lookup zones:

- *Standard primary*—The DNS zone file is stored as a regular read/write text file in the %systemroot%\system32\dns folder. Use this zone type on DNS servers that are not domain controllers.
- *Standard secondary*—A read-only zone file is copied from a configured standard primary zone. Use this zone type to copy zone files from other DNS zones to provide fault tolerance and load balancing.
- *Active Directory integrated*—The zone data is stored in the Active Directory database rather than a zone file. The zone data is replicated throughout all domain controllers and follows the Active Directory replication cycle.

When a standard primary or standard secondary zone is created, a DNS zone file is also created and stored in the %systemroot%\system32\dns folder. The zone file contains configuration information and resource records that list each computer name and IP address entry. Active Directory zones store the resource records in the Active Directory database.

There are a number of resource record types, as explained in Table 7-10.

Table 7-10 DNS resource record types

Resource Record Type	Purpose
SOA (start of authority)	Indicates the authoritative name server for the zone as well as administrative information, such as the serial number, zone transfer intervals, and TTL (Time to Live, for indicating how long information should be cached)
A (address or host)	Indicates the IP address for a specific host name
NS (name server)	Defines the name servers responsible or authoritative for a specific zone
CNAME (canonical name or alias)	Allows you to specify additional names or aliases for computers that have host names
MX (mail exchanger)	Specifies a server to which e-mail applications can send mail
PTR (pointer)	Used in reverse lookup zones to provide IP to domain name resolution
SRV (service)	Registered by Windows 2000 services so that clients can find a service by querying DNS

Figure 7-22 shows the DNS console with an example of different types of resource records listed in the details pane.

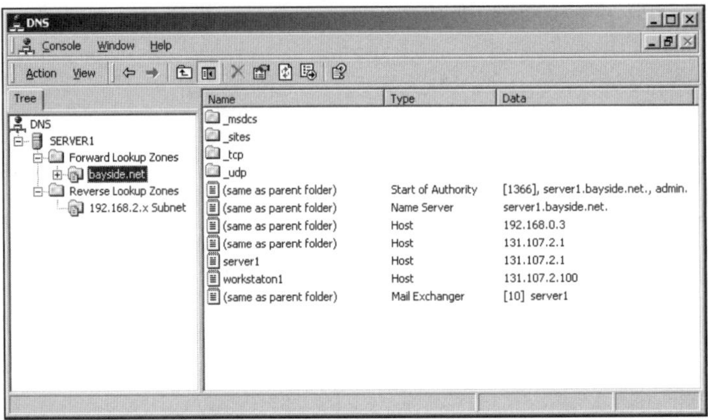

Figure 7-22 Configuring DNS

The first step to configuring DNS is to create a forward lookup zone. To create the forward lookup zone, open the DNS console and right-click the Forward Lookup Zones folder. Click the New Zone command on the shortcut menu to start the New Zone Wizard. After you click past the welcome screen, you are given the option to choose the type of zone that you want to create, as shown in Figure 7-23. The New Zone Wizard then steps you through the simple task of creating the zone, and then creates the zone, the zone file, and the necessary initial resource records.

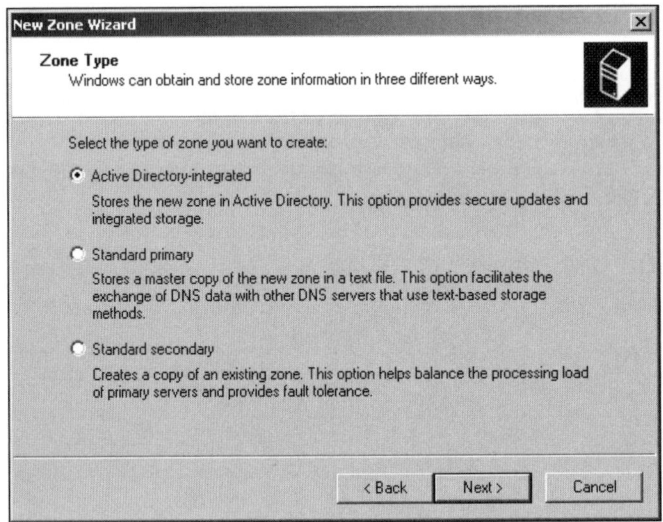

Figure 7-23 Creating a forward lookup zone

If you are configuring DNS on a member server, the Active Directory integrated option is not available. This is only available on DNS servers that are also domain controllers. If you are configuring DNS on a domain controller, it is recommended you choose Active Directory integrated for security and ease of administration purposes.

The next step is to create the reverse lookup zone. A reverse lookup zone is configured in much the same way as a forward lookup zone, except that you initially click the Reverse Lookup Zones folder in the scope pane of the DNS console, and then click the New Zone option on the shortcut menu. Once you have clicked past the welcome screen, you are given the option to choose the type of zone to create. The wizard then prompts you to enter the network ID or a specific name for the reverse lookup file. By default, the network ID and subnet mask determine the name of the zone file. For example, if your network ID is 154.169 the name of the reverse lookup file becomes 169.154.in-addr.arpa.dns.

Creating Resource Records

Once you have configured the zone database file, you can then configure the resource records, such as the computer aliases or mail exchanger records. Windows 2000 clients are capable of dynamically adding their own resource records to the zone file, eliminating the need for an administrator to do it manually. There are instances, however, when you must manually create a resource record. For example, if there are legacy clients on the network (such as Windows NT 4.0) configured with static IP addresses, resource records have to be manually added to the zone file.

You can create a resource record by right-clicking the zone file in which you want to create the record and then clicking the type of record you want to create. You can also choose the Other New Records option for a complete list and description of additional record types.

Configuring Dynamic DNS Updates

As you learned earlier, DNS now supports dynamic updates of the resource records. An administrator no longer has to manually update the zone file because clients and name servers on the network can automatically update the database file on their own. For example, when a client leases a new IP address from the DHCP server, it can automatically update the mapping of its name to its IP address in the zone file.

When a client receives an acknowledgement from a DHCP server that it has successfully leased an IP address, the client then sends a DNS update request to the DNS server to update its A record in the zone file. The DHCP server then sends an update to the DNS server on behalf of the client to update the client's PTR record.

Keep in mind that only Windows 2000 clients support dynamic updates. If there are legacy clients on the network, DHCP must be configured to update the A records and the PTR records with the DNS server on behalf of the clients.

Before you can use dynamic updates, you must first configure the DNS service to allow them. This can be done by opening the properties dialog box for the zone for which you wish to enable dynamic updates. There are three available options for configuring dynamic updates. You can choose No, which means dynamic updates are disabled for the zone, or you can choose Yes to enable them. The third option, Only secure updates, also enables dynamic updates, but updates are only accepted from computers that have a computer account within Active Directory. Using this option means that only users that are authorized can update the zone file, providing more security. The Only secure updates option is only available on DNS servers that are also domain controllers and have Active Directory integrated zones.

To enable dynamic updates:

1. From within the DNS console, click the forward lookup zone under the Forward Lookup Zones folder.
2. Right-click the zone, and click **Properties** on the shortcut menu.
3. In the Properties dialog box for the zone, click **Yes** from the Allow Dynamic Updates list arrow.
4. Click **OK**. The Allow dynamic updates options are illustrated in Figure 7-24.

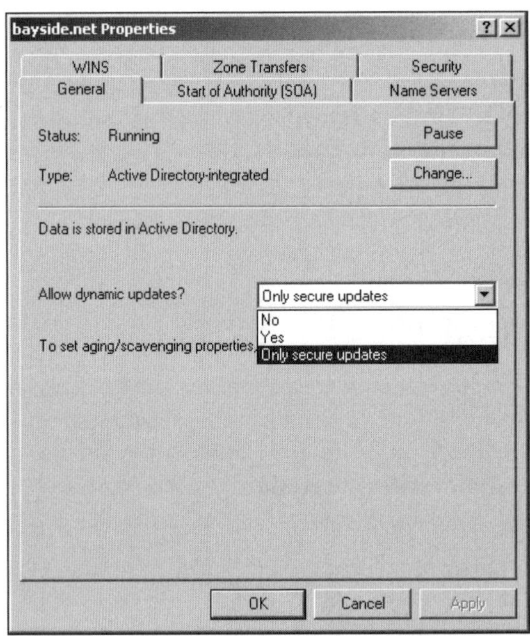

Figure 7-24 Configuring dynamic updates

The clients on the networks that support dynamic updates (Windows 2000 and XP clients) must also be configured to automatically update their records with a DNS server. As shown in Figure 7-25, you can configure this by choosing Properties on the shortcut menu for the LAN connection that you want to configure. In the Properties dialog box for the LAN connection, click TCP/IP, and then click the Properties button. In the Internet Protocol (TCP/IP) Properties windows, click the Advanced button, and then click the DNS tab. Make sure the following two options are selected:

- *Register this connection's addresses in DNS*—This option allows clients to register their computer name and IP address with the DNS server.
- *Use this connection's DNS suffix in DNS registration*—This option allows the client to register the computer name along with the DNS suffix. Use this option only if the DNS suffix is different from the domain name.

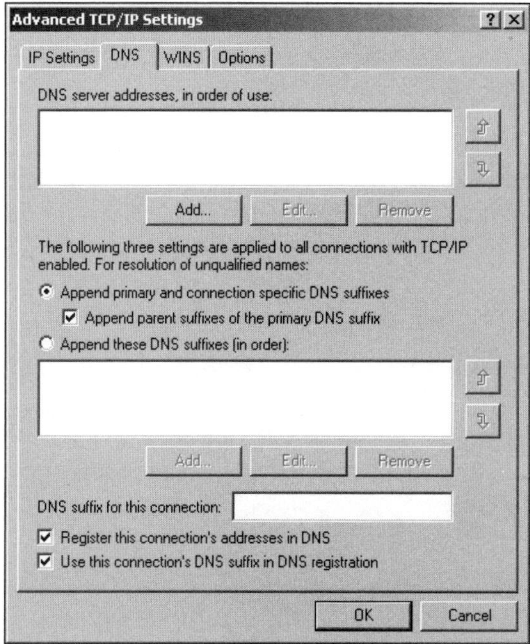

Figure 7-25 Configuring dynamic DNS on client computers

Testing the DNS Server

After your DNS server has been installed and configured, you may want to test the server to ensure that lookup queries and resource records are properly configured. There are two utilities that can be used to perform these tests:

- *DNS Monitor*—In the DNS console, right-click your server, and click Properties. Click the Monitoring tab, as shown in Figure 7-26. The DNS Monitor can perform a simple query against itself to verify correct configuration. You can also test the DNS server by forwarding a recursive query to another configured DNS server.
- *Nslookup*—This utility is installed with TCP/IP and is the classic diagnostic command line utility used for DNS. You can use nslookup to view resource

records and perform queries on any DNS server. Search Windows help for more information on nslookup. The nslookup screen is shown in Figure 7-27.

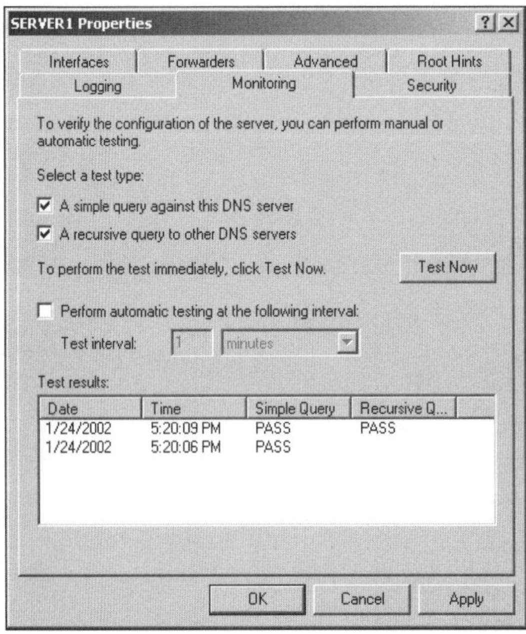

Figure 7-26 Monitoring a DNS server

```
C:\WINNT\System32\cmd.exe - nslookup

C:\>nslookup
Default Server:  danville.intersales.corp
Address:  10.0.0.100

> help
Commands:   (identifiers are shown in uppercase, [] means optional)
NAME            - print info about the host/domain NAME using default server
NAME1 NAME2     - as above, but use NAME2 as server
help or ?       - print info on common commands
set OPTION      - set an option
    all                 - print options, current server and host
    [no]debug           - print debugging information
    [no]d2              - print exhaustive debugging information
    [no]defname         - append domain name to each query
    [no]recurse         - ask for recursive answer to query
    [no]search          - use domain search list
    [no]vc              - always use a virtual circuit
    domain=NAME         - set default domain name to NAME
    srchlist=N1[/N2/.../N6] - set domain to N1 and search list to N1,N2, etc.
    root=NAME           - set root server to NAME
    retry=X             - set number of retries to X
    timeout=X           - set initial time-out interval to X seconds
    type=X              - set query type (ex. A,ANY,CNAME,MX,NS,PTR,SOA,SRV)
    querytype=X         - same as type
    class=X             - set query class (ex. IN (Internet), ANY)
    [no]msxfr           - use MS fast zone transfer
    ixfrver=X           - current version to use in IXFR transfer request
server NAME     - set default server to NAME, using current default server
lserver NAME    - set default server to NAME, using initial server
finger [USER]   - finger the optional NAME at the current default host
root            - set current default server to the root
ls [opt] DOMAIN [> FILE] - list addresses in DOMAIN (optional: output to FILE)
    -a          -  list canonical names and aliases
    -d          -  list all records
    -t TYPE     -  list records of the given type (e.g. A,CNAME,MX,NS,PTR etc.)
view FILE           - sort an 'ls' output file and view it with pg
exit            - exit the program

>
```

Figure 7-27 Viewing the nslookup command

Troubleshooting Name Resolution Problems

You should now be able to understand how DNS is used to assist Windows 2000 and XP clients to resolve host names to IP addresses, and how they locate network services. Legacy Windows clients, such as Windows 9x or Windows NT, use an additional form of network identification and communication called NetBIOS names. Just as DNS is used to resolve host names to IP addresses, there has to also be a method to resolve NetBIOS names to IP addresses. Windows 2000 can use a service called the **Windows Internet Name Service (WINS)** to assist in resolving NetBIOS names to IP addresses. A WINS server is very similar to a DNS server in that it maintains a list of IP addresses and NetBIOS names. In addition to name resolution, it is used to assist pre-Windows 2000 clients in finding network resources such as a domain controller. A WINS server can be installed the same way as DNS, by accessing Add/Remove Programs, clicking Add/Remove Windows Components, and then clicking the Details of the Network Services category.

When a WINS server has been implemented, and when a client needs to resolve a NetBIOS name, Windows 2000 follows a specific process in the attempt to discover the IP address. Being familiar with this process can assist you in diagnosing NetBIOS name resolution problems on the network.

1. The client attempts to communicate with another computer using a NetBIOS utility such as net use. The first place that is checked for name resolution is the NetBIOS name cache. The NetBIOS name cache contains the most recently used NetBIOS names. You can view the NetBIOS name cache by typing nbtstat -c at the command prompt.
2. If the name is not in the cache, the WINS server is queried.
3. If the WINS server is not available, a network broadcast takes place to find out if the target computer can be reached. Because broadcasts are not usually configured to pass through routers, if the target computer is in a different subnet, name resolution may still not take place.
4. At this point, the next step requires a special file called the Lmhosts file. This is an ASCII file that is stored in the %systemroot%\System32\drivers\etc folder on the computer. The computer's IP address and NetBIOS name are listed in the file in order to provide IP to name resolution. This file may be edited with a regular text editor such as Notepad.
5. If name resolution fails up to this point, the next method is to attempt to read another text file called the Hosts file. This file is also stored in the %systemroot%\System32\drivers\etc folder. Very similar to an Lmhosts file, this file is usually used to resolve DNS domain names to IP addresses.

6. The final method of resolution is to check a configured DNS server to see if a DNS name is the same as the NetBIOS name. If resolution does not take place after this step, the client receives an error message.

If you do not want to use a WINS or DNS server and you need to communicate with a computer over a router, edit the Lmhosts (WINS) or Hosts (DNS) files to provide the name and IP address of the target computer. Both of these files must be saved without any file extension.

If you are attempting to troubleshoot a host name problem, host name resolution also follows a process similar to NetBIOS name resolution:

1. When a client attempts to contact another computer by using a utility based on a Host name or TCP/IP, such as ping, the first step is that the computer checks to make sure that the target name is not its own.
2. The next step is to query the Hosts file for an entry that states the host name and IP address.
3. The final step is to query a DNS server. If the DNS server is configured to allow WINS forward lookups, name resolution may continue to a WINS server.
4. If the WINS server fails to provide a resolution, a local broadcast takes place in an attempt to find the target computer.
5. The final step is to query the Lmhosts file in an attempt to find the name to IP address resolution. If name resolution does not take place after this step, the client receives an error message.

The final step of troubleshooting NetBIOS or host name resolution is to ensure that the client configurations have been set correctly. To access the configuration settings, double-click the Network and Dial-up Connections on Control Panel. Right-click your network adapter, and choose Properties. Double-click Internet Protocol (TCP/IP) to access the TCP/IP Properties. Click the Advanced button to view both the client DNS and WINS configurations. Click Add to add the appropriate server's IP address to the list, as shown in Figure 7-28.

A DHCP server can automatically provide network clients with WINS and DNS server configurations, as well as define the name resolution process.

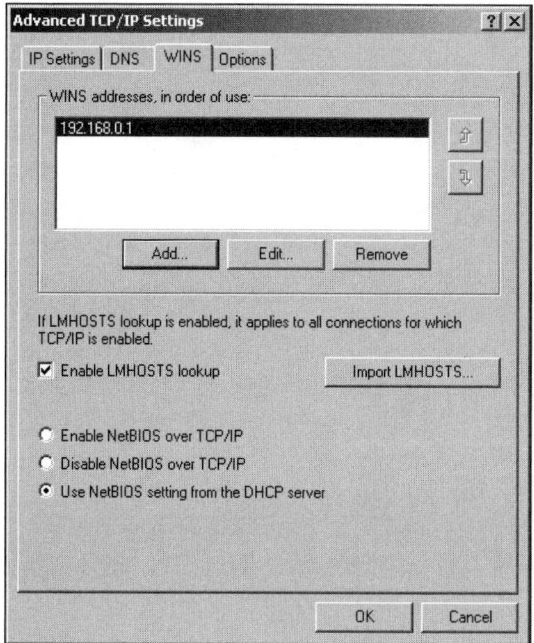

Figure 7-28 Configuring a client's WINS settings

Chapter Summary

- TCP/IP consists of a suite of protocols that are used to configure, manage, and troubleshoot network connectivity. Some of these protocols include TCP, UDP, ARP, and IP.
- All hosts on a TCP/IP network require an IP address and a subnet mask. A default gateway is needed to communicate outside of the local subnet. IP addresses can be assigned statically to a host computer, or be dynamically assigned by using a DHCP server.
- There are several utilities, such as ipconfig and ping, that can be used to verify and troubleshoot TCP/IP.
- Once the DHCP service is installed, a unique scope must be created and activated and the DHCP server authorized in Active Directory. Various scope options, such as the IP address of the default gateway, can also be added.
- Windows 2000 DHCP clients automatically update resource records with the DNS server. The DHCP server can be configured to perform all updates and perform updates on behalf of legacy clients.
- DNS is used for name resolution and to locate network services.

- There are three types of DNS zones: primary, secondary, and Active Directory integrated. Primary servers are authoritative for a zone and the secondary servers act as a backup, maintaining a copy of the zone file. An Active Directory integrated zone stores the zone information in Active Directory. The information is replicated to all domain controllers.
- When configuring a DNS server, you can choose whether or not to allow dynamic updates. You can also choose to only allow those computers with accounts in Active Directory to perform updates.
- The ipconfig and nslookup commands can be used to troubleshoot name resolution problems.

KEY TERMS

Active Directory integrated zone — The zone data is stored in the Active Directory database rather than in a zone file.

Address Resolution Protocol (ARP) — Works at the Internet layer and is responsible for mapping IP addresses to MAC addresses assigned to the network interface adapter. These can be either dynamic or static entries. Dynamic entries are stored in the ARP cache for two to 10 minutes. Static entries stay in the cache until the computer is restarted.

default gateway — This is the 32-bit number of the router on the local network, which is used to communicate with hosts outside of the local subnet.

Domain Name System (DNS) — Used for two essential tasks: host name to IP address resolution and for the location of network services, such as domain controllers that provide user authentication.

Dynamic Host Configuration Protocol (DHCP) — Used to centralize the administration of IP addresses and various options, and eliminate the administrative overhead of statically assigning the information to each network host.

forward lookup zone — Used to perform the standard host name to IP address forward lookup queries.

fully qualified domain name (FQDN) — Describes the location of the host in relation to the DNS namespace. For example a computer named "webserver" in the marketing domain of Bayside.com would have the FQDN of *webserver.marketing.bayside.com*.

host — Any computer that is a member of a specific DNS domain within the network structure.

Internet Control Message Protocol (ICMP) — Operates at the network layer and is used to exchange status and error information between two hosts.

Internet Group Management Protocol (IGMP) — Operates at the network layer and is used to manage network and host information when multicasting is used.

Internet Protocol (IP) — The Internet layer protocol responsible for the addressing and routing of packets so that they are delivered to the correct host on the local network or across routers to a host on another subnet.

IP address — The 32-bit number that uniquely identifies a host on a TCP/IP network.

ipconfig — A command used to verify the addressing parameters assigned to a computer.

ipconfig/all — The ipconfig command plus the all parameter is used to produce a full display of assigned parameters.

iterative query — If the DNS server cannot resolve a name, it gives the requestor a pointer to another DNS server that is authoritative for the next level of the FQDN supplied.

multicasting — The sending of a message to multiple clients, or a group of clients.

pathping — A command that combines the functions of the ping and tracert commands. The pathping command checks network connectivity by sending echo request messages to each router between a source and destination host and then computing the result based on packets returned from each router.

ping — A command used to test for connectivity between hosts on the network by sending ICMP packets to a remote computer and listening for an echo reply from the remote host.

recursive query — A command that specifies the return of a complete and full answer to the query, not a pointer to another DNS server.

reverse lookup zone — A specific type of zone that performs reverse IP address to host name resolution queries.

scope — A range of IP addresses configured on a DHCP server that can be handed out to network clients.

standard primary zone — The DNS zone file is stored as a regular read/write text file in the %systemroot%\system32\dns folder.

standard secondary zone — A read-only zone file is copied from a configured standard primary zone.

subnet mask — The 32-bit number that identifies the network to which a TCP/IP host belongs.

superscope — A grouping of scopes created for multiple subnets on a physical network.

tracert — A command used to determine the route taken to a destination by sending ICMP echo packets with varying time-to-live (TTL) values to the destination.

Transmission Control Protocol (TCP) — Operates at the transport layer and is responsible for the reliable transmission of data on a TCP/IP network.

Transmission Control Protocol/Internet Protocol (TCP/IP) — Consists of a suite of protocols and utilities that are used for network communication and troubleshooting on local networks and the Internet.

User Datagram Protocol (UDP) — A connectionless protocol that functions at the transport layer and provides no guarantee of delivery.

Windows Internet Name Service (WINS) — A Windows 2000 service that is used to resolve NetBIOS names to IP addresses.

winipcfg — A command used on Windows 9x machines to display the TCP/IP configuration settings.

zone file — A DNS configuration file that holds all of the resource records for the domain, such as computer name records, mail exchanger records, and service records.

zone transfer — The copying of the DNS database information between the primary and secondary zones.

REVIEW QUESTIONS

1. Your network consists of many subnets and managing the DHCP scopes has become difficult. What feature of Windows 2000 DHCP can you use to make the administration of multiple scopes more manageable?
   a. multicast scopes
   b. client reservations
   c. superscopes
   d. dynamic DNS
2. Your network consists of multiple subnets and multiple gateways connecting the different segments. When configuring the 003 scope option, at which level should the option be configured?
   a. server
   b. DHCP
   c. client
   d. scope
3. Scope options configured at the server level override options configured at the scope and client level. True or False?
4. You install the DHCP service on one of your network servers. You configure an IP scope, some additional scope options, and activate the scope. You soon discover that clients on the network are not receiving IP addresses. What is likely causing the problem?
   a. You must configure a minimum of two scopes.
   b. Clients are configured with static IP addresses.
   c. The DHCP service is not started.
   d. The DHCP server must be authorized in Active Directory.
5. Your network consists of two subnets. You create two scopes on your DHCP server. Scope1 (for subnet 1) has a range of 192.168.2.10 to 192.168.2.30. Scope2 (for subnet 2) has a range of 192.168.3.10 to 192.168.3.20. The subnets are connected via a single router. You configure the 003 router option at the server level and type the IP address of 192.168.2.31. Users on subnet 1 now report that they can access resources on their own subnet, but cannot access resources on subnet 2. What is likely causing the problem?
   a. The router is not operational.
   b. The 003 router option should be configured at the scope level.
   c. The DHCP server is offline.
   d. Clients on subnet 1 are not receiving IP addresses.

6. Which of the following TCP/IP commands can be used to verify the IP addressing parameters assigned to a computer?
   a. arp
   b. ping
   c. tracert
   d. ipconfig
7. Which of the following TCP/IP commands can be used to verify network connectivity with a host on another subnet?
   a. ping
   b. ipconfig
   c. tracert
   d. arp

8. Your network consists of Windows 2000 clients and some legacy clients. You have a DHCP server and a DNS server on your network. You want Windows 2000 clients to perform the DNS updates on their own and the DHCP server to perform the updates for those clients that do not support the dynamic update feature. What two options should be selected when configuring DHCP? (Choose two answers.)
   a. Always Update DNS
   b. Automatically Update DNS for Clients that Do Not Support Dynamic Update
   c. Never Update DNS for Windows 2000 Clients
   d. Automatically Update DHCP Client Information in DNS
9. Your network consists of several IP subnets connected by routers. One of your goals is to minimize the number of broadcasts on the network. Clients on each subnet are configured for dynamic IP addressing. You install the DHCP service on one of the Windows 2000 Servers. What else must you do so clients on each subnet can obtain IP addressing information?
   a. Install the DHCP relay agent on the DHCP server.
   b. Install the DHCP relay agent on one server on each subnet.
   c. Install the DHCP relay agent on all client workstations.
   d. Configure the routers to forward DHCP broadcasts.
10. The DHCP relay agent can be installed on the DHCP Server. True or False?
11. You are planning to install the DNS service. You want the zone file to be replicated to all domain controllers. What type of zone will you configure?
    a. primary zone
    b. replicated zone
    c. Active Directory integrated zone
    d. standard secondary zone

12. Which command can be used to clear out the entries stored in the local DNS resolver cache?
    a. ipconfig /registerdns
    b. ipconfig /flushdns
    c. nslookup /flushdns
    d. ipconfig /cleardns
13. To use dynamic updates on a network, what components have to be configured?
    a. DHCP servers
    b. DHCP clients
    c. routers
    d. DNS servers
14. What utility can you use to verify the host name associated with an IP address?
    a. ipconfig
    b. nslookup
    c. hostname
    d. ping
15. You are a network administrator for a medium-size network. All clients have been upgraded to Windows 2000. All servers that are running Windows NT 4.0 are to be upgraded to Windows 2000 Server in the near future. Clients are configured for dynamic DNS, but the entries are not appearing in the zone file. What is causing the problem?
    a. DHCP needs to be configured to perform updates.
    b. DNS needs to be configured to allow updates.
    c. Clients are not configured correctly.
    d. Servers need to be upgraded to Windows 2000.
16. A DNS server can be configured to only accept updates from computers that have accounts in Active Directory. True or False?
17. Which of the following records indicates the IP address associated with a host name?
    a. CNAME
    b. A
    c. MX
    d. SRV

18. Which type of zone is recommended if you are installing DNS on a domain controller?
    a. primary
    b. standard secondary
    c. Active Directory integrated
    d. domain
19. What resource record enables a host to have an alias name?
    a. A
    b. CNAME
    c. PTR
    d. SRV
20. What does Windows 2000 support so that DNS records can be dynamically updated?
    a. automatic IP updates
    b. dynamic IP updates
    c. automatic DNS
    d. dynamic DNS

Hands-on Projects

Project 7-1

In this Hands-on Project, you validate your local computer configuration and connectivity by utilizing TCP/IP diagnostic utilities.

1. Log on to your computer with the administrator account.
2. Click **Start**, click **Run**, and then type **cmd** in the Open text box. Click **OK**. The command prompt opens.
3. At the command prompt, type **ipconfig**, and then press **Enter**.
4. Fill in the following information from the data displayed after typing ipconfig:
    a. Connection-specific DNS Suffix ________________
    b. IP address ________________
    c. Subnet Mask ________________
    d. Default Gateway ________________
5. At the command prompt, type **ipconfig /all**, and then press **Enter**. Notice the additional information presented.

6. At the command prompt, type **ping 127.0.0.1**, and press **Enter**. This is the address that represents your local computer. You then receive four replies indicating that TCP/IP is installed correctly.
7. Obtain the IP address from your partner or second computer. Type **ping <*partnerIP*>** to test connectivity to your partner's computer.
8. If you have Internet connectivity, at the command prompt, type **pathping –h 5**. This generates ping and router statistics for five hops.
9. For a final test, type **netdiag** at the command prompt. Look for any errors in the information that is displayed.
10. Close all windows, and log off.

Project 7-2

In this Hands-on Project, you install the DHCP service on your server.

1. Log on to your computer with the administrator account.
2. Click **Start**, point to **Settings**, and then click **Control Panel**.
3. Double-click **Add/Remove Programs**, and then click **Add/Remove Windows Components**.
4. Scroll down and click **Networking Services**, and then click the **Details** button.
5. Check the **Dynamic Host Configuration Protocol (DHCP)** option. Make sure that only the DNS and DHCP options are checked, and then click **OK**. Click **Next**. The Windows Components Wizard continues and installs the DHCP service. Click **Finish**.
6. Close all windows.

Project 7-3

In this Hands-on Project, you configure a DHCP scope and authorize the DHCP server into Active Directory.

1. Click **Start**, point to **Programs**, point to **Administrative Tools**, and then click **DHCP**.
2. Click your server name, and then right-click. Then click **New Scope**. The New Scope Wizard appears. Click **Next**.
3. Type **Bayside IP range** for the Name, and then click **Next**.
4. In the Start IP address box, type **10.0.0.1**.
5. In the End IP address box, type **10.0.0.10**. Click **Next**.
6. Click **Next** in the Add Exclusions dialog box.
7. Change the Lease Duration to **3** days, and then click **Next**.
8. Click **No, I will configure these options later**. Click **Next**, and then click **Finish**.

9. To authorize the server into Active Directory, right-click **DHCP**, and click **Manage authorized servers**.
10. Click the **Authorize** button, and then type the IP address of the server.
11. Click **OK,** and then click **Yes**.
12. Close all windows.

Normally, at this point you would also need to activate the scope; however, for classroom purposes do not activate the DHCP scope.

Project 7-4

In this Hands-on Project, you verify TCP/IP configurations on client computers. You begin by viewing the TCP/IP properties to see how IP addresses are obtained, and you verify that dynamic IP registration is enabled.

1. Right-click **My Network Places**, and click **Properties**.
2. Right-click your network adapter, and click **Properties**.
3. Double-click the **Internet Protocol (TCP/IP)** component to open its properties.
4. If you were using a DHCP server, which setting would you choose?
5. Leave the current IP settings, and click the **Advanced** button.
6. Click the **DNS** tab. Make sure that the **Register this connection's addresses in DNS** option is checked.
7. Click **OK**, and close all windows.

Project 7-5

In this Hands-on Project you create a new forward lookup zone and a reverse lookup zone for the company washex.com, and then configure it for dynamic updates.

1. Click **Start**, point to **Programs**, point to **Administrative Tools**, and then click **DNS**.
2. Click the plus sign next to your server name.
3. Left-click and then right-click **Forward Lookup Zones**, and click **New Zone**. The New Zone Wizard opens. Click **Next**.
4. Click **Standard Primary**, and then click **Next**.
5. Type **washex.com** for the Name of the zone. Click **Next**.
6. Click **Next** at the Zone File dialog box. Click **Finish**.
7. Click the plus sign (+) next to Forward Lookup Zones.
8. Click **washex.com**, and then right-click **washex.com**, and click **Properties**.
9. Click the drop-down menu next to Allow dynamic updates, and then click **Yes**.

10. Click **OK**.
11. Left-click and then right-click **Reverse Lookup Zones**, and click **New Zone**. The New Zone Wizard opens. Click **Next**.
12. Click **Active Directory-integrated**, and then click **Next**.
13. For the network ID, type **10.0.0**. Then click **Next**, and click **Finish**.
14. Close all windows.

Project 7-6

In this Hands-on Project, you change the DNS server to be Active Directory integrated, change the zone to support secure dynamic updates, and then add an MX record for your mail server and a CNAME for your Web server.

1. Click **Start**, point to **Programs**, point to **Administrative Tools**, and then click **DNS**.
2. Click the plus sign (+) next to your server name.
3. Click the plus sign (+) next to Forward Lookup Zones.
4. Click **washex.com**, and then right-click **washex.com**, and click **Properties**.
5. On the General tab, click the **Change** button next to Type.
6. Click **Active Directory integrated** and then click **OK**. Click **OK** at the prompt.
7. Click the drop-down menu next to Allow dynamic updates, and then click **Only Secure updates**. Click **OK**.
8. Right-click **washex.com**, and click **New Mail Exchanger**.
9. In the Mail server text box, type **mail1**, and then click **OK**.
10. Right-click **washex.com**, and click **New Alias.**
11. In the Alias name text box, type **www**.
12. In the Fully qualified name for target host text box, type ***<yourservername>*** **.bayside.net**.
13. Close all windows.

Project 7-7

In this Hands-on Project, you view the Hosts file to ensure you understand how to edit these files to provide name resolution.

1. Right-click **My Computer,** and click **Explore**.
2. Click the plus sign (+) to expand drive C.
3. Click the plus sign (+) to expand the **WINNT** folder.
4. Click the plus sign (+) to expand the **SYSTEM32** folder.
5. Click the plus sign (+) to expand the **DRIVERS** folder.
6. Click the plus sign (+) to expand, and then click the **ETC** folder.

7. Right-click the **Hosts** file, and click **Open With**.
8. Click the **Notepad** application, and then click **OK**.
9. Under the 127.0.0.1 entry, type the IP address of your server.
10. Next to your IP address, leave a space, and type your first name.
11. Save the file as **HOSTS** with no file extension.
12. Open a command prompt, and type **ping <*your first name*>**. You should get a reply because you have designated your server IP address to map to your first name in the Hosts file.
13. Close all windows.

CASE PROJECTS

Case Project 7-1

Your network currently implements static IP addressing. With the rapid increase in network growth and the implementation of multiple IP subnets, you are proposing a switch from static IP addressing to dynamic addressing.

1. In your proposal, include a description as to why it is a good idea that your network implements DHCP.
2. List the steps involved in installing and configuring a DHCP server.
3. The network consists of six different subnets that are connected with routers. Each of the subnets has a different gateway. How will you configure the scope options on the DHCP server? The network also has a DNS server and a WINS server.
4. The DHCP server will be placed on one of the subnets. Describe the three options you have for ensuring that clients on other subnets can still get IP addresses from a DHCP server on another subnet.

Case Project 7-2

You are a consultant for Bayside and have been asked to participate in the rollout of Windows 2000 (both clients and servers) for one of Bayside's major clients. The infrastructure consists of three separate companies, each of which will be configured as their own domain (including their own DNS domain so each can maintain control). You have been specifically asked to implement the DNS structure.

1. What type of DNS servers will you implement for each of the separate companies? How will redundancy be implemented? Explain your answer.
2. How will you configure the DNS servers between the domains so users can resolve host names outside of their local domain?
3. Administration of zone files should be minimal. How can dynamic DNS be implemented to reduce administration? How will it be configured on the network? Will the DHCP servers be required to perform updates on behalf of the clients?

CHAPTER

8

MONITORING AND TROUBLESHOOTING WINDOWS 2000

After reading this chapter and completing the exercises, you will be able to:

- Monitor Windows 2000 Server health and performance
- Troubleshoot Windows 2000 startup procedures
- Use advanced startup options and other tools used in operating system recovery
- Use the Windows 2000 backup utility

Many businesses today rely heavily on their servers for day-to-day operations. Expectations are set for network server availability and performance. When a server goes down or starts to perform poorly, many routine functions are affected and the complaints soon filter in. This means that as a network administrator you need to ensure that a server is capable of meeting performance expectations and that server downtime is minimal.

This chapter begins by looking at server performance and why it is important to monitor the health of your server. You are introduced to tools, such as the Windows 2000 System Monitor and the Performance Log and Alert components, which can be used to monitor the performance of a server. You are also shown how the information you gather can alert you to to server problems so that you can diagnose them.

This chapter also discusses the troubleshooting of system startup procedures. You should be familiar with the tools and options that are available with Windows 2000 to troubleshoot an operating system that fails to start. The more familiar you are with the tools, the faster you can troubleshoot the problem, and the sooner you can get the server back online.

Monitoring Windows 2000 Server Health and Performance

Maintaining your server is very similar to maintaining an automobile. When you purchase a new automobile, it must be serviced on a regular basis to ensure its performance over time. Many of the new cars and trucks today also come with tools that can alert you to problems when they occur. Server maintenance is very similar. Often, administrators configure servers for network use, while not realizing that over time, server performance can deteriorate for a number of reasons.

One of the more important reasons for monitoring the health of your server is that it can help alert you to problems before they occur or become more serious. Over time, networks change; the demands placed on a server can vary or increase. Monitoring server performance can help you determine what normal behavior is for your server under the current demands and alert you to any performance issues that may be occurring if the normal behavior changes. This normal behavior is known as **baseline** performance.

Windows 2000 comes with several built-in tools that can be used to monitor server health and performance, including:

- System Monitor
- Performance Logs and Alerts
- Event Viewer
- Task Manager

The following sections introduce you to these tools, providing you with a description of how they can be used to monitor your server and how to use them.

System Monitor

System Monitor is one of the most useful tools for collecting data on real-time server performance. It also allows you to track how system resources are being used and how they are behaving under the current workload. System Monitor collects data that can be used for the following tasks:

- *Server performance*—If System Monitor is used on a regular basis, it can help an administrator understand how the server performs under the current workload.
- *Problem diagnosis*—The data that is collected can be used to alert you to server components that may not be performing optimally, causing a bottleneck within the server.
- *Capacity planning*—You can use the information to see how server usage is changing over time and plan ahead for future upgrades.
- *Testing*—If configuration changes are made, you can use the data to observe the impact that the changes have on the server.

For those of you familiar with Windows NT 4, Performance Monitor has now been renamed to System Monitor.

Using System Monitor, you can define the components you want to monitor and the type of data you want to collect. You choose the **performance objects** you want to monitor, such as memory, and the specific type of **performance counters** or data associated with the object for which you want to gather data. You can further customize the data you want to capture by specifying the source or computer you want to monitor. System Monitor can be used to gather data from the local computer or from a network computer for which you have permission.

The information you capture can be displayed in one of three formats. The default format is a graph view, but information can also be viewed in a histogram and report view.

8

Capturing Data Using System Monitor

You can access the System Monitor tool by clicking the Performance console located under Administrative Tools. System Monitor opens by default in the graph view with the graph being blank, as shown in Figure 8-1.

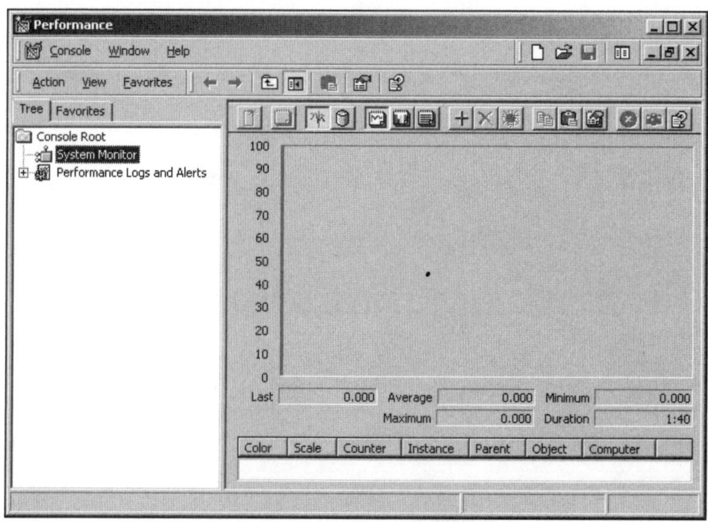

Figure 8-1 Default System Monitor view

To begin capturing data, you must choose the performance counters and objects you wish to monitor. From within the Performance console, you can click the + (plus sign) located on the tool bar. This opens the Add Counters window, as shown in Figure 8-2.

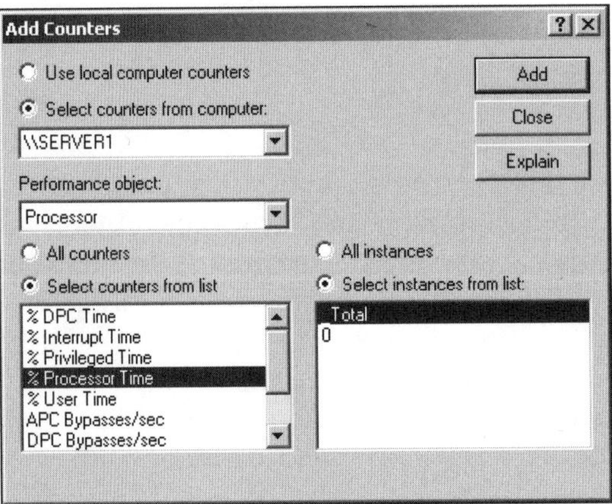

Figure 8-2 Add Counters window

As you notice from the Add Counters window, you can choose whether to use the counters on the local computer or a computer from the network. Use the Performance object list arrow, to choose the object to monitor, such as Processor, as shown in Figure 8-3. Once you choose an object, the related counters are displayed. Different objects have different performance counters available.

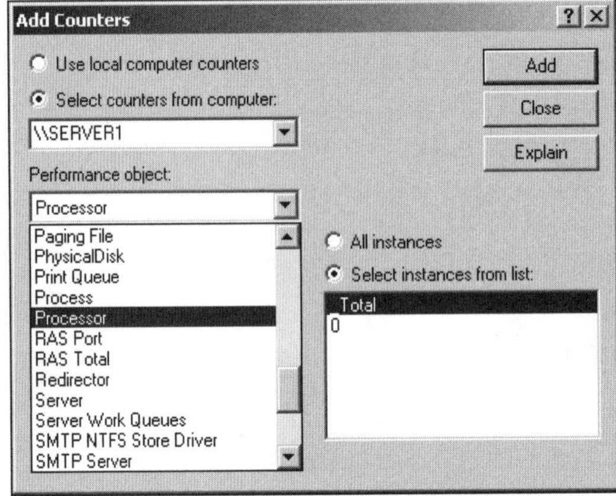

Figure 8-3 Selecting a performance object

The next step is to choose to monitor All counters or Select counters from list. To add a counter to the graph, click the counter in the list, and click the Add button. To add more than one counter at a time, hold down the Ctrl key, click the counters you want to add to the graph, and click Add.

If there are multiple instances of a performance object on the computer, such as multiple processors or physical hard drives, you can choose to monitor All instances or Select instances from list.

There are many performance counters available in System Monitor, and it is very difficult to know what each one does. In the Add Counters window there is an Explain button that provides a description of each counter associated with an object.

Once the Add Counters window is closed, System Monitor automatically begins gathering data at one-second intervals based on the counters that you added. You can change the interval by right-clicking anywhere within the graph, then clicking Properties, clicking the General tab, and changing the Update automatically every <*number*> seconds parameter, as shown in Figure 8-4. You can also use manual update or update on demand by clearing this check box and using the Update Data option (the camera icon) on the tool bar.

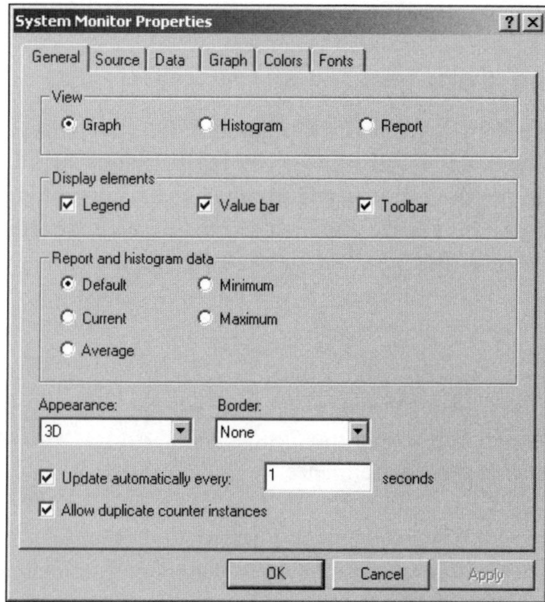

Figure 8-4 Changing the update interval

As already mentioned, the default view for System Monitor is the graph view. To change to one of the other available views, click the View Histogram or View Report icon on the tool bar. You can also right-click anywhere in the graph, click Properties, and choose the view you want to use from the General tab. Figure 8-5 shows an example of the Report View. All three of these views can have various elements modified such as graph colors and titles. To modify these elements, right-click the graph or report, and click Properties.

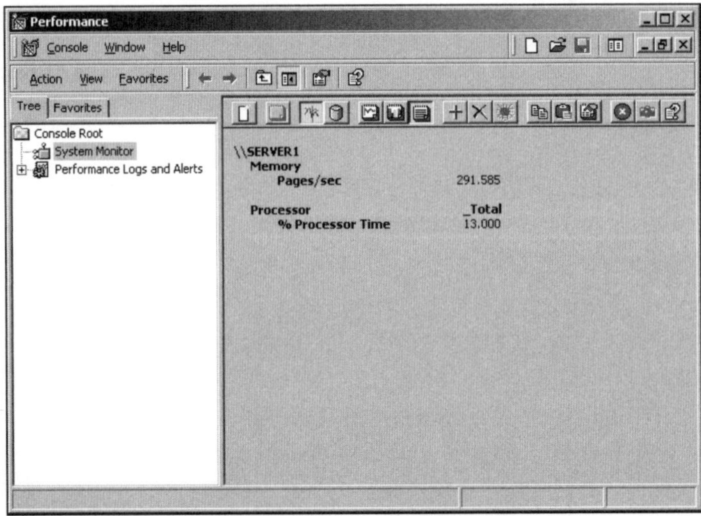

Figure 8-5 Changing views in System Monitor

Performance Objects and Counters

Monitoring performance on your server should be a regular maintenance task. The information you gather can help to establish a baseline server performance or identify what is normal server performance under the current workload. As you continue to monitor your server over time, you can compare the data against the baseline to identify how performance is changing as the network changes and workloads increase. Doing so allows you to pinpoint bottlenecks, such as components that may be hindering server performance, before they become a serious problem.

Any time you upgrade or add a component to a system, whether it is a hardware or software component, you should run System Monitor to determine the effect the change has on server performance.

When monitoring server performance, there are a few performance objects that should be included, as well as specific performance counters associated with each one. For the processor performance object, these include:

- *% Processor Time*—Measures the percentage of time that the processor is executing a non-idle thread. If the value is continually at, or over, 80%, a CPU upgrade may be required.
- *% Interrupt Time*—Measures hardware interrupts. If you experience a combination of Processor Time exceeding 90% and % Interrupt Time exceeding 15%, check for malfunctioning hardware or device drivers.

For the memory performance object, these include:

- *Pages/Second*—Measure the number of pages read in or out to disk to resolve hard page faults. If this number exceeds 20 or more page faults per second, add more RAM to the computer.
- *Page Faults/Second*—Measures the number of hard page faults

For the physical disk performance object, this includes:

- *% Disk Time*—Measures the percentage of elapsed time that the selected disk drive is busy. If above 90%, try moving the page file to another physical drive, or upgrade the hard drive.

For the logical disk performance object, this includes:

- *Disk Queue Length*—If averaging over 2, then drive access may be a bottleneck. You may want to upgrade the drive or hard drive controller. Implementing a Stripe Set with multiple drives may also fix this problem.

In Windows NT, all disk counters were turned off by default. In Windows 2000, the physical disk object is turned on by default and the logical disk object is turned off by default. To obtain performance counter data for logical disk drives, you must type diskperf –yv at the command prompt.

Gathering the data is the easy part. The difficult part is interpreting the information to determine what component is affecting performance. The difficulty lies in the fact that the performance of some components can affect other components. It may appear from the data that one component is performing poorly when this can be the result of another component performing poorly. For example, if you determine that your processor is running over 80%, your first instinct may tell you to upgrade the processor or install multiple processors if the motherboard supports it. Through further analysis, however, you may find a lack of memory is the bottleneck that is causing excess paging. You would have discovered this by monitoring the Pages/Second Memory counter. Thus monitoring multiple components on a regular basis should give you an idea of how they perform together and make troubleshooting server performance that much easier.

Performance Logs and Alerts

Another tool available within the Performance console is the **Performance Logs and Alerts**. This tool allows you to automatically collect data on the local computer or from another computer on the network and view it using System Monitor or export the data into a program such as Excel.

Performance Logs and Alerts allows you to perform the following tasks:

- Collect data in a comma-separated or tab-separated format so it can easily be imported into another program for analysis
- View data both while it is being collected and after it has been collected

- Configure parameters such as start and stop times for log generation, file names, and file size
- Configure and manage multiple logging sessions from a single console window
- Set up alerts so a message is sent, a program is run, or a log file started when a specific counter exceeds or drops below a configured value

The Performance Logs and Alerts can be accessed through the Performance console. There are three options available under Performance Logs and Alerts, as shown in Figure 8-6: counter logs, trace logs, and alerts. Clicking each of these options displays the logs and alerts that you have already configured.

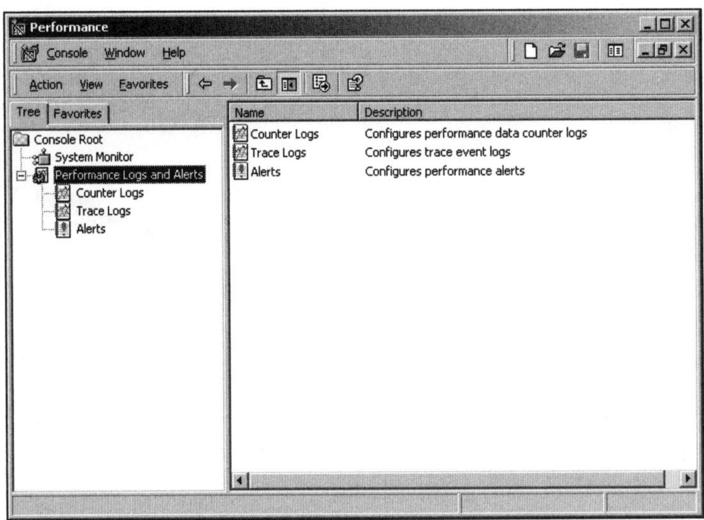

Figure 8-6 Performance Logs and Alerts

Counter logs take the information that you view using System Monitor, and save it to a log file. One of the main advantages of using counter logs is that logging can be configured to start and stop at different intervals. **Trace logs** are similar to counter logs only they are triggered to start when an event occurs. You can use **alerts** to configure an event to occur when a counter meets a predefined value.

Configuring Alerts

Logging does increase overhead on a server, so it is not something you want to have running all the time. It is essential that you set up a regular schedule for collecting data and ensure that the data is reviewed to make sure no problems are developing or occurring. Because logging should not be running all the time, alerts can be set up to notify you of a potential problem. For example, you can configure an alert to monitor the processor usage and notify you if it exceeds 80%.

To create an alert, use the following steps:

1. Right-click the **Alerts** object in the Performance Logs and Alerts node, and then click **New Alert Settings** on the shortcut menu.
2. When the New Alert Settings dialog box opens, type in a name for the alert, as shown in Figure 8-7, and then click **OK**.

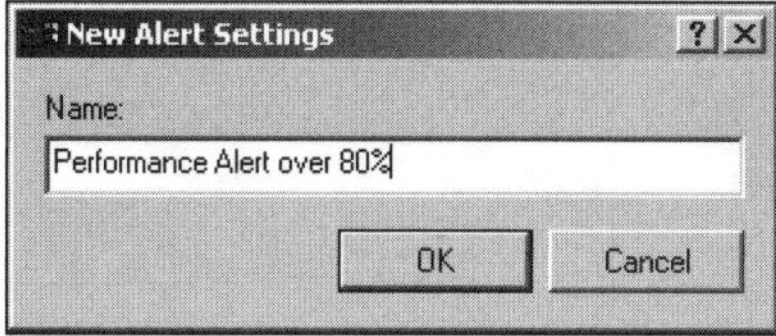

Figure 8-7 The New Alert Settings dialog box

3. In the Alert Settings dialog box, type a comment describing the alert, and then click **Add**.
4. As shown in Figure 8-8, the Select Counters dialog box opens for you to choose the objects and counters to monitor for the alert.

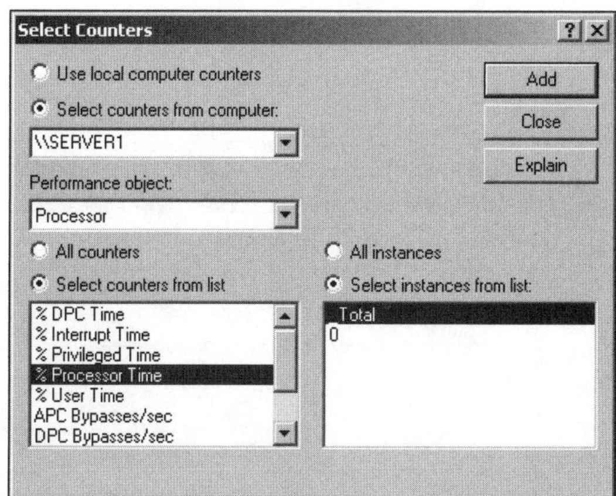

Figure 8-8 The Select Counters dialog box

5. When you have specified the required counters, click the **Close** button to return to the Alert dialog box.
6. From the Alert when the value is list, specify Under or Over, and specify the value the counter must reach to trigger an alert. You can also specify the update interval in the Sample data every: section.
7. Click the **Action** tab and specify the action that should be taken when the alert is triggered. The default action is to Log an entry in the application event log. The completed dialog box is shown in Figure 8-9.

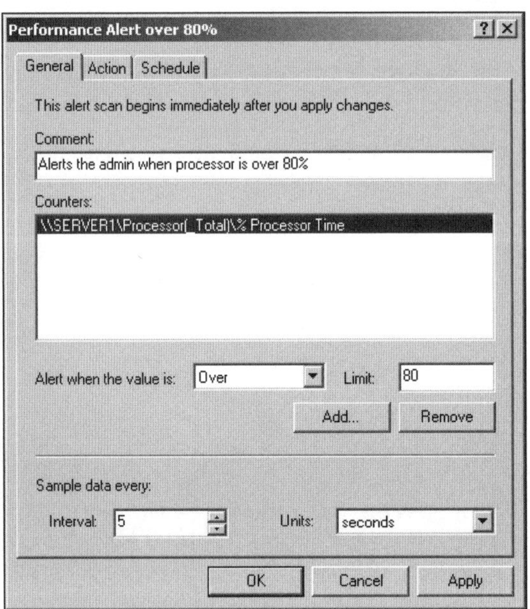

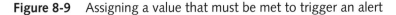

Figure 8-9 Assigning a value that must be met to trigger an alert

Table 8-1 summarizes the available options on the Action tab.

Table 8-1 Actions that can be taken when an alert is triggered

Option	Description
Log an entry in the application event log	Adds an entry to the application log when the event is triggered
Send a network message to	Messenger service sends a message to the specified computer when the alert is triggered
Start performance data log	Counter log is run when the alert is triggered
Run this program	Specified program is run when the alert is triggered
Command line arguments	Specified command line arguments are copied when the Run this program option is used

Event Viewer

Another tool available with Windows 2000 is the **Event Viewer**. Event Viewer can be used to gather information and troubleshoot software, hardware, and system problems.

Events that occur on a system are tracked and recorded in different log files. You can use Event Viewer to view the contents of the log files. For example, you can use Event Viewer to view the contents of the system log to determine when, and possibly why, a specific service failed to start.

Whenever you are troubleshooting a problem with a server, one of the first places to look to gather information about the cause is the Event Viewer. Entries in the log files can alert you to warnings and errors that are occurring, the component or application that is generating the message, and possibly why the problem is happening. Most entries also include an event ID that can be researched on Microsoft's Web site to gather more detailed information on the problem and find a possible solution.

Access *support.microsoft.com* for additional resources that can be used in researching event ID messages.

Events are written to one of three log files:

- ***Application log***—Contains information, warnings, and errors generated by programs installed on the system
- ***Security log***—Events pertaining to the audit policy are written to the security log. For example, if the audit policy is tracking failed logon attempts, an event is written to the security log each time a user is unsuccessful in logging on. By default, security logging is disabled until an audit policy is configured.
- ***System log***—Contains information, warnings, and errors generated by Windows 2000 system components, such as drivers and services

A domain controller has two additional logs: the directory service log, which records events logged by Active Directory, and the file replication service log, which logs file replication events. A server installed with the DNS service also includes the DNS server log, which records events related to the DNS server service.

You can open Event Viewer by clicking Start, pointing to Programs, and then pointing to Administrative Tools. To view the contents of a log file, click the log file from the scope pane. The events are then displayed in the details pane, as shown in Figure 8-10.

By default, any user can view the contents of the application and system log. The security log can only be viewed by administrators, and those users who have been assigned the Manage Auditing and Security Log right.

The system and application logs display the following types of events:

- *Information*—When a component or application successfully performs an operation; information events are identified by an "I" in Event Viewer
- *Warning*—When an event occurs that may not be a problem at the current time, but may become a problem in the future; warnings are indicated by an exclamation point
- *Error*—When a significant event has occurred, such as a service failing to start or a device driver failing to load; errors are indicated by an "x"

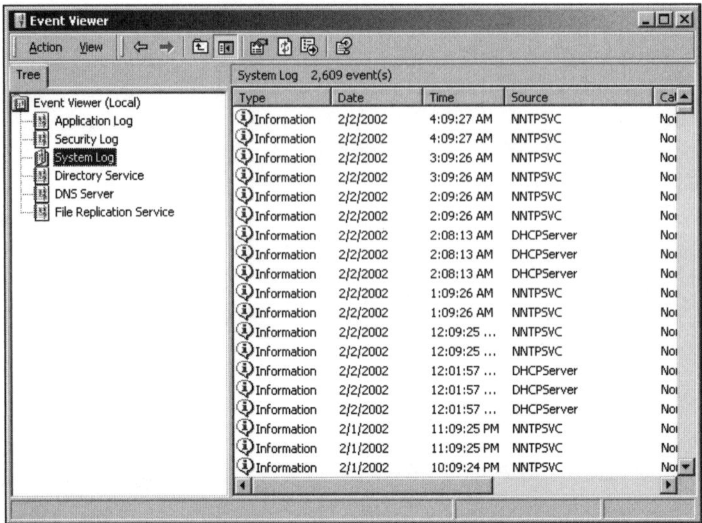

Figure 8-10 The contents of a log file using Event Viewer

There are two other types of events that are logged. These are successes and failures of actions that are performed on the network based on the configuration of an audit policy. Refer to Chapter Five for the configuration of security audit policies.

Interpreting Events

When you click a log file within Event Viewer, the details pane lists all the events that have occurred and provides general information about each one, such as:

- Type of event (information, warning, or error)
- The date and time that the event occurred
- The source of the event (the component or application that logged the event)
- The category and event ID
- The computer on which the event occurred

You can view more detailed information about an event by double-clicking the event in the details pane. This opens the Event Properties dialog box, as shown in Figure 8-11.

The event header provides the same information that was listed above. The event description provides an administrator with a description of what occurred and why the event is significant, which is usually the most useful information.

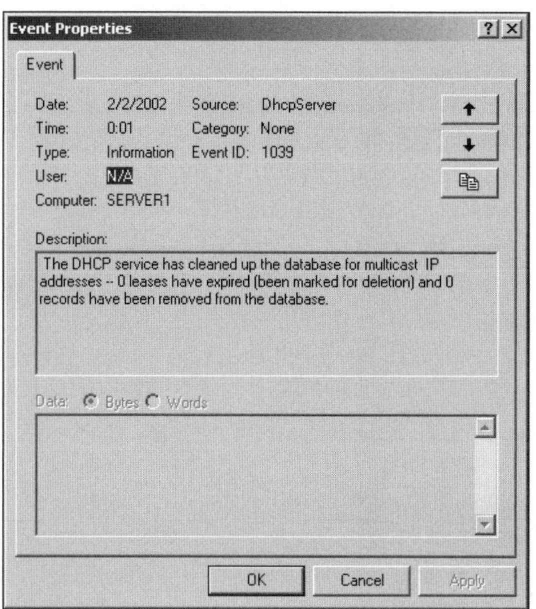

Figure 8-11 Event Properties dialog box

The data field displays information that is generated by the program or component. It contains binary data that can be used to support technicians to troubleshoot the problem.

Task Manager

Another tool that you can use to monitor server health and performance is **Task Manager**. It is one of the fastest ways to check server performance and determine what processes are running on the system.You can launch the tool by right-clicking the taskbar, and clicking Task Manager, or by pressing Ctrl+Alt+Del and clicking Task Manager.

Once Task Manager is open, it displays three tabs: Applications, Processes, and Performance, as shown in Figure 8-12.The Applications tab tells you what applications are currently running and what their status is (running or not responding). This tab is most useful for ending a program that is frozen or has stopped responding.

The Processes tab, as shown in Figure 8-13, shows information about the processes currently running on the system. The Processes tab displays information such as the name of the process, the percentage of CPU being used by the process, and the amount of memory each process is consuming.To modify these columns, access the Select Columns command in the View menu.

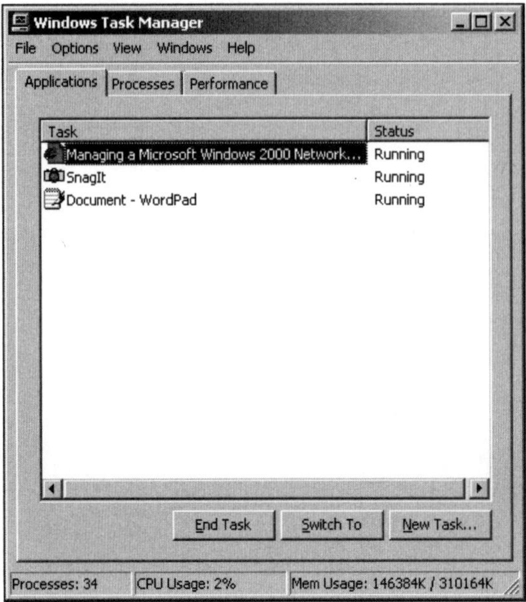

Figure 8-12 Task Manager

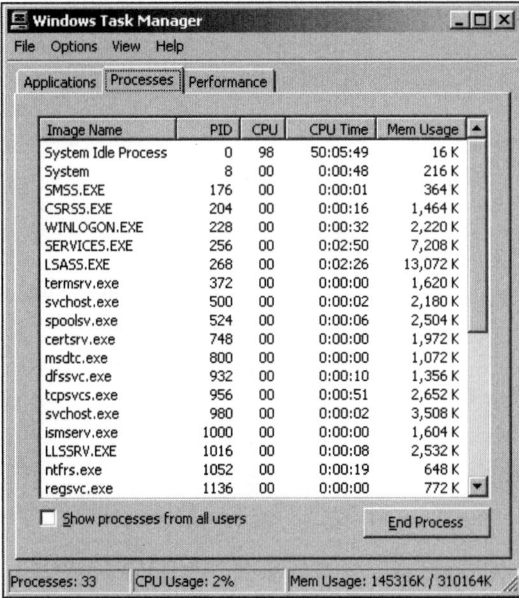

Figure 8-13 The Processes tab within Task Manager

The Performance tab, as shown in Figure 8-14, provides a quick view of the system's current performance. It is not meant to provide detailed performance information, but is a quick way of checking performance to determine if there is a problem. You can then use another tool such as System Monitor for further investigation. Table 8-2 summarizes the information that is provided on the Performance tab.

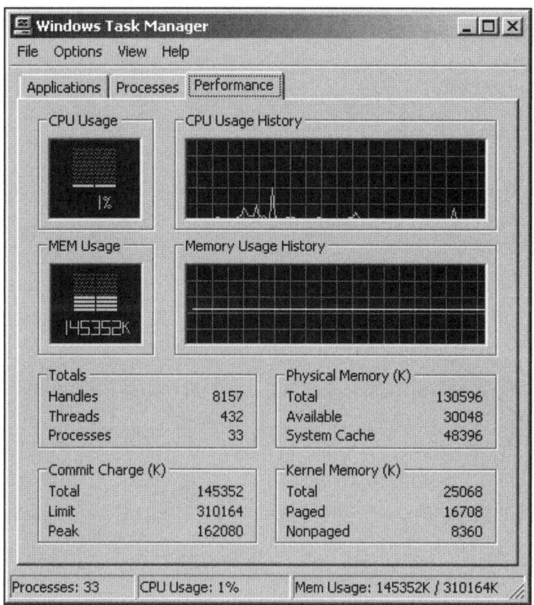

Figure 8-14 The Performance tab within Task Manager

Table 8-2 The Performance tab

Component	Description
CPU Usage/CPU Usage History	Shows the percentage of CPU being used and graphs CPU usage for the last minute
Mem Usage/Mem Usage History	Shows the amount of memory currently in use
Totals	Displays the total number of handles, threads, and processes
Physical Memory	Displays the total amount of memory, how much is available, and the amount of memory used for the system cache
Commit Charge	The amount of memory that has been committed to all applications currently running
Kernel Memory	The amount of memory that has been allocated to kernel functions, the amount of memory that could be paged to disk, and the amount of nonpaged memory

Identify and Disable Unnecessary Services

When it comes to optimizing and securing your server, one of the first things you can do is disable any unnecessary components, such as services. When a service is unnecessarily installed during setup or is no longer in use, it should be disabled. Running unnecessary services can cause overhead on a system. For example, when you install Windows 2000, Internet Information Services is installed. If your computer is not publishing Web information, the service should be disabled.

The services that you disable depend on the role the server plays on the network. For example, a Web server requires different services than a print server. The other thing you need to consider is service dependencies. Before you stop or disable a service, check to see if there are any other services running that depend on the service.

Services are likely to be affected if a service they depend on is stopped or disabled.

Use the following steps to disable any unnecessary services running on your system:

1. Click **Start**, point to **Programs**, point to **Administrative Tools**, and click **Services**.
2. Double-click the service you want to disable.
3. Click the General tab of the service's Properties dialog box, click the Startup type list arrow, and then click **Disabled**, as shown in Figure 8-15.

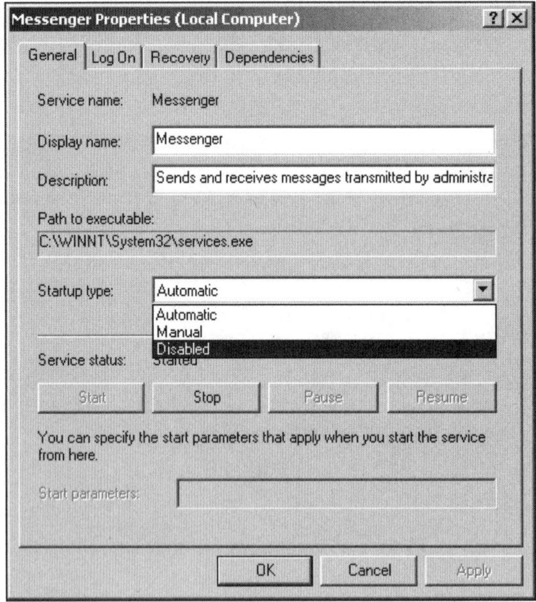

Figure 8-15 Disabling a service

The Properties dialog box also has a Dependency tab, as shown in Figure 8-16. Use this tab to view the services that are dependent upon the one you are disabling.

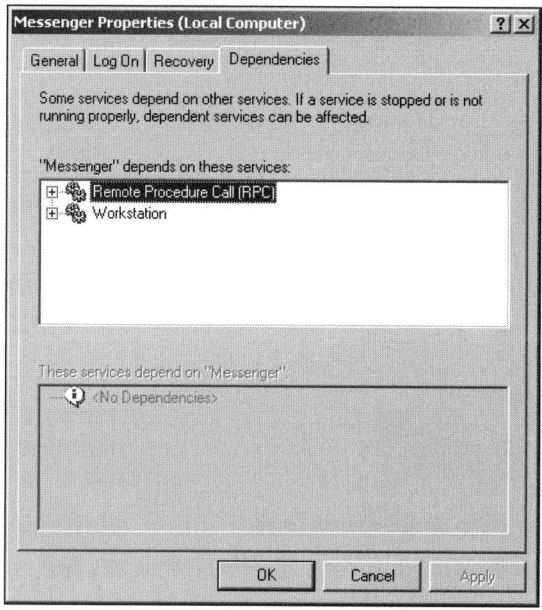

Figure 8-16 Viewing a service's dependencies

8

Monitoring your server's health and performance, and using this information to optimize it is only part of your job as a network administrator. Another important task that comes with the job is ensuring server availability and minimizing downtime. The following section provides information on troubleshooting Windows 2000 startup procedures and introduces you to the tools available to troubleshoot problems.

Troubleshooting Windows 2000 Startup Procedures

System startup problems can occur for a variety of reasons, including missing files, corrupt files, and configuration errors. In order to successfully troubleshoot problems related to startup, it is essential that you have an understanding of the Windows 2000 startup process.

One of the most common reasons for experiencing startup problems is because of missing files. In order for a system running Windows 2000 to successfully start, it requires certain files to be located on the system and the boot partition.

The system partition is usually drive C:, while the boot partition is the partition in which the WINNT folder resides.

Windows 2000 requires the following files to be located on the system partition in order to start up successfully:

- *Ntldr*—This file loads the operating system.
- *Boot.ini*—This file is used by Ntldr to create the Boot Loader Operating System Selection menu.
- *Ntdetect.com*—This file is used to gather a list of hardware components installed on the system and passes the information back to Ntldr.
- *Ntbootdd.sys*—This file is only used for those systems booting from a SCSI disk with the BIOS disabled.

Windows 2000 also requires the following files be located on the boot partition in order to start up:

- *Ntoskrnl.exe*—This is the Windows 2000 kernel file that is located in the *systemroot*/System32 folder.
- *System*—This file contains configuration settings and is responsible for controlling the device drivers and services loaded during initialization.
- *Device drivers*—These files are required for different device drivers.
- *Hal.dll*—This is the interface between the kernel and 2000 Executive and the system hardware.

The Windows 2000 Startup Process

You need to understand the process that occurs when a system running Windows 2000 boots up. The boot sequence occurs in two separate stages: the startup phase and the load phase. Having a general understanding of the process can make troubleshooting startup problems easier.

Prior to the startup phase, the system performs a power-on self test (POST). During the POST, the system determines the amount of physical memory and the hardware components present. A failure at this stage would indicate a hardware problem. If all the hardware components are functioning, then the boot device is located and the master boot record (MBR) is loaded into memory and executed. The MBR scans the partition table to locate the active partition. The boot sector from the active partition is loaded into memory and executed. The Ntldr is located on the active partition and initialized. At this point the startup phase begins.

The following actions occur during the startup phase:

1. The processor is switched from real mode to 32-bit flat memory mode in order for Ntldr to function.
2. Ntldr starts the appropriate minifile system drivers that are used to load Windows 2000 from different file systems.

3. If the Boot.ini file is present, Ntldr reads it and presents the Boot Loader Operating System selection menu. If you do not make a selection, the operating system listed as the default in the boot.ini file is loaded.
4. Ntldr runs Ntdetect.com, which generates a list of hardware and passes the list back to Ntldr.
5. Ntldr loads the Ntoskrnl.exe, Hal.dll, and the system hive.
6. Device drivers that are configured to load at startup are loaded.
7. The Ntoskrnl.exe is started.

At this point the startup phase is complete, the load phase begins, and control is given to the Ntoskrnl.exe file. The load phase occurs in four distinct steps: kernel load, kernel initialization, services load, and the Win32 subsystem start.

During the kernel load phase, the HAL and the System.dat are loaded. The HAL is the interface between the hardware and the operating system. The System.dat loads the drivers and services required for startup.

Next, the kernel initialization phase loads the kernel and initializes any drivers that are required. The System.dat also loads any drivers and services that need to be loaded during this phase.

During the services load phase, the remaining subsystems and any services required for Windows 2000 are started by the Session Manager. The registry is parsed to determine which programs are configured to run when the system is started.

The final phase occurs when the Win32 subsystem loads. The Winlogon.exe and the Local Security Authority are started and display the Ctrl+Alt+Del logon box. Keep in mind that the startup process is not considered successful until the user is able to log on.

The following sections cover the tools available in Windows 2000 for troubleshooting startup problems.

ADVANCED STARTUP OPTIONS

Several things can cause a system not to start, such as the installation of new software or device drivers, or changes made to the system's configuration. If your computer fails to start, you can try using one of the advanced startup options to troubleshoot the problem. For example, you can start the computer in **safe mode**, which only loads the default Windows 2000 settings and the device drivers necessary to start the operating system. If you have installed new software that you think is causing the problem, you can uninstall it once in safe mode.

You can access the advanced startup options during system startup by pressing F8 while viewing the Boot Loader Operating System Selection menu. The screen that appears presents you with a list of startup options, summarized in Table 8-3. The table provides a description of each option and what each one is useful for.

Table 8-3 Advanced startup options

Startup Option	Description
Safe mode	Only the basic files and drivers required to start Windows 2000 are loaded. The default Windows 2000 settings are used. This option is useful when an application needs to be uninstalled or a component disabled.
Safe mode with networking	This option starts the computer the same as in safe mode, but provides network connections. Use this option if you need access to the network to repair the problem.
Enable boot logging	This option starts Windows 2000 while creating a log file that lists all the installed drivers and services that were loaded or not loaded. Use this option to determine the exact cause of startup problems. The file is called ntbtlog.txt, and is stored in the Winnt folder.
Enable VGA mode	This option starts Windows 2000 with the basic VGA driver for the video card. This is useful if you've installed a new video driver that is causing Windows 2000 to not start.
Last known good configuration	Selecting this option starts Windows 2000 using registry information from the last saved logon. This option is useful if incorrect configuration changes have been made.
Directory services restore mode	Selecting this option enables you to restore the Sysvol and Active Directory Services on a domain controller. The system must be a domain controller to have this option available.
Debugging mode	Debugging information is sent to another computer via a serial cable connection while Windows 2000 starts. Use this option to provide software developers with information about the problem.

Last Known Good Configuration

The **last known good configuration** allows you to recover your system from failed driver and registry changes. For example, installing a device driver that is incorrect for your hardware can cause a system to fail on startup. The last known good configuration information is stored in the registry and is updated each time the computer restarts and the user successfully logs on.

Normally when a computer is restarted, the default configuration is used. Each time you make configuration changes, they are copied to the default configuration the next time the computer is restarted. If the changes damage the default configuration, your computer may not be able to successfully start.

The last known good configuration can be thought of as a backup that can be used to restart the system in the event that the default configuration fails. Use the following steps to start your computer using the last known good configuration:

1. Restart the computer.
2. When you see the message Please choose an operating system to start, press F8.
3. Use the arrow keys to highlight Last Known Good Configuration, and press **Enter**, as shown in Figure 8-17.

```
Windows 2000 Advanced Options Menu
Please select an option:

    Safe Mode
    Safe Mode with Networking
    Safe Mode with Command Prompt

    Enable Boot Logging
    Enable VGA Mode
    Last Known Good Configuration
    Directory Services Restore Mode (Windows 2000 domain controllers only)
    Debugging Mode

    Boot Normally
    Return to OS Choices Menu

Use ↑ and ↓ to move the highlight to your choice.
Press Enter to choose.
```

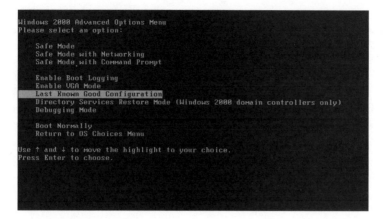

Figure 8-17 Selecting the Last Known Good Configuration option

4. Use the arrow keys to choose the operating system for which you want to use the last known good configuration, and press **Enter**.
5. On the Hardware Profile/Configuration Recovery menu, choose the specific hardware profile with which you want to boot into the Last Known Good Configuration option, and then press **Enter**. You can switch between the last known good configuration or the default configuration by pressing the D (default) or L (last known good configuration) keys on the keyboard. See Figure 8-18.

```
     Hardware Profile/Configuration Recovery Menu

This menu allows you to select a hardware profile
to be used when Windows 2000 is started.

If your system is not starting correctly, then you may switch to a previous
system configuration, which may overcome startup problems.
IMPORTANT: System configuration changes made since the last successful
startup will be discarded.

    Profile 1

Use the up and down arrow keys to move the highlight
to the selection you want. Then press ENTER.
To switch to the default configuration, press 'D'.
To Exit this menu and restart your computer, press F3.

Seconds until highlighted choice will be started automatically: 19
```

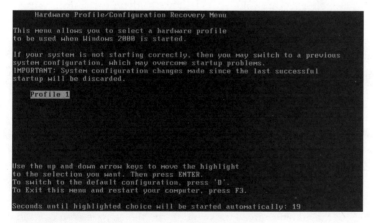

Figure 8-18 Selecting the hardware profile

Because the last known good configuration is updated each time you log on, make sure you do not log on if startup problems occur. Once you do, the last known good configuration is updated with the incorrect configuration changes.

The last known good configuration is useful in situations where Windows 2000 configuration changes have been made. It cannot resolve problems such as missing or corrupt files or if you restart and log on after the configuration changes have been made.

Recovery Console

Another tool that can be used for system recovery is the **Recovery Console**. The Recovery Console is an advanced tool for experienced administrators, allowing them to gain access to a hard drive formatted with the NTFS or FAT file system on computers running Windows 2000. It can be used to perform the following tasks:

- Start and stop services
- Format drives
- Read and write data on a local hard drive
- Copy files from a floppy or CD to a local hard drive
- Perform administrative tasks

Installing the Recovery Console

The Recovery Console can be started in one of two ways. The first option is to either run it from the Windows 2000 setup disks or the Windows 2000 CD. The second option is to install it on your computer. To install it, insert the Windows 2000 CD, and at the command prompt, switch to your CD-ROM drive, and type the following command: \i386\winnt32.exe /cmdcons. When prompted, click Yes to install the Recovery Console and follow the on-screen instructions. Once the Recovery Console is installed, it is listed as an option from the list of available operating systems, as shown in Figure 8-19. The Recovery Console can then be started by selecting it on the Boot Loader Operating System Selection menu.

If you choose not to install the Recovery Console on your system, it can be started by inserting the first setup floppy, or the CD (if your system can boot from the CD-ROM). Follow through the text-based portion of setup and when prompted, press R for recovery, then press C to start the Recovery Console.

You must be an administrator to run the Recovery Console, so you are prompted for the administrator's password to run the console. You can allow users the ability to run the console by using a Group Policy to enable the Automatic administrative logon when using the recovery console option.

```
Please select the operating system to start:

    Microsoft Windows 2000 Server
    Microsoft Windows 2000 Recovery Console

Use ↑ and ↓ to move the highlight to your choice.
Press Enter to choose.

For troubleshooting and advanced startup options for Windows 2000, press F8.
```

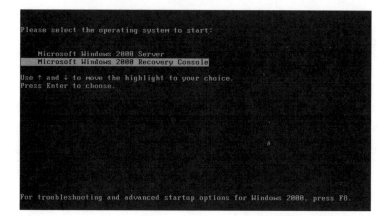

Figure 8-19 Selecting the Windows 2000 Recovery Console

There are a variety of commands available through the Recovery Console. The following list includes some of the common commands that are used. For a complete list of commands that are available, use the Help command from within the console.

- *Copy*—Copies a file from removable media to the system folders
- *Disable*—Disables a system service or a device driver
- *Enable*—Enables or starts a system service or a device driver
- *Exit*—Closes the Recovery Console and restarts your computer
- *Fixboot*—Writes a new partition boot sector onto the system partition
- *Fixmbr*—Repairs the master boot record of the boot partition
- *Listsvc*—Lists all the services on the computer

Parallel Installations

In most cases you should be able to get your system running again using one of the advanced startup options or by using the Recovery Console. If you are unsuccessful using any of these tools, one of the last things you can try is a **parallel installation**. A parallel installation is a second installation of the operating system in a different directory, on a separate partition, or on a different physical disk.

If you cannot restart your system with the original operating system, a parallel installation provides you with access to any partitions formatted with NTFS. This allows you to access any files and any registry data to repair the problem.

When you are performing the installation of the second operating system, make sure to include all of the troubleshooting and recovery tools.

The Windows 2000 Backup Utility

Windows 2000 includes a backup utility that allows you to restore an operating system or data in the event of a total hardware or storage media failure. Windows 2000 backup is a much-needed improvement over previous versions of Windows. Using this new backup utility you can perform a variety of tasks, such as:

- Back up and restore files and folders
- Schedule a backup
- Back up Windows 2000 System State data
- Restore all or a portion of the Active Directory database
- Create an emergency repair disk (ERD)

The Windows 2000 Backup utility now supports a wide variety of storage devices and media, such as tape drives, recordable CD-ROM drives, logical drives, and removable disks.

Backing Up and Restoring Files and Folders

The most common use of the Windows 2000 Backup utility is to back up critical data and operating system files to ensure a quick recovery in the event of a disaster. To start the backup utility, click Start, point to Programs, point to Accessories, point to System Tools, and then click the Backup icon. The backup utility opens, as shown in Figure 8-20.

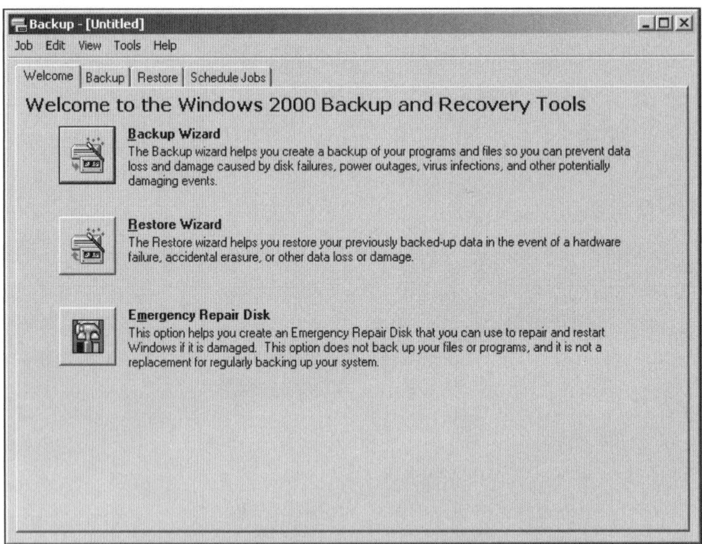

Figure 8-20 Starting the Windows 2000 Backup utility

The easiest way to configure a backup is to use the Backup Wizard. The Backup Wizard begins by allowing you to choose what exactly to back up, as shown in Figure 8-21.

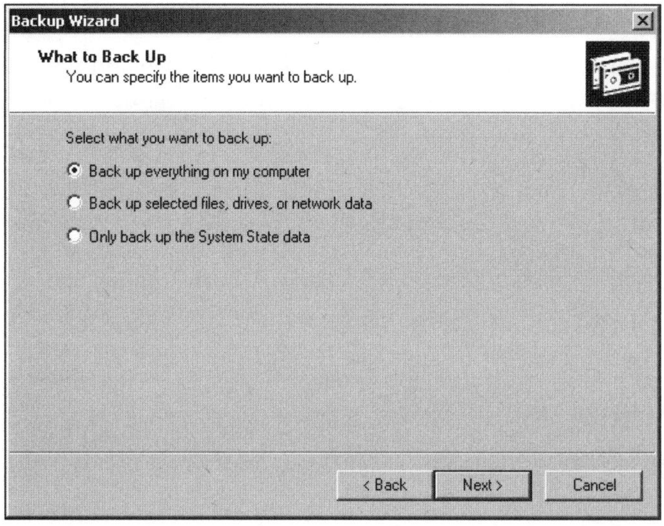

Figure 8-21 Choosing what to back up using the backup utility

If you choose to back up selected files, drives, or network data, you are given the choice to check off exactly which files and folders you want to back up, as shown in Figure 8-22.

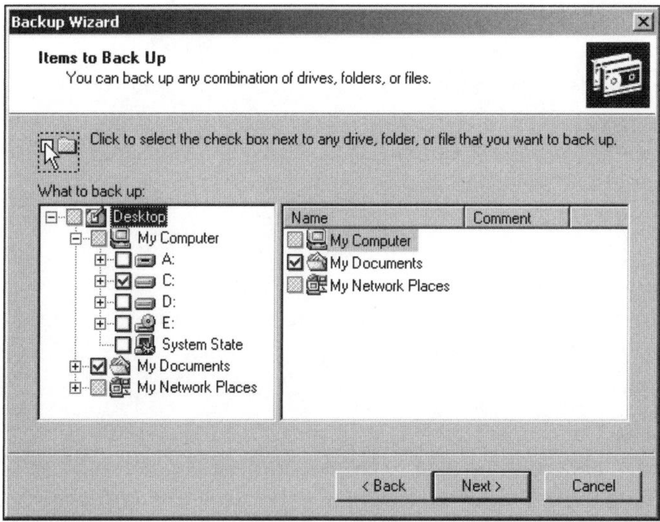

Figure 8-22 Selecting items to back up

The final steps for the backup include specifying the media type, where to store the backup, and advanced backup options such as backup type, backup schedule, data verification, and hardware compression.

You can restore files and folders by using the RestoreWizard. The Restore Wizard allows you to specify the folders and files to restore, a restore location, and advanced restore options such as whether to replace existing files with the backed up versions.

Backing Up the System State

The Windows 2000 Server System State includes the following system components:

- Active Directory (when installed)
- Sysvol folder (when Active Directory is installed)
- Registry
- Component Services Class Registration database
- System startup files
- Certificate Services database (when Certificate Services are installed)
- DNS zones (when DNS is installed)
- Server cluster data (when Cluster services are installed)

These components should also be backed up regularly with your standard backup schedule. In the event of an Active Directory or system startup failure, a last resort can be to restore the System State data.

One limitation to the Windows 2000 Backup utility is that you cannot back up individual components of the System State data. Third-party backup applications allow individual component backups.

If you are restoring the System State because of a corrupt Active Directory database, you must restart the computer and choose the Directory Services Restore Mode advanced startup option. You can then use the backup utility to restore the latest System State data from backup. After you restart the computer and Windows 2000 starts normally, Active Directory is automatically reindexed, and updates Active Directory and the file replication service.

In the event that you are attempting to restore a portion of the Active Directory tree, a few additional steps may be required. For example, if an OU was inadvertently deleted by an administrator, you can still use Windows 2000 Backup to restore the System State in an attempt to restore the deleted OU. One problem with this scenario is that when an Active Directory object is restored from backup, the replica domain controllers still think that the object should be deleted. When replication takes place with the other domain controllers, the newly restored object is again deleted.

This problem can be overcome by performing an authoritative restore. An **authoritative restore** marks specific objects in the Active Directory as the master copy, and forces the other domain controllers to receive the change.

An authoritative restore can be accomplished by restarting the computer in directory service restore mode, restoring the most recent System State from backup, and then running the Ntdsutil utility at a command prompt in authoritative restore mode. For more information on the Ntdsutil utility, check Windows 2000 Help.

Creating an Emergency Repair Disk

The emergency repair disk (ERD) is used to fix various system problems in Windows 2000. You can use the ERD to repair the system files, startup environment, and the partition boot sector.

You can create the ERD by clicking the Emergency Repair Disk button within the Windows 2000 Backup utility. Once you have inserted a floppy disk, the system copies all of the ERD information to the disk.

Windows NT 4 had a command called RDISK that created the ERD. Windows 2000 no longer includes this command, as the backup utility is now used to create the ERD.

To use the ERD, you can boot the computer using your Windows 2000 CD-ROM or boot floppy disks. When prompted to repair the system, press R on the keyboard. The Repair Options menu appears allowing you to repair the computer system using the ERD created earlier.

Chapter Summary

- The Performance console has two tools that can be used to monitor server health and performance: System Monitor and Performance Logs and Alerts.
- Alerts can be configured for specific objects and counters. Once a counter exceeds or drops below the configured value, an alert is triggered. The alert can send a message, start a counter log, write an event to the application log, or run a program.
- Event Viewer can be used to view the contents of the system logs, application logs, and security logs. Processes and applications write events to the log files. Administrators can use this information to identify and troubleshoot server problems.
- Task Manager provides information on processes and applications running on a system. It also provides general information on a system's current performance.
- When optimizing the performance of your computer, use the Services icon to disable any unnecessary services to eliminate overhead.

- The Windows 2000 startup process occurs in two distinct phases: the startup phase and the load phase.
- Windows 2000 includes advanced startup options that can be used to troubleshoot and repair startup problems. The advanced startup options can be accessed by pressing F8 at the Boot Loader Operating System Selection menu.
- The last known good configuration can be used to restart your computer if the default configuration becomes damaged due to Windows 2000 configuration changes.
- Windows 2000 includes a text mode command interpreter called the Recovery Console that allows an administrator to access the hard drive of a computer running Windows 2000. The Recovery Console can be installed on the computer and started from the Boot Loader Operating System Selection menu or it can be started directly from the Windows 2000 CD or setup floppies.
- If you are unable to recover a system using any of the Windows 2000 utilities, you can perform a parallel installation or perform a restore from backup to repair the primary operating system or data files.

KEY TERMS

alerts — An alert performs a specified action once a counter meets the specified setting. Once an alert is triggered, a message can be sent, a program can be run, a counter log started, or an event can be written to the application log.

application log — Where applications that are written to Microsoft standards record event information. The application developer determines the type of information an application writes to the log file.

authoritative restore — Marks specific objects in the Active Directory as the master copy, and forces the other domain controllers to receive the change.

baseline — A performance benchmark that is used to determine what is normal server performance under a specific workload.

counter log — Performance data that is collected into a comma-separated or tab-separated format.

Event Viewer — A utility used to view the contents of the system, security, and application logs.

Last Known Good Configuration — An advanced startup option that can be used to recover a system from failed Windows 2000 configuration changes.

parallel installation — A second installation of an operating system into a different directory, on a different partition, or on a different hard drive as the primary.

performance counter — A data item associated with a particular performance object used to measure a certain aspect of performance.

Performance Logs and Alerts — A tool included with Windows 2000 that enables you to create counter logs, trace logs, and configure alerts.

performance objects — A system component that can be monitored using System Monitor.

Recovery Console — A command line interpreter that can be used to gain access to a local hard drive in the event that the system fails to boot.

safe mode — A method of starting Windows 2000 with only the basic drivers and services.

security log — Events pertaining to the audit policy are written to the security log.

system log — Where system components such as services and device drivers record information, warnings, and errors.

System Monitor — A tool that allows you to gather and view real-time performance statistics of a local or network computer.

Task Manager — A tool used to view the processes and applications currently running on a system. Also provides basic resource usage statistics.

trace log — Where data provider collects performance data when an event occurs.

Review Questions

1. What feature of Windows 2000 can you use to have a message sent to your computer when a performance counter exceeds a certain value?

   a. counter logs

   b. alerts

   c. Event Viewer

   d. Task Manager

2. What tool can be used to view the contents of the system log?

   a. System Monitor

   b. Performance Console

   c. Event Viewer

   d. Task Manager

3. You are running several programs on your computer. One of them appears to have stopped responding. What tool can you use to check the status of the application?

   a. Performance Monitor

   b. System Monitor

   c. Application Manager

   d. Task Manager

4. What type of log would you create to have performance data collected and saved into a comma-separated file?
   a. trace log
   b. database log
   c. counter log
   d. system log
5. Only administrators can view the contents of the system and application logs. True or False?
6. What is the default view when System Monitor is first opened?
   a. histogram
   b. graph
   c. counter
   d. report
7. You have started to receive complaints from users on the network that the server has been performing poorly. What tool can you use to monitor and view real-time performance of the server?
   a. Event Viewer
   b. Performance Monitor
   c. Performance Logs and Alerts
   d. System Monitor
8. A service fails to start on your server. In which log file is the event recorded?
   a. application
   b. system
   c. services
   d. counter
9. What is the name of the file that contains a list of operating systems displayed at the Boot Loader Operating System Selection menu?
   a. Boot.ini
   b. System.ini
   c. OperatingSystems.ini
   d. Ntldr.ini
10. When is the Windows 2000 startup process considered to be successful?
    a. after the startup phase finishes
    b. after the user logs on
    c. after the load phase
    d. after the user logs on and launches an application

11. Which of the following actions can be taken when an alert is triggered? (Choose all that apply.)
    a. A message can be sent to a computer.
    b. An event can be written to the application log.
    c. A program can be run.
    d. A counter log can be started.
12. You load a new device driver on your server. The server fails to boot when it is restarted. What advanced startup option can you use to recover the server?
    a. safe mode
    b. Last Known Good Configuration
    c. safe mode with networking
    d. debugging mode
13. Which of the following options can be used to start the Windows 2000 Recovery Console? (Choose all that apply.)
    a. Install it on the local computer and choose it from the list of available operating systems.
    b. Install and share the Recovery Console on a network server and connect to the share from the local computer using safe mode with Networking.
    c. Boot from the Windows 2000 CD-ROM, and choose R for recovery.
    d. Restart the computer, press F8 to access the advanced startup options, and choose the Recovery Console.
14. Which of the following files must be located on the boot partition in order for Windows 2000 to successfully boot? (Choose all answers that apply.)
    a. Ntoskrnl.exe
    b. Boot.ini
    c. Ntbootdd.sys
    d. Hal.dll
15. You can use the last known good configuration to recover from missing or corrupt files. True or False?
16. A missing file is preventing your server from starting. Which of the following options can you use to recover the system?
    a. safe mode
    b. Recovery Console
    c. Task Manager
    d. Last Known Good Configuration

17. You want to determine which services and drivers are, and are not, being loaded during startup. Which advanced startup option should you use?
    a. debugging mode
    b. safe mode
    c. Enable Boot Logging
    d. step-by-step confirmation
18. By default, any user can run the Recovery Console. True or False?
19. What tool can be used to view all processes and applications currently running on a system?
    a. App Manager
    b. System Monitor
    c. Event Viewer
    d. Task Manager
20. If your server fails to boot, the first thing you should do is a parallel installation. True or False?

HANDS-ON PROJECTS

Project 8-1

In this Hands-on Project, you use System Monitor to collect data on your server's performance.

1. Log on to your computer with the administrator account.
2. Click **Start**, point to **Programs**, point to **Administrative Tools**, and then click **Performance**.
3. Click **System Monitor** in the scope pane of the console.
4. In the details pane, click **Add** (which looks like a + sign).
5. Click the **Explain** button to open the Explain window.
6. Under Performance object, click the list arrow, and choose **Processor**.
7. Verify that the option **Select counter from list** is checked.
8. In the counters list, choose **% Processor Time**, and then click **Add**.
9. Under Performance object, click the list arrow, and choose **Memory**.
10. In the counters list, choose **Available MBytes and Page Faults/sec**. Hold down the Ctrl key to choose more than one counter at a time.
11. Click **Add**, and then click **Close**.
12. Right-click the detail pane on the far right, and click **Properties**.

13. On the General tab, ensure that **Graph** is selected, and then click **OK**.
14. With the System Monitor running, click **Start**, point to **Programs**, point to **Accessories**, and then click **WordPad**.
15. Click **Start**, point to **Programs**, point to **Administrative Tools**, and then click **Active Directory Users and Computers**.
16. Click the **Performance** button on the taskbar to view the results of applications starting. Notice the spikes during processor usage and pagefile usage. If the pagefile is being used constantly, this indicates a need for more RAM.
17. In the toolbar, switch between Chart, Histogram, and Report views. Open and close other applications to obtain performance results.
18. Close all applications and windows.

Project 8-2

8

In this Hands-on Project, you configure a System Monitor alert to alert you to processor usage of over 80%.

1. Click **Start**, point to **Programs**, point to **Administrative Tools**, and then click **Performance**.
2. Click **Performance Logs and Alerts** in the scope pane of the console.
3. In the details pane, right-click **Alerts**, and then click **New Alert Settings**.
4. Name the new alert **Processor Alert**. Click **OK**.
5. Click **Add**.
6. Verify that **Processor** is selected under the Performance object section.
7. Under Select counters from list, choose **% Processor Time**, and then click **Add**. Click **Close**.
8. Click the list arrow next to Alert when the value is, and choose **Over**.
9. Type **80** in the Limit text box.
10. Type **1** in the Interval text box.
11. Click the **Action** tab, and verify that the **Log an entry in the application event log** option is checked.
12. Check the **Send a network message to** option, and then type **administrator** (or whomever you are logged on as). Click **OK**. If you receive an alert immediately, click **OK**.
13. Click **Start**, point to **Programs**, point to **Administrative Tools**, and then click **Active Directory Users and Computers**. Open various other programs. Notice that you receive an alert stating that the processor has reached its threshold.
14. Click **Start**, point to **Programs**, point to **Administrative Tools**, and then click **Event Viewer**.
15. Click the **Application** log.

16. In the details pane, click the information entry with the source SysmonLog. Notice that it states that the processor has tripped its threshold.
17. Click the **Performance** button on the taskbar to return to the Performance console.
18. Click the **Alerts** node, right-click your Processor Alert, and then click **Delete**.
19. Click **OK**.
20. Close all windows.

Project 8-3

In this Hands-on Project, you use Task Manager to view running Applications, processes, and system performance.

1. Click **Start**, point to **Programs**, point to **Accessories**, and then click **WordPad**.
2. Click **Start**, point to **Programs**, point to **Accessories**, and then click **Paint**.
3. Right-click the taskbar, and then click **Task Manager**.
4. On the Applications tab, view the applications that are running.
5. Choose the untitled **Paint** application, and then click **End Task**.
6. Click the **Processes** tab. Click the **CPU** column to place the CPU percentage in numerical order.

This is a quick way of determining which process is using the most CPU cycles.

7. Click the **Performance** tab.
8. Open various applications to view the CPU Usage History.
9. Close all windows.

Project 8-4

In this Hands-on Project, you view the advanced startup options available in Windows 2000. You also view the startup log file to verify which drivers loaded during the operating system startup.

1. Restart your computer.
2. When the Starting Windows or operating system menu appears, press **F8**.
3. Select **Safe Mode**, and then press **Enter**. Choose your server if prompted, and press **Enter**.
4. Log on as the administrator. Safe mode starts up with minimal drivers, which would allow you to fix a number of startup problems that may occur to prevent you from booting normally.

5. Click **Start**, point to **Programs**, point to **Administrative Tools**, and then click **Services**. Notice that very few services are started.
6. Restart your computer. When the operating system menu appears, press **F8** on the keyboard.
7. Click **Enable Boot Logging,** and press **Enter**. Choose your server if prompted, and press **Enter**.
8. Windows 2000 boots up normally. Log on as the administrator.
9. Browse to the **C:\Winnt\ntbtlog.txt** file, and open it. Observe which drivers were and were not loaded during startup.
10. Close all windows.

Project 8-5

In this Hands-on Project, you create an emergency repair disk (ERD).

1. Click **Start**, point to **Programs**, point to **Accessories**, click **System Tools**, and then click **Backup**.
2. Click the **Emergency Repair Disk** button.
3. Insert a blank, formatted floppy disk into drive A. Check the **Also backup the registry to the repair directory** option. Click **OK**.
4. Click **OK** when the ERD creation is complete.
5. Close Windows 2000 Backup.
6. To use the ERD, you must reboot the computer using the Windows 2000 CD-ROM, and then insert the ERD when prompted to repair the installation.

8

CASE PROJECTS

Case Project 8-1

You are responsible for the administration of three Bayside servers. You have recently installed a new service on your server. The service is set to start automatically and runs continuously to service user requests. Your managers are concerned about server performance after the service is installed, and you assure them that performance should not suffer. Answer the following questions based on the scenario.

1. After you install the service, what is one of the first things that should be done?
2. During peak hours, one of your managers stops in to see how the server is performing under the added workload. What tool can you use to quickly show your manager the current processor usage on the server?

3. You have a slight concern that the service may indeed have an impact on the amount of time the processor is utilized. The % utilization was running at times near 50% before the service was installed. You would like to be notified if the processor utilization goes above 60%. Explain how this can be done. What other actions can be configured if this occurs?
4. Because the server is working under an increased workload, you want to disable any unnecessary services to eliminate the overhead associated with running them. What should you consider before disabling any services on the server?

Case Project 8-2

A new administrator has been hired at Bayside to work during evenings and weekends under your direction. One evening he decides to install a new device driver on one of the servers to enhance performance. Before checking with you or any other administrators on staff, he installs the device driver. You receive a call that upon restart the new administrator discovered that the server no longer boots successfully. The server needs to be available to users in the morning.

1. What options in Windows 2000 are available to recover from a failed reboot? What is each option used for?
2. What recovery tool would be appropriate for this situation?
3. You noticed after the server is recovered that the Recovery Console was not listed as an option during the operating system selection. It is company policy that this tool be installed on all servers. How can the tool be installed? If you needed to use the Recovery Console and it wasn't installed, how could you start it?

CHAPTER

9

ADMINISTERING REMOTE ACCESS SERVICES

After reading this chapter and completing the exercises, you will be able to:

- Configure remote access and virtual private network (VPN) connections
- Implement and troubleshoot remote access policies
- Configure and troubleshoot network address translation (NAT)
- Configure and troubleshoot Internet connection sharing
- Configure and manage Terminal Services

Remote access services can be implemented to allow users to connect to your network from any remote location. Windows 2000 provides many new and improved features to increase the usability and security of your remote access solutions. The Routing and Remote Access Services (RRAS) component of Windows 2000 provides the capability to configure remote access by implementing dial-up or virtual private network (VPN) connections to the internal network. Support for a number of new authentication and encryption protocols helps to secure any communication that is established through the standard dial-up or VPN connections.

This chapter explains how to configure and troubleshoot RRAS to provide remote access and VPN connections. A new feature called remote access policies is also discussed, which can assist in controlling access to your RRAS server.

With the popularity and availability of high-speed Internet connections via cable or ADSL, a need has developed to provide shared Internet access to multiple network clients. Windows 2000 provides two features that can fill this need. The first feature is Network address translation (NAT), which is another RRAS configured component that can allow multiple network clients access to the Internet. The second feature is Internet connection sharing (ICS), which is a very similar technology, but is used in smaller or home-based networks. This chapter discusses the difference between NAT and ICS, and how to configure and troubleshoot both of these services to provide shared Internet access for your network users.

This chapter also discusses how to implement and troubleshoot Terminal Services for remote access. Terminal Services is a new feature available in Windows 2000 that can provide network clients with access to shared applications that are installed on a central server. Terminal Services can also enable administrators to perform remote administration tasks on the servers from any device that can support the Terminal Services client component.

CONFIGURING REMOTE ACCESS AND VIRTUAL PRIVATE NETWORK CONNECTIONS

One of the requirements in almost any organization is to give users remote access to the internal network. In some cases, providing this remote access may be quite simple. For example, an organization may decide to give remote access to a single network resource, such as e-mail, to only a few executives. The organization might limit the remote access even more by giving the executives access to the corporate network only from their home computer and only when they dial into the company's **remote access server**. A remote access server is a computer running Windows 2000 and the Routing and Remote Access Service (RRAS) that authenticates remote or mobile users. In other cases, the requirement to provide remote access to the network can be much more complicated. A company may have a large number of users who require remote access because they spend most of their time outside the office. For example, a company may have a mobile sales force or executives who travel a great deal. These people require access to the corporate network from almost anywhere in the world. These users may be using laptops or sitting at kiosk computers in an airport. In addition to almost universal access, the users may require access to a variety of resources including e-mail, an Intranet Web server, a database server to run a client application, and files on the corporate file servers.

When a client needs to connect to a network from a remote location, two methods may be used to provide the connection. One method is to use standard dial-up connections. When a client uses a dial-up connection, communication is established via communication networks such as a Public Switched Telephone Network (PSTN).

The client typically uses a modem or ISDN connection to dial up to the remote server and establish a connection to the internal network. To provide the remote access connection, Windows 2000 supports a number of remote access protocols. The most common protocol is the **Point-to-Point Protocol (PPP)**. PPP enables remote access clients and servers to communicate over a dial-up connection from any operating system that supports the PPP standards. One disadvantage to using a dial-up method is that users may have to incur long-distance charges in order to connect over long distances.

The second method that can be implemented to provide remote access is to use a **virtual private network (VPN)**. A VPN uses a LAN protocol and PPP, which are both encapsulated within a VPN protocol, to send data over a public network. This encapsulation creates an encrypted tunnel through the public network to the internal network.

Two common VPN protocols are **Point-to-Point Tunneling Protocol (PPTP)** and **Layer 2 Tunneling Protocol (L2TP)**. PPTP and L2TP are both used to establish a secure tunnel between two endpoints over an insecure network. These protocols are included with Windows 2000, and provide the security needed to make virtual private networks a common choice for remote network access. Table 9-1 explains the differences between PPTP and L2TP.

Table 9-1 Differences between PPTP and L2TP

PPTP	L2TP
Network must be IP based.	Network can be IP, Frame Relay, X.25, or ATM based
Does not provide header compression	Provides header compression for better performance
Does not provide tunnel authentication	Provides tunnel authentication for increased security
Uses built-in PPP encryption	Uses IPSec to provide encryption
Most clients can use PPTP	Only Windows 2000 and XP computers can use L2TP

One of the main advantages to using a VPN is that clients can connect to a local ISP, and then connect to their internal network from anywhere in the world via the Internet.

Remote access is implemented on a Windows 2000 server by configuring the Routing and Remote Access Service (RRAS). RRAS provides a variety of routing and remote access solutions such as dial-up, virtual private networking (VPN), and network address translation (NAT). To provide these services, there are three primary tasks that you have to complete:

- Configure RRAS with the appropriate remote access configuration.
- Configure clients to connect to the RRAS server.
- Configure user rights, security, and conditions in order to successfully and securely connect to the RRAS server.

Windows 2000 Server can be configured to provide remote access to clients using a number of different methods. Some of these methods include analog modems, ISDN adapters, and other broadband hardware such as DSL or cable modems. Clients can then access the server through a standard dial-up connection or through connections established via the Internet. The RRAS server can authenticate users and provide a gateway to the network resources available on the internal network.

The next several sections describe, in more detail, the methods used to create and configure dial-up and VPN connections. Various authentication and encryption protocols that you can use to help secure your remote access connections are also outlined, as well as suggestions for troubleshooting remote access connection problems.

Configuring Dial-up Connections

Many organizations still provide dial-up remote access for users who travel extensively. Despite the fact that dial-up access is slow (with a 56 Kbps maximum connection speed) and often unreliable, dial-up access is often also the only option that the remote user has available. Few hotel rooms have high speed Internet connections that you can use to connect to your company network; however, almost all hotel rooms have a data line that you can use to dial out using your laptop's modem. The primary advantage of dial-up access is that it is available almost anywhere.

The first step in providing remote access to clients is to configure the physical modem on the server to which the clients connect. If the users are dialing in using analog modems, you need to install and configure the modem or modems on the server. If the connection is an ISDN or X.25 connection, then you have to configure the hardware device for the connection. In most cases, the modem is detected by Plug and Play in Windows 2000 and automatically installed during the installation process or when you scan for hardware changes in Device Manager. If the modem is not detected, then use the Add New Hardware Wizard to add the correct modem. After you have added the modem(s), the next step is to configure Windows 2000 Server as a remote access server.

To configure a remote access server to accept dial-up connections, complete the following steps:

1. Click **Start**, point to **Programs**, point to **Administrative Tools**, and then click **Routing and Remote Access**. The Routing and Remote Access console opens, as shown in Figure 9-1.

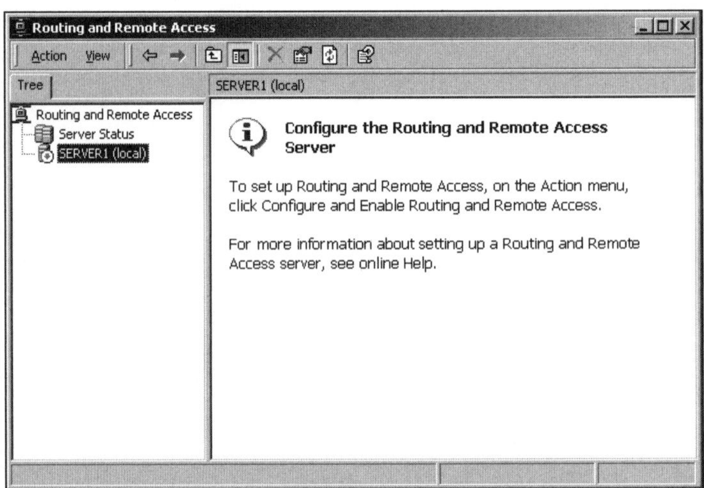

Figure 9-1 The Routing and Remote Access console

2. After you right-click the server listed in the console pane, click **Configure and Enable Routing and Remote Access** as displayed in the shortcut menu. The Routing and Remote Access Setup Wizard starts. Click **Next**.

3. Select which remote access configuration you want to make available to clients. As you can see in Figure 9-2, the first four choices are common preconfigured settings such as an Internet connection server, remote access server, virtual private network (VPN) server, and a network router. The final option starts the RRAS server with basic options that need to be configured manually to provide the appropriate access.

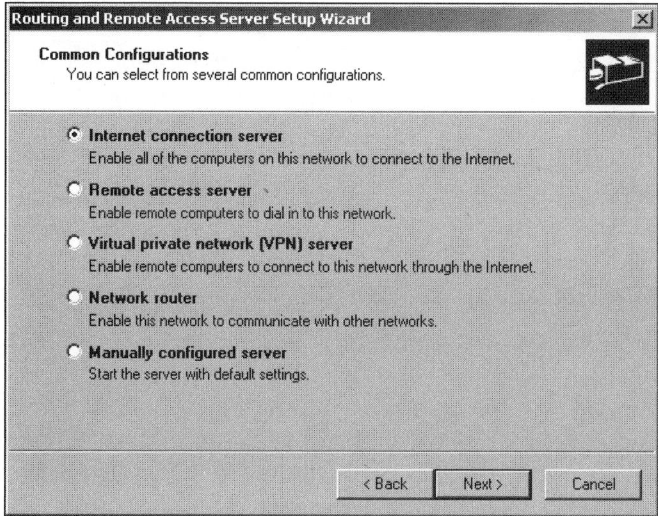

Figure 9-2 Selecting a RRAS configuration

4. To enable dial-up access, click the **Remote access server** option, and then click **Next**.
5. The Remote Client Protocols dialog box opens, which lists all of the configured network protocols on the server. This step only allows you to verify the installed protocols. When you click **Next**, you are then asked to choose the network adapter that links to the dial-up connection. This is usually the network that provides IP addressing via DHCP and general access. Click **Next** again.
6. Choose between assigning the remote user an IP address automatically via a DHCP server, or from a specified range of preconfigured addresses.
7. Finally, indicate whether you want to choose the option to set up the RRAS server to use **RADIUS**. RADIUS is used as a central management and authentication database when you have a large number of RRAS servers in your organization.

When you are finished configuring the dial-up server, the Routing and Remote Access console appears, as shown in Figure 9-3.

9

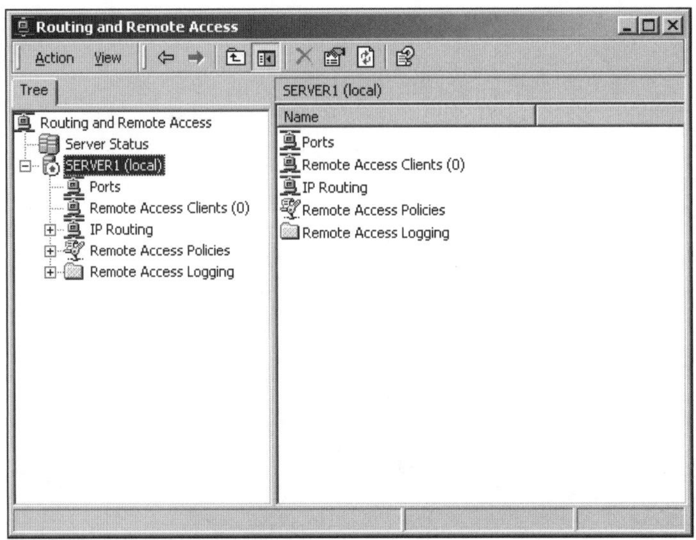

Figure 9-3 The RRAS console

Now that you have installed the dial-up server, you may want to configure IP addressing options, protocol options, and remote access clients. You perform these three tasks at this time in the event that you require modifications from the initial installation of the RRAS configuration. We discuss each in turn next.

Configuring IP Addressing Options for the Dial-up Server

Depending on the choice that you made during the installation, the server may or may not be using DHCP to assign IP address information to the dial-up clients. If you want to change this configuration after the installation, you can do so by accessing the server properties in RRAS by right-clicking the server name, clicking Properties, and then clicking the IP tab, as shown in Figure 9-4.

If you have enabled the server to use DHCP and want to change the setting, select Static address pool. You then need to configure the IP addresses that the server hands out to dial-up clients. To do so, click Add**.** Type the IP address range that you want to assign to the clients, and click OK**.**

If you are using DHCP to assign IP addresses to the dial-up clients, the clients receive an IP address and the subnet mask from the RAS server, but not the other DHCP settings such as WINS server or DNS server IP addresses. In most cases, you should configure the clients to get this additional information. To do so, you must install a DHCP relay agent as a routing protocol, and then add the dial-up interface to the list of interfaces that act as a DHCP relay agent.

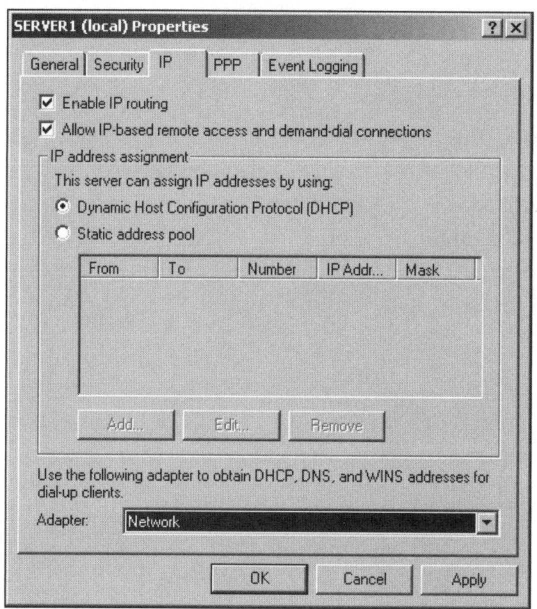

Figure 9-4 Configuring DHCP in RRAS

If DHCP is being used, the RRAS server initially obtains 10 IP addresses from the DHCP service. The first IP address is assigned to the RRAS server itself, and then the next nine addresses are available to be assigned to dial-up clients. If all nine addresses are allocated to remote clients, the RRAS server leases 10 more addresses from the DHCP server.

If remote clients cannot browse the network, check the IP address that has been assigned by the RRAS server. If the DHCP server was not available when the RRAS server asked for 10 IP addresses, it then starts to hand out addresses in the 169.254.0.1 through 169.254.255.254 range. This range is the automatic IP addressing range used by Windows, and may not be routable in your network.

Multilink and Bandwidth Allocation Protocol Options

If your server has more than one physical connection that can be used for dial-up access, Windows 2000 Server can be configured to support multilinking, or combining multiple physical connections into one connection in order to increase bandwidth. You can configure multilinking using multiple modems, ISDN, or X.25 connections. By using the Point-to-Point (PPP) multilink protocol, the client can dial in to the server on multiple lines, and these lines are combined together into one logical connection.

Windows 2000 Server also uses Bandwidth Allocation Protocol (BAP) to help dynamically manage multiple links. For example, if a user is connected on both of the B channels for an ISDN connection, BAP can be configured so that when the use of one of the channels falls below a set limit for a period of time, that channel is dropped. The channel would then be available to another client.

Both multilink and BAP are configured on the PPP tab in the Server Properties dialog box, as shown in Figure 9-5. To configure multilink and BAP, select both the options for Multilink connections and Dynamic bandwidth control using BAP or BACP. This is all that is needed to enable the server to use both multilinking and BAP. You still need to use the remote access policies to further configure multilinking and BAP, including setting controls on how many links a client can use and to configure BAP settings.

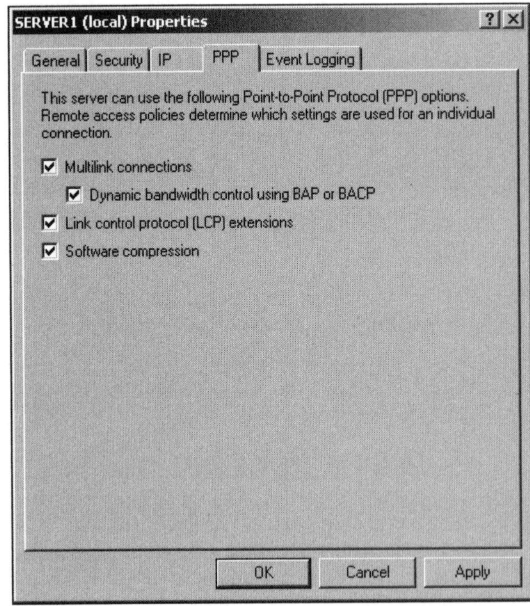

Figure 9-5 Configuring Multilink and BAP

Configuring Remote Access Clients

After the server has been prepared, the next step is to configure the dial-up clients. The client configuration can be completed either manually or through a Connection Manager (CM) application. In Windows 2000, individual connections can be manually configured using the Network Connection Wizard

To configure a dial-up connection manually, complete the following steps:

1. Click **Start**, point to **Settings**, and then click **Network and Dial-up Connections**.
2. Click **Make New Connection**. The Network Connection Wizard opens.

3. Click the **Next** button to view the various types of network connections that can be created using the Wizard. Figure 9-6 shows the various connection types that you can choose.

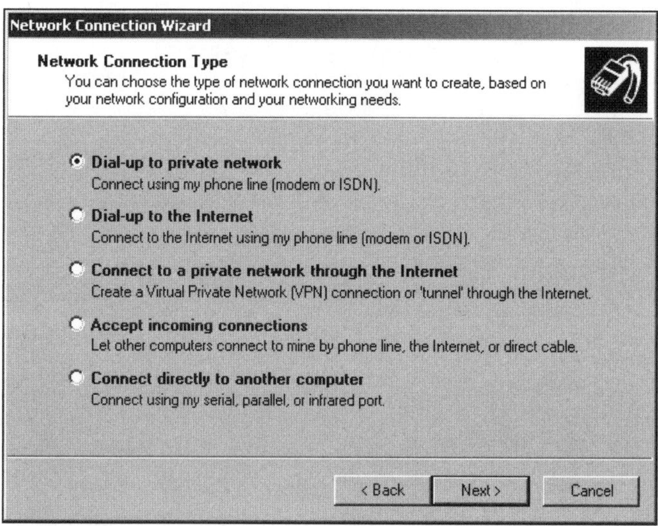

Figure 9-6 Configuring a dial-up client

4. To connect using a dial-up connection, click the **Dial-up to private network** option button, and then click **Next**.
5. The next step has you configure the Phone Number, Area Code, and Country/Region Code, if necessary.
6. The Connection Availability dialog box appears. You can specify whether the connection is for all users, or only for a specific user. If you want everyone who logs on to the computer to be able to use the connection, then accept the default of creating the connection for all users, and click **Next**.
7. The final step allows you to choose whether you want to enable Internet connection sharing (ICS) for this connection. ICS makes it possible for multiple users in a small office to share a single connection to the Internet or another network.
8. Type a name for the connection, and then click **Finish**.

Implementing Virtual Private Network Access

An increasingly popular alternative to providing the traditional dial-up remote access is to provide virtual private network (VPN) access. A VPN is used to ensure that your data communication on a public network, such as the Internet, is secure. This is implemented by having the VPN create an encrypted tunnel through the Internet.

To create a tunnel, a client computer establishes a PPP connection to an Internet Service Provider (ISP), which gives the client access to the Internet. After the PPP link is established, the client negotiates a second connection to a remote access server at the corporate network that is also connected to the Internet. In this second negotiation, the client and the server agree on how the packets over the virtual connection are encapsulated and encrypted. Then, the two computers can send data across the Internet connection with the assurance that the data is secure.

A VPN can be created over any existing connection to the Internet. For example, in many parts of North America, cable modem or digital subscriber line (DSL) access to the Internet is widely available and very fast. The VPN can be created using this fast connection to the Internet, thus providing the client with secure and fast access to the corporate network.

Figure 9-7 illustrates how a VPN is created using a dial-up or cable modem connection to the Internet.

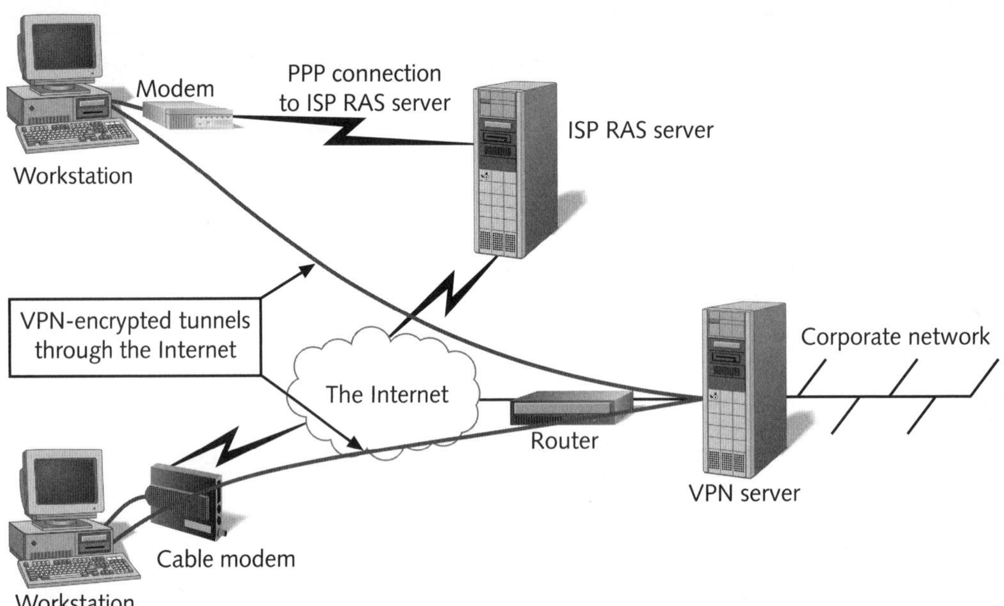

Figure 9-7 VPNs

In many ways, configuring both the server and client for VPN is similar to configuring them for dial-up remote access. From the client, the VPN connection is configured as a network and dial-up connection. From the server, the Routing and Remote Access Service is used to configure the VPN server.

VPN Server Configuration

As discussed, Windows 2000 supports two VPN protocols: Point-to-Point Tunneling Protocol (PPTP) and Layer Two Tunneling Protocol (L2TP). Configuring the VPN server is similar for either protocol. The first step is to install two network adapters in the VPN server. One of the adapters must have a permanent connection to the Internet, and the other adapter is connected to the internal corporate network. Each of the adapters should be installed and tested before continuing.

After installing and testing the network adapters, follow these steps to configure the VPN server:

1. Configure the network adapter connected to the Internet with a valid static IP address, subnet mask, and default gateway. Your ISP provides you with the correct information.
2. Configure the network adapter connected to the corporate network with a valid internal IP address, subnet mask, and name server address (that is, DNS or WINS). The card should not be configured with a default gateway.
3. Open Routing and Remote Access on the Administrative Tools menu.
4. If the RRAS server has not been configured, right-click the RRAS server, and click **Configure and Enable Routing and Remote Access**. You can then choose the **Virtual Private Network (VPN) server** option. If the server has already been configured, right-click the **RRAS server**, and click **Properties**.
5. Verify that both the Router check box and the Remote access server check box are selected, as shown in Figure 9-8.

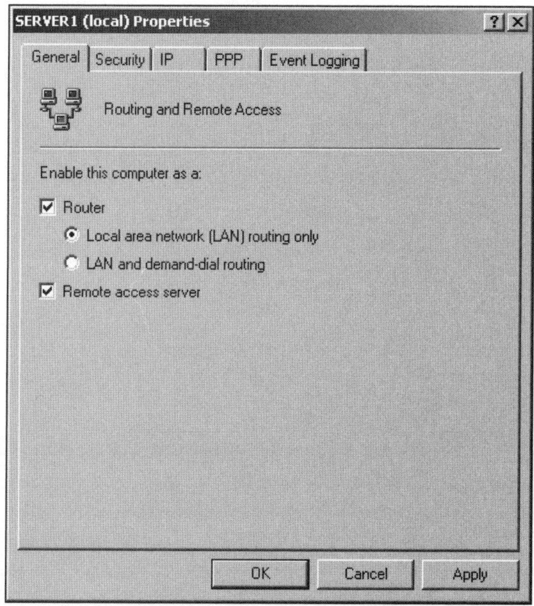

Figure 9-8 Configuring a VPN server

6. Click the **IP** tab, and verify that Enable IP Routing is selected. Select whether the clients receives IP addresses from a static pool or from DHCP on the network. Click **OK**.
7. Expand the **RRAS server** container, and then right-click **Ports**, and click **Properties**.
8. Verify that WAN Miniport (PPTP) is selected, and then click the **Configure** button. The Configure Device - WAN Miniport (PPTP) dialog box opens, as shown in Figure 9-9.

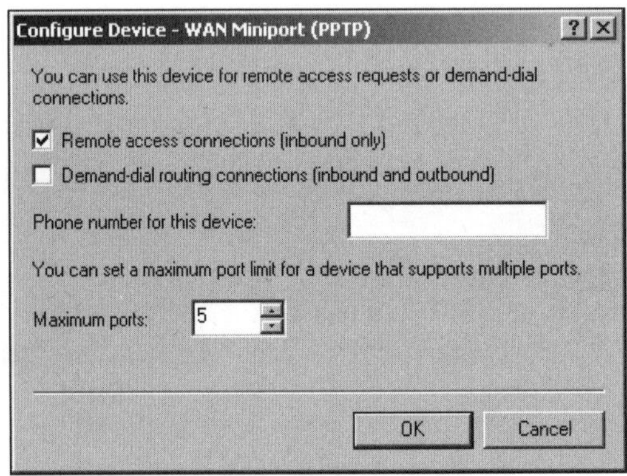

Figure 9-9 Configuring PPTP ports

9. Select either Remote access connections (inbound only) or Demand-dial routing connections (inbound and outbound). Specify the maximum number of PPTP ports available. Configure the server with enough PPTP ports to make sure that a port is available for each concurrent client that may connect. Click **OK**.
10. If you also have clients that are connecting using L2TP, repeat the port configuration for WAN Miniport (L2TP).
11. Click **OK** to accept the changes.

VPN Client Configuration

Configuring a VPN client is also similar to configuring the dial-up client. To configure the VPN client, use the following procedure:

1. If you are connecting to an ISP using a dial-up account, create the dial-up connection first using the procedure described in the previous set of steps. If you are using a permanent connection to the Internet such as a cable modem or DSL connection, you do not have to configure an initial connection.
2. Click **Start**, point to **Settings**, and then click **Network and Dial-up Connections**.
3. Double-click **Make New Connection**.

4. The Network Connection Wizard starts. Click **Next**.
5. You are given the option of creating several different types of network connections. Click **Connect to a private network through the Internet**. Click **Next**.
6. In some configurations you are given a choice of whether you want to first dial an initial connection before creating the VPN, as shown in Figure 9-10. If you are using an ISP dial-up account to access the Internet, click the dial-up connection name. If your connection to the Internet is always active, click **Do not dial the initial connection**. Click **Next**.

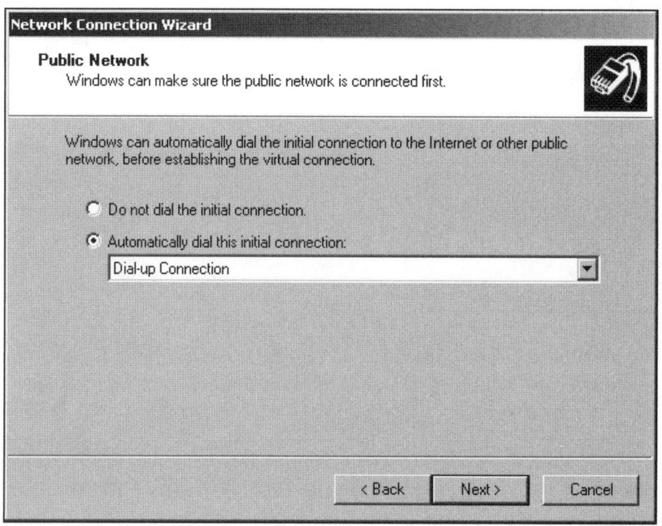
Network Connection Wizard
Public Network
Windows can make sure the public network is connected first.
Windows can automatically dial the initial connection to the Internet or other public network, before establishing the virtual connection.
Do not dial the initial connection.
Automatically dial this initial connection:
Dial-up Connection
< Back
Next >
Cancel

Figure 9-10 Configuring a VPN client

7. Type in the IP address or host name for the VPN server to which you are connecting. Click **Next**.
8. Choose whether to configure the connection for all users on the computer. Click **Next**.
9. Choose whether to share the connection with other computers on your network using Internet connection sharing. Click **Next**, and then click **Finish**.

Configuring Remote Access Authentication

The first step to making remote access as secure as possible is to configure the remote access authentication. Windows 2000 Server provides several options that can be used to authenticate users who connect to a remote access server using either dial-up or VPN. The type of protocol you use depends on the level of security required and the type of clients requiring access. You also have the option of implementing unauthenticated access.

Authentication protocols can be configured through the Routing and Remote Access console by right-clicking your RAS server, and clicking Properties. From the Properties dialog box, click the Security tab, and click the Authentication Methods button. The Authentication Methods dialog box opens allowing you to enable the required authentication protocols, as shown in Figure 9-11.

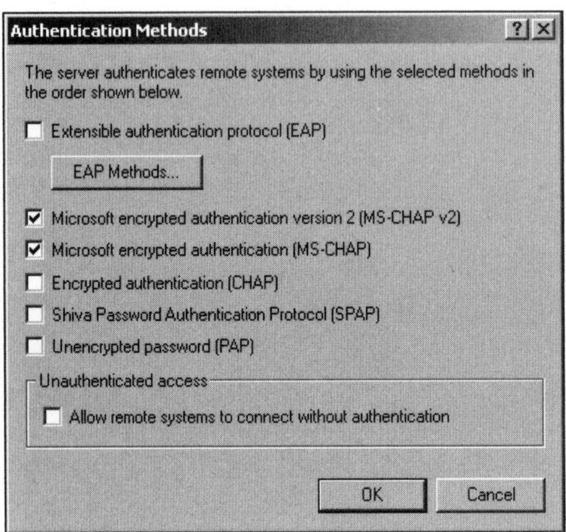

Figure 9-11 Configuring RRAS authentication

By default, the only two authentication protocols that are enabled are MS-CHAP v2 and MS-CHAP. After a protocol has been enabled, it can be used to authenticate users.

The following authentication methods are supported by Windows 2000:

- Microsoft Challenge Handshake Authentication Protocol (MS-CHAP), versions 1 and 2
- Challenge Handshake Authentication Protocol (CHAP)
- Shiva Password Authentication Protocol (SPAP)
- Password Authentication Protocol (PAP)
- Extensible Authentication Protocol (EAP)

We discuss each in turn, along with the unauthenticated access option.

MS-CHAP

Microsoft Challenge Authentication Protocol (MS-CHAP) uses a challenge and response handshake for authentication. To begin the authentication process, the RRAS server sends a challenge that includes a challenge string and session identifier to the client. The client responds with a username, session identifier, password, and a nonreversible encryption of the challenge string that it received from the server. The server checks and authenticates the response if it is valid. MS-CHAP is quite secure because the password is never sent on the network in an unencrypted form.

MS-CHAP v2

MS-CHAP v2 is similar to MS-CHAP, but with enhanced security options, including the following:

- LAN Manager authentication is not supported, thus improving security.
- The cryptographic key used for encrypting data is based on the user's password and the challenge string, rather than on the password only.
- Two-way authentication is supported, which means that the client can also authenticate the server.
- A different key is used to encrypt data each time a user connects, and a different key is used to send and receive data.

During MS-CHAP v2 authentication, the RAS server sends a challenge that includes a session identifier and challenge string. The client responds with the username and a peer challenge string that it generates. The client also sends a one-way encryption of its peer challenge string, the server challenge string, the session identifier, and the user's password. The server checks this response, and then informs the client if authentication was successful, and sends a response based on its challenge string, the peer challenge string, the client's encrypted response, and the user's password. The client must now authenticate the server's response. The client does not use the connection if unable to authenticate the server's response.

MS-CHAP (version 1 or 2) is needed for password changes during logon and for using **Microsoft Point-to-Point Encryption (MPPE)** for PPP or PPTP encryption. MPPE is an encryption technique that uses encryption keys varying in length from 40 bits to 128 bits so that packets traveling between the remote access client and the remote access or tunnel server are secure. MPPE is used when IP security is not available.

CHAP

Challenge Handshake Authentication Protocol (CHAP) is a challenge response authentication protocol that uses the industry standard Message Digest 5 (MD5) hashing for encryption. It is supported by various vendors and can be enabled on a Windows 2000 RAS server to enable authentication for non-Microsoft clients.

SPAP

Shiva Password Authentication Protocol (SPAP) uses a reversible encryption method employed by Shiva to encrypt a user's password, although it is not as secure as MS-CHAP or CHAP. The drawback of using this authentication method is that the password is always encrypted in the same reversible form. If you have Shiva clients connecting to your RAS server, this authentication protocol must be enabled.

PAP

Password Authentication Protocol (PAP) is the least secure authentication method because user passwords are sent in clear text. This means that anyone capable of capturing the authentication packet can read the password, which can lead to an unauthorized user gaining access to your network. This authentication method should only be used if the client does not support any of the other protocols listed previously.

EAP

Windows 2000 supports **Extensible Authentication Protocol (EAP)** as a remote access authentication protocol. EAP is different than the other options in that it is really a standard for designing other authentication processes. Two options are currently supported for Windows 2000 authentication: EAP-Message Digest 5 Challenge Handshake Authentication (MD5 CHAP) and EAP-TLS. EAP-MD5 CHAP uses challenges and responses sent as EAP messages between the client and server. It is typically used to support authentication based on usernames and passwords. EAP-TLS is used with certificate-based security. For example, you would use EAP-TLS if you were using smart cards for logon and authentication. EAP-TLS is only supported if your RAS server is part of an Active Directory domain.

EAP also provides an Application Programming Interface (API) that supports the creation of any device or process to perform the authentication. This means that EAP can be used when developing a new authentication process, such as a retina scan, simply by designing the new process to use the EAP APIs.

Unauthenticated Access

Windows 2000 Server supports remote access connections that do not require any authentication. This option uses the Guest account to gain access to network resources, so the account needs to be enabled and strict permissions need to be set for the account.

If you are using a Windows 2000 RRAS server as the remote access server and Windows 95 or later Microsoft clients, you usually accept the default of supporting only MS-CHAP v1 and v2 authentication. In a more secure environment, you can enforce the use of MS-CHAP v2 only. (To use MS-CHAP v2 with Windows 9x clients, you must upgrade the dial-up client.) The most secure option for remote access authentication is EAS-TLS, because the user must not only know a password or PIN number, but must also have physical possession of the smart card.

Another option for securing remote access is to use a random password-generating device for both the client and the server. In this case, the user is given a small device that generates a unique password every few minutes. When the user tries to access the remote access server, the user must type in the password that is currently displayed on the device. The server uses the same algorithm to generate passwords, so it has the same current password for the user and the user is authenticated. The advantage of this type of device is that it protects you in case an attacker manages to install an application on your computer that captures your keystrokes as you type in your password. Because the password is only valid for a very short time period, the attacker cannot use the password to log in again. This type of system requires dedicated third-party hardware and software to implement.

Configuring Encryption Protocols

Encryption protocols are used to encrypt the data sent between a client and an RAS server. This ensures that the data passed between a client and server is secure. Where confidentiality is required, such as for financial data, the remote access server can be configured to require encryption of all data or the connection is refused. In cases such as a VPN, encryption should always be required if data is being sent across a public network.

If you are using MS-CHAP version 1 or 2 or EAP, there are two forms of encryption that can be used: Microsoft Point-to-Point Encryption and **IP Security (IPSec)**. IPSec consists of a suite of cryptography-based protection services and protocols that provide machine-level authentication and data encryption.

The MPPE protocol encrypts data for PPP connections including PPTP. MPPE can use 40-bit, 56-bit, or 128-bit encryption schemes. For connections that use L2TP, IPSec is used for authentication and encryption of data. Before any information is sent between the two computers, IPSec negotiates the highest encryption for encrypting data and passwords. IPSec uses 56-bit Data Encryption Standard (DES) encryption or triple DES (3DES) encryption. (3DES provides the highest level of security.)

Encryption protocols can be enabled through the profile of the remote access policy (creating a remote access policy is covered later in the chapter). Within the Routing and Remote Access console, click the Remote Access Policies container. Right-click the policy you want to edit, and click Properties. In the Properties dialog box, click the Edit Profile button. Click the Encryption tab to view the various levels of encryption available, as shown in Figure 9-12.

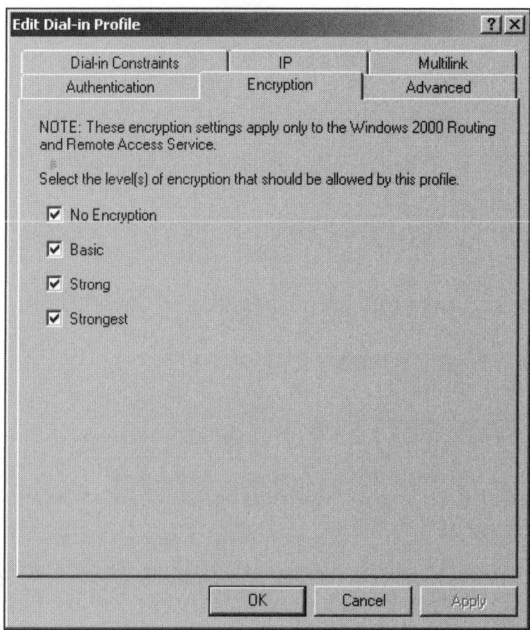

Figure 9-12 Configuring RRAS encryption

There are three options available with the base installation. If you have Windows 2000 SP2 installed, four choices are available. Table 9-2 summarizes these four options.

Table 9-2 Encryption options

Option	Description
No Encryption	Encryption is not enabled for the remote access policy
Basic	Uses MPPE 40-bit or IPSec 56-bit encryption
Strong	Uses MPPE 56-bit or IPSec 56-bit encryption
Strongest	Uses MPPE 128-bit or IPSec 3DES encryption; only available if Windows 2000 SP2 is installed

Troubleshooting Remote Access

If you cannot successfully connect to a dial-up or VPN-based RAS server, check the following list of possible solutions:

- Verify that all dial-up credentials such as username and password are correct.
- Ensure that remote access is enabled on the RRAS server.
- Check to see that ports such as PPTP or L2TP are enabled for inbound remote access connections. These ports may also be used up, which would prevent additional connections.
- Ensure that the remote access server and remote access client are configured with at least one common authentication and encryption method between the two.
- Check the remote access policy to be sure that it is configured to allow access.
- Verify that there are enough addresses in the static IP address range.
- Ensure that a DHCP relay agent has been configured. This should be the first thing you check if clients cannot see resources inside the network. Remember that the DHCP relay agent provides the additional options that are needed to browse the network, such as a WINS or DNS IP address.
- Ensure that packet filters are not being used that may restrict access.
- Check to be sure that the network adapter that is connected to the Internet is configured with a static IP address.

Implementing and Troubleshooting Remote Access Policies

In early versions of Windows, permission to dial into a RAS server was controlled by enabling dial-in permission directly to a user account. One of the major drawbacks to this was that each user account had to be configured and if there were a large number of users on the network, it dramatically increased administration. Windows 2000 uses the dial-in properties of user accounts as well as remote access policies to grant users the ability to dial into a RAS server. The combination of the two now reduces the administration associated with granting dial-in access, and provides an administrator with greater flexibility for authorizing connection attempts.

Remote access permissions can be configured by using the Active Directory Users and Computers console, right-clicking a user object, and then clicking the Dial-in tab under the properties of a user account, as shown in Figure 9-13. In the properties of the user account, you can choose to Allow access, Deny access, or Control access through Remote Access Policy.

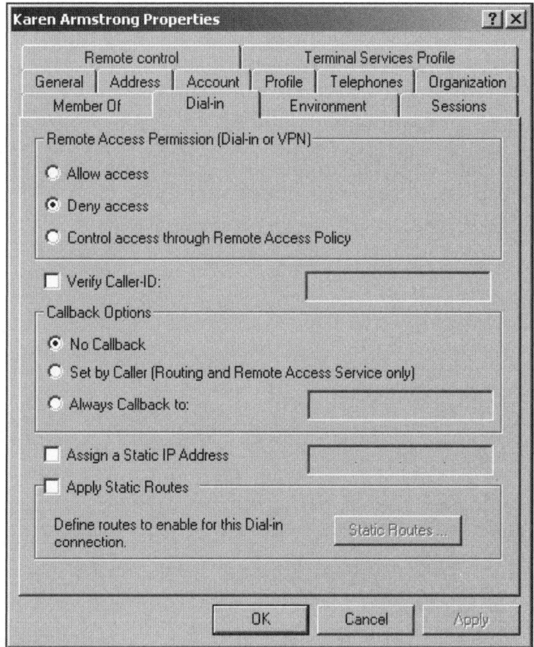

Figure 9-13 Granting permissions

The control access through Remote Access Policy setting is only available for domains running in native mode.

In the following sections, you learn the elements in a remote access policy, the steps that you need to take to create a policy, and some troubleshooting tips that you might find useful while working with a remote access policy.

Elements of a Remote Access Policy

A **remote access policy** consists of the following three elements that must be evaluated before a user is allowed to dial-in:

- Conditions
- Permissions
- Profile

Each element is described in turn and then the process of applying a remote access policy is outlined.

Conditions

The remote access policy conditions are attributes that are compared to the connection attempt. For example, the conditions can include attributes such as the phone number the user is calling from, the day of the week and time of day the user is permitted to dial-in, or the group or groups of which the user must be a member. For each user that dials in, the RAS server evaluates the conditions to make sure they match the connection attempt. The RAS server evaluates all remote access policies that are configured until it finds one that matches the connection attempt.

Permissions

The permissions for a remote access policy are a combination of user account permissions as well as those defined in the policy. If the connection attempt matches the condition in one of the remote access policies, the remote access permissions are then evaluated. If the user is denied access under their account properties, the user is not permitted dial-in access. If the user is allowed access, the policy evaluation continues. If the dial-in permission under the properties of the user account is set to Control access through Remote Access Policy, the permissions configured in the policy are evaluated and the user is either allowed or denied access.

The default remote access permission assigned through a policy is Deny access.

Profile

The final stage in the policy evaluation is to match the connection attempt to the remote access policy profile. If the connection is authorized, meaning the user has been granted access either through their user account settings or through a remote access policy, the settings configured in the profile are evaluated. The profile consists of settings such as dial-in constraints, multilink properties, authentication protocols, and encryption properties. If the connection attempt matches the profile settings, the user is granted dial-in access.

When a User Attempts a Connection

The following steps illustrate the process that occurs when a user attempts a connection:

1. The remote access policy is checked. If there is no policy, the connection attempt is rejected. If there are multiple policies, the first policy in the list is evaluated. If the conditions do not match the connection attempt, the next policy in the list is evaluated. If none of the conditions in any of the policies match the connection attempt, the attempt is denied.
2. If the conditions in one of the policies match the connection attempt, the permissions are then evaluated.
3. If the user has been denied access, the connection attempt is rejected. If the user has been granted access, the user account and remote access profile settings are evaluated. If the settings match the connection attempt, dial-in access is granted. If the settings do not match the connection attempt, access is denied.
4. If the Permission Control access through Remote Access Policy is selected, the permissions in the remote access policy are evaluated. If the Deny Remote Access Permission is selected, access is denied. If the Grant Remote Access Permission is selected, the user account and profile settings are evaluated. If the user account and profile settings do not match the connection attempt, access is denied. If the user account and profile settings do match the connection attempt, access is granted.

Creating a Remote Access Policy

When Routing and Remote Access Services are installed, a default policy called Allow access if dial-in permission is enabled is created. The default permission set in the policy is to deny access. If you configure user account properties to control access through a remote access policy, the default permission needs to be changed or all connection attempts are denied.

A remote access policy can be created using the Routing and Remote Access snap-in. Use the following steps to configure a remote access policy:

1. Click **Start**, point to **Programs**, point to **Administrative Tools**, and then click **Routing and Remote Access**.
2. Expand your remote access server, right-click the **Remote Access Policies** container, and then click **New Remote Access Policy**.
3. In the Policy Name dialog box, type in a friendly name for the new policy. Click **Next**.
4. Click **Add** in the Conditions dialog box to select the conditions that are included in the policy. Add each condition to be included by selecting it from the list of attributes, and clicking **Add**. Some sample conditions include day and time restrictions and group membership. Figure 9-14 illustrates these conditions added to the new policy. Click **Next**.

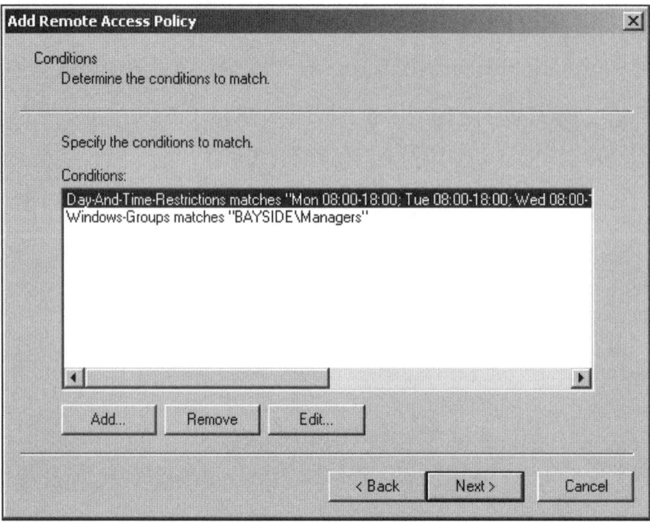

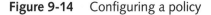

Figure 9-14 Configuring a policy

5. In the Permissions dialog box, select whether remote access is to be granted or denied if the remote access policy conditions are met. Be very cautious when denying access. If a remote access policy is set to deny access, no other polices are evaluated, and the connection attempt is rejected. Click **Next**.
6. From the User Profile dialog box you can click the **Edit Profile** button to edit the remote access profile, or you can choose **Finish**.
7. If you click Edit Profile, the Edit Dial-in Profile dialog box appears, as shown in Figure 9-15. Table 9-3 summarizes the different tabs available. These tabs provide various possible configuration choices such as authentication, encryption, and other advanced connection options. After you have configured the profile settings, click **OK**, and then click **Finish**.

Table 9-3 Editing the Dial-in Profile

Tab	Description
Dial-in Constraints	Configures the disconnect times, maximum idle time, day and time restrictions, whether access is restricted to a single number, and whether to restrict access based on the media used
IP	Configures how the client dialing in receives an IP address; IP filters can also be determined to restrict the protocols that a client can use
Multilink	Configures whether clients can use multilink, the number of connections they can use, at what point a link is dropped; BAP can also be enabled from this tab
Authentication	Configures authentication protocols that are available for the policy
Encryption	Configures the encryption level
Advanced	Used to set RADIUS-specific attributes that can further restrict access

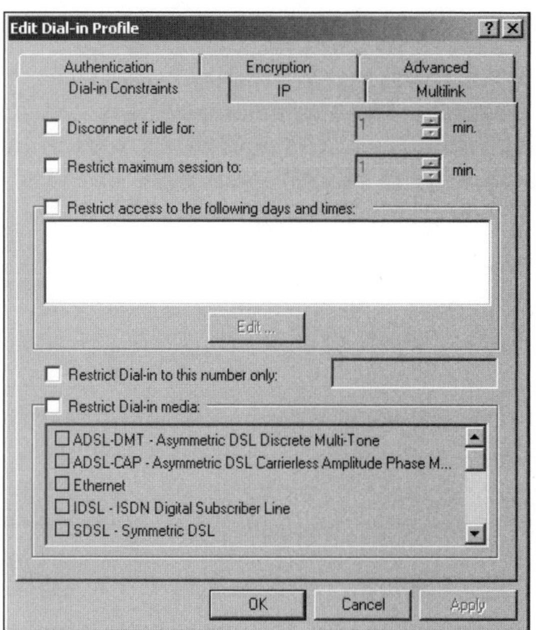

Figure 9-15 Configuring a RRAS profile setting

After the policy has been created, it is listed under the Remote Access Policies container within the Routing and Remote Access snap-in. (Refer to Figure 9-3 to see the Remote Access Policies container.) The policy can be edited at any time by right-clicking the policy, and choosing Properties.

If there is no policy configured, any connection attempts are denied regardless of the dial-in permissions assigned under the user account properties.

Using the Routing and Remote Access console, you can configure multiple policies for different security groups that have different requirements. If there are multiple policies, each policy is evaluated in the order in which it appears under the Remote Access Policy container. When a connection request is received, the conditions are evaluated against the first policy in the list. If the conditions do not match the connection attempt, the remaining policies are evaluated in the order they appear until a match is found. After a match is found, the permissions and profile of that policy are then evaluated against the connection attempt. If the permissions and profile of that policy do not match the connection attempt, access is denied and no other policies are evaluated.

You can change the order in which the policies are evaluated by right-clicking a policy and clicking either Move Up or Move Down, depending on how you want to reorder the list. It is recommended that the policy configured for the majority of remote access users be listed first so that fewer policies have to be evaluated when a user attempts to dial-in.

Troubleshooting Remote Access Policies

There are several problems that can arise with remote access policies. Having a thorough understanding of how remote access policies are applied can assist you in quickly determining the source of the problem. If connection attempts to the remote access server are being rejected, check the following list of possible solutions:

- Verify that the connection attempt matches the profile of at least one remote access policy.
- Check to be sure the user is not a member of any groups that have been denied access. Be careful of any group nesting that may be taking place, which might be configured to deny remote access.
- Ensure that the user attempting to connect has been granted permission to dial in either through a user account property or through a remote access policy.
- Check to be sure the dial-in settings configured for the user account are not conflicting with those of the remote access policy.
- Verify that the connection attempt matches all of the settings configured in the profile of the policy.

Configuring and Troubleshooting Network Address Translation

Network address translation (NAT) allows a group of computers to access the Internet using a single Internet connection and a single IP address. The computer that is configured with NAT can act as a network translator, assign IP addresses, and act as a proxy server.

If an office wanted to connect their computers to the Internet, they would have to obtain a public IP address for each computer. NAT provides a simple solution to this by allowing the use of private IP addresses on the internal network and mapping the private addresses to a public address when a computer requires access to the Internet. For example, a small office could assign the computers IP addresses in the range of 172.16.0.0 to 172.31.255.255, and obtain a single IP address from its ISP. When a computer on the internal network accesses the Internet, the private IP address is translated into the public IP address. The mappings of the internal client addresses and the public address are stored in a table so the server routes the request to the correct client.

NAT can perform address translation in two different ways, depending on whether you have a single public IP address or multiple public addresses. If there is a single IP address, NAT changes the source IP address to that of the public one and then changes the port number to a random one. If there are multiple IP addresses, NAT can perform a one-to-one IP address translation.

A computer running NAT provides several different services, which allow multiple computers to share a single Internet connection:

- *Address translation*—The computer running NAT translates the internal IP addresses to a public address forwarding the packets between the private network and the Internet.
- *IP addressing*—The NAT computer runs a simplified version of TCP/IP providing IP addressing information to clients on the internal network. The computers on the internal network are configured as DHCP clients. The NAT computer can then assign them an IP address, subnet mask, and the IP address of the default gateway, as well as the IP address of the DNS server.
- *Name resolution*—The NAT computer, in a sense, becomes the DNS server for the internal clients. Any name resolution requests are received by the NAT computer, forwarded to the appropriate DNS server on the Internet, and returned to the requesting client.

Installing NAT

You can configure NAT by installing and enabling Routing and Remote Access Services using the steps outlined earlier in the chapter. Make sure you select the options for Internet connection server and setting up a router with network address translation. After the wizard is complete, all the necessary configuration changes are made to the computer.

If you already have RRAS enabled on your computer and want to configure it as a NAT computer as well, use the following steps:

1. Configure the IP address of the internal network adapter, setting it to **192.168.0.1** with a subnet mask of **255.255.255.0**. (It is not required that you use this particular IP address.) You can do this by right-clicking the network adapter found in the Network and Dial-up connections. In the Properties dialog box, click **TCP/IP**, and then click the **Properties** button.
2. Enable routing on the appropriate port by right-clicking the **Ports** container under your RAS server within the Routing and Remote Access snap-in, and then clicking **Properties**. On the Devices tab, click the device you want to configure, and click the **Configure** button. Check the **Demand-dial routing connections (inbound and outbound)** check box. Click **OK**.
3. If you have a dial-up connection to the Internet, create a demand-dial interface connecting to your ISP by right-clicking the **Routing Interfaces** container under your RAS server within the Routing and Remote Access snap-in. You can then click **New Demand-dial Interface** to start the wizard.
4. Create a default static route that uses the Internet interface by expanding your RAS server and IP Routing container. Right-click the **Static Routes** container, and click **New Static Route**. Click the interface to use for the

default route and type **0.0.0.0** for both the destination and network mask. Click the check box for the **Use this route to initiate demand-dial connections** option. Type **1** for the metric. Click **OK**.

5. Add the NAT routing protocol by right-clicking the **General** container under IP Routing, and click **New Routing Protocol**. Click **Network Address Translation**, and click **OK**.
6. Add the Internet and LAN interfaces to the NAT protocol by right-clicking **Network Address Translation (NAT)** under the IP Routing container, and clicking **New Interface**. Click the interface to add, and click **OK**.
7. Enable NAT addressing by right-clicking **Network Address Translation (NAT)** under the IP Routing container, and clicking **Properties**. Click the **Address Assignment** tab, and click **Automatically assign IP addresses by using DHCP**. If necessary, configure the range of IP addresses assigned to clients. Click **OK**.

After NAT is installed, it can be configured using the Routing and Remote Access snap-in. To configure NAT, right-click the Network Address Translation icon within the Routing and Remote Access console, and click Properties. The Network Address Translation (NAT) Properties dialog box appears, as shown in Figure 9-16. Table 9-4 summarizes the available tabs.

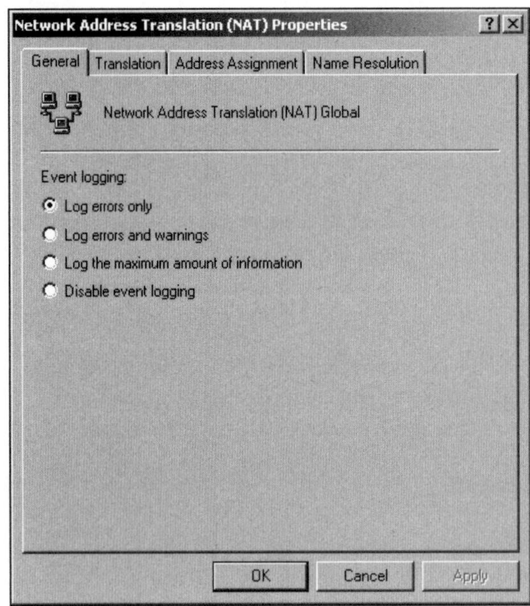

Figure 9-16 Configuring network address translation (NAT)

Table 9-4 Configuring NAT

Tab	Description
General	Use to configure event logging; you can choose to Log errors only, Log errors and warnings, Log the maximum amount of information (use this option if you have just installed NAT and want to get an idea of what is happening), and Disable event logging
Translation	Use to configure timeout values for translations; using the Applications button, you can configure which applications are available to internal users across the Internet
Address Assignment	Use to enable the DHCP service for NAT and configure a range of IP addresses to be assigned to internal clients
Name Resolution	Use to configure which clients the NAT server resolves IP addresses for and how name resolution is handled

NAT provides you with the option to use your own DHCP server or use the Address Assignment features built into NAT itself. This is one of the main differences between NAT and Internet connection sharing (ICS). ICS does not give you the option to configure an alternate IP address range or use a different DHCP server. ICS is discussed in more detail later in the chapter.

Troubleshooting NAT

Problems with NAT can usually be attributed to incorrect configuration settings. Problems can be simple to troubleshoot if you understand how NAT works and how it is configured.

If you are experiencing a problem, work through the following:

- If clients are not receiving IP addresses from the NAT computer, verify that network address translation addressing has been enabled. Also, verify that there is no other DHCP server running on the network.
- If name resolution is not working for NAT clients, check to be sure that name resolution has been enabled using the Name Resolution tab under the NAT properties. Also, check the configuration of the NAT computer using the ipconfig command to verify DNS settings.
- If packets are not being properly translated, verify that both the Internet and LAN interface have been added to the NAT protocol. Verify the range of IP addresses that has been configured on the NAT computer. Using the Translation tab under the NAT properties, verify that the program being used is in the list of supported programs using the Translation tab under the NAT properties. Last, verify that IP packet filtering is not preventing certain Internet traffic from being sent and received.

CONFIGURING INTERNET CONNECTION SHARING

Internet connection sharing (ICS) provides an easy way of connecting multiple computers in a home office or small business to the Internet. Using ICS provides all computers on the network with HTTP, FTP, and e-mail access using a single Internet connection.

Enabling ICS on a computer (a member server or computer running Windows 2000 Professional) provides NAT services, IP addressing, and name resolution for computers on the internal network. Each computer can then access the Internet as if they had their own direct connection.

After installing ICS on the computer connected to the Internet, the IP address of the internal network adapter is automatically set to 192.168.0.1. A simplified version of DHCP is installed, which assigns internal clients an IP address (from the network ID of 192.168.0.0/24). A DNS proxy service is also installed to pass internal DNS requests to the DNS server that the computer running ICS is configured to use.

ICS and NAT are both used to connect a small or home office to the Internet. The differences between the two are summarized in Table 9-5.

Table 9-5 Difference between ICS and NAT

ICS	NAT
Supports a single office interface	Supports multiple office interfaces
Uses a single public IP address	Can use a single public IP address or multiple public IP addresses
Assigns internal clients IP addresses from a fixed range	Can configure the range of IP addresses assigned to internal clients
Provides automatic configuration by enabling connection sharing	Requires some manual configuration

Enabling Internet Connection Sharing

ICS is relatively straightforward to enable. It does not require any configuration unless you want to change the applications and services available to users on the internal network.

Use the following steps to enable and configure ICS:

1. Click **Start**, point to **Settings**, and click **Network and Dial-up Connections**.
2. Right-click the adapter that is connected to an Internet connection, and click **Properties**.
3. Click the **Sharing** tab, and click the **Enable Internet Connection Sharing for this connection** check box, as shown in Figure 9-17.
4. To configure ICS, click the **Settings** button.

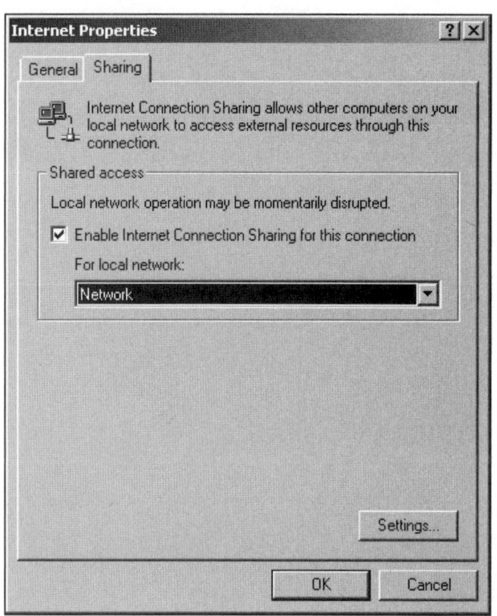

Figure 9-17 Enabling Internet connection sharing (ICS)

5. Click the **Applications** tab, and then click **Add** to open the Internet Connection Sharing Application dialog box. This dialog box allows you to configure application programs that you want to make available for users on the network that share the Internet connection, as shown in Figure 9-18.

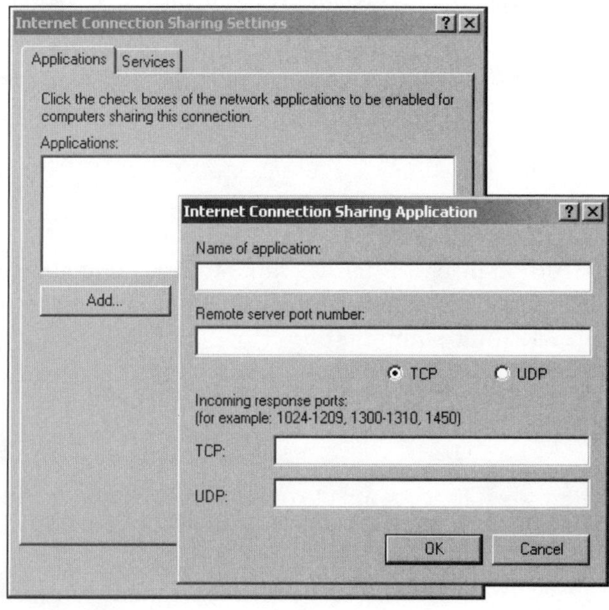

Figure 9-18 Configuring applications to work through ICS

6. Click the **Services** tab. Click the services that you want enabled, as shown in Figure 9-19. Services that are not listed can be added by clicking the **Add** button. Click **OK**.

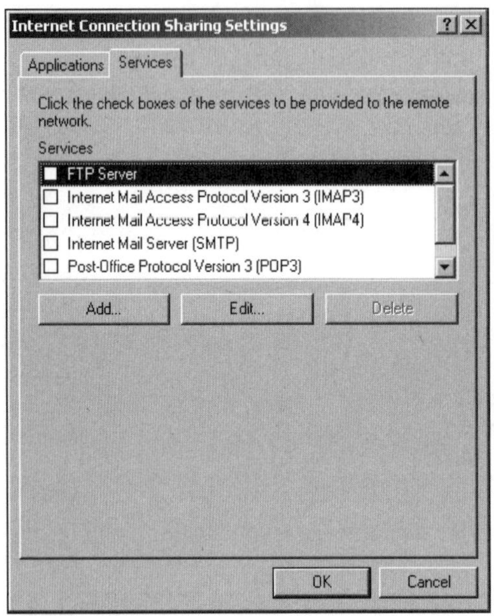

Figure 9-19 Configuring ICS services

7. Click **Yes** to verify that you want to enable ICS for the Internet connection.

After ICS is installed, the computer's IP address should be set to 192.168.0.1 with a subnet mask of 255.255.255.0. Those computers that access the Internet through the computer running ICS should be configured to obtain an IP address automatically.

Troubleshooting ICS

As with most other services and applications you install and configure on a computer, problems are bound to arise. Although ICS is fairly simple to use, there are some common problems that you may encounter. The following list gives some ways you can verify ICS configuration and troubleshoot common problems.

- After ICS is installed, use the ipconfig command to verify that the network adapter has been assigned the IP address of 192.168.0.1, and the subnet mask is 255.255.255.0.
- If client computers are unable to connect to the Internet, use the ipconfig command to verify that an IP address in the range of 192.168.0.2 through to 192.168.0.254 has been assigned, and the subnet mask is 255.255.255.0. Use the ping command to verify TCP/IP connectivity with the computer running ICS.

- Verify that there is no DHCP server already running on the network. This inhibits the DHCP service included with ICS from functioning.
- If the client computers are unable to connect to Web sites, verify the DNS address configured on the computer running ICS.
- If clients can only connect to the Internet after you manually establish a connection, verify that demand dialing is enabled on the ICS computer.

CONFIGURING TERMINAL SERVICES FOR REMOTE ACCESS

Terminal Services provides remote access to a server desktop through "thin client" software, which serves as a terminal emulator. Terminal Services transmits only the user interface of the program to the client. The client then returns keyboard and mouse clicks back to be processed by the server. **Terminal Services** is mainly used for two purposes: for centralized access to applications and for remote administration.

Terminal server can be used to centralize control of applications, allowing organizations to maintain control over specific applications such as financial applications. It is also used for remote administration. A server administrator can use it to remotely access management tools, such as Active Directory Users and Computers, the Computer Management tool, the DNS tool, and others that appear in the Administrative Tools menu. A terminal server can also be used as MMC snap-ins. Remote access enables a server administrator to manage one or more servers from her or his workstation on the same network, or to dial in from home or while traveling.

Another reason for using a terminal server is to enable thin clients—such as specialized PCs that have minimal Windows-based operating systems—to access a Windows 2000 server, so that most CPU-intense operations (creating a spreadsheet for example) are performed on the server. Some examples of thin client computers are Hewlett-Packard's Netstation, Maxspeed's MaxTerm, Neoware's NeoStation, and Wyse Technologies' Winterm terminals.

In this last section of the chapter, you learn how to install and manage Terminal Services.

Installing Terminal Services

Terminal Services can be installed from the Add/Remove Windows Components section from within the Add/Remove Programs applet found in Control Panel. Because Terminal Services can be installed in one of two modes, before you install it, determine whether you want the server to function as an application server to clients, or as a remote administration server for server administrators. This is required because the installation cannot be set up for both on a single server. The only way to change the configuration to the other mode is to reinstall Terminal Services. Also, if you plan to set up an application server, then one Windows 2000 server must also be configured as a Terminal Services licensing server.

To install Terminal Services:

1. Click **Start**, point to **Settings**, and click **Control Panel**.
2. Double-click the **Add/Remove Programs** icon, and click **Add/Remove Windows Components**.
3. Check the box in front of Terminal Services, and make sure that the box is not gray, (a gray box means that not all components are installed). If the box is gray, double-click **Terminal Services**, check all of the subcomponents, and click **OK** in the Terminal Services dialog box.
4. If this is the first or only Windows 2000 server configured as a terminal server, also click **Terminal Services Licensing** in order to license clients to use Terminal Services. Note that if you are installing Terminal Services for remote administration, you do not need to install Terminal Services Licensing.
5. Click **Next** in the Windows Components Wizard dialog box.
6. Select whether this server is to be a remote administration server for server administrators or an application server, as shown in Figure 9-20. Click **Next**.

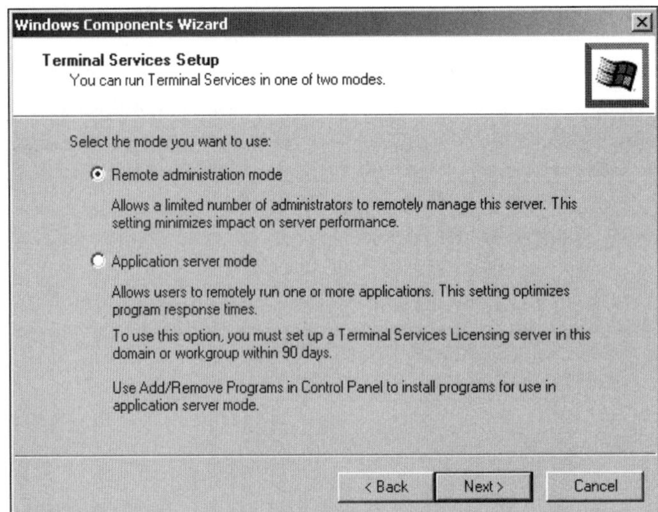

Figure 9-20 Configuring Terminal Services

7. In Step 6, if you selected to configure for the application server mode, two dialog boxes are displayed next. The first enables you to specify the security level for access to software applications. You can either use permissions that are compatible with Windows 2000 security or permissions that are less secure for compatibility with some older software applications. The second dialog box shows applications that are currently installed, such as Microsoft Office, and that may need to be reinstalled to function using Terminal Services.

8. In Step 4, if you selected to install Terminal Services Licensing in the next dialog box, click **Your entire enterprise** if this server is to be used to manage licenses for all clients in an enterprise. Click **Your domain or workgroup**, if this server is to be used to manage licensing only for clients in a domain or on a stand-alone server. Also, select the folder location for the license database. Click **Next**.
9. If requested, insert the Windows 2000 Server CD-ROM, specify the path to the CD-ROM drive and the \I386 folder, and click **OK**.
10. Click **Finish**.
11. Select the option to restart the server to enable the new services.

Managing Terminal Services

There are various tools available to administer a computer running Terminal Services once it is installed. In the Administrative Tools folder within Control Panel there are four tools that can be used for Terminal Services administration: Terminal Services Client Creator, Terminal Services Manager, Terminal Services Configuration, and Terminal Services Licensing (if Terminal Services is installed in application mode).

Table 9-6 describes the Terminal Services administration tools.

Table 9-6 Terminal Services administrative tools

Administrative Tool	Description
Terminal Services Client Creator	Used to create a floppy disk for Terminal Services client installations
Terminal Services Manager	Used to monitor and control client access to one or more terminal servers
Terminal Services Configuration	Used to configure terminal server settings and connections
Terminal Services Licensing	Used to store and track Terminal Services client access licenses

In the following sections, you learn how to configure remote connections and a Terminal Services client, how to install applications, and how to configure Terminal Services user properties. After you complete these sections, you have all the knowledge you need to create and configure a Terminal Services server and provide client access in order to use available server-based applications or perform remote administration.

Configuring Remote Connections

Begin by using the Terminal Services Configuration tool to configure the remote connection properties, as shown in the following steps. Only one connection is configured for each NIC in the server, which is used to handle multiple clients.

1. Click **Start**, point to **Programs**, point to **Administrative Tools**, and click **Terminal Services Configuration**.

2. Double-click **Terminal Services Configuration**, if necessary, to view the Connections and Server Settings folders in the tree.
3. Click **Connections** to view the connection set up during installation.
4. If you have more than one NIC, you can create another connection by right-clicking **Connections**, and clicking **Create New Connection**.

To manage the properties of a connection, double-click the connection in the right details pane, such as RDP-Tcp. Figure 9-21 shows the Properties dialog box and Table 9-7 describes the capabilities found on each tab.

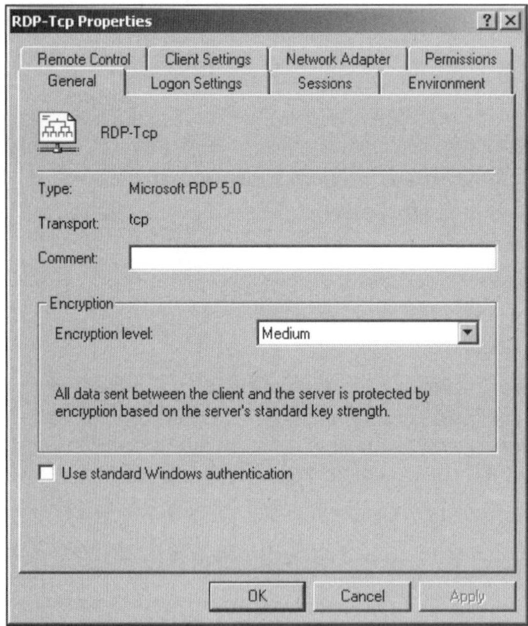

Figure 9-21 The Properties dialog box

Table 9-7 Property tabs for a terminal connection

Tab	Description
General	Used to configure authentication and encryption
Logon Settings	Used to configure how the user logs on, by supplying information or with preconfigured information
Sessions	Used to configure timeout settings
Environment	Used to configure a program to run automatically when a user connects
Remote Control	Used to enable remote control of a client
Client Settings	Used to configure client settings such as drive mappings and port mappings
Network Adapter	Used to configure the number of simultaneous connections
Permissions	Used to control user access based on standard permissions, such as allow or deny access

Some of the settings outlined above can also be configured on a user-by-user basis under the properties of a user account. Any settings configured for the connection override those configured on a user account.

One property that should be checked from the start is permission security. If the terminal server is used by server administrators for remote administration, make sure that access is set up only for the appropriate administrators group, such as Administrators or Domain Admins. If the terminal server is configured as an application server, first use the Active Directory Users and Computers tool or the Local Users and Groups tool (on a stand-alone server) to create one or more groups of users who have access to the terminal server. Then use the Terminal Services Configuration tool to set up the permissions.

Another property that should be checked is the implementation of encryption and authentication. Click the General tab to check these properties. Authentication can be set to use either no authentication or standard Windows authentication when the clients are Windows 95, 98, NT, or 2000. The encryption options are:

- *Low*—Data sent from the client to the server is encrypted.
- *Medium*—Data sent from the client to the server and from the server to the client is encrypted using the default server encryption (uses 40-bit or 56-bit encryption).
- *High*—Data sent from the client to the server and from the server to the client is encrypted using the highest encryption level at the server (uses 128-bit encryption).

Configuring a Terminal Services Client

The Terminal Services Client Creator can be used to create installation floppies to install the Terminal Services Client. Before you start, format four floppy disks for Windows 3.11, or two disks for Windows 95 or higher and for UNIX systems. After you start the Terminal Services Client Creator tool, the Create Installation Disk(s) dialog box opens, as shown in Figure 9-22.

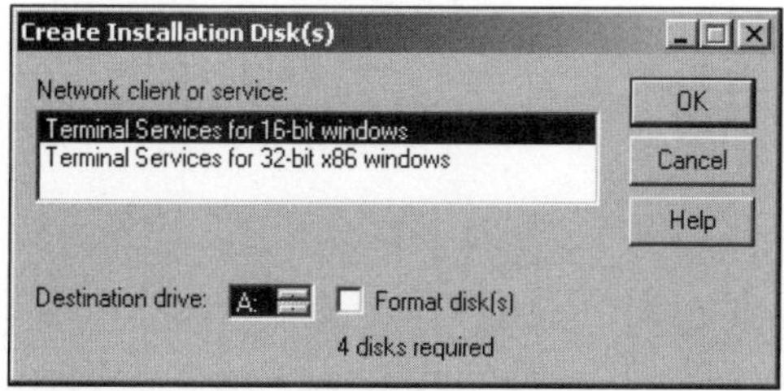

Figure 9-22 Creating Terminal Services client diskettes

Select the client for which you want to create an Installation disk set. Insert the first disk, and click OK to begin making the disk set. Click OK again to confirm that you want to start making the disks.

To install the terminal server client software on the floppy disks, as you might for a computer running Windows 95 or Windows 98, insert the first disk in the computer. Click Start, click Run, and enter a:\setup in the Open box. Click OK to start the Setup program, which installs the software and creates a program group of the programs used to access the terminal server.

Installing Applications

When you configure a terminal server to function in the applications server mode, applications are installed to be compatible with this mode. For this reason, you may need to reinstall some applications, as indicated by the Windows Components Wizard when you install Terminal Services. Use the Add/Remove Programs applet in Control Panel to install new applications after the Terminal Services are installed, and use the same applet to uninstall and reinstall programs that were installed prior to setting up the server for Terminal Services.

On a terminal server, software applications are installed only via the install mode, which is automatically invoked when you install applications by clicking Add/Remove Programs in Control Panel, clicking the Add New Programs button, and clicking the CD or Floppy button to start the program installation. You should not install programs by using the Start menu and Run Option, or by double-clicking the installation program from Windows Explorer or My Computer.

Configuring Terminal Services User Properties

When Terminal Services is installed in Windows 2000, it adds extra configuration options to the properties of user accounts. There are four extra tabs available when Terminal Services is installed, as shown in Figure 9-23.

- *Terminal Services Profile*—Use this tab to enable the user as a Terminal Services client, to configure a special profile used when users connect to a terminal server, and to configure a home directory.
- *Remote control*—Use this tab to configure remote control properties for the user account. These settings can also be configured under the properties for the connection, and if so, override any settings specified under the user account properties.
- *Sessions*—Use this tab to configure a maximum session time and disconnect options. These properties can also be configured under the properties for the connection, and if so, override any settings configured under the user account.
- *Environment*—Use this tab to configure a program to automatically run when the user connects to the terminal server.

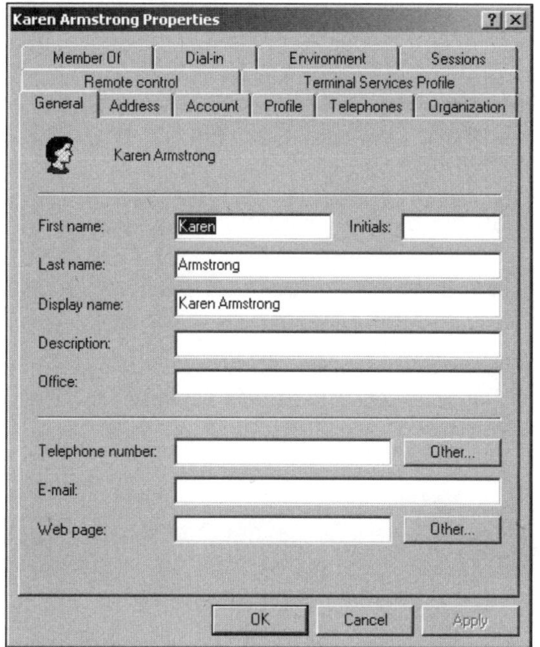

Figure 9-23 Configuring user properties

CHAPTER SUMMARY

- A remote access server is a computer running Windows 2000 with Routing and Remote Access Services enabled. A remote access server authenticates remote and mobile users, providing a gateway to internal network resources.
- Remote access solutions can be implemented including dial-up, VPN, and NAT.
- Each RAS server can be configured using the Routing and Remote Access console.
- Windows 2000 supports two VPN protocols: PPTP and L2TP. L2TP is more secure, but requires Windows 2000 or XP machines.
- Authentication and encryption protocols can be used to secure communications between the RAS server and a dial-up client.
- Windows 2000 supports the following authentication protocols: MS-CHAP versions 1 and 2, CHAP, SPAP, PAP, and EAP.
- Dial-in access can be controlled through user account properties and through Remote Access policies. Remote Access policies consist of conditions, permissions, and profiles. Policies are evaluated in the order in which they appear under the Remote Access Policies container.

- Network address translation (NAT) and Internet connection sharing (ICS) provide a way of connecting computers in a small or home office to the Internet using a single connection.
- Terminal Services is a feature included with Windows 2000 that enables clients to access Windows 2000 and other Windows-based applications on a terminal server. It also gives administrators the ability to remotely administer network servers. Terminal Services can be installed in one of two modes: application or remote administration.

Key Terms

Challenge Handshake Authentication Protocol (CHAP) — A cross-platform authentication protocol designed for IP- or PPP-based exchange of passwords.

Extensible Authentication Protocol (EAP) — EAP is a standard for developing authentication methods. It allows a client and RAS server to negotiate the exact authentication scheme.

Internet connection sharing (ICS) — A feature included with Windows 2000 that enables a small or home office to connect to the Internet. ICS allows a single dial-up connection to be shared among multiple computers.

IP Security (IPSec) — IPSec consists of a suite of cryptography-based protection services and protocols that provide machine-level authentication and data encryption.

Layer 2 Tunneling Protocol (L2TP) — An advanced VPN protocol that is used to establish a secure tunnel between two endpoints over an insecure network. This protocol uses advanced authentication and encryption with the help of IPSec. Only Windows 2000 and XP machines currently support L2TP.

Microsoft Challenge Authentication Protocol (MS-CHAP) — A Microsoft-enhanced version of CHAP that can negotiate encryption levels and that uses a highly secure encryption algorithm to encrypt communications between client and host.

Microsoft Point-to-Point Encryption (MPPE) — An encryption technique that uses encryption keys varying in length from 40 bits to 128 bits so that packets traveling between the remote access client and the remote access or tunnel server are secure. Used when IP security is not available.

network address translation (NAT) — A feature included with Windows 2000 that enables a small or home office to connect to the Internet using a single connection. It provides address translation as well as DNS and DHCP services

Password Authentication Protocol (PAP) — The least secure authentication protocol that sends passwords between a client and a server in clear text.

Point-to-Point Protocol (PPP) — Enables remote access clients and servers to communicate over a dial-up connection from any operating system that supports the PPP standards.

Point-to-Point Tunneling Protocol (PPTP) — A VPN protocol that is used to establish a secure tunnel between two endpoints over an insecure network.

remote authentication dial-in user service (RADIUS) — A client/server protocol and software that enables remote access servers to communicate with a central server to authenticate dial-in users and authorize their access to the requested system or service.

remote access policy — A set of conditions that determines how users access the network remotely. A remote access policy consists of conditions, permissions, and profile settings.

remote access server — A computer running Windows 2000 and the Routing and Remote Access Service that authenticates remote or mobile users.

Shiva Password Authentication Protocol (SPAP) — A reversible encryption method employed by Shiva.

Terminal Services — A built-in feature of Windows 2000 that allows clients to access Windows 2000 and other Windows-based programs remotely. It is also used to remotely access desktop and installed applications for remote troubleshooting.

virtual private network (VPN) — Uses a LAN protocol such as TCP/IP which is encapsulated within a WAN protocol to send data over a public network

Review Questions

1. Which of the following are elements of a remote access policy?
   a. profile
   b. authentication
   c. permissions
   d. conditions
   e. RADIUS
2. The default remote access policy grants users permission to dial in. True or False?
3. You are configuring remote access so users can dial in. You delete the default remote access policy, and configure the properties of each user account to grant dial-in access. Users report that they are receiving an access denied message when they attempt to connect. What might be the cause of the problem?
   a. Users who need access to dial-in are not members of the correct group.
   b. There is no remote access policy configured.
   c. There is no Group Policy configured.
   d. The permission in the remote access policy is set to deny access.
4. If the permission and profile of a remote access policy do not match the connection attempt, the next policy in the list is evaluated. True or False?
5. You are configuring ICS on a network computer with a dial-up connection to the Internet. The computers on the network are currently receiving IP addresses from a DHCP server on the network. You enable ICS on the dial-up connection

and connect to the Internet; however, none of the internal computers can access the Internet via the shared connection. What might be causing the problem?

a. ICS needs to be enabled on the LAN connection.

b. There is a DHCP server already on the network.

c. The computers must be assigned a static IP address.

d. The DNS option needs to be configured on the DHCP server.

6. You have set up a TCP/IP-based Windows 2000 terminal server. A user calls because she is trying to use the service for the first time by dialing in from home, but is not succeeding. What should she check?

   a. that her home computer is using TCP/IP

   b. that her home computer is using multilink

   c. that her home computer is using PPP

   d. All of the above

7. You are the server administrator for a company and are on call several evenings a week to handle problems that may occur. Unfortunately, you live about 40 minutes from work, and often have to go in to work in the evenings for tasks that only take a couple of minutes. How can you make your life easier by accessing administrative programs from home?

   a. Configure a terminal server as an application server.

   b. Configure a terminal server as a remote administration server.

   c. Configure a terminal server as a thin client.

   d. Purchase a third-party utility, as Windows 2000 does not provide remote access capabilities.

8. How can you make a client installation disk for a Terminal Services Windows 3.11 client?

   a. Use Active Directory Users and Computers.

   b. Use the Terminal Services Client Creator tool.

   c. Use the Terminal Services Manager.

   d. Use the Client Installation tool.

9. ICS allows you to configure the range of IP addresses to be assigned to clients on the internal network. True or False?

10. A small business is using NAT. The internal network is using the IP address network number of 192.168.0.0. The company has been assigned the external IP address of 198.10.2.25 by its ISP. To what IP address does NAT map the private IP addresses?

    a. 192.168.0.1

    b. 198.10.2.1

    c. 192.10.2.25

    d. 192.168.0.25

11. Your network is implementing smart cards for user authentication. Which of the following protocols need to be configured?
    a. PAP
    b. SPAP
    c. MS-CHAP
    d. EAP
    e. CHAP
12. If the dial-in permission is configured using the properties of a user account, remote access policies are not used. True or False?
13. Of the following authentication protocols, which one provides the highest level of security?
    a. CHAP
    b. PAP
    c. MS-CHAP v2
    d. MS-CHAP v1
    e. SPAP
14. All of your RAS server clients are configured to use 56-bit encryption key MPPE, but when you use a network analyzer, it appears that none of the communications is actually encrypted. Which of the following might be the problem?
    a. The remote access policy has been configured with No Encryption, and should be configured for Strong.
    b. The remote access policy must be set for Basic encryption.
    c. The RAS must be set up to use EAP.
    d. Multilink and BAP must be enabled.
15. You have set up a RAS server that is to be accessed by clients running Windows 2000 Professional. What authentication should you configure for the RAS server?
    a. MS-CHAP v2
    b. PAP
    c. CHAP
    d. EAP
16. Your RAS server is configured to enable Multilink as a way to enable the combining of connections when users need more bandwidth, such as when they are using multimedia applications. However, when a user connects, the server does not seem to dynamically adjust for the amount of bandwidth needed by a user. What should you configure the RAS server to use along with multilink?
    a. PPP
    b. PPTP
    c. BAP
    d. L2TP

17. Your organization is setting up multiple RAS servers and wants to establish one set of remote access policies and one place from which to coordinate all of the VPN servers. What feature can you implement to provide centralized management of the RAS servers?
    a. NAT
    b. RADIUS
    c. VPN
    d. Terminal Services
18. Your RAS server is assigning IP addresses to dial-up clients. However, the clients are not receiving the IP addresses of the WINS and DNS servers. What step might you have omitted?
    a. Install the DHCP relay agent.
    b. Statically configure these additional parameters on clients.
    c. Configure the DHCP options on the RAS server.
    d. Disable IP forwarding.
19. Which of the following protocols can be used to establish a VPN connection?
    a. NAT
    b. PPTP
    c. SPAP
    d. L2TP
    e. PAP
20. What authentication protocol should be enabled if there are non-Windows clients dialing into a RAS server?
    a. MS-CHAP
    b. PAP
    c. EAP
    d. CHAP

HANDS-ON PROJECTS

Project 9-1

In this Hands-on Project, you configure Routing and Remote Access Services as a VPN server.

1. Log on to your Windows 2000 computer with an administrator account.
2. Click **Start**, point to **Programs**, point to **Administrative Tools**, and click **Routing and Remote Access**.

3. In the scope pane, click your server. Note the red down arrow indicating that RAS is not running.
4. Right-click your server, and click **Configure and Enable Routing and Remote Access**.
5. Click **Next**.
6. Click **Virtual private network (VPN) server**, and click **Next**.
7. Keep the default selection of all protocols, and click **Next**.
8. Select your network card from the list, and click **Next**.
9. Click **From a specified range of addresses**, and click **Next**.
10. Click **New**.
11. Enter a start IP address of **131.107.1.20**.
12. Enter a stop IP address of **131.107.1.30**.
13. Click **OK**, and then click **Next**.
14. Keep the default selection of not setting up a RADIUS server, and click **Next**.
15. Click **Finish**. If you receive a message about relaying DHCP, then click **OK** to clear the message.
16. Expand the server in the left console pane, and click **Ports**. Verify that you have two types of VPN ports: PPTP and L2TP.
17. Close all windows, and log off.

Project 9-2

In this Hands-on Project, you create a user account with permissions to connect to your server using a VPN connection.

To create a new user account:

1. Log on to your Windows 2000 computer with an administrator account.
2. Click **Start**, point to **Programs**, point to **Administrative Tools**, and click **Active Directory Users and Computers**.
3. Right-click **Users**, point to **New**, and click **User**.
4. Name the user **VPNuser1** with the same logon name. Click **Next**.
5. Set the password as **connect**, click **Next**, and then click **Finish**.

To configure VPNuser1 dial-in options:

1. Give VPNuser1 permission to access the network remotely by right-clicking the **VPNuser1** user object, and clicking **Properties**.
2. Click the **Dial-in** tab.
3. Click the **Allow Access** option button. Click **OK**.
4. Close all windows.

Project 9-3

In this Hands-on Project, you test the VPN by connecting to your VPN server using the user account created in the previous project.

To create a client VPN connection:

1. Click **Start**, point to **Settings**, and click **Network and Dial-up Connections**.
2. Double-click **Make New Connection**. Specify location information if prompted, and then click **OK** to close the Phone and Modem Options dialog box.
3. Click **Next** to start the Network Connection Wizard.
4. Click **Connect to a private network through the Internet**, and click **Next**.
5. Enter the IP address of your network card, and click **Next**.
6. Click **Only for myself**, and click **Next**. Click **Finish**.

To connect to a VPN server:

1. At the VPN logon prompt, type **VPNuser1** as the user name.
2. Type **connect** as the password.
3. Click the **Connect** button.
4. Click **OK** to close the Connection Complete window if it appears.
5. View the status of the VPN connection by right-clicking **Virtual Private Connection** (found on the desktop or the connection icon in the task bar tray), and then click **Status**. Note the status of the connection as well as the amount of traffic that has gone through the connection.
6. Click **Properties**.
7. Click the **Security** tab.
8. Click **Advanced**.
9. Click **Settings**. Note that there are varying levels you can choose for data security, as well as logon security (authentication).
10. Click **Cancel** twice.
11. Disconnect the VPN connection by clicking **Disconnect**.
12. Close all windows.

Project 9-4

In this Hands-on Project, you configure and test a remote access policy that only allows access between 6 pm and 8 pm, Monday through Friday.

To configure a RAS policy:

1. Click **Start**, point to **Programs**, point to **Administrative Tools**, and click **Routing and Remote Access**.

2. Click **Remote Access Policies**. Note that there is one policy in place by default.
3. Right-click **Remote Access Policies**, and click **New Remote Access Policy**.
4. Enter **Evening Only** as the Policy friendly name, and click **Next**.
5. In the Conditions dialog box, click **Add**.
6. Double-click **Day-And-Time-Restriction**.
7. Highlight the area from **6pm to 8pm, Monday to Friday**, and click the **Permitted** option button. Click **OK**
8. Click **Next**.
9. Click the **Grant remote access permission if the conditions match** option button, and click **Next**.
10. Click **Edit Profile**. Click the check box next to **Disconnect if idle for**, and type **20** in the text box.
11. Click **OK,** and then click **Finish**.
12. Right-click the **Evening only** policy, and click **Move Up**. This places the most restrictive policy at the bottom.

To test the new policy:

1. Click **Start**, point to **Programs**, point to **Administrative Tools**, and click **Active Directory Users and Computers**.
2. Right-click **VPNuser1**, and click **Properties**.
3. Click the **Dial-in** tab, then click the **Control access through Remote Access Policy** option button, and then click **OK**.
4. Close all windows.
5. Click **Start**, point to **Settings**, point to **Network and Dial-up Connections**, and click your VPN connection.
6. Enter **VPNuser1** as the user name.
7. Enter **connect** as the password.
8. Click **Connect**. You get an error indicating that you do not have permission to dial-in. Why do you get this error?
9. Click **Cancel**.

To disable Routing and Remote Access:

1. Click **Start**, point to **Programs**, point to **Administrative Tools**, and click **Routing and Remote Access**.
2. Right-click your server, and click **Disable Routing and Remote Access**.
3. Click **Yes**.
4. Close all windows, and log off.

Project 9-5

In this Hands-on Project, you configure Routing and Remote Access as a network address translation server.

1. Log on to your Windows 2000 computer with an administrator account.
2. Click **Start**, point to **Programs**, point to **Administrative Tools**, and click **Routing and Remote Access**.
3. Right-click the server name, or click **Action**, and click **Configure and Enable Routing and Remote Access**.
4. Click **Next** at the RRAS Wizard welcome screen to view the common configurations of RRAS.
5. To configure the NAT options, click **Internet Connection Server**, and click **Next**.
6. Click **Set up a router with the Network Address Translation (NAT) routing protocol**, and click **Next**.
7. Choose the **External** network interface as the Internet connection. (If you do not have two network cards, choose the interface that is shown.)
8. Click **Next**, and then click **Finish**.

Project 9-6

In this Hands-on Project, you configure various settings on the NAT server to ensure that it is properly configured.

To verify network interface assignment:

1. Expand the **IP Routing** node in the left pane.
2. Click the **Network Address Translation (NAT)** node.
3. In the right-most pane, right-click the **External** interface. Click **Properties**.
4. Click the **General** tab, and ensure that the **Public interface connected to the Internet** option button is chosen. Click **OK**.

To configure DHCP and DNS:

1. In the left pane, right-click **Network Address Translation (NAT)**, and click **Properties**.
2. Click the **Address Assignment** tab.
3. To automatically assign computers IP addresses, check the **Automatically assign IP addresses by using DHCP** option. Leave the default IP address range as is.
4. To ensure that clients get DNS settings, click the **Name Resolution** tab.
5. Check the **Clients using Domain Name System (DNS)** option.
6. Click **OK**.

To uninstall all previous RRAS configurations:

1. Right-click your server, and click **Disable Routing and Remote Access**.
2. Click **Yes**.
3. Close all windows, and log off.

Project 9-7

In this Hands-on Project, you install Terminal Services in remote administration mode.

1. Log on to your Windows 2000 computer with an administrator account.
2. Click **Start**, point to **Settings**, and click **Control Panel**.
3. Double-click **Add/Remove Programs**.
4. Click **Add/Remove Windows Components**.
5. Click the **Terminal Services** option, and click **Next**.
6. Click **Next** to keep the default Remote Administration Mode. If required, insert the Windows 2000 CD-ROM or browse to the D:\W2KAS folder on your computer. Click **OK**.
7. Click **Finish**. Click **Yes** to restart your server.

Project 9-8

In this Hands-on Project, you configure Terminal Services to require high encryption, and automatically end an idle session after 10 minutes.

To edit the encryption level of Terminal Services:

1. Log on to your Windows 2000 computer with an administrator account.
2. Close any windows that may be open as a result of the previous project.
3. Click **Start**, point to **Programs**, point to **Administrative Tools**, and click **Terminal Services Configuration**.
4. Click the **Connections** folder.
5. Right-click **RDP-Tcp**, and click **Properties**.
6. Change the Encryption Level list arrow box to **High**.

To configure an idle session to end after 10 minutes:

1. Click the **Sessions** tab.
2. Click the check box next to **Override user settings**.
3. Click the drop-down menu next to **Idle session limit**, and click 10 minutes. Click **OK**.
4. Close all windows, and log off.

CASE PROJECTS

Case Project 9-1

The International Produce Association is a nonprofit association of produce growers, researchers, buyers, sellers, and shippers that provides a wide range of information about growing, processing, and shipping produce worldwide. The association is located in Toronto and has member groups throughout the world. One of the International Produce Association's most popular services is maintaining a database of research information for all members. The database is accessed via a Windows NT 4.0 RAS server. You have been hired to set up a Windows 2000 RAS server where the database will eventually be located.

1. As you are creating your proposal for the International Produce Association, include in the document the steps for installing and configuring a RAS server. Also include a brief explanation of VPN and how it may be useful for the organization.
2. Outline the different authentication and encryption protocols that can be implemented. Most of the users run Windows 98 or later on their desktops. Based on this, make a recommendation for an authentication protocol.
3. Four users are responsible for the administration of the RAS server. Provide a preliminary training paper for the administrators on the basic concepts of remote access policies and how they are applied.
4. Before implementation, you establish a test lab. After the RAS server and remote access policy is configured, you attempt to dial in as one of the members. You receive an access denied message. What are some of the things you should verify to troubleshoot the problem?

Case Project 9-2

One of the members of the International Produce Association has approached you in regards to his own small office. He is a shipper/receiver for produce companies, and has a small office with eight computers. Currently, each computer has its own Internet connection. You have been asked if there is a more economical way for the small office to provide Internet access for each computer.

1. What option would you recommend for the small office, and why?
2. After your proposal is reviewed, it is decided to implement ICS in the office. Your next step is to outline in a document the steps entailed in enabling and configuring ICS.
3. The small office does not require a network administrator on site, but does have one they can call when problems arise. One of your tasks included in this project is to configure the server so remote administration can be performed. What Windows 2000 service can be implemented for remote administration? Outline the process of installing and configuring it.

CERTIFICATION OBJECTIVES FOR MCSA GUIDE TO MANAGING A MICROSOFT WINDOWS 2000 NETWORK (EXAM #70-218)

CREATING, CONFIGURING, MANAGING, SECURING, AND TROUBLESHOOTING FILE, PRINT, AND WEB RESOURCES

Objective	Chapter: Section	Hands-on Project(s)
Publish resources in Active Directory. Types of resources include printers and shared folders. • Perform a search in Active Directory Users and Computers. • Configure a printer object.	Chapter 5: Publishing Resources in Active Directory	Project 5-4 Project 5-5
Manage data storage. Considerations include file systems, permissions, and quotas. • Implement NTFS and FAT file systems. •Enable and configure quotas. • Implement and configure Encrypting File System (EFS). •Configure volumes and basic and dynamic disks. • Configure file and folder permissions. • Manage a domain-based distributed file system (DFS). • Manage file and folder compression.	Chapter 5: Creating and Managing Shared Folders Chapter 5: Managing Data Storage Chapter 5: Configuring and Managing a Distributed File System	Project 5-6 Project 5-9

Objective	Chapter: Section	Hands-on Project(s)
Create shared resources and configure access rights. Shared resources include printers, shared folders, and Web folders.	Chapter 5: Creating and Managing Shared Folders	Project 5-1
• Share folders and enable Web sharing. • Configure shared folder permissions.	Chapter 5: Creating and Modifying Web Folders	Project 5-2
• Create and manage shared printers. • Configure shared printer permissions.	Chapter 5: Creating and Modifying Printer Resources	Project 5-3
Configure and troubleshoot Internet Information Services (IIS). • Configure virtual directories and virtual servers. • Troubleshoot Internet browsing from client computers. • Troubleshoot intranet browsing from client computers • Configure authentication and SSL for Web sites. • Configure FTP services. • Configure access permissions for intranet Web servers	Chapter 6: All Sections	Project 6-1 Project 6-2 Project 6-3 Project 6-4 Project 6-5 Project 6-6
Monitor and manage network security. Actions include auditing and detecting security breaches. • Configure user-account lockout settings. • Configure user-account password length, history, age, and complexity. • Configure Group Policy to run logon scripts. • Link Group Policy objects. • Enable and configure auditing. • Monitor security by using the system security log file.	Chapter 5: Auditing Access to Shared Resources	Project 5-7 Project 5-8

CONFIGURING, ADMINISTERING, AND TROUBLESHOOTING THE NETWORK INFRASTRUCTURE

Objective	Chapter: Section	Hands-on Project(s)
Troubleshoot routing. Diagnostic utilities include the **tracert** command, the **ping** command, and the **ipconfig** command. • Validate local computer configuration by using **ipconfig**, **arp**, and **route** commands. • Validate network connectivity by using the **tracert**, **ping**, and **pathping** commands.	Chapter 7: Troubleshooting TCP/IP and Network Connectivity	Project 7-1
Configure and troubleshoot TCP/IP on servers and client computers. Considerations include subnet masks, default gateways, network IDs, and broadcast addresses. • Configure client computer TCP/IP properties. • Validate client computer network configuration by using the **winipcfg**, **ipconfig**, and **arp** commands. • Validate client computer network connectivity by using the **ping** command.	Chapter 7: Configuring TCP/IP on Windows 2000 Computers	Project 7-1 Project 7-4
Configure, administer, and troubleshoot DHCP on servers and client computers. • Detect unauthorized DHCP servers on a network. • Configure authorization of DHCP servers. • Configure client computers to use dynamic IP addressing. • Configure DHCP server properties. • Create and configure a DHCP scope.	Chapter 7: Administering DHCP in Windows 2000	Project 7-2 Project 7-3
Configure, administer, and troubleshoot DNS. • Configure DNS server properties. • Manage DNS database records such as CNAME, A, and PTR. • Create and configure DNS zones.	Chapter 7: Administering DNS in Windows 2000	Project 7-5 Project 7-6

Objective	Chapter: Section	Hands-on Project(s)
Troubleshoot name resolution on client computers. Considerations include WINS, DNS, NetBIOS, the Hosts file, and the Lmhosts file. • Configure client computer name resolution properties. • Troubleshoot name resolution problems by using the **nbtstat**, **ipconfig**, **nslookup**, and **netdiag** commands. • Create and configure a Hosts file for troubleshooting name resolution problems. • Create and configure an Lmhosts file for troubleshooting name resolution problems.	Chapter 7: Troubleshooting Name Resolution Problems Chapter 7: Troubleshooting TCP/IP and Network Connectivity	Project 7-1 Project 7-7

Managing, Securing, and Troubleshooting Servers and Client Computers

Objective	Chapter: Section	Hands-on Project(s)
Install and configure server and client computer hardware. • Verify hardware compatibility by using the qualifier tools. • Configure driver signing options. • Verify digital signatures on existing driver files. • Configure operating system support for legacy hardware devices.	Chapter 2: All Sections	Project 2-1 Project 2-2 Project 2-3 Project 2-4
Troubleshoot starting servers and client computers. Tools and methodologies include Safe Mode, Recovery Console, and parallel installations. • Interpret the startup log file. • Repair an operating system by using various startup options. • Repair an operating system by using the Recovery Console. • Recover data from a hard disk in the event that the operating system will not start. • Restore an operating system and data from a backup	Chapter 8: Troubleshooting Windows 2000 Startup Procedures Chapter 8: Advanced Startup Options Chapter 8: The Windows 2000 Backup Utility	Project 8-4 Project 8-5

Objective	Chapter: Section	Hands-on Project(s)
Monitor and troubleshoot server health and performance. Tools include System Monitor, Event Viewer, and Task Manager. • Monitor and interpret real-time performance by using System Monitor and Task Manager. • Configure and manage System Monitor alerts and logging. • Diagnose server health problems by using Event Viewer. • Identify and disable unnecessary operating system services.	Chapter 8: Monitoring Windows 2000 Server Health and Performance	Project 8-1 Project 8-2 Project 8-3
Install and manage Windows 2000 updates. Updates include service packs, hot fixes, and security hot fixes. • Update an installation source by using slipstreaming. • Apply and reapply service packs and hot fixes. • Verify service pack and hot fix installation. • Remove service packs and hot fixes.	Chapter 2: Managing Windows 2000 Updates	Project 2-5 Project 2-6

Configuring, Managing, Securing, and Troubleshooting Active Directory Organizational Units and Group Policy

Objective	Chapter: Section	Hands-on Project(s)
Create, manage, and troubleshoot User and Group objects in Active Directory. • Create and configure user and computer accounts for new and existing users. • Troubleshoot groups. Considerations include nesting, scope, and type. • Configure a user account by using Active Directory Users and Computers. Settings include passwords and assigning groups. • Perform a search for objects in Active Directory. • Use templates to create user accounts. • Reset an existing computer account.	Chapter 3: Administering Active Directory Objects Chapter 3: Group Types	Project 3-1 Project 3-2 Project 3-3

Objective	Chapter: Section	Hands-on Project(s)
Manage object and container permissions. • Use the Delegation of Control wizard to configure inherited and explicit permissions. • Configure and troubleshoot object permissions by using object access control lists (ACLs).	Chapter 3: Administering Permissions in Active Directory	Project 3-4
Diagnose Active Directory replication problems. • Diagnose problems related to WAN link connectivity. • Diagnose problems involving replication latency. Problems include duplicate objects and the LostandFound container.	Chapter 3: Managing Active Directory Replication	Project 3-5
Deploy software by using Group Policy. Types of software include user applications, antivirus software, line-of-business applications, and software updates. • Use Windows Installer to deploy Windows Installer packages. • Deploy updates to installed software including antivirus updates. • Configure Group Policy to assign and publish applications.	Chapter 4: Deploying Software using Group Policy	Project 4-6
Troubleshoot end-user Group Policy. • Troubleshoot Group Policy problems involving precedence, inheritance, filtering, and the **No Override** option. • Manually refresh Group Policy	Chapter 4: Introduction to Group Policy Chapter 4: Managing Group Policy Inheritance	Project 4-5
Implement and manage security policies by using Group Policy. • Use security templates to implement security policies. • Analyze the security configuration of a computer by using the **secedit** command and Security Configuration and Analysis. • Modify domain security policy to comply with corporate standards.	Chapter 4: Introduction to Group Policy	Project 4-1 Project 4-2 Project 4-3 Project 4-4

Configuring, Securing, and Troubleshooting Remote Access

Objective	Chapter: Section	Hands-on Project(s)
Configure and troubleshoot remote access and virtual private network (VPN) connections. • Configure and troubleshoot client-to-server PPTP and L2TP connections. • Manage existing server-to-server PPTP and L2TP connections. • Configure and verify the security of a VPN connection. • Configure client computer remote access properties. • Configure remote access name resolution and IP address allocation.	Chapter 9: Configuring Remote Access and Virtual Private Network Connections	Project 9-1 Project 9-2 Project 9-3
Troubleshoot a remote access policy. • Diagnose problems with remote access policy priority. • Diagnose remote access policy problems caused by user account group membership and nested groups. • Create and configure remote access policies and profiles. • Select appropriate encryption and authentication protocols.	Chapter 9: Implementing and Troubleshooting Remote Access Policies	Project 9-4
Implement and troubleshoot Terminal Services for remote access. • Configure Terminal Services for remote administration or application server mode. • Configure Terminal Services for local resource mapping. • Configure Terminal Services user properties.	Chapter 9: Configuring Terminal Services for Remote Access	Project 9-7 Project 9-8
Configure and troubleshoot Network Address Translation (NAT) and Internet Connection Sharing. • Configure Routing and Remote Access to perform NAT. • Troubleshoot Internet Connection Sharing problems by using the **ipconfig** and **ping** commands.	Chapter 9: Configuring and Troubleshooting Network Address Translation Chapter 9: Configuring Internet Connection Sharing	Project 9-5 Project 9-6

Glossary

access control entry (ACE) — An entry in an object's discretionary access control list (DACL) that grants permissions to a user or group. An ACE is also an entry in an object's system access control list (SACL) that specifies the security events to be audited for a user or group.

Active Directory (AD) — A directory service included with Windows 2000 server-based systems that provides a single point of administration, authentication, and storage for user, group, and computer objects.

Active Directory client extensions — These allow legacy operating systems to perform searches in Activity Directory; they also provide site awareness and access to Windows 2000 distributed file systems.

Active Directory Domains and Trusts — An Active Directory MMC tool that allows you to configure trust relationships between domains as well as the UPN suffix for the forest.

Active Directory integrated zone — The zone data is stored in the Active Directory database rather than in a zone file.

Active Directory schema — Contains the definition of all object classes and attributes used in the Active Directory database.

Active Directory Sites and Services — An Active Directory MMC console that allows you to configure site objects and site links, and configure replication costs and times between sites.

Active Directory Users and Computers — An Active Directory MMC console that allows you to create various objects such as organizational units, user accounts, groups, computers, and contacts.

Add/Remove Hardware Wizard — Enables you to add or remove hardware and troubleshoot any hardware-related problems.

Address Resolution Protocol (ARP) — Works at the Internet layer and is responsible for mapping IP addresses to MAC addresses assigned to the network interface adapter. These can be either dynamic or static entries. Dynamic entries are stored in the ARP cache for two to 10 minutes. Static entries stay in the cache until the computer is restarted.

administration Web site — A Web site that is configured to allow administrators to manage the Web server from a remote location using a Web browser. During installation, this site is assigned a random port number and is configured with a restriction that only allows access from the 127.0.0.1 IP address. This IP address is actually the local server itself. To allow remote administration, this restriction would have to be modified.

alerts — An alert performs a specified action once a counter meets the specified setting. Once an alert is triggered, a message can be sent, a program can be run, a counter log started, or an event can be written to the application log.

alias — A name used to hide the real name of a directory and to simplify the directory name that would be used to access the information.

anonymous access — Allows users to access a Web site without having to provide a username and password.

application log — Where applications that are written to Microsoft standards record event information. The application developer determines the type of information an application writes to the log file.

attribute level permissions — Define which attributes of a certain object a user or group can view or modify within Active Directory.

attributes — Used to define the characteristics of an object class within Active Directory.

audit policy — Defines the events on the network that Windows 2000 records in the security log as they occur.

auditing — The process that tracks the activities of users by recording selected types of events in the security log of a server or a workstation.

authentication — Refers to determining whether a user has a valid user account with the proper permissions to access a resource such as a shared folder or Web site.

authoritative restore — Marks specific objects in the Active Directory as the master copy, and forces the other domain controllers to receive the change.

bandwidth throttling — Allows you to limit the network bandwidth that is available for Web and FTP connections to the server.

baseline — A performance benchmark that is used to determine what is normal server performance under a specific workload.

Basic authentication — Prompts users for a username and password to be able to access the Web resource. The username and password are then transmitted as clear text.

basic disk — The traditional storage type that divides physical disk space into primary partitions, extended partitions, and logical drives.

Basic Input/Output System (BIOS) — A program stored on a flash memory chip attached to the motherboard that establishes the initial communication between the components of the computer, such as the hard drive, CD-ROM, floppy disk, video, and memory.

Challenge Handshake Authentication Protocol (CHAP) — A cross-platform authentication protocol designed for IP- or PPP-based exchange of passwords.

compression — Data is stored in a format that takes up less disk space, enabling you to store more data.

computer account — An Active Directory object that represents a physical computer that is a member of the domain.

Computer Management console — A predefined Microsoft Management Console (MMC) application that allows you to administer a variety of computer-related tasks on the local computer or a remote computer.

container — An object that is used to organize related objects within the Active Directory hierarchy. Container objects can consist of other child containers or leaf objects, such as organizational units.

counter log — Performance data that is collected into a comma-separated or tab-separated format.

data recovery agent — Individual responsible for recovering encrypted data in the event a user's private key is lost.

default domain controllers policy — The name of the default Group Policy object that is linked to the domain controllers organizational unit. Used primarily for configuration of policy settings that are only to be applied to the domain controllers in the domain (i.e., auditing).

default domain policy — The name of the Group Policy object that is linked to the domain container in Active Directory; used primarily for configuration of domain-wide password policies.

default FTP site — An FTP server that responds to TCP/IP port 21 on all configured IP addresses of the server that are not assigned to another site.

default gateway — This is the 32-bit number of the router on the local network, which is used to communicate with hosts outside of the local subnet.

default NNTP virtual server — A newsgroup server that responds to port 119 on all configured IP addresses of the server that have not been assigned to another site.

default SMTP virtual server — An e-mail component server that responds to port 25 on all IP addresses of the server that have not been assigned to another site.

default Web site — A Web site configured with FrontPage extensions that responds to TCP/IP port 80 on all unassigned IP addresses of the server. This Web site is initially empty and may be used to create a custom Web site for your organization.

Delegation of Control Wizard — An Active Directory MMC tool that guides you through the process of determining the permissions that you want to delegate, and then configures the permissions for the object and child objects.

Device Manager — Used to view and modify hardware device properties, update device drivers, and uninstall unneeded hardware.

DFS link — A pointer to the physical location of a share on the network.

DFS topology — The logical structure of a distributed file system, which includes the DFS root and DFS link.

DFS root — The top level of a DFS tree structure that contains links to the shared folders on the network.

Digest authentication — Prompts users for a username and password to be able to access the Web resource. The username and password are hashed to prevent hackers from obtaining the information.

discretionary access control list (DACL) — A part of the security descriptor of an object that contains a list of user or group references that have been allowed or denied permissions to the resource.

disk quotas — A Windows 2000 feature that is used as a means of monitoring and controlling the amount of disk space available to users.

distinguished name (DN) — An LDAP component used to uniquely identify an object throughout the entire LDAP hierarchy by referring to the relative distinguished name, domain name, and the container holding the object.

distributed file system (DFS)— A file system that organizes shared folders located throughout a local or wide area network into a single logical tree structure.

distribution group — A group that is only used for an e-mail distribution list.

domain — A logically structured organization of objects, such as users, computers, groups, and printers, that are part of a network and share a common directory database. Domains are defined by an administrator and administered as a unit with common rules and procedures.

domain local group — Can only be assigned permissions to a resource available in the domain in which it is created. However, group membership can come from any domain within the forest. Created on domain controllers within the domain.

Domain Name System (DNS) — Used for two essential tasks: host name to IP address resolution and for the location of network services, such as domain controllers that provide user authentication.

driver signing — Ensures that a driver for a specific device has been verified by Microsoft and a unique digital signature has been incorporated into the driver.

dynamic disk — A new storage system supported by Windows 2000 that divides physical disk space into volumes.

Dynamic Host Configuration Protocol (DHCP) — Used to centralize the administration of IP addresses and various options, and eliminate the administrative overhead of statically assigning the information to each network host.

encrypting file system (EFS) — The Windows 2000 file system that enables you to encrypt files and folders on NTFS volumes for security purposes.

Event Viewer — A component you can use to view and manage event logs, gather information about hardware and software problems, and monitor security events. Event Viewer maintains logs about program, security, and system events.

Extensible Authentication Protocol (EAP) — EAP is a standard for developing authentication methods. It allows a client and RAS server to negotiate the exact authentication scheme.

File Signature Verification — This utility can identify unsigned files and give you information such as the file name, location, modification date, and version number.

File Transfer Protocol (FTP) — Used to transfer files between two computers that are both running TCP/IP.

Folder redirection — A Group Policy feature that enables you to redirect the contents of the Application Data, Desktop, My Documents, My Pictures, and Start menu folders from a user's profile to a network location.

forest — A collection of Active Directory trees that do not share a contiguous DNS naming convention, but do share a common global catalog and schema.

forest root domain — The first domain created within the Active Directory structure.

forward lookup zone — Used to perform the standard host name to IP address forward lookup queries.

fully qualified domain name (FQDN) — Describes the location of the host in relation to the DNS namespace. For example, a computer named "webserver" in the marketing domain of Bayside.com would have the FQDN of *webserver.marketing.bayside.com*.

global catalog — An index of the objects and attributes used throughout the Active Directory structure. It contains a partial replica of every Windows 2000 domain within Active Directory, enabling users to find any object in the directory.

global group — A group that is mainly used for organizing other objects into administrative units. A global group has the ability to be assigned permissions to any resource in any domain within the forest. The main limitation of a global group is that it can only contain members of the same domain in which it is created.

globally unique identifier (GUID) — A unique 128-bit number assigned to the object when it is created.

Gpresult — This utility can be used to discover Group Policy-related problems and to illustrate which Group Policy objects were applied to a user or computer. Gpresult also lists all group memberships of the user or computer being analyzed.

group — A container object that is used to organize a collection of users, computers, contacts, or other groups into a single object reference.

Group Policy — Enables the centralized management of user desktop settings, desktop and domain security, and the deployment and management of software throughout your network.

Group Policy object (GPO) — An Active Directory object that is configured to apply Group Policy and linked to either the site, domain, or organizational unit level.

host — Any computer that is a member of a specific DNS domain within the network structure.

host header — The fully qualified DNS name that is used to access a Web site on an IIS Server.

hot fixes — Interim updates to Windows 2000 that are released between major service pack releases. These are used to fix operating system bugs and security issues.

incremental templates — A set of text-based security template files that you can use to apply uniform security settings on computers within an enterprise. The templates modify security settings incrementally and do not include the default security settings.

Integrated Windows authentication — Does not ask the user for a password, but rather uses the clients currently logged-on credentials to supply a challenge/response to the Web server.

Internet connection sharing (ICS) — A feature included with Windows 2000 that enables a small or home office to connect to the Internet. ICS allows a single dial-up connection to be shared among multiple computers.

Internet Control Message Protocol (ICMP) — Operates at the network layer and is used to exchange status and error information between two hosts.

Internet Group Management Protocol (IGMP) — Operates at the network layer and is used to manage network and host information when multicasting is used.

Internet Information Services (IIS) — Is used to provide access utilizing a number of protocols such as Hypertext Transfer Protocol (HTTP), File Transfer Protocol (FTP), Network News Transfer Protocol (NNTP), and Simple Mail Transfer Protocol (SMTP).

Internet Protocol (IP) — The Internet layer protocol responsible for the addressing and routing of packets so that they are delivered to the correct host on the local network or across routers to a host on another subnet.

Internet Services Manager — The administrative tool used to manage the Internet Information Services server components.

interrupt request (IRQ) — A signal sent by a device to notify the processor when the device is ready to accept or send information. Each device typically has a unique IRQ number.

IP address — The 32-bit number that uniquely identifies a host on a TCP/IP network.

ipconfig — A command used to verify the addressing parameters assigned to a computer.

ipconfig/all — The ipconfig command plus the all parameter is used to produce a full display of assigned parameters.

IP Security (IPSec) — IPSec consists of a suite of cryptography-based protection services and protocols that provide machine-level authentication and data encryption.

iterative query — If the DNS server cannot resolve a name, it gives the requestor a pointer to another DNS server that is authoritative for the next level of the FQDN supplied.

Key Distribution Center (KDC) — A Kerberos version service that runs on a domain controller. It issues ticket-granting tickets (TGTs) and service tickets for obtaining network authentication in a domain.

Last Known Good Configuration — An advanced startup option that can be used to recover a system from failed Windows 2000 configuration changes.

Layer 2 Tunneling Protocol (L2TP) — An advanced VPN protocol that is used to establish a secure tunnel between two endpoints over an insecure network. This protocol uses advanced authentication and encryption with the help of IPSec. Only Windows 2000 and XP machines currently support L2TP.

leaf — An object that represents resources within a selected domain. Leaf objects are stored within a container and cannot contain other objects, for example user or group objects.

Lightweight Directory Access Protocol (LDAP) — An access protocol that defines how users can access or update directory service objects.

local group — Can only be assigned permissions to a resource available on the local machine in which it is created.

master properties — IIS parameters that are configured on the server and inherited by all Web and FTP sites hosted on the server.

metabase — IIS 5.0 stores its configuration settings in a database referred to as the IIS metabase.

Microsoft Challenge Authentication Protocol (MS-CHAP) — A Microsoft-enhanced version of CHAP that can negotiate encryption levels and that uses a highly secure encryption algorithm to encrypt communications between client and host.

Microsoft Hardware Compatibility List (HCL) — A list of hardware devices that have been tested by Microsoft to determine whether they can work with Windows 2000.

Microsoft Management Console (MMC) — A customizable management interface that can contain a number of management tools to provide a single, unified application for network administration.

Microsoft Point-to-Point Encryption (MPPE) — An encryption technique that uses encryption keys varying in length from 40 bits to 128 bits so that packets traveling between the remote access client and the remote access or tunnel server are secure. Used when IP security is not available.

Microsoft Saved Console (MSC) — The filename extension of a console saved using the Microsoft Management Console.

mixed mode — Domains consisting of Windows 2000 domain controllers and Windows NT backup domain controllers (BDCs).

multicasting — The sending of a message to multiple clients, or a group of clients.

multi-master replication — A replication model in which any domain controller accepts and replicates directory changes to any other domain controller. This differs from other replication models in which one computer stores the single modifiable copy of the directory and other computers store backup copies.

native mode — Domains consisting of Windows 2000 domain controllers only. No Windows NT BDCs exist in the domain.

network address translation (NAT) — A feature included with Windows 2000 that enables a small or home office to connect to the Internet using a single connection. It provides address translation as well as DNS and DHCP services.

object — A collection of attributes that represent items within Active Directory, such as users, groups, computers, and printers.

object classes — Define which types of objects can be created within Active Directory, such as users, groups, and printers.

object-level permissions — Define which types of objects a user or group can view, create, delete, or modify within Active Directory.

organizational unit (OU) — An Active Directory logical container used to organize objects within a single domain. Objects such as users, groups, computers, and other OUs can be stored in an OU.

originating update — The initial change to the Active Directory database performed on a specific domain controller, e.g., creating a user.

orphan pruner — A process that removes orphaned printer objects from the Active Directory. The orphan pruner verifies that all printer objects are still valid in Active Directory

parallel installation — A second installation of an operating system into a different directory, on a different partition, or on a different hard drive as the primary.

Password Authentication Protocol (PAP) — The least secure authentication protocol that sends passwords between a client and a server in clear text.

pathping — A command that combines the functions of the ping and tracert commands. The pathping command checks network connectivity by sending echo request messages to each router between a source and destination host and then computing the result based on packets returned from each router.

performance counter — A data item associated with a particular performance object used to measure a certain aspect of performance.

Performance Logs and Alerts — A tool included with Windows 2000 that enables you to create counter logs, trace logs, and configure alerts.

performance objects — A system component that can be monitored using System Monitor.

ping — A command used to test for connectivity between hosts on the network by sending ICMP packets to a remote computer and listening for an echo reply from the remote host.

Point-to-Point Protocol (PPP) — Enables remote access clients and servers to communicate over a dial-up connection from any operating system that supports the PPP standards.

Point-to-Point Tunneling Protocol (PPTP) — A VPN protocol that is used to establish a secure tunnel between two endpoints over an insecure network.

Power Users group — Power Users have less system access than adminstrators but more than users. By default, members of this group have Read/Write permissions to other parts of the system in addition to their own profile. Power Users can perform many system-wide operations, such as changing system time and display settings, and creating user accounts and shares.

print device — The actual hardware device that produces the printed document. A local print device connects directly to a port on the print server. A network print device connects to a print server through its own network adapter and connection to the network.

print driver — Files that contain information that Windows 2000 uses to convert raw print commands to a language that the printer understands.

print server — The computer in which the printers and print drivers are located. This is usually where you set up and configure the shared printing system.

printer — A configuration object in Windows 2000 that controls the connection to the print device.

printer pool — Consists of a single printer that is connected to a number of print devices.

printer priorities — Configuring multiple printers to print to the same print device. One printer is then configured to print before any of the other printers by adjusting the priority setting from one (lowest priority) to 99 (highest priority).

published — An Active Directory object that represents a link or direct information on how to use or connect to the shared resource.

published folder — An Active Directory object that points to a related shared folder on a file server.

Recovery Console — A command line interpreter that can be used to gain access to a local hard drive in the event that the system fails to boot.

recursive query — A command that specifies the return of a complete and full answer to the query, not a pointer to another DNS server.

relative distinguished name (RDN) — An LDAP component used to identify an object within the object's container.

remote access policy — A set of conditions that determines how users access the network remotely. A remote access policy consists of conditions, permissions, and profile settings.

remote access server — A computer running Windows 2000 and the Routing and Remote Access Service that authenticates remote or mobile users.

remote authentication dial-in user service (RADIUS) — A client/server protocol and software that enables remote access servers to communicate with a central server to authenticate dial-in users and authorize their access to the requested system or service.

replica set — A set of shared folders that is replicated or copied to one or more servers in a domain.

replicated update — An update to the Active Directory database that has been copied from another domain controller.

replication latency — The time that it takes to replicate an Active Directory update to another domain controller.

reverse lookup zone — A specific type of zone that performs reverse IP address to host name resolution queries.

Routing and Remote Access Services (RRAS) — A Windows 2000 service that allows users to access a company network or access the Internet through a variety of ways, such as dial-up, VPN, or NAT services.

safe mode — A method of starting Windows 2000 with only the basic drivers and services.

script — A file that includes various commands to automate routine operations.

scope — A range of IP addresses configured on a DHCP server that can be handed out to network clients.

secedit.exe — A command-line tool that allows you to perform security configuration and analysis. The secedit.exe command-line tool allows the following high-level operations: analyze, configure, export, and validate.

Secure Socket Layer (SSL) — This protocol is used to encrypt Web traffic between a client and the Web server.

Security and Configuration Tool Set — A security toolset consisting of security templates that can be used to analyze and apply security configurations.

security accounts manager (SAM) database — The local directory service that stores user and group information for standalone Windows NT and 2000 computers.

security group — A group that can be used to define permissions on a resource object.

security log — A Windows 2000 event log used to record security events such as auditing information.

Security Policy template — A template used to apply various security settings to an Active Directory container or object.

service packs — Periodic updates to the Windows 2000 operating system to fix reported bugs and security issues.

shared folder — A data resource container that has been made available over the network to authorized network clients.

Shiva Password Authentication Protocol (SPAP) — A reversible encryption method employed by Shiva.

site — A combination of one or more Internet Protocol (IP) subnets connected by a high-speed connection.

site link — A low bandwidth or unreliable/occasional connection between sites. The site links can be adjusted for replication availability, bandwidth costs, and replication frequency. They enable control over replication and logon traffic.

slipstreaming — A process that integrates a Windows 2000 service pack with the original Windows 2000 installation files.

snap-ins — The management tools that are added to a Microsoft Management Console interface.

standard primary zone — The DNS zone file is stored as a regular read/write text file in the %systemroot%\system32\dns folder.

standard secondary zone — A read-only zone file is copied from a configured standard primary zone.

subnet mask — The 32-bit number that identifies the network to which a TCP/IP host belongs.

superscope — A grouping of scopes created for multiple subnets on a physical network.

System File Checker — A command-line utility that scans and verifies all of the protected system files on your computer.

system log — Where system components such as services and device drivers record information, warnings, and errors.

System Monitor — A tool that allows you to gather and view real-time performance statistics of a local or network computer.

Task Manager — A tool used to view the processes and applications currently running on a system. Also provides basic resource usage statistics.

taskpad — Allows you to simplify administrative procedures by providing a graphical representation of the tasks that can be performed in an MMC console.

Terminal Services — A built-in feature of Windows 2000 that allows clients to access Windows 2000 and other Windows-based programs remotely. It is also used to remotely access desktop and installed applications for remote troubleshooting.

ticket-granting ticket (TGT) — A ticket issued by the Kerberos version Key Distribution Center (KDC) for purposes of obtaining a service ticket from the ticket-granting service (TGS).

trace log — Where a data provider collects performance data when an event occurs.

tracert — A command used to determine the route taken to a destination by sending ICMP echo packets with varying time-to-live (TTL) values to the destination.

transitive trust — The ability for domains to trust one another, even though they do not have a direct explicit trust between them.

Transmission Control Protocol (TCP) — Operates at the transport layer and is responsible for the reliable transmission of data on a TCP/IP network.

Transmission Control Protocol/Internet Protocol (TCP/IP) — Consists of a suite of protocols and utilities that are used for network communication and troubleshooting on local networks and the Internet.

tree — A hierarchical collection of domains that share a contiguous DNS namespace.

universal group — Can be assigned permissions to any resource in any domain within the forest. Universal groups can consist of any user or group object except for local groups.

urgent replication — The immediate replication that takes place when any changes that are made to the Active Directory database are considered security sensitive, such as account lockouts.

user account — An object that is stored in Active Directory that represents all of the information that defines a physical user who has access permissions to the network.

User Datagram Protocol (UDP) — A connectionless protocol that functions at the transport layer and provides no guarantee of delivery.

user principal name (UPN) — Consists of the user logon name and a domain name identifying the domain in which the user account is located.

virtual directory — A mapping to a physical directory containing content to be included on a Web site.

virtual private network (VPN) — Uses a LAN protocol such as TCP/IP which is encapsulated within a WAN protocol to send data securely over a public network.

Web folder — A folder that is intended to be accessed from the Internet or an internal intranet using the HTTP or FTP protocols.

Windows 2000 Readiness Analyzer — A Windows 2000 utility used to check for hardware and software compatibility.

Windows File Protection — Helps to prevent the replacement of protected Windows 2000 files such as .sys, .dll, .ocx, .ttf, .fon, and .exe files.

Windows installer package (MSI) — A file that contains all of the information needed to install an application in a variety of configurations.

Windows Internet Name Service (WINS) — A Windows 2000 service that is used to resolve NetBIOS names to IP addresses.

Windows Update — A Microsoft Web site used to automatically download and install Windows 2000 service packs and hot fixes.

winipcfg — A command used on Windows 9x machines to display the TCP/IP configuration settings.

ZAP file — A text file that can be used by Group Policy to deploy an application; it has a number of limitations compared to an MSI file.

zone file — A DNS configuration file that holds all of the resource records for the domain, such as computer name records, mail exchanger records, and service records.

zone transfer — The copying of the DNS database information between the primary and secondary zones.

Index

A

T

U